Peirong Lin

**Countering Mission Drift in a Faith-based Organization:
An Interdisciplinary Theological Interpretation Focused on
the Case Study of World Vision's Identity Formation**

edition pro mundis

Vol. 20

Vol. 1: Inka und Torsten Marold. Immanuel: Die Geschichte der Geburt eines anenzephalen Kindes.

Vol. 2: Thomas Zimmermanns. Grundriß der politischen Ethik: Eine Darstellung aus biblisch-reformatorischer Sicht.

Vol. 3: Thomas Schirrmacher. Marxismus - Opium für das Volk.

Vol. 4: Thomas Schirrmacher, Walter Schrader, Hartmut Steeb (Hg.). The Right to Life for Every Person / Lebensrecht für jeden Menschen.

Vol. 5: Wilhelm Faix. Die christliche Familie heute: Ergebnisse einer Untersuchung.

Vol. 6: Meego Remmel. The Role of Christian Ethics in Postmarxist and Postmodern Estonia.

Vol. 7: Thomas Schirrmacher. Säkulare Religionen: Aufsätze zum religiösen Charakter von Nationalsozialismus und Kommunismus.

Vol. 8: John Warwick Montgomery. Christ our Advocates: Studies in Polemical Theology, Jurisprudence and Canon Law.

Vol. 9: Gudrun V. Lang, Michael F. Strohmer (Hg.). Europa der Grundrechte? Beiträge zur Grundrechtecharta der Europäischen Union.

Vol. 10: Judith Fischer. Christen in der CDU/CSU am Beispiel des EAK. Unter besonderer Berücksichtigung des EAK in Baden-Württemberg.

Vol. 11: Gudrun V. Lang (Hg.). Helden der Menschenwürde: Texte zum Symposium im Gedenken an die Widerstandsgruppe ‚Weiße Rose' zum 60. Todestag von Hans Scholl, Sophie Scholl, Christoph Probst.

Vol. 12: Horst Waldemar Beck. Marken dieses Äons: Wissenschaftskritische und theologische Diagnosen.

Vol. 13: Thomas Zimmermanns. Rechtsstaat Bundesrepublik – wohin? Christliches und humanistisches Menschenbild.

Vol. 14: Thomas Schirrmacher, Daniel Suter, Markus Wäfler, Stéphane Derron. Christ und Politik: 50 Antworten auf Fragen und kritische Einwände.

Vol. 15: Thomas Zimmermanns. Demokratie aus christlicher Sicht.

Vol. 17: Stephan Holthaus (Hg.). Die Evangelikalen – wie sie wirklich sind: Daten und Fakten, die jeder kennen sollte.

Vol. 18: Thomas Schirrmacher, Titus Vogt. „Ein neues normatives Familienmodell" als „normative Orientierung" – eine soziologische und theologische Kritik des Familienpapiers der EKD.

Vol. 19: Johannes Kandel. Streitkultur statt Harmonisierung.

Vol. 20: Peirong Lin. Countering Mission Drift in a Faith-based Organization: An Interdisciplinary Theological Interpretation Focused on the Case Study of World Vision's Identity Formation

Peirong Lin

Countering Mission Drift in a Faith-based Organization:

An Interdisciplinary Theological Interpretation Focused on the Case Study of World Vision's Identity Formation

WIPF & STOCK · Eugene, Oregon

Wipf and Stock Publishers
199 W 8th Ave, Suite 3
Eugene, OR 97401

Countering Mission Drift in a Faith-based Organization
An Interdisciplinary Theological Interpretation Focused
on the Case Study of World Vision's Identity Formation
By Lin, Peirong
Copyright©2019 Verlag fur Kultur und Wissenschaft
ISBN 13: 978-1-7252-5226-4
Publication date 9/21/2019
Previously published by Verlag für Kultur und Wissenschaft, 2019

Contents

Contents – Overview

Abstract..21

Acknowledgments..22

CHAPTER 1
Introduction..25

PART A: DESIGN PHASE..41

CHAPTER TWO
Establishing the basis of the Christian Development Organization...........43

CHAPTER THREE
Discovering Three Different Ways of Understanding the Christian Values in an Organization 63

PART B: COLLECTION PHASE..91

CHAPTER FOUR
Introducing World Vision As Organization in Case Study 93

CHAPTER FIVE
Uncovering World Vision's Partnership Christian Understanding..........105

CHAPTER SIX
Measuring World Vision's Organizational Culture in Two Different Locations..133

PART C: ANALYSIS PHASE 211

CHAPTER SEVEN
Analyzing the Field Research...213

PART D: RECOMMENDATIONS PHASE 259

CHAPTER EIGHT
APPROPRIATING The Trinity as Central for World Vision 261

CHAPTER NINE
Strengthening Leadership in the Organization 309

CHAPTER TEN
Conclusion 363

APPENDICES 373

Appendix 1: Organizational Culture Questionnaire 375

Appendix 2: Questions for Focus Group Discussions and Interviews 404

Appendix 3: Relational Proximities as answered by respondents in
WV Nepal and WV PNG 405

Appendix 4: Summary of Organizational Cultural Dimensions in Nepal
and Papua New Guinea 422

Consolidated Bibliography 425

Contents – Details

Contents 5
    Contents – Overview 5
    Contents – Details 7
    List of Tables 13
    List of Figures 19

Abstract 21

Acknowledgments 22

CHAPTER 1
Introduction 25
    1.1 Subject and Relevance 25
    1.2 Research Question & Practical Theological Interpretation 27
        1.2.1 Descriptive Empirical Tasks Appropriating Sociology
               and Organizational Studies 29
        1.2.2 Interpretative Task Appropriating Organizational
               Studies 31
        1.2.3 Normative Task Appropriating Reformational
               Philosophy 31
        1.2.4 Pragmatic Task Appropriating Theology 32
    1.3 Research Strategy – Case Study 34
        1.3.1 Design Phase 37
        1.3.2 Collection Phase 38
        1.3.3 Analytical Phase 39
        1.3.4 Recommendation Phase 40

PART A: DESIGN PHASE 41

CHAPTER TWO
Establishing the Basis of the Christian Development Organization 43
    2.1 Civil Society and its Institutions: Situating the Christian
        Development Organization 43
        2.1.1 Pursuing Good in a Pluralistic Civil Society 44
        2.1.2 Institutions in Civil Society 45
    2.2 Organizations as a Type of Institution Studied in this
        Dissertation 48
        2.2.1 Characteristics of Organizations 49

    2.2.2 Critical Approach to Organizations 50
  2.3 Religion and Organizations 53
    2.3.1 Role of Religion in Society 54
    2.3.2 Religious Organizations 55
    2.3.2 Religious Identity in Organizations 59

CHAPTER THREE
Discovering Three Different Ways of Understanding the Christian
Values in an Organization 63
  3.1 First Way: Appropriating Typologies to Categorize Religious
      Organizations 64
  3.2 Second Way: Relating Christian Understanding to
      Organizational Characteristics and Variables 65
    3.2.1 Goal Oriented Nature of the Organization 67
    3.2.2 Activity Systems 68
    3.2.3 Boundary Maintenance 69
    3.2.4 Environment 71
  3.3 Third Way: Studying the Impact of Christian Values in the
      Organization's Culture 73
    3.3.1 The Organization Comprising a Group of Individuals 74
    3.3.2 Meaning Held by Organizations 75
    3.3.3 Influences of External Environment in Organizational
          Culture 83
    3.3.4 Intentional Control in Organizational Culture 86
  3.4 Concluding Design Phase 90

PART B: COLLECTION PHASE 91

CHAPTER FOUR
Introducing World Vision as Organization in Case Study 93
  4.1 Collecting Data at Two Levels 94
    4.1.1 Level of World Vision as a Partnership 95
    4.1.2 Level of World Vision at its Branch Offices 95
  4.2 Data Collection Used in the Case Study 101
    4.2.1 Role of Panel in Determining Data Collection 102
    4.2.2 Qualitative Research: Review of Core Documents, Focus
          Group Discussions and Interviews 102
    4.2.3 Quantitative Research: Questionnaire 103
  4.3 From Methodology to Documentation 104

CHAPTER FIVE
Uncovering World Vision Partnership's Christian Understanding 105
- 5.1 Reviewing the Religiosity of the Organizational Characteristics 105
  - 5.1.1 Goal Oriented 105
  - 5.1.2 Boundary Maintenance 109
  - 5.1.3 Activity Systems 111
  - 5.1.4 Organizational Characteristics Marked by Rich Christian Religiosity 113
- 5.2 Mapping the Evolution of World Vision 113
  - 5.2.1 Birth Phase 115
  - 5.2.2 Survival Phase 117
  - 5.2.3 Growth Phase 121
  - 5.2.4 Revival Phase 124
  - 5.2.5 Evolution of the Christian Understanding in World Vision 129
- 5.3 Collecting Information on World Vision as a Partnership: Concluding Thoughts 132

CHAPTER SIX
Measuring World Vision's Organizational Culture in Two Different Locations 133
- 6.1 Uncovering Christian Values of World Vision Based on Organizational Culture Dimensions 134
  - 6.1.1 Ideas about the Basis of Truth and Rationality in the Organization 134
  - 6.1.2 Ideas of Nature of Time and Time Horizon 135
  - 6.1.3 Motivation 136
  - 6.1.4 Stability versus Change/Innovation/Personal Growth 137
  - 6.1.5 Orientation to Work/Task/Coworkers 137
  - 6.1.6 Isolation versus Collaboration/Cooperation 138
  - 6.1.7 Control/Coordination/Responsibility 139
  - 6.1.8 Orientation and Focus 140
  - 6.1.9 Summary of Values Required to Maintain Christian Identity 140
- 6.2 Outlining the Field Research Design to Measure Organizational Culture 143
  - 6.2.1 Questionnaire 143
  - 6.2.2 Focus Group Discussions and Interviews 144
- 6.3 Documenting Research Results 144
  - 6.3.1 Data Collection in WV Nepal 144

      6.3.2 Data Collection in WV Papua New Guinea 181
  6.4 Concluding the Collection Phase 209

PART C: ANALYSIS PHASE 211

CHAPTER SEVEN
Analyzing the Field Research 213
  7.1 The Different Organization 'Selves' and the Mediated Self in Identity Formation of World Vision 214
      7.1.1 Self as Object 214
      7.1.2 Self as Story 215
      7.1.3 Self as Subject 215
      7.1.4 Uncovering Tacit Christian Identity Through Study of Organizational Culture 216
      7.1.5 Relationships as key in mediating content and process....217
  7.2 Introduction to the Normative Practice Model 219
      7.2.1 Practices within Society Expressed in Institutions like Organizations 220
      7.2.2 Norms rooted in the Christian View of Reality as described in Dooyeweerdian's social philosophy 222
      7.2.3 Plurality in Practices and its Impact on Organizations 226
  7.3 World Vision as Part of the Development Practice 229
      7.3.1 Development as Long-term Process of Change 230
      7.3.2 Development as Progressive, Indicator-led change 232
      7.3.3 Development as Deconstructing Change 233
      7.3.4 A Normative Understanding of Development? 233
  7.4 Analysis of Field Research using the Normative Practice Model 234
      7.4.1 Introduction of the Structural Side 235
      7.4.2 Introduction of the Directional Side 247
      7.4.3 Introduction of the Contextual Side 250
      7.4.4 Summary Analysis based on the Normative Development Practice Model 257
  7.5 From Analysis to Recommendations 258

PART D: RECOMMENDATIONS PHASE 259

CHAPTER EIGHT
Appropriating The Trinity as Central for World Vision 261
  8.1 Content Analysis and the Proposed Recommendation 262
      8.1.1 Recognizing the Particularity of the Christian faith 262
      8.1.2 Trinity as the Main Theological Motif 264

Contents

    8.2 Appropriating the Constructive Theological Approach for World Vision 266
        8.2.1 Integrative 267
        8.2.2 Coherent 267
        8.2.3 Inclusive 268
        8.2.4 Dialogical 269
        8.2.5 Hospitable 270
    8.3 The Trinity 271
        8.3.1 Importance of the Trinity in Christian Tradition 272
        8.3.2 The Trinity as Revelation in the World 273
        8.3.3 *Missio Dei* rooted in the Triune God 275
        8.3.4 The Individual Contribution of the Divine Persons to the Understanding of the Development Practice 284
    8.4 From Content Recommendations to Process Recommendations 306

CHAPTER NINE
Strengthening Leadership in the Organization 309
    9.1 Identifying Issues in Processes at World Vision and their Link to Leadership 310
    9.2 Appropriating the Theology of Work as the Hermeneutical Lens for Leadership 312
        9.2.1 The Ontological Dimension of Work 315
        9.2.2 The Instrumental Dimension of Work 319
        9.2.3 The Relational Dimension of Work 337
    9.3 Leadership and the Individual Leader 342
        9.3.1 Understanding of Self 344
        9.3.2 Communication between Authentic Leaders and Followers 354
    9.4. Concluding the Recommendations on Processes 361

CHAPTER TEN
Conclusion 363
    10.1 Case Study Strategy to Answer Research Question 363
        10.1.1 Design Phase 364
        10.1.2 Collection Phase 365
        10.1.3 Analytical Phase 366
        10.1.4 Recommendation Phase 367
        10.1.5 Implications of Research 369
    10.2 Future Research Opportunities 370
        10.2.1 Implement Recommendations Listed in the Dissertation.370

10.2.2 Expansion in scope: More Organizations, More Offices 370
10.2.3 National Cultural Implications 371
10.2.4 Virtues Required in Leaders of World Vision......................371

APPENDICES 373

Appendix 1: Organizational Culture Questionnaire 375
1. Introduction 375
2. Organizational Cultural Dimensions 378
   2.1   Basis of Truth and Rationality in the Organization...........378
   2.2   Nature of Time and Time Horizon 380
   2.3   Motivation 383
   2.4   Stability vs Change/ Innovation/ Personal Growth...........385
   2.5   Orientation to Work/Task/Coworkers 388
   2.6   Isolation vs Collaboration/Cooperation...............................388
   2.7   Control/Coordination/Responsibility..................................389
   2.8   Orientation and Focus 391
3. Stakeholders Relationships 392

Appendix 2: Questions for Focus Group Discussions and Interviews.......404

Appendix 3: Relational Proximities as answered by respondents in
WV Nepal and WV PNG 405
   WV Nepal 405
   WV Papua New Guinea 413

Appendix 4: Summary of Organizational Cultural Dimensions in Nepal
and Papua New Guinea..422

Consolidated Bibliography 425
   Primary Sources 425
   Secondary Sources...427

List of Tables

Table 2.1: Differences in the Multiple Perspectives of Organizational Theory 52

Table 3.1: Organizational Variables Related to Religiosity 66

Table 3.2: Categories of Meaning in an Organization Related to External Adaptation and Survival and Internal Integration 76

Table 3.3: Mechanisms Available to Leaders 89

Table 4.1: Description of Organizational Culture Dimensions 98

Table 5.1: Life Cycle Stage Characteristics 114

Table 6.1: Summary of World Vision Values and Practices According to Organizational Culture Dimensions 141

Table 6.2: Length of Service with World Vision Nepal 145

Table 6.3: Religion of Respondents at World Vision Nepal 145

Table 6.4: Overall Importance of the Organization's Religious Motivation and Values in Choosing a Job at World Vision Nepal 146

Table 6.5: Influence of World Vision's Mission Statement at World Vision Nepal 147

Table 6.6: The Relative Importance for Decision Making at World Vision Nepal 149

Table 6.7: Scriptures in Decision Making Process at World Vision Nepal 150

Table 6.8: Obstacles in Using Scriptures in the Decision Making Process at World Vision Nepal 151

Table 6.9: Extent of Importance in Goal Setting at World Vision Nepal..................152

Table 6.10: Extent that Goals are Time Bound with Timelines Observed at World Vision Nepal..................154

Table 6.11: World Vision Nepal Seeks God's Direction in the Setting of Goals..................154

Table 6.12: How World Vision Nepal Seeks God's Direction in the Setting of Goals..................155

Table 6.13: Obstacles in Seeking God's Direction in the Setting of Goals at World Vision Nepal..................156

Table 6.14: Reasons for Working with World Vision Nepal..................157

Table 6.15: Motivating and Demotivating Factors at World Vision Nepal..................159

Table 6.16: Understanding of Change at World Vision Nepal..................160

Table 6.17: Changes that Take Place Most Often at World Vision Nepal 161

Table 6.18: Main Reasons for Changes in the Office at World Vision Nepal..................161

Table 6.19: God's Guidance Sought in Consideration of Changes at World Vision Nepal..................162

Table 6.20: When God's Guidance is Considered in the Change Process at World Vision Nepal..................162

Table 6.21: How God's Guidance is Considered in the Changes Experienced by World Vision Nepal..................163

Table 6.22: Obstacles in Seeking God's Guidance in Changes that Take Place at World Vision Nepal..................164

Table 6.23: Priority for World Vision Nepal from the Most Important to the Least Important 165

Table 6.24: World Vision Nepal's Views on Relationships with Internal Stakeholders 166

Table 6.25: The Role of Relationships for Internal Stakeholders at World Vision Nepal 167

Table 6.26: How Work is Accomplished at World Vision Nepal 168

Table 6.27: Decisions Making at World Vision Nepal 168

Table 6.28: God's Guidance in Decision Making at World Vision Nepal .. 169

Table 6.29: How God's Guidance is Sought in the Decision Making Process at World Vision Nepal 170

Table 6.30: Views on Relationships with External Stakeholders at World Vision Nepal 171

Table 6.31: The Role of Relationships in the Office with External Stakeholders at World Vision Nepal 172

Table 6.32: Summary of World Vision Nepal Values 173

Table 6.33: Ranking of the Following Stakeholders in the Way it Influences the Strategy and Direction at World Vision Nepal 175

Table 6.34: Average Rating on Relationships with Stakeholders at World Vision Nepal 175

Table 6.35: Average Perceived Influence of Different Stakeholders at World Vision Nepal 176

Table 6.36: Average Perception Regarding Relational Proximity for Senior Management at World Vision Nepal 177

Table 6.37: Perception Regarding Relational Proximity for Middle Management at World Vision Nepal 178

Table 6.38: Perception Regarding Relational Proximity for Support Staff at World Vision Nepal 179

Table 6.39: Perception Regarding Relational Proximity for Field staff at World Vision Nepal..180

Table 6.40: Length of Service at World Vision Papua New Guinea 182

Table 6.41: Religion of Respondents at World Vision Papua New Guinea..182

Table 6.42: Importance of World Vision Papua New Guinea's Religious Motivation and Values in Choosing a job...................................183

Table 6.43: The Influence of World Vision's Mission Statement on World Vision Papua New Guinea 183

Table 6.44: Extent of Importance for Decision Making at World Vision Papua New Guinea..184

Table 6.45: Scriptures in Decision Making Process at World Vision Papua New Guinea 185

Table 6.46: Obstacles in Using Scriptures in the Decision Making Process at World Vision Papua New Guinea 185

Table 6.47: Extent of Importance in Goal Setting at World Vision Papua New Guinea 186

Table 6.48: Extent that Goals are Time Bound with Timelines Observed at World Vision Papua New Guinea................................187

Table 6.49: World Vision Papua New Guinea Seeks God's Direction in the Setting of Goals 187

Table 6.50: Seeking God's Direction in the Setting of Goals at World Vision Papua New Guinea 188

Table 6.51: Obstacles in Seeking God's Direction in the Setting of Goals at World Vision Papua New Guinea...................................188

Table 6.52: Reasons for Working with World Vision Papua New Guinea 189

Table 6.53: Motivating and Demotivating Factors at World Vision Papua New Guinea 190

Table 6.54: Understanding Change at World Vision Papua New Guinea 191

Table 6.55: Changes that Take Place Most Often at World Vision Papua New Guinea 192

Table 6.56: Main Reasons for Changes at World Vision Papua New Guinea 192

Table 6.57: Seeking God's Guidance in the Consideration of Changes at World Vision Papua New Guinea 193

Table 6.58: When God's Guidance is Considered in the Change Process at World Vision Papua New Guinea 193

Table 6.59: How God's Guidance is Considered in the Changes Experienced by World Vision Papua New Guinea 194

Table 6.60: Obstacles in Seeking God's Guidance in Changes Experienced at World Vision Papua New Guinea 194

Table 6.61: Priority for World Vision Papua New Guinea from the Most Important to the Least Important 195

Table 6.62: Views on Relationships with Internal Stakeholders at World Vision Papua New Guinea 196

Table 6.63: The Role of Relationships for Internal Stakeholders at World Vision Papua New Guinea 197

Table 6.64: The Accomplishment of Work at World Vision Papua New Guinea 197

Table 6.65: Decisions at World Vision Papua New Guinea 198

Table 6.66: God's Guidance in Decision Making at World Vision Papua New Guinea 199

Table 6.67: How God's Guidance is Sought in the Decision Making Process at World Vision Papua New Guinea 199

Table 6.68: Views on Relationships with External Stakeholders at World Vision Papua New Guinea 200

Table 6.69: Role of Relationships with External Stakeholders at World Vision Papua New Guinea 201

Table 6.70: Summary of World Vision PNG Values 201

Table 6.71: Ranking of the Following Stakeholders in the Way it Influences the Strategy and Direction at World Vision Papua New Guinea 203

Table 6.72: Average Rating on Relationships with Internal Stakeholders at Papua New Guinea 204

Table 6.73: Average Perceived Influence of Different Stakeholders at World Vision Papua New Guinea 204

Table 6.74: Average Perception Regarding Relational Proximity for Senior Management at World Vision Papua New Guinea 205

Table 6.75: Perception Regarding Relational Proximity for Middle management at World Vision Papua New Guinea 206

Table 6.76: Perception Regarding Relational Proximity for Support Staff at World Vision Papua New Guinea 207

Table 6.77: Perception Regarding Relational Proximity for Field Staff at World Vision Papua New Guinea 208

List of Figures

Figure 1.1: Phases of Case Study and its Relation to the Theological Interpretation Tasks 37

Figure 2.1: Organizational Theories 51

Figure 2.2: Three Dimensions of Self and their Relations in an Organization 60

Figure 3.1: Mintzberg's Five Preferred Configuration of Organizations Projected onto a Power Distance x Uncertainty-avoidance Matrix 88

Figure 4.1: Collecting Information about the Organizational Identity 94

Figure 5.1: Critical Path in World Vision Development Program Approach 126

Figure 5.2: Decision Makers in World Vision 129

Figure 6.1: Schematic Framework for Measuring Organizational Culture 133

Figure 7.1: Sides of the Normative Practice Model 235

Figure 7.2: Reality of Aid Development 252

Figure 9.1: Leadership Moment in Organizational Processes 312

Figure 9.2: The Three Dimensions of Work Theology 314

Figure 9.3: Illustration of Fundamental Needs 322

Figure 9.4: Basic Structure of Spiritual Guidance Model 328

Figure 9.5: Spiritual Guidance Model with the Hermeneutical and Agogic Framework Model 333

Abstract

In this dissertation, the case study of World Vision is presented as a useful contribution in the discussion of mission drift: where faith-based organizations drift away from their founding mission, purpose and identity. The practical theological interpretation, appropriating different academic disciplines in dialogue with theology, is undertaken in this case study. There are four phases described in this approach: design, collection, analysis and recommendation.

In the first phase, design, the key terms of the dissertation are explicated. Key discussions include situating the faith-based organization in civil society, discussing the implications of different organizational approaches, as well as the formation of religious identity within the organization using the identity formation model. This model understands identity as an ongoing dialectic between the process and content of the organization. In addition, three different ways of uncovering the Christian understanding of an organization are also outlined. In the second phase, collection, the actual collection of the empirical research is documented. This include the description of the specific research method, the documentation of the Christian understanding at a partnership level as well as in in two separate locations, Papua New Guinea and Nepal. In the third phase, analyzing, the findings of the empirical research are analyzed firstly using the identity formation model, and more normatively, through the use of the normative practice model. This normative practice model roots the reality of the practice in the created order. In the final phase, recommendations are made in light of the analysis. These recommendations are also framed using the identity formation model with content and process recommendations given. Content recommendations include constructively approaching the Trinity in the reflection of the structure and direction of the development practice within the organization. Process recommendations include appropriating the theology of work as the hermeneutical lens for leadership. In addition, with the understanding of the leader as an active agent that drives the leadership process, authentic leadership theory is studied to provide further understanding for the authentic leader. Specific recommendations are given in light of this theory.

Acknowledgments

The challenge of Jesus is not to solve all the world's problems before the end of time but to remain faithful at any cost.[1]

The truth of these words was made real to me in these years of labor. I am grateful and humbled to finally be at this stage of publishing this dissertation. I am firstly thankful to God for His divine inspiration and provision through it all.

In addition, I am grateful to World Vision for allowing me to use them as the case study for my dissertation. I have been inspired by the strength and service of so many World Vision staff members and have fond memories of my own service there. These memories and people have in many ways motivated me in my project. I am particularly grateful to Mr. Ajit Hazra, South Asia and Pacific Region, Faith & Development Director, for his encouragement as well as providing me with access to the organization. I am also thankful for staff members in World Vision Nepal and Papua New Guinea for their valuable input. I hope that my research will be of some service to World Vision.

I am indebted to my promoters, Prof. Patrick Nullens, Prof. Henk Jochemsen and co-promoter, Prof. Pieter Boersema. Thank you for believing in the viability of this project, your patience and your wisdom. I appreciate the different conversations we had to spark my thinking, your assistance to develop logical thoughts and finally, the discussions on how we can bring the different academic disciplines together. I am privileged to have your guidance in my project.

I am also thankful to the official readers of this dissertation, Prof. Maarten Verkerk, Prof. John Choi, Dr. Steven van den Heuvel for their invaluable comments as well as Prof. Martin Webber, Ruth Nivelle and Matthias Mangold for their editing support.

Sincere appreciation to the Evangelische Theologische Faculteit, ETF and to my colleagues who make ETF come alive. This includes being part of the Institute of Leadership and Social Ethics, ILSE. Thank you for being a place of rigorous learning, gracious mentoring as well as joyous working together. It is my prayer that the purposes of ETF (and ILSE) will continue to be realized.

---

[1] Henri Nouwen, "Remaining Faithful," accessed January 10, 2018, http://henrinouwen.org/meditation/remaining-faithful/.

Acknowledgments

I am also grateful to my family and friends who believed in my dream and stood by me through the different seasons of this project. Both virtually and in person, your acts of love have sustained me. I remember the prayers, encouragement, care, sacrifice, food and humor. I praise God for the gift of you and remain yours through time.

Finally, I recognize the small drop that my research contributes to this big ocean of knowledge. While not wanting to solve all the world's problems, I hope that my project, bridging praxis and theory, would be a stepping stone to further engagement in this regard.

CHAPTER I

Introduction

Faith-based organizations are part of the landscape of societies. A current concern of these kind of organizations is the phenomenon known as mission drift, a moving away from its original founding mission. This dissertation draws from the example of World Vision in order to better understand the phenomenon of mission drift before providing relevant recommendations. A theological interpretation through an interdisciplinary approach is appropriated.

In this chapter, the dissertation is broadly introduced. It describes first the subject and relevance of the dissertation, presenting World Vision as the case study focused on. The research question is then outlined, concentrating on how the method of theological interpretation reduces mission drift. The *status questionis* of the different relevant disciplines used in the theological interpretation has been incorporated in this section. In the final section, the research strategy is delineated. This research strategy specifies the case study as the methodology used in the dissertation, introducing each phase and its relation to the theological interpretation.

1.1 Subject and Relevance

A crisis that faith-based organizations have been categorized to experience has been termed "mission drift". This is described as a phenomenon where "faith-based organizations will inevitably drift from their founding mission, away from their core purpose and identity."[2] The discussion of "mission drift" is not only a practitioner's concern, but has also been studied and debated in scholarship.[3] With mission a key theme in theology, this dissertation contributes to this scholarship through practical theological interpretation of this phenomenon via a real-life example. This practical

---

[2] Peter Greer and Chris Horst, *Mission Drift* (Bloomington, MN: Bethany House, 2014), 15, 18.

[3] See Anselm Reimer, "How Do We Maintain a Credible Diaconia for the Future? Some Thoughts from a German Protestant Perspective," *Diaconia* 2, no. 2 (2011): 170–74, and Johannes Eurich, "Diaconia Under Mission Drift," *Diaconia* 3, no. 1 (2012): 58–65.

theological interpretation reflects on the different sub-disciplines in theology as well as other academic disciplines alongside the real-life example of World Vision, an example of a Christian faith-based organization.

World Vision, a Christian development organization, is an example of an organization that took the phenomenon of mission drift seriously in its organizational journey. It self identifies itself as a "global Christian relief, development and advocacy organization dedicated to working with children, families and communities to overcome poverty and injustice."[4] Founded in 1960 in the USA, it has grown drastically in size. As of 30 September 2015, World Vision reports working in 99 countries with more than 44,000 staff. It claims to benefit 41 million children around the globe.[5]

Shortly after its fiftieth birthday, the top leadership of World Vision initiated a change management process because it had observed that large growth and broad reach of the organization resulted in the "strain on systems, capacity and people."[6] In defining the agenda of this change management process, the first strategic mandate identified was to "reinforce our Christian foundations, identity and witness."[7] From this agenda, it was clear that the management of World Vision were aware and wanted to address the mission drift within the organization. The way that World Vision sought to solve this problem was through the focus on the management of the organization. They first defined key objectives, developed an operational plan as well as a shared business scorecard for the entire partnership. The language and method used in this process parallels that found in strategic management, a branch of business management studies.[8] Strategic management is firmly rooted in the modern construct, with its appeal

---

[4] World Vision International, accessed March 23, 2016, http://www.wvi.org.
[5] World Vision International, 2015 Annual Review, accessed March 23, 2016, http://www.wvi.org/sites/default/files/20161030_WVIAnnualReview.pdf
[6] World Vision International, "From Genesis to Exodus: Our Future Legacy," (2008).
[7] World Vision International, "The Will to Make It So," (2008). This is an internal document circulated by World Vision International to clarify the journey and to introduce the strategic mandates of World Vision in 2008. Strategic Mandates have been defined by World Vision as the "operational agenda moving forward. It represents five drivers for the partnerships where the whole partnership needs to steward in a coherent way."
[8] Strategic management is about the deliberate management of key actions that managers undertake to increase their company's performance. For more information, see Charles W. L. Hill, Gareth R. Jones, and Melissa A. Schilling, *Strategic Management: Theory: An Integrated Approach*, 11th ed. (Stamford, CT: Cengage Learning, 2014).

to progress and rationalization.⁹ This management approach, located in the modern approach to organizations, is positivistic in nature with the belief that there is a solution 'out there'.¹⁰

While applauding the effort taken by World Vision to reinforce their Christian foundations, the management focus is argued to be lacking because it does not directly engage with the content of mission drift. The term mission drift presupposes an understanding of the mission as well as the sender of this mission, themes that are studied in theology. It is not possible for due attention to the mission and the sender of the mission, God, to be well represented in the modern organizational approach chosen by World Vision, with its focus on efficiency, rationality and positivity.

As an alternative to the approach chosen by World Vision, a theological approach, namely practical theological interpretation, is appropriated in this dissertation. This approach recognizes theology as "an ongoing, second-order, contextual discipline that engages in the task of critical and constructive reflection on the beliefs and practices of the Christian church for the purpose of assisting the community of Christ's followers in their missional vocation to live as the people of God in the particular social-historical context to which they are situated."¹¹ This understanding of theology actively engages and reflects on Christian beliefs and tradition for the purpose of supporting the Christian community. It engages with the different theological sub-disciplines as well as with other relevant academic disciplines. Intentionally practical, it focuses on an identified problem within a specific community, World Vision. Through the detailed description of the process taken, this is useful for other similar organizations facing similar situations.

1.2 Research Question & Practical Theological Interpretation

Taking World Vision as an example of an organization dealing with mission drift, the research question in this dissertation can be formulated as

---

⁹ Rationalization, a legacy of Taylorism is the belief in the powers of objective measurement and the discovery of laws governing work efficiency. See Mary Jo Hatch, *Organization Theory: Modern, Symbolic, and Postmodern Perspectives*, 3rd ed. (Oxford: Oxford University Press, 2013), 31.

¹⁰ Mary Jo Hatch, *Organization Theory: Modern, Symbolic, and Postmodern Perspectives*, 3rd ed. (Oxford: Oxford University Press, 2013), 48.

¹¹ John R. Franke, *The Character of Theology: An Introduction to Its Nature, Task, and Purpose* (Grand Rapids: Baker Academic, 2005),44.

follows: "how can the four different tasks involved in practical theological interpretation, as well as the appropriation of different academic disciplines and theological sub-disciplines, be used to strengthen the Christian identity of the organization thereby countering mission drift?"

This research question is answered using the case study of World Vision. The attention on one organization and on change is an established methodology in social research that is useful in generating concrete solutions.[12] This focus on one particular context for the purpose of practical recommendations has also been seen in theological disciplines such as practical theology and missiology.

Practical theological interpretation involves the deliberate emphasis on theology in solving a practical situation. It looks for a theological interpretation to the situation and the process of arriving at the solution. In this dissertation, the framework offered by practical theologian Richard Osmer is loosely followed alongside the research method of the case study. Osmer's framework of practical theological interpretation is well established and broadly received within the practical theological discipline. It is a useful framework consisting of four distinct but interrelated tasks: descriptive empirical, interpretative, normative and pragmatic application.[13] These tasks are applied in the case study to elucidate the situation, understood collectively as necessary to the hermeneutical circle.[14]

The framework offered by Osmer intentionally reflects on the different theological sub-disciplines as well as with other academic disciplines. This broad engagement opens up the potential of developing new approaches to "defining and analyzing a research problem that more closely represents the reality in which such problems are situated."[15] These different disciplines are brought together through a specific form of rational communication, as they support the understanding of different systems in the web of life.[16] The particular way in which the different disciplines interact in this dissertation follow the tradition of Hans Frei "ad hoc correlational model of cross-disciplinary dialogue". Appropriating this tradition, theology enters into a dialogue with other fields. "It transforms their insights

---

[12] David E. Gray, *Doing Research in the Real World* (London: SAGE Publications, 2004), 2.
[13] Richard R Osmer, *Practical Theology: an Introduction* Grand Rapids: Eerdmans Publishing, 2008), 4.
[14] Ibid., 10.
[15] Patricia L. Rosenfield, "The Potential of Transdisciplinary Research for Sustaining and Extending Linkages Between the Health and Social Sciences," *Social Science and Medicine* 35, no.11 (1992): 1343.
[16] Richard R Osmer, Practical Theology: an Introduction, 162, 164.

as they as they are placed in the altogether different language game of theology."[17] These different academic disciplines are appropriated and brought into dialogue with theology.

The academic disciplines appropriated in this dissertation include organizational studies, sociology and reformational philosophy. These different disciplines are chosen as a direct reference to the research question. They are introduced below and categorized via the different tasks involved in this theological interpretation.

1.2.1 Descriptive Empirical Tasks Appropriating Sociology and Organizational Studies

The descriptive empirical task seeks to draw a clear picture of the problem at hand. It answers the question "What's going on?"[18] To arrive at a clearer picture, social sciences have been used to capture the understanding of the people and the situation involved, as well as the social trends that impact the context of the ministry.[19] Sociology as well as organizational studies are used in this dissertation as they contribute to the empirical enquiry of the organization. These disciplines are useful as they describe the external context of the organization, as well as the inner workings of the organization. The way that these different disciplines contribute to drawing a clearer picture to the research problem is described.

The focus in this dissertation is World Vision, a faith-based organization. Faith-based organizations have been defined as "any organization that derives inspiration and guidance for all its activities from the teachings and principles of the faith or from a particular interpretation or school of thought within that faith."[20] A sociological introduction of the context faith-based organizations exist in is useful for background information. Faith-based organizations have often been described as belonging to a broader sphere, categorized as the civil society. The term "civil society" is a popular catchall term for the broader civic action done by institutions or networks that advances the common good of society independent

---

[17] Richard R Osmer, Practical Theology: an Introduction, 169.
[18] Ibid., 33.
[19] Ibid., 41.
[20] Gerard Clarke and Michael Jennings, Development, Civil Society and Faith Based Organizations: Bridging the Sacred and the Secular (Basingstoke: Palgrave Macmillan, 2008), 6.

of the state and the market, yet at the same time, closely related to them both and even at times permeating them.[21]

World Vision, a Christian development organization, draws its specific understanding of what constitutes as good from its faith understanding. This implies the importance of understanding how religious faith actually influences society. The description of religious organizations as well as the extent to which the external environment influences the way that faith impacts the organization is investigated. In addition, the way in which identity is developed in an organization is examined.

The focus of the research question is on the inter-workings of the organization, namely how religious faith in organizational settings has been studied. Thus far, organizational literature has examined how different organizational variables are influenced by religiosity.[22] In addition, typologies have also been created to indicate the role of faith within various organizations, ranging from faith-permeated organizations to secular organizations.[23] The extent that the organizational variables of World Vision are influenced by religiosity will be investigated empirically in this dissertation. While useful, the focus is on explicit variables that are outwardly measurable. This does not take into the account the potential influence of staff members to the overall religiosity of the organization. As a supplement, this dissertation includes the perception of the staff members, namely the extent to which staff members are influenced by the faith content of the organization. Staff members' perceptions are valued particularly in the socio-interpretative approach of organizational studies. This moves beyond assuming a direct causal relationship between the explicit variables. From this perspective, the organization is understood as the "product of beliefs held by members of society."[24] The perceptions of the staff members become key to what the organization expresses in society.

Organizational culture is a good tool to understand the perception of staff members. This organizational culture is made up of the unconscious assumptions shared by members of the organization. It has been defined

---

[21] Jonathan Chaplin, *Herman Dooyeweerd: Christian Philosopher of State and Civil Society* (Notre Dame, IN: University of Notre Dame, 2011), 9.

[22] See for example Thomas H. Jeavons, "Identifying Characteristics of 'Religious' Organizations," in *Sacred Companies Organizational Aspects of Religion and Religious Aspects of Organizations*, ed N.J Demerath III, Peter Dobkin Hall, Terry Schmitt and Rhys H. Williams, (New York: Oxford University Press, 1998), 79-95.

[23] Rick James, "What is distinctive about FBOS," *INTRAC* 22 (February 2009): accessed April 1, 2014, http://www.intrac.org/data/files/resources/482/Praxis-Paper-22-What-is-Distinctive-About-FBOs.pdf.

[24] Mary Jo Hatch, *Organization Theory*, 42.

as "a pattern of shared basic assumptions learned by a group as it solved problems of external adaptation and internal integration, which has worked well enough to be considered valid and, therefore, to be taught to new members as the correct ways to perceive, think and feel in relation to these problems."[25] Measuring the organizational culture supplements the explicit information about the role of Christian faith in the organization as described in typologies as well as identifying religious characteristics. This provides a fuller picture on the faith impact within the organization.

1.2.2 Interpretative Task Appropriating Organizational Studies

The interpretative task consists of "wisely judgment."[26] In this phase, interpretation takes into consideration "1) relevant particulars of specific events and circumstances, 2) discernment of the moral ends at stake and 3) determination of the most effective means to achieve these ends in light of the constraints and possibilities of a particular place and time."[27]

To take into account the relevant circumstances of World Vision, organizational identity theory is appropriated. From this theory, identity in an organization has been described as a dialectic between the processes in the organization as well as the content.[28] This understanding of identity is useful to categorize and interpret the information gathered from the empirical task into a framework for further normative interpretation. It focuses on the understanding of identity as experienced by the organization.

1.2.3 Normative Task Appropriating Reformational Philosophy

The normative task involves the direct dialogue of the situation from a particular point of view. It focuses on what "ought to be going on" with the situation at hand. Osmer outlines the normative task in three different ways: theological interpretation, ethical reflection and deriving norms from good practice.[29]

---

[25] Edgar Schein, *Organizational Culture and Leadership*, (San Francisco: Jossey- Bass, 2010), 18.
[26] Richard R Osmer, *Practical Theology: an Introduction*, 80.
[27] Ibid., 84.
[28] Arne Carlsen, "On the Tacit Side of Organizational Identity: Narrative Unconscious and Figured Practice," *Culture and Organization* 22, no. 2 (2016): 107–135.
[29] Richard R Osmer, *Practical Theology: an Introduction*, 132-160.

In this dissertation, we look at theological interpretation and ethical reflection through the lens of reformational philosophy. Reformational philosophy is a branch of philosophy that is clearly rooted in the Christian faith. Key in understanding reformational philosophy is the idea that reality is not neutral, but always has a starting point. For reformational philosophy, the starting point stems from the Christian God as the creator. To derive at a normative understanding of development, the kind of work that World Vision is argued to be doing, the normative practice model, an established model rooted in reformational philosophy, is used to frame the discussion on development. This normative practice model has been developed as an alternative to applied ethics in which ethical principles are applied to ethical dilemmas. This model takes seriously the actual practice, recognizing a specific practice as constituted by a constellation of norms. This normative structure of a practice resists the tendency of following popular ethical trends within the social, scientific or economic domains blindly.

As a brief introduction at this juncture, the normative practice model comprises of three sides: structural, directional and contextual. The structural side focuses on the nature of practice related to the constellation of norms of practice, which in this case is related to the development practice. The directional, or regulative side, of the practice describes worldview based ideas of the practitioners that give the actual performance its specific character. This always occurs in a in a specific context with its specific restrictions and opportunities, the contextual side. By using the model, it is possible to interpret the existing literature regarding development, as well as the actual state of affairs as depicted by the empirical findings from World Vision, from a Christian view of reality. From the comparison between the normative with the actual, recommendations and further steps are suggested. This is included in the pragmatic task as described next.

1.2.4 Pragmatic Task Appropriating Theology

The pragmatic task consists of forming and enacting strategies of action that influence events in ways that are desirable. This involves practical actions that the organization can undertake which include the leadership involved in leading this change.[30] In this dissertation, a deliberate theological approach, particularly constructive theological approach, is empha-

---

[30] Richard R Osmer, *Practical Theology: an Introduction*, 176.

sized in the pragmatic task. This ensures the focus on theology in responding to the gaps identified.

The term constructive theology was coined by systematic theologian Veli-Matti Kärkkäinen. It describes theology as "an integrative discipline that continuously searches for a coherent, balanced understanding of Christian truth and faith in light of Christian tradition (biblical and historical) and in the context of the historical and contemporary thought, cultures and living faiths."[31] This approach focuses on the possibility of theology being integrative, coherent, inclusive, dialogical and hospitable. Constructive theology is compatible to the context that the faith-based organization is in. These organizations exist in very varied religious contexts that require sensitivity in its theological approach. They work with varied stakeholders that may or may not share their overall theological mission. A constructive theological approach is useful to support the organization as they stay faithful to their mission in the context that they are in. While this notion of constructive theology will be expounded in later chapters, explaining some key principles which undergird the understanding of this approach can be useful to clarify their appropriateness in this dissertation.

Firstly, constructive theology implies a non-foundationalist understanding to theology. It "envisions theology as an ongoing conversation between Scripture, tradition, and culture through which the Spirit speaks in order to create a distinctively Christian "world" centered on Jesus Christ in a variety of local settings."[32] This openness is particularly useful for the context of the faith-based organization that is deeply immersed in a public context. There is an "awareness of the contextual nature of human nature" that "mandates a critical awareness of the role of culture and social location in the process of theological interpretation and construction."[33] Secondly, the theological interpretation that ensues is expected to be coherent and dialogical. This affirms the understanding of theology as a second order discourse that "describes the grammar or internal logic of first-order language and assesses such language critically."[34] Such an approach embraces the first order language consisting of other academic disciplines that articulate human thought further. The insights from these academic

---

[31] Veli-Matti Kärkkäinen, *Christ and Reconciliation* (Grand Rapids, MI: Eerdmans, 2013), 13.
[32] John R. Franke, *The Character of Theology: An Introduction to Its Nature, Task, and Purpose,* 79.
[33] Ibid.
[34] Richard R Osmer, *Practical Theology: an Introduction,* 169.

disciplines are then appropriated on a need-to basis depending on the research question and are critically analyzed for use in Christian theology.[35]

In addition, an ecumenical approach is also implied in the appropriation of constructive theology. With the subject matter of this dissertation focused on faith-based organizations, the pluralistic contexts in which faith-based organizations work are taken seriously. These organizations work alongside other kinds of institutions in the public sphere. This can result in finer points of dogma that differentiate denominations to take a backseat role, as the differences within denominations are seen to play a less relevant role in the pluralistic context.[36] A deliberate ecumenical approach categorizes the Christian faith-based organizations together as a collective category of organizations in their dialogue with the broader pluralistic society. This takes into account the broader context that the organization is in, described in further detail in the inclusive and hospitable aspects of Kärkkäinen's constructive theology.

Finally, a broad engagement of different theological disciplines, described by Kärkkäinen as integrative, is also deliberately included in the constructive theological approach. The integrative aspect refers to the possibility to "utilize the results, insights, and materials of all theological disciplines. This includes fields such as religious studies, ethics and missiology."[37] Together, these different theological disciplines can support each other in forming strategies of action.

Thus far, the four different tasks that make up the overall theological interpretation have been outlined. These tasks are not separate, but rather inform each other in arriving at the overall theological interpretation. They are all crucial to the answering of the research question: how to strengthen Christian identity in faith-based organizations. Having introduced the different tasks and disciplines that will be appropriated in this dissertation, the next section outlines the research design that is used.

1.3 Research Strategy – Case Study

The chosen research strategy for the practical theological interpretation in this dissertation is through the focus on a case study. Case studies have been defined as an "empirical inquiry that investigates a contemporary

---

[35] Richard R Osmer, *Practical Theology: an Introduction*, 169.
[36] Barbara Hargrove, *The Sociology of Religion: Classical and Contemporary Approaches*, 2nd ed. (Arlington Heights, IL: Harlan Davidson, 1989).
[37] Veli-Matti Kärkkäinen, *Trinity and Revelation* (Grand Rapids, MI: Eerdmans, 2014), 14.

phenomenon within its real-life context, especially when the boundaries between phenomenon and context are not clearly evident."[38] This method is chosen in this dissertation because of the space it provides for intense scrutiny of a real-life context with the use of multiple sources of evidence.[39] It enables a detailed documentation of the processes taken to understand the phenomenon at hand which can be useful for other organizations facing similar situations. The case study at hand is the Christian development organization World Vision. World Vision is chosen because of its own recognition of its struggle with mission drift. In addition, it is an established organization within its field which makes it a representative example for other faith-based organizations.

Different sources of evidence in World Vision are scrutinized in this case study approach. This includes the formal documents of World Vision, tracing the narrative of the organization using the theory of organizational life cycle, as well as the organizational culture of the staff members in two different locations. This implies using a single case study with an embedded design where two subunits are studied. This use of the two subunits and the single case study enables us to grasp a deeper understanding of the actual experience of World Vision, both as a partnership as well as in the branch offices.

The use of the case study approach is not without its detractors. It has been critiqued as a 'soft option' lacking rigor, often seen as an exploratory precursor to a more established approach.[40] At the same time, from a positivist perspective, the case study approach is dismissed as an inadequate strategy because of its lack of empirical generalizability, with the in-depth review of only one case.[41] This critique however loses its claim from a different epistemological perspective such as the interpretative perspective. An interpretative perspective takes seriously the interpretation of the organization. Case studies are particularly useful for such a perspective as they provide valuable in-depth information about staff's interpretation as well as regarding the way meaning is mediated in the organization. As well described by Yin, case studies "focus on expanding and generalizing theory and not to enumerate frequencies."[42]

---

[38] Robert K. Yin, *Case Study Research: Design and Methods*, 5th ed. (Los Angeles: SAGE Publications, 2013), 13.
[39] Alan Bryman, *Social Research Methods*, 3rd ed. (New York: Oxford University Press, 2008), 57.
[40] Colin Robson, *Real World Research*, 3rd ed. (West Sussex: John Wiley & Sons, 2011), 137.
[41] Robert K. Yin, *Case Study Research: Design and Methods*, 19.
[42] Ibid., 48.

In addition, to ensure that the case study has undergone sufficient rigor, the adherence to four different kinds of validity typical of social sciences research is observed. These different kinds of validity include construct validity, internal validity, external validity and reliability.[43] A brief introduction to how this dissertation observes the different validity are mentioned at this juncture.

Construct validity refers to the need to "identify correct operational measures for the concepts being studied."[44] To ensure construct validity in this case study, different data sources are included in the data collection phase. Internal validity seeks to establish a causal relationship in the research.[45] To ensure internal validity, the identity formation model is used throughout this case study. It is first introduced in the design phase, used for data collection and analysis as well as for framing of the recommendations. External validity refers to broader domain whereby the study's findings can be generalized beyond the case study.[46] This case study is intended for the generalization for the broader faith-based organization domain who are facing mission drift. Finally, reliability refers to the possibility of the research being repeated with the same results.[47] One way that reliability is ensured is the careful documentation of the processes involved in this case study. Much effort is taken to detail the different processes that take place. In addition, clear transparent data has also been recorded during the data collection phase for transparency and reliability.

As a research strategy, the case study is made up of an empirical process including design, collection, analysis and recommendation phases.[48] Figure 1.1 illustrates the different phases in the case study and the way they relate to the different tasks in the practical theological interpretation described earlier. The key academic disciplines that are being employed at each juncture are also displayed.

---

[43] For further information, refer to Robert K. Yin, *Case Study Research: Design and Methods*, 45-49.
[44] Ibid.,46.
[45] Ibid.,47.
[46] Ibid.,48.
[47] Ibid., 49.
[48] Gray, *Doing Research in the Real World*, 127.

Introduction 37

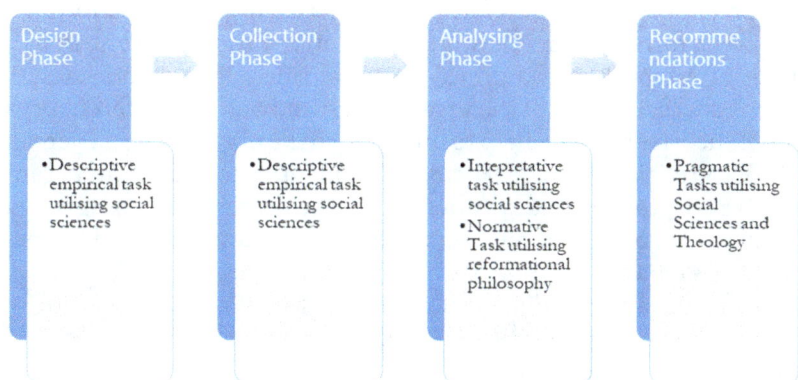

Figure 1.1 Phases of Case Study and its Relation to the Practical Theological Interpretation Tasks

The first phase—the design phase—begins with setting the context of the case study. Research tools are designed to match the research objectives. This phase corresponds to the descriptive empirical task utilizing social sciences. The second phase is the collection phase—this is where the actual empirical research of World Vision is documented. This phase also corresponds to the descriptive empirical task. In the third phase, the findings are analyzed with the help of both social sciences as well as reformational philosophy. This includes both the interpretative and normative tasks of the practical theological interpretation. Finally, in the fourth phase, recommendations are given. These recommendations are done by focusing particularly on the pragmatic task, emphasizing on theology. The different phases and the way they relate to the chapters in this dissertation are outlined below.

1.3.1 Design Phase

In the design phase, the focus of the project is outlined. The leaders from the Christian Commitments department of World Vision were closely involved in determining the focus and research question from the start. During this planning process, the scope of the research is marked. In addition, a clearer idea of how this research might contribute to the ministry of World Vision is outlined. Chapters two and three are devoted to this phase.

As part of the descriptive empirical task, social sciences, namely sociology and organizational studies are employed in this stage. In chapter two, existing research on organizations as well as the relationship between religion and organization is described. It begins by situating the Christian development organization, a form of faith-based organization, within civil society. As a form of institution, an organization orders society through its systems of established and prevalent social rules. This chapter describes different characteristics of the organization and outlines different organizational theories that will help to understand the organization. Thereafter, the link to religion is made. Focusing on identity formation in organizations, this chapter concludes by describing the process of forming religious identity within organizations as a dialectic, a process mediated by the organization's content and process.

The third chapter outlines different ways that World Vision's Christian understanding can be described. Three different ways are detailed in this chapter. The first way utilizes established methods of studying the faith component through the use of typologies. The second comprises of studying organizational variables influenced by religious ideas. The third method focuses on studying the organizational culture in each office. This study of the organizational culture measures the extent to which staff members embrace World Vision's Christian values. This method moves beyond the official statements to understand how these statements actually influence organizational assumptions held by staff members.

Together, chapters two and three form the necessary theoretical basis for the case study. It situates World Vision, a Christian development organization, as part of an institution within civil society. It looks at the process of religious identity formation in an organization: the dialectic between the content and process of the organization.

1.3.2 Collection Phase

The collection phase is the actual implementation and documentation of the case study. In this dissertation, the specific type of case study used is the "single case, embedded" where a single case incorporates a number of different units of analysis.[49] This case study is implemented in two different locations: Nepal and Papua New Guinea. Conducting the case study in two locations is done to shed further light on the possible impact of the environmental context to the overall Christian identity of World Vision offices. Nepal and Papua New Guinea have been chosen because of their similar size of operations in each country. The overall Christian identity is studied through the model of identity formation, taking seriously both the content and processes of the organization.

---

[49] Gray, *Doing Research in the Real World*, 134.

Introduction 39

The field research design, as well as the documented findings are detailed in chapters four to six. Chapter four describes specific research methods employed in this field research. These include description of specific data collection sources along with the discussion of the limitation of the field research as well as issues of validity and reliability. Chapter five further details the context of World Vision, primarily through an answer to the question: How is World Vision's Christian understanding expressed in its organizational variables and how has this Christian understanding evolved in the development of the organization? This outlines the official statement of World Vision based on their policies. To further understand the organization, the chapter further describes how the organization has evolved with relation to its Christian identity. A critical hermeneutic approach is considered in the review of documents, emphasizing on the specific social and historical context in which the document originated.

Having provided context to World Vision as an organization in chapter five, attention is turned to uncovering the organizational culture in two separate locations, Nepal and Papua New Guinea (chapter six). Together, a snapshot of World Vision's Christian identity is taken and is useful for further analysis.

1.3.3 Analytical Phase

For the analytical phase, chapter seven reports the analysis of the case study in two ways. First, the case study is analyzed through the previously described identify formation model. This model describes the organization as three different 'selves' that interact in order to make up the resultant tacit identity. This includes the self as object, content and subject. In addition to looking at each individual self, the analysis outlines the resultant tacit identity as explicated by the organizational culture. This form of analysis is reflected in the interpretative task of the practical theological interpretation framework.

The second form of analysis begins from a clearly Christian worldview: the use of the normative practice model. The normative practice model moves towards the normative task, taking seriously the Christian view of reality that is important to the interpretation of the findings. It analyses the findings based on one of the three sides of the normative practice: structural, contextual and directional. Through the normative practice model, the analysis ensures that the Christian perspective is firmly sustained.

1.3.4 Recommendation Phase

The final phase consists of recommendations in light of the prior steps of design, collection and analysis. As a way of organizing, the recommendations are framed using the identity formation model. In chapter eight, content recommendations are described and in chapter nine, recommendations related to the processes in the organization are suggested. In making these recommendations, the constructive theological approach is emphasized to support the organization stay faithful to their mission and counter mission drift.

Having introduced the dissertation project in this chapter, we begin the next chapter with the design phase.

PART A: DESIGN PHASE

CHAPTER TWO

Establishing the Basis of the Christian Development Organization

This chapter begins the first phase of the dissertation, the design phase. In this first chapter, a deeper understanding of the context that the faith-based organization exist in as well as a broader understanding of the organization as a form of institution is described. This includes the discussion of the civil society as the domain where faith-based organizations operate in as well as the understanding of the organization. This is useful for understanding the context where the Christian organization is in. In addition, recognizing that the mission of a faith-based organization finds its basis in its religious origins, the way that religion influences society as well as how religious organizations have fared in society is looked at. Finally, the religious identity formation of organization is discussed. This understanding of identity formation forms the basis of understanding identity within the organization in this dissertation project. Throughout this chapter, different theories are explicated as they form the starting point of the project.

2.1 Civil Society and its Institutions: Situating the Christian Development Organization

World Vision, as a Christian development organization, belongs to a category of organizations known as faith-based organizations. This category of organization has been defined as "any organization that derives inspiration and guidance for all its activities from the teachings and principles of the faith or from a particular interpretation or school of thought within that faith."[50] Their faith often acts as the starting point for the work that they do within society. Examples of such organizations are faith-based NGOs, or

---

[50] Gerard Clarke and Michael Jennings, *Development, Civil Society and Faith Based Organizations: Bridging the Sacred and the Secular* (Basingstoke: Palgrave Macmillan, 2008), 6.

faith-based social services and educational organizations.[51] These organizations exist within the broader society, in what is often termed as the "civil society." The term "civil society" is a popular catchall term for the broader civic action performed by institutions or networks that advances the common good of society independent of the state and the market, yet at the same time, closely related to them both and even at times permeating them.[52] An introduction to this civil society is pursued to further understand the context that the faith-based organization is working in.

2.1.1 Pursuing Good in a Pluralistic Civil Society

The term "civil society" is first used to describe a sphere that exist in political modernity, where individual freedom is valued positively.[53] This freedom refers to the liberation from "premodern customary, religious and political constraints, ushering in hitherto unavailable possibilities for new forms of social interaction among emancipated individuals and differentiated institutions."[54] Today, the term civil society is used more widely. Consequentially, this civil society is made up of different institutions that have distinctive historical roots. These different historical roots result in the institutions advancing different normative claims within the civil society. This has been described as normative institution pluralism.[55] In the same way, the understanding of common good that civil society advances is not singular, but rather made of different ideas of what good constitutes. This normative institutional pluralism brings together different ideas of good in the civil society. This can also include the good that comes from minority religions in different societies. This diversity is an important aspect of the civil society and any just and well-ordered society should actively protect the "integrity and autonomy" of these different kinds of social institutions.[56]

---

[51] Ronald J. Sider and Heidi R. Unruh, "Typology of Religious Characteristics of Social Service and Educational Organizations and Program," *Nonprofit and Voluntary Sector Quarterly* 33, no. 1 (2004): 109-134.

[52] Jonathan Chaplin, *Herman Dooyeweerd: Christian Philosopher of State and Civil Society* (Notre Dame, IN: University of Notre Dame, 2011), 9.

[53] This term was first coined among intellectual circles in the eighteen century and revived in the 1980s among Eastern Europeans and Latin American intellectuals as they were looking for a term to describe a sphere outside of a dominant autocratic state. Helmut K. Anheier, *Nonprofit Organizations: Theory, Management, Policy* (Cornwall: Routledge, 2005), 56.

[54] Jonathan Chaplin, *Herman Dooyeweerd: Christian Philosopher of State and Civil Society* (Notre Dame, IN: University of Notre Dame, 2011), 9.

[55] Jonathan Chaplin, *Herman Dooyeweerd: Christian Philosopher of State and Civil Society*, 14.

[56] Ibid.

World Vision, the case study in this dissertation is one of many institutions that form Christian pluralism. Christian pluralism relates to the diversity caused by different Christian denominations and their understanding of created human reality. The teachings from different Christian traditions continue to exist in some shape and form in civil society today. These teachings, unique to the Christian tradition, is what differentiates these institutions from the others in the broader civil society. There is validity to these teachings even in societies where Christianity is in the minority as what is good is common to all. Organizations that belong to Christian pluralism have clear Christian teachings that influence the understanding of common good necessary to the broader civil society. It is therefore important for such institutions to prioritize their understanding of theology in their operations instead of existing social consensus and political expediency.[57]

2.1.2 Institutions in Civil Society

The term "institution" has been widely used in different social sciences such as economics, politics, and sociology because of its importance in society.[58] Despite differing emphases in different disciplines, it is commonly agreed that institutions are systems of established and prevalent social rules that structure social interactions, including language, money, law, organizations, etc.[59] They are generally considered to be enduring features of social life since they give order to society.[60] Some ways that institutions have been discussed include their function, structures, and social processes related to the transmission of the rules of the institution.[61] To discuss institutions in depth is beyond the scope of this chapter. Instead, what is envisaged is an outline of three cursory remarks of institutions that is useful in the subsequent discussion of organizations, a form of institutions.

---

[57] Silvio Ferrari, "Religion and the Development of Civil Society," *International Journal for Religious Freedom* 4, no. 2 (2011): 29–36.
[58] Geoffrey M. Hodgson, "What Are Institutions?" *Journal of Economic Issues* 40, no. 1 (March 2006): 1–25.
[59] Geoffrey M. Hodgson, "What Are Institutions?" 1.
[60] Anthony Giddens, *The Constitution of Society: Outline of the Theory of Structuration* (Cambridge: Polity Press, 1984).
[61] Seumas Miller, "Social Institutions," in *The Stanford Encyclopedia of Philosophy*, Winter 2014 edition, ed. Edward N. Zalta (2014), accessed August 7, 2015, http://plato.stanford.edu/archives/win2014/entries/social-institutions/.

2.1.2.1 Institutions as Molecular

A molecular approach to institutions takes seriously both the purpose of the institution as well as the people involved. This molecular approach is adopted in this dissertation. This understanding of institutions as molecular is an alternative to both the atomistic and holistic view of institutions. On one end of the spectrum, institutions can be studied by focusing on the individuals that make them up. This has been termed the "atomic" account of institutions.[62] In this instance, the focus is on the individual. Social forms of the institutions are seen as secondary, supporting the individual agent in the moral deliberation of institutions. At the other end of the spectrum, institutions are studied "holistically," with a focus on the inter relationships of institutional structures and their contribution to the overall society.[63] Such studies focus on the function of the social form as expressed in institutional structures. In this approach, the individual is merely understood as fulfilling a role in the institution to which he or she belongs. A key concern of such approaches is the seemingly moral decay of society as a result of the breakdown of "strong, mutually supportive social institutions."[64]

One main reason why the molecular approach is adopted is because of its equal emphasis on both the importance of rules in the institution, as well as the institution's structural relationships and its intended impact on society.[65] This understanding of institution is seen as analogous to a molecule; where "an institution has constitutive elements determined by its rules which are in return determined by the people involved, yet the influence of society and other institutions continues to be important as the institution considers its role within society."[66] With the molecular approach, both people and institutional structures are important.

In addition, this molecular approach encourages a comprehensive study of the institution. It includes the need to study people who make up the institution and influence the organization and the subsequent rules, as well as constructed systems, relationships that the institution has with other institutions, and the overall functioning of the institution in society.

---

[62] Charles Taylor, *Philosophy and the Human Sciences: Philosophical Papers*, vol. 2 (Cambridge: Cambridge University Press, 1985).
[63] The holistic approach consists of the different structural functional way of looking at institutions. Proponents of a functional approach include sociologists such as Emile Durkheim, Radcliffe-Brown and Talcott Parsons.
[64] Miller, "Social Institutions."
[65] Ibid.
[66] Ibid.

2.1.2.2 Institutions as Comprising Systems of Established and Prevalent Social Rules

Institutions order society through their systems of established and prevalent social rules. The term "rule" is broadly understood as "a socially transmitted and customary normative injunction or immanently normative disposition, that in circumstances X do Y."[67] These rules facilitate a certain way of doing things through ordered thought, expectation and action by enforcing form and consistency on human activities.[68] Instead of instantly appearing in society or as a result of genetic inheritance, rules are formed as a process of social transmission.

The extent that rules are transmitted in society depends on the extent that they are embedded in shared habits of thought and behavior. Defined as "unconscious, submerged repertoires of potential thought or behavior; they can be triggered or reinforced by an appropriate stimulus or context."[69] It is not difficult to see how culture is made up of shared habits of thought and behavior. Therefore, the more similarity the rules have to the culture of a society, the more likely it is that these rules, and the accompanying institutions become established in the society.

At the same time, instead of just passive and entirely subject to the culture of a society, it is also possible for institutions to influence society. As part of society, institutions have power to mold society through their influence with the people with whom they work. As structures, they are able to influence individual aspirations through the structuring, constraining and enabling individual behaviors. Through the process of repetition, it is possible for an act to become an accepted norm for the people within a given social context.[70] Institutions are unique. Not only is the acceptance of institutions influenced by the context and extent to which rules have something in common with existing shared habits, institutions also have the ability to influence culture through influencing people within society.

2.1.2.3 Institutions as Purpose-driven

Thus far this discussion of institutions has focused on the adoption of the molecular approach, as well as the way the rules are transmitted. A final

---

[67] Hodgson "What are Institutions?" 3, see Ostrom 1986 and Crawford and Ostrom 1995 for detailed analyses of the nature of institutional rules.
[68] Hodgson, "What Are Institutions?" 2.
[69] Hodgson, "What Are Institutions?" 6.
[70] Ibid., 7.

aspect important for this discussion is the appropriation of a teleological account of institutions for understanding the purpose of the institution. A teleological account of institution adopts a definition of institution that includes a description of the "common good or social benefit" it seeks to advance in society.[71] A teleological understanding of the institution thus underscores the importance of the intended purpose of the institution. It emphasizes the importance of focusing on the particular understanding of common good that the institution seeks to advance in civil society.

At the same time, while focusing on the telos of the institution, it is important to note that the people involved in the institution are constituent to arriving at the telos. French philosopher, Paul Ricoeur in describing the good life incorporated the individual self – human agency alongside the function of the institution.[72] People influence the understanding of the good life in institutions, and work in institutions to achieve the good life. This good life is dependent on the institutions understanding of good. In addition, people are required in arriving at the telos of the institution. Both human agency as well as the structure, function and relationships of the institutions are taken seriously.

Having discussed the civil society as the domain where faith-based organizations exist in society, as well as introducing institutions as populating the civil society, the chapter now turns its focus to organizations, a particular kind of institution which concern this dissertation. The description of institutions as molecular, with a system of rules that is purpose-driven in society informs the discussion on organizations below.

2.2 Organizations as a Type of Institution Studied in this Dissertation

Organizations have been described as the "fundamental building blocks of modern societies and the basic vehicles through which collective action occurs."[73] They are characterized as goal-directed, boundary-maintaining, and socially constructed systems of human activity.[74] A description of different characteristics of the organization follows below, including an out-

---

[71] Hodgson, "What Are Institutions?" 7.
[72] Paul Ricoeur and Kathleen Blamey, *Oneself as Another* (Chicago: University of Chicago Press, 1994), 172, 199.
[73] Howard E. Aldrich and Martin Ruef, *Organizations Evolving* (London: SAGE Publications, 2003), 1.
[74] Ibid., 3.

2.2.1 Characteristics of Organizations

Goal direction provides the *raison d'être* for the organization. Together, members of the organization work towards the purpose of the organization. These goals influence the make-up of the organization and differentiate one organization from the other. This understanding of goal direction orientation has also been described as the *Zweck* of the organization. This *Zweck* forms the purpose of the organization, fulfilling needs in society.[75] This is linked to norms held by the organization[76] or otherwise described as the telos of the institution.

Boundary Maintenance relates to how the organization decides who should belong to it. This includes clear systems and processes that enforce membership distinctions in organizations. Such boundaries differentiate the organization from its environment.[77] At the same time, processes set up also include scenarios where members exit the organization, voluntarily or involuntarily.[78] Besides thinking about the processes involved in bringing people into the membership, the individual is also important. This individual brings along with him or her one's own individuals skills and knowledge, the fit between who the individual is and the task at hand, personal needs and preferences as well as bringing a broader background to the organization.[79] This brings to mind the molecular approach, which focuses on the interface between the purpose of the organization and the people involved as described in the molecular structure.

Organizations also develop activity systems for organizational members to achieve their goals. These activity systems are deliberate forms, rules procedures, strategies and technologies constructed for interaction between organizational members, or for members and different technologies

---

[75] Stefan Kühl, *Organisationen: Eine sehr kurze Einführung* (Dordrecht: Verlag für Sozialwissenschaften, 2011), 18.
[76] Richard W. Scott and Gerald F. Davis, *Organizations and Organizing: Rational, Natural and Open Systems Perspectives* (New York: Routledge, 2016), 24.
[77] Aldrich and Ruef, *Organizations Evolving*, 4.
[78] Kühl, *Organisationen*, 18.
[79] W. Richard Scott, *Institutions and Organizations: Ideas, Interests, and Identities* (Los Angeles: SAGE Publications, 2014), 96.

in place.[80] This can include both formal elements developed by the organization as well as informal elements. Formal elements include practices related to technology, how jobs are designed, and the overall organizational structure. Informal aspects focus on emergent characteristics dependent on the people of the organization. These comprise aspects such as the resulting social networks of the organizations as it relates to its environment, or the actual decision makers and processes in the organization.[81] This is related to the systems of rules that institutions are characterized by.

Finally, while not a direct characteristic of the organization, the environment is a key contributing factor to the organization's final expression. Organizations interact in and operate out of a societal environment. This context provides the main source for the organization to find members as well as a source of opportunities, constraints, demands and threats with which the organization has to grapple.[82] The environment also comprises of the social norms and customs accepted in society. These norms and customs in the environment impact the extent that the goals of the organization, otherwise described as rules, are reached. The immediate environment discussed in this dissertation is the civil society in each country. Organization works towards seeking acceptance in society through regulatory structures, government agencies, laws and courts, professions as well as interest groups.[83]

Apart from identifying the characteristics of an organization, the way an organization is approached and studied is focused on next. Different organizational approaches lead to different emphases and conclusions. Instead of blindly applying theories, it is important to be aware of the assumptions involved in the different approaches. An introduction to different approaches of organizational theory is presented before the discussion of application of these theories.

2.2.2 Critical Approach to Organizations

To understand the diversity and approaches in organizational theories, sociologists have tried to organize the different theories along two interlocking axes: the determinist – interpretivist axis and the technocratic-critical

---

[80] Aldrich and Ruef, *Organizations Evolving*, 4.
[81] Scott and Davis, *Organizations and Organizing*, 24.
[82] Ibid., 19–20.
[83] Mary Jo Hatch, *Organization Theory: Modern, Symbolic, and Postmodern Perspectives*, 3rd ed. (Oxford: Oxford University Press, 2013), 76.

axis (Figure 2.1). Theories on the determinist end of the determinist-interpretivist axis focus on the scientific and objective way in which organizations can be assessed, often relating specifically to underlying structural conditions and requirements. Theories on the interpretivist end of the same axis emphasize the indeterminate and contingent nature of reality, the significance of human interaction, unintended consequences of human action and the influence of interpretation. For the technocratic-critical axis, theories on the technocratic end of the axis are essentially pragmatically oriented where what matters is the improvement of organizational efficiency. On the other end of that axis, social effects of the organization upon its members and the society within which it operates are valued.[84]

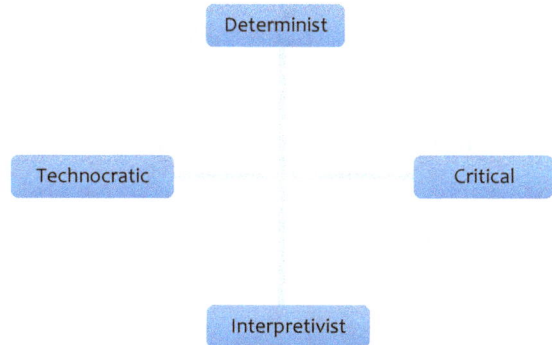

Figure 2.1 Organizational Theories

Source: Keith Grint, *The Sociology of Work: Introduction*, 3rd ed. (Cambridge: Polity Press, 2005), 114.

Describing the two axes explicates different assumptions underlying the different organizational approaches. Another way that organizational theory has been categorized is in its evolution through time. These approaches have been categorized from prehistory, to modern to symbolic to postmodernism.[85]

---

[84] Keith Grint, *The Sociology of Work: Introduction*, 3rd ed. (Cambridge: Polity Press, 2005), 112–114.
[85] Hatch, *Organization Theory*, 15, 20.

Perspective	Subject/Focus	Method	Result
Classical	• The effects of organization on society • Management of the organization	• Observation and historical analysis • Personal reflection on experience	• Typologies and theoretical frameworks • Prescription for management practice
Modern	• The organization through "objective" measures	• Descriptive Measures • Correlation among standardized measures	• Comparative studies • Multivariate statistical analyses
Symbolic/Interpretative	• The organization through "subjective perceptions"	• Participant observation • Ethnographic interviewing	• Narrative texts such as case studies and organizational ethnographies
Postmodern	• Organization theory and theorizing practices	• Deconstruction • Critique of theorizing practices	• Reflexivity and reflexive accounts

Table 2.1 Differences in the Multiple Perspectives of Organizational Theory

Source: Mary Jo Hatch, *Organization Theory: Modern, Symbolic, and Postmodern Perspectives*, 2nd ed. (New York: Oxford University Press, 1997), 49.

Table 2.1 illustrates differences in the multiple perspectives of organizational theory based on the focus, method and result. In her book, organizational theorist Mary Jo Hatch looked at how organizational theory has evolved in time. She focused on modern, symbolic/interpretative and postmodern perspectives of organizational theory. It is not difficult to relate links among these different perspectives to those described by sociologists along two interlocking axes.

A modern approach of organizations focuses on objectivism, well designed structures, rules and routines. This is similar to the determinist, technocratic approach suggested by sociologists. The symbolic approach of organizations focuses rather on interpretation of the organization, where the organization is seen as continually constructed or deconstructed by its members. It is subjective, with context playing a large role. This recalls organizational approaches closer to the interpretivist spectrum. The postmodern approach does not try to look for a holistic understanding of the organization. Instead it focuses on existing practices, managerial, ideological, and power relations. This approach is clearly interpretivist as well as critical according to the axes.

In choosing the organizational approach, the overall aims of this research is important. As described in the introduction, the research question focuses on the strengthening of the Christian identity of the organization through practical theological interpretation of World Vision. This dissertation seeks to broaden the search for answers on shaping Christian Identity beyond the modern organizational approach that World Vision has employed. This implies firstly the assumed role of the modern approach in organizations. In addition, it seeks to include, where appropriate, both the symbolic/interpretative approach as well as the postmodern approach. Inclusion of these two approaches with a broader focus on the human agency involved in the organization supplements the modern approach. Together, these different approaches do justice to the molecular approach of institutions that has been advocated. A deeper understanding of the people and their interpretation, the study of the narrative of the organization as well as the objective organizational characteristics are all taken into account. Not sticking to one fixed organizational approach, different approaches are useful to support the overall practical theological interpretation.

Following the descriptions of civil society, institutions, and organizations, the final section of this chapter outlines key sociological theories related to the link between religion and organizations. With the focus on faith-based organizations, the way religion is expressed in society, as well as how it influences the organization become important.

2.3 Religion and Organizations

Thus far, we have not looked specifically at the role of religion in society. This understanding of religion can however impact faith-based organizations who as part of Christian pluralism, draw their inspiration of good from the teachings of faith. Recognizing that religion is not separate from society and organizations, theories related to the role of religion in society are first introduced. The way religion can impact organizations are then looked at thereafter.

2.3.1 Role of Religion in Society

Sociologists have often focused on the two main aspects of religion: the substantive and the functional[86]. Descriptions of the substantive aspect of religion as described by the founding fathers of sociologists include: "religiosity" by Georg Simmel,[87] "a belief in spiritual things" as described by Edward Taylor,[88] founder of British social anthropology or simply the "sacred"[89] as described by modern sociologist Richard Fenn. This substantive aspect of religion focuses on the religious content.

The other way that religion has been studied is in its effect on society. This focuses on the functional aspect of religion. It looks at what religion does and how it affects the society of which it is part of. From this point of view, religious representations are collective representations that express collective realities. "Religious rites are ways of acting born only in the midst of assembled groups and whose purpose is to evoke, maintain, or recreate mental states of those groups."[90] While it is possible for religion to impact society structurally, this does not imply that religion impacts societies to the same extent.

The extent that religion influences society has been studied by sociologist Karel Dobbelaere who uses the concept of secularization to analyze the role of religion in different societies.[91] He looks at three levels of secularization: societal, organizational and individual.[92] He argues that different societies are influenced by religion differently; some societies are impacted by religion directly from a societal level while others are more influenced from an organizational level.[93] Depending on other factors in society, religion has a varied impact on society. This can range from having

---

[86] Grace Davie, *The Sociology of Religion* (London: SAGE Publications, 2007), 19.
[87] A more complete quote by Georg Simmel is "Religion then is the empirical transpositions of religiosity, a realization at the organizational level of this religiosity through the various modalities of church, sect, denomination and movement". Georg Simmel, *Essays on Religion,* trans. H. J. Helle (New Haven, CT: Yale University Press, 1906), 41.
[88] See Edward Taylor, *Primitive Culture* (London: John Murray, 1903).
[89] Richard Fenn, *Key Thinkers in the Sociology of Religion* (London: Continuum, 2009), 1–3.
[90] Emile Durkheim, *The Elementary Forms of the Religious Life: The Totemic System in Australia* (New York: Free Press, 1912), 9.

a societal impact as outlined by Durkheim, or perhaps a different kind of impact. What is important to note is that religion continues to play a role in society.

This understanding of religion as substantive and functional is useful in understanding the impact of religion in society and in organizations. It differentiates the content, studied from the substantive, from the functional, which focuses on the impact of religion on society. From a functional perspective, religion continues to impact society at different levels. The discussion by Doddelbare clarifies the different kinds of society that a faith-based organization can be operating in. Depending on the societal context, there can be different implications to the overall success in the transmission of rules of the organization as well as the assumptions held by the people who are part of the environment. It can be at varying degrees of difficulty in transmission due to the societal context. In the next section, religious organizations and their impact in society is investigated.

2.3.2 Religious Organizations

Two main points are raised in the discussions of religious organizations. In the first point of discussion, established theories of religious organizations are focused on. These sociological theories provide insight on how religious organizations perform in society. In the second point of discussion,

---

[91] One key theory in the sociology of religion is the secularization hypothesis. As the founders of sociology worked from an enlightened worldview, they believed in the development of society evolving from the stage of theological to metaphysical and finally to the scientific stage. Each stage was considered to be more preferable compared to the previous, leading to the esteemed value of science and the reliance of human agency that was popularized during the thinking of that time, which also resulted in the waning influence of religion. See Grace Davie, *The Sociology of Religion* (London: SAGE Publications, 2007), 47.

[92] See Karel Dobbelaere, *Secularization: An Analysis at Three Levels* (Brussels: Peter Lang, 2002).

[93] When religion is able to influence on a societal scale, religious content and social processes form part of the structures held by society. These processes include the importance of ecclesiastical authority within society as it has provided social legitimization. Doddelbare describes the historic church in western Europe as falling into this category. When religion influences on an organizational and individual level, this indicates that no one church holds power over all of society. This however does not mean a decline of influence of religion in the American society but rather a different expression of religion. Instead of religious activity centering around one church, religious activity has continued through different religious organizations present in society as well as through individuals.

both the substantive and functional aspects of religion are focused on in the organization. The theory of identity formation in an organization is used to bring these two aspects together in the understanding of the religious organization.

2.3.1.1 Bureaucratic Religious Organizations

The first theory that is discussed is the bureaucratization of religious organizations. This was one central idea adopted by religious sociologists from broader fields of sociologists was that which considers religious organizations as bureaucracies. Several studies in the 1960s – 1970s looked at the impact of bureaucratization in protestant denominations.[94] The argument argued that as denominations became more bureaucratic, the focus of the denomination will tend towards the functional aspect of religion.[95] As decision makers become more professional, decisions are made based on the value of their professional function.[96] Theology, the substance of faith, then takes a back seat to the day to day operations dominated by functional issues related to bureaucracy.[97]

The incompatibility between bureaucracy and religious idealism often underlies this understanding of bureaucracy, with religion and rationality as 'antithetical' to one another.[98] The concept of bureaucracy was the evolving modern society that Weber tried to understand. One key aspect of this modern society was an increasingly need for rationality. With science taking a more central role in society came a decline in the magical interpretation of the world. This also meant replacement of 'affective' and traditional action with rational action – things were done when benefits outweighed costs, or because they were built upon rational principles and common sense[99]. The essential points of bureaucracy include legality, with the bureaucracy on the basis of procedures with a body of rules, as well as

---

[94] Examples of studies include P. M. Harrison, *Authority and Power in the Free Church Tradition* (Princeton, NJ: Princeton University Press, 1959), G. Winter, *The Emergent American Society: Large Scale Organization* (New Haven, CT: Yale University Press, 1967), and K. P. Takayama, "Administrative Structures and Political Processes in Protestant Denominations," *Publius* 4, no. 2 (1974): 5–37.
[95] Chang, "Escaping the Proscrustean Bed," 127.
[96] See, for example, Winter, *The Emergent American Society*.
[97] Chang, "Escaping the Proscrustean Bed," 127.
[98] Ibid.
[99] Keith Grint, *The Sociology of Work: Introduction*, 3rd ed. (Cambridge: Polity Press, 2005), 108.

Establishing the Basis of the Christian Development Organization

rationality – operation on the principles of expert knowledge and calculability.[100] This perspective became so prevalent that people began to hold the view that decision makers concerned with making both moral choices and organizationally efficient choices need to be secularized,[101] leaving their faith ideals behind for the progress of the organization.[102]

Describing the impact of bureaucratization serves as a warning about the possibility for bureaucratization, and for the need to actively reflect on the faith content of the organization. Drawing from previous good practice, the growth and expansion of the Methodist and Baptist churches are good examples of where faith ideals have supplemented organizational efficiency in religious organizations resulting in a positive outcome. In these occurrences, religious zeal was seen as the inspiration for greater organizational efficiency in organizations, which resulted in influential proponents of religion.[103]

2.3.1.2 Neo-institutional Theory: The Influence of the External Environment

Another theory related to religious organizations is the neo-institutional theory. This focuses on the role of the environment in its impact on organizational behavior. This theory describes the role of external cultural processes related to the institutional sector as pressurizing organizations to

---

[100] Keith Grint, *The Sociology of Work: Introduction*, 3rd ed. (Cambridge: Polity Press, 2005), 109.
[101] Ibid., 128.
[102] When describing this theory, it is not the intention of Weber to insist on the incompatibility between bureaucracy and religious idealism. What was intentioned was instead the description of an observable phenomenon. Max Weber developed the theory of bureaucracy in the context of work settings. His first discussion of bureaucracy along with its central themes of authority and rationality was documented in his book *The Theory of Social and Economic Organization* published in 1924 in German and translated in English in 1947. In his understanding of rationality, Weber differentiated different kinds of reality, including among formal rationality and substantive rationality. His description of formal rationality involved techniques of calculation based on established rules and ways of measurements involved. Substantive rationality however was related to the values, where what is valued is dependent on values held. He did not seek to overturn the importance of values, but rather to show the different rationality involved in society. See Stephen Kalberg, "Max Weber's Types of Rationality: Cornerstones for the Analysis of Rationalization Process in History," *American Journal of Sociology* 85, no. 5 (March 1980): 1145–79.
[103] Chang, "Escaping the Proscrustean Bed," 129.

conform to the rules of the institutional sector. This influence is related to the power relations involved within the organization as well as external stakeholders such as customers, suppliers and regulators instead of focusing only on its internal staff members.[104]

Pressures that the organization may face include standardization of occupational categories, skills, rights and privileges that are associated with the practice.[105] Another pressure related to this neo-institutionalism is managerialism. Managerialism has been "generally understood as the dominance of management practices and ideas" within non-profit organizations, to which religious organizations are part of. One main reason for this managerialism is because of the legitimating effect it has on organizations.[106] Organizations are thought to be legitimate when there is a perception that "their actions are desirable, proper or appropriate." This legitimacy is "seen as providing a roof that will protect the organization from the effects of unfavorable actions in the future."[107]

One of the main critiques of the neo-institutional theory is its sole focus on external forces. External processes are seen to homogenize the organization with no attention given to individual organizations.[108] In this instance, the organization is seen as a passive agent with no ability to assert itself. This is too pessimistic in light of the discussion of institutions and organizations as earlier described in this chapter. Taking a molecular approach, organizations exist as a system of rules with a specific telos with people involved. It is not passive, but rather an active agent that seeks to transmit rules to society. While focusing on the external environment, this does not mean that the internal members of the organization are helpless. The transmission of rules within society is a two-way process that internal staff member can also get involved in.

As with bureaucratic theory, neo-institutional theory is helpful in providing plausible explanations to the way religious organizations perform in society. These theories seek to further explain the trends observed

---

[104] Chang, "Escaping the Proscrustean Bed," 129. For more information, see Richard W. Scott, *Organizations: Rational, Natural, and Open Systems* (Englewood Cliffs, NJ: Prentice-Hall, 1987).
[105] Chang, "Escaping the Proscrustean Bed," 129, 130.
[106] See Michael Meyer, Renate Buber and Anahid Aghamanoukjan, (2013) "In Search of Legitimacy: Managerialism and Legitimation in Civil Society Organizations." *Voluntas* 24 (2013): 167–93.
[107] Michael Meyer, Renate Buber and Anahid Aghamanoukjan, (2013) "In Search of Legitimacy: Managerialism and Legitimation in Civil Society Organizations," 169.
[108] Paul J. DiMaggio, "Interest and Agency in Institutional Theory," in *Institutional Patterns and Organizations*, ed. L. Zucker (Cambridge, MA: Ballinger, 1988), 3–22.

Establishing the Basis of the Christian Development Organization

in society. This, however, does not mean that all organizations need to evolve in such a direction. These theories, purely descriptive in nature do not provide useful recommendations on how to avert such situations.

Having looked at theories involved with religious organizations, the final section of this chapter looks in detail at the process of religious identity formation in an organization. This takes into consideration both the content and the processes involved in the understanding of religion. This theory of identity formation remains central throughout the dissertation. It is used as a means to understand the existing Christian identity of the organization, for analysis of the existing identity and finally, also used as a framework in describing recommendations.

2.3.2 Religious Identity in Organizations

The process of identity formation in an organization brings together the different theories that have been discussed throughout this chapter. Firstly, the understanding of the molecular institution influences the understanding of the religious identity of the organization. Religious identity is neither only a management constructed image, nor is it constructed only by the perception of the staff members. It is both: the "narrative unconscious in the stories that people live by," as well as the "formative organizational practice."[109] Secondly, this process of identity formation also recognizes the different organizational approaches involved within the organization. It takes seriously the management aspect as assumed in the modern approach, as well as the socio-interpretative and postmodern organizational approach that focuses on the perspectives of the staff members as well as the broader narrative.

In this section, the way that the religious identity of an organization is formed is understood using the theory of the tacit identity of the organization. It understands that "identity formation is both cultural embedded in complex and taken-for-granted ways and undertaken as part of organizational practice."[110] A description of the identity formation process is described next.

2.3.2.1 Tacit Religious Identity in Organizations

As illustrated in figure 3.2, tacit identity has been described as the ongoing dialectic between the process and content of the organization.

---

[109] Arne Carlsen, "On the Tacit Side of Organizational Identity: Narrative Unconscious and Figured Practice," *Culture and Organization* 22, no. 2 (2016): 107.
[110] Ibid.

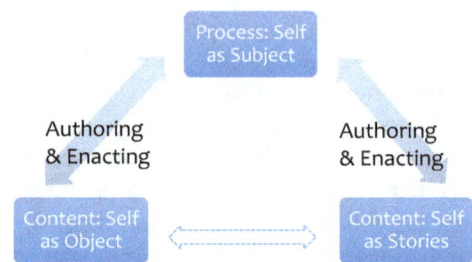

Figure 2.2 Three Dimensions of Self and their Relations in an Organization

Source: Arne Carlsen, "On the Tacit Side of Organizational Identity: Narrative Unconscious and Figured Practice," *Culture and Organization* 22, no. 2 (2016): 114.

The understanding of process and content of the organization is a result of analyzing the organization as 'self' from three different lenses: self as object, subject and stories. Self as object and story together form the content of identity while self as subject is involved in the processes. Instead of choosing one way of looking at the organization, the self as object, stories and subject together presents a more comprehensive way of looking at how identity is formed in the organization. It recognizes the different selves involved in developing identity. This takes into account the different traditions and the emphases that each self may have.[111] In the following section, the way the process and content of the organization interact is described in more detail.

2.3.2.2 Process of Identity

To study the process of identity means to understand the organization as a subject. This study focuses on the possibility for organizational identity to be socially constructed through organizational processes. It describes two main processes related to the social construction of organizational identity: self-authoring and self-enacting.[112] Authoring relates to the selection of organizational experiences and the attributing of meaning in the form of self-conceptions and self-stories whilst enacting refers to the living of these self-conceptions and stories.

---

[111] Carlsen, "On the Tacit Side of Organizational Identity," 115.
[112] Anne Carlsen incorporated the work of William James, volume 2, chapter 9 and 10 in William James, "A World of Pure Experience," in *Writings of William James, a Comprehensive Edition*, ed. John J. McDermott (Chicago, IL: University of Chicago Press, 1977).

To focus on the process is to focus on the stakeholders involved in the different organizational processes and the plausible management implications. This is very much related to the socio-interpretative organizational approach described earlier. Such a focus recognizes the importance of practices in the organization, or activity systems within the organization in constructing organizational identity. Experiences within an office context provide an opportunity for staff members to frame the meaning based on their own self-conception of the organization. From this point of view, "the processes of self are processes of participation in and performance of embodied, valued producing activity."[113] These practices described as "formative practices" are influential for the overall understanding of self as subject.[114]

2.3.2.3 Content of Identity

The content of identity can be investigated both from the study of the organization as an object or through the story or narrative lived by the organization.

Self as object was one of the early foci of organizational identity research.[115] Looking at self as object looks at identity as image. It asks the question how does the organization want to be perceived? In this sense, identity construction is therefore a reflection of creating this image.[116] Such an approach is very much related to the modern approach to organizations.

Self as story takes seriously the situatedness of the organization in its location, its temporality, and its purpose within society.[117] It affirms the importance of narrative in providing continuity and purpose in human experiences. People continuously construct and reconstruct to make sense of their past and anticipate their future. In the same way, organizational members look at the situatedness of the organization as they try to understand its identity. This focuses on the socio-interpretative approach to organizations. Looking at the narrative clarifies where the identity arises from: the host culture of the organization, or from specific events considered key in the story of the organization.

---

[113] Carlsen, "On the Tacit Side of Organizational Identity," 116.
[114] Philip Selznich, *Leadership in Administration. A Sociological Interpretation* (Berkeley, CA: University of California, 1957).
[115] See K. Corley et al., "Guiding Organizational Identity Through Aged Adolescence," *Journal of Management Inquiry* 15, no. 2 (2006): 85–99.
[116] M. Hatch and M Schultz, "The Dynamics of Organizational Identity," *Human Relations* 55, no. 8 (2002): 989–1018.
[117] Carlsen, "On the Tacit Side of Organizational Identity," 129.

2.3.2.4 Forming Religious Tacit Identity in an Organization

Together, the organization as content and process interact with each other to form the tacit identity of the organization. This focus on the tacit religious identity implies more than the management control that happens at the organization. It is more than a surface phenomenon. It takes into account the importance of interpretation by the staff members as well as the story of the organization.

This approach of understanding the religious tacit identity validates the different organization selves: story, content and subject. Each of these selves are important and together, result in a mediated religious identity. This approach takes seriously the different selves of the organization mediated through "a refrain and style of self-authoring and self-enacting persisting through time."[118] It incorporates different organizational approaches and the two aspects of religion: function and structure.

In this chapter, we begin the design phase of this case study by introducing key terms related to this dissertation. We first looked at the civil society as the domain that faith-based organizations work in. Secondly, institutions as well as organizations as a form of institution are outlined. In the third section of this chapter, the way that religious organization is understood in society is further explored. In the final part of this chapter, the mediated process involved in the religious identity of the organization has been outlined. This process of religious identity is a key theory that frames the dissertation. It is used in the design of the field research, the analysis and subsequent recommendations.

Having argued for a specific list of theories in this chapter, the next chapter continues the design phase by outlining the different ways that a Christian understanding of the organization can be articulated.

---

[118] Carlsen, "On the Tacit Side of Organizational Identity," 135.

CHAPTER THREE

Discovering Three Different Ways of Understanding the Christian Values in an Organization

In the previous chapter, we have outlined different theories that provide context to the faith-based organization. In this chapter, we continue in the design phase with the focus on the faith-based organization, studying specifically the different ways Christianity can influence the organization.

Three different ways that Christianity can influence the organization are outlined in this chapter. These different ways reflect different organizational approaches that have been used to broach this subject. Approaching the organization through different approaches is useful as it broadens the sources of selves of the organization relevant for uncovering religious identity.

The first and most traditional way to outline an organization's Christian understanding is typologies. Typologies seek to categorize different faith-based organizations based on a certain criterion. These typologies list different organizations on a continuum. This method, particularly useful for comparing religious impact in different organizations, is an example of a classical approach to organizations. The second way described in this chapter outlines the impact of religious variables on different organizational variables. With a focus on an individual organization, this method clearly links Christian understanding with different organizational characteristics: its goal oriented nature, boundary maintenance, activity systems as described in the first chapter. This approach is clearly modern as it focuses on descriptive measures, outlining "objective" measures of the organization. The third way to describe Christian understanding in this chapter is in the emphasis on organizational culture, focusing on the extent to which members' express religious understanding in different organizational culture dimensions. This method moves beyond official statements to understand how religious understanding influences the organization. This type of method focuses on the symbolic/interpretative approach. This chapter outlines each of these three approaches.

3.1 First Way: Appropriating Typologies to Categorize Religious Organizations

Typologies are often created to categorize organizations along a spectrum. They clarify the role of religion in the organization and have been used to guide interaction between religious organizations and other organizations. Often, these typologies evaluate organizations in three main areas: organizational control, expression of religion, and program implementation. Organizational control considers variables such as funding resources, decision making power, and processes; expressions of religion include self-identity of the organization, religiosity of participants and definition of outcome measures; finally, program implementation includes selection of services provided, integration of religious elements in service delivery, and participation in religious activities.[119]

An example of a typography includes one developed for church based social programs that incorporate an explicit religious character or message[120]. It uses key organizational variables as well as specific aspects related to the program that the organization is undertaking. On one end of the spectrum, organizations are considered to be "faith-permeated" and on the other end, "secular" organizations. The middle of this spectrum includes organizations ranging from "faith-centered," "faith-affiliated,'" "faith-background organizations," to "faith-secular partnerships." The purpose of developing this typology was to highlight the wide spectrum of organizations called "faith-based." Recognizing that making decisions regarding faith-based organizations as a collective can potentially lead to misrepresentation, typologies can offer a proposed solution for clarity that can lead to further dialogue and research about the role of faith-based organizations. These typologies can assist in studying, funding and making policies regarding social services and educational entities with a connection to religion. In this typology, both program characteristics and organizational variables are studied. Measured organizational variables include the mission statement, founding of the organization, affiliation to other partners, selection of controlling board, selection of staff, as well as subse-

---

[119] Wolfgang Bielefeld and William Suhs Cleveland, "Defining Faith-Based Organizations and Understanding Them through Research," *Nonprofit and Voluntary Sector Quarterly* 42, no. 3 (2013): 442–67.

[120] Ronald J. Sider and Heidi R. Unruh, "Typology of Religious Characteristics of Social Service and Educational Organizations and Program," *Nonprofit and Voluntary Sector Quarterly* 33, no. 1 (2004): 109-134.

quent personnel religious practices. Program characteristics include existence of the religious environment, religious content of the program content, integration of religious components and the expected connection between religious content and the desired outcome.

Typographies are developed to be easily observable with verifiable characteristics with the purpose of categorizing them for policy purposes.[121] While useful for comparison within a broader organizational field, these categories can become limiting, remaining at the level of comparative analysis when understanding the religious aspect of the organization. In addition, to boldly claim an organization to be "secular" or "faith permeating" can be simplistic since this typology does not easily reflect the nuanced impact of religion. At best the use of typologies provides insight into the content of religious understanding of the organization based on selected variables. Focused on comparing different organizations, they are not able to gain a comprehensive understanding of an individual organization in question. In the next approach, the organization in itself is studied. The religious understanding of the organization is described in terms of its organizational variables. This reflects a modern approach to the organization that seeks to provide "objective" measures of the organization.

3.2 Second Way: Relating Christian Understanding to Organizational Characteristics and Variables

As previously described, characteristics of an organization have been described as goal directedness, boundary maintenance and activity systems. The environment was also described as key to the understanding of an organization. This section describes the relation of religiosity to organizational characteristics. Examples of different organizational variables affected by religiosity are also listed. These variables are mainly derived

---

[121] For other examples of typologies, see Stephen V. Monsma, *When Sacred and Secular Mix: Religious Non-Profit Organizations and Public Money* (Lanham, MD: Rowman and Littlefield,1996), who ranks FBOs involved in social welfare and educational institutions as high, medium or low on a Religious Practices scale; or Steven R. Smith and Michael R. Sosin, "The Varieties of Faith Related Agencies," *Public Administration Review* 61, no. 6 (2001): 651–670 who look at three main dimensions: 1) resource dependency, 2) authority and 3) organizational culture; and Julia Berger, "Religious Nongovernmental Organizations: An Exploratory Analysis," *Voluntas: International Journal of Voluntary and Nonprofit Organizations* 14, no. 1 (2003): 22–23, who looks at the orientation and the pervasiveness of the religious dimension in the organization.

from the work of Thomas H. Jeavons,[122] as well as other variables mentioned in religious typologies not mentioned by Jeavons.[123] Table 3.1 shows the summarized version of organizational variables related to religiosity.

Characteristics of the Organization	Related Organizational variables that depict the religious characteristics of organizations	Other models
Goal Oriented Nature	<ul><li>Organizational Goals, Products and Services</li><li>Organizational Self Identity</li><li>Sources of Material Resources</li></ul>	<ul><li>Program Characteristics</li><li>Definition of outcome measures</li><li>Religious Environment</li></ul>
Activity Systems	<ul><li>Information and Decision Making Process</li></ul>	<ul><li>Content</li></ul>
Boundary Maintenance	<ul><li>Organizational power</li><li>Organizational Participants and their inclusion</li></ul>	<ul><li>Constituencies</li><li>Personnel</li></ul>
Environment	<ul><li>Organizational Fields</li><li>Partnerships</li></ul>	

Table 3.1 Organizational Variables Related to Religiosity

---

[122] Thomas H. Jeavons, "Identifying Characteristics of 'Religious' Organizations," in *Sacred Companies Organizational Aspects of Religion and Religious Aspects of Organizations*, ed N.J. Demerath III et al. (New York: Oxford University Press, 1998), 79–95.

[123] These other typologies include Heidi R. Unruh, "Religious Elements of Church-Based Social Service Programs: Types, Variables and Integrative Strategies," *Review of Religious Research* 45, no. 4 (2004): 317–335, Hendrik Sander Westerveld, "Moved by God's Compassion with this World," ThM thesis, University of Tilburg, 2011, 34–37, Bielefeld and Cleveland, "Defining Faith-Based Organizations," 442–67.

Sources: Thomas H. Jeavons, "Identifying Characteristics of 'Religious' Organizations," in *Sacred Companies Organizational Aspects of Religion and Religious Aspects of Organizations*, ed N.J. Demerath III et al. (New York: Oxford University Press, 1998), 79–95, Heidi R. Unruh, "Religious Elements of Church-Based Social Service Programs: Types, Variables and Integrative Strategies," Review of Religious Research 45, no. 4 (2004): 317–335, Hendrik Sander Westerveld, "Moved by God's Compassion with this World," ThM thesis, University of Tilburg, 2011, 34–37, Bielefeld and Cleveland, "Defining Faith-Based Organizations," 442–67.

3.2.1 Goal Oriented Nature of the Organization

The first characteristic, the goal oriented nature of the organization focuses on goals that realize the purpose of the organization. One reason that faith based organizations exist is to address particular needs in society, where these needs are recognized and addressed based on the specific faith's understanding of justice and charity.[124]

One kind of impact that theology has on the actual work that organizations do has been described as a process called "a representation of abstraction level." It describes how Christian understanding actually influences the purpose or collective end of Christian development organizations.[125] This process begins with a theory where religion influences one's worldview and ethical framework. Religion affects the "assumptions" that one has on faith and development. These assumptions thereafter cascade into rules that organizations should observe as they influence program and project objectives, as well as competences in the concrete development work that the organization sets out to do. The final level of abstraction is "concrete practice," the overall experience of the recipient receiving the development aid. The goals of the organization as related to its purpose is what is described as "concrete practice."

With regard to organizational variables, the organizational goals, products and services can reveal the religious motivations of the organization. These can include processes by which these goals and products are produced. Another way of looking at this is the program characteristics that the organization seeks to achieve. To what extent are religious components integrated in the program? To what extent are expectations of religious content related to the desired outcome of the program? To what extent are definitions of outcome measures related to the goals?

---

[124] Jo Anne Schneider, "Comparing Stewardship Across Faith-Based Organizations," *Nonprofit and Voluntary Sector Quarterly* 43, no. 3 (2012): 517–39.

[125] This model is termed "Abstraction levels for reflection: development aid and identity." It is described by Hendrik Sander Westerveld, "Moved by God's Compassion with this World," 22.

The organizational self-identity is revealed by the name of the organization, or its corresponding logo. Does the name of the organization or its corresponding logo point directly towards a certain religious tradition? Sources of material resources focuses on the basis of resources the organization receives. Who provided information and on what basis? Does it come from a specific religious tradition and how did these resources become associated with the organization? Is this due to the specific religious values expounded by the organization?

Other aspects of program characteristics relate to the organizational self-identity and the sources of material resources. From the perspective of the religious environment, do programs take place in a space whose main function is for religious purposes? Are objects with religious meaning present in the program space? Also, to what extent are beneficiaries expected to attend religious meetings as part of the program?

3.2.2 Activity Systems

As previously discussed, activity systems are systems constructed in the organization to achieve its goals. One way that activity systems related to Christian understanding is the impact of the faith tradition on stewardship support structures. Stewardship has been defined as the overall administration and guidance of nonprofit organizations by the founding or supporting faith community, based on their practical theology.[126] In a study done to analyze support structures of faith-based organizations, results showed that these support structures were dependent on the practical teaching of its founding faith communities. Three different systems were described with differences arising from the different faith traditions. These included the institutionalized system, congregational systems, and network systems. These are summarized in what follows.

Institutionalized systems have centralized structures with which faith-based organizations of the same faith tradition work. These faith traditions, for example, Jewish and Catholic, tend to be well-established, recognizing the work that faith-based organizations do as part of their responsibility. These institutionalized structures include centralized fundraising, volunteer recruitment, training and sometimes facilities management, managed by authorized members of the faith tradition. A tradition of centralized planning exists with the ability to share resources across different organizations of the same faith traditions. Congregational systems are less

---

[126] Jo Anne Schneider, "Comparing Stewardship across Faith-Based Organizations," *Nonprofit and Voluntary Sector Quarterly* 43, no. 3 (2012): 517–39.

centralized compared to institutionalized systems. In this instance, congregations in well-established protestant denominations are seen as the main channel for implementing activities determined by their faith. Churches adopt projects and have representatives as advisory members of these different faith-based organizations. These organizations are dependent on individual congregations for board appointments, financial support and even the supply of volunteers. The final type of system, network systems, are relatively new and are not necessarily dependent on only one congregation. Instead, they are supported by social networks with a more flexible system, where decisions made do not reflect a particular congregation. These organizations are supported by a network of individuals focused on a particular ministry with the same understanding on how faith should influence work. As looser systems, network systems do not have a clear expected source for resources but are rather dependent on like-minded believers with similar goals.

The organizational variable information and decision-making process has impact on activity systems. It considers key information considered important and necessary for organizational operations, how this information is derived and the extent to which decision-making processes are affected or shaped by religious beliefs.[127] This can also be described as 'content' in dimensions of determining religious identity. Content is related to how the organization, in its approach, tries to account for what drives the founders, members and employees.[128] This is often expressed through activity systems that members of the organization develop within an organization.

3.2.3 Boundary Maintenance

Boundary maintenance involves both processes related to membership and people in the organization. Just as with activity systems, the impact of different faith traditions leading to different kinds of systems has been explored, in the same way, impact of these faith traditions on boundary maintenance of the organization has also been studied.[129]

Caputo describes faith-based organizations as either institutionalized systems, congregational systems, or network systems.[130] For faith tradi-

---

[127] Jeavons, "Identifying Characteristics of 'Religious' Organizations," 79–95.
[128] Sider and Unruh, "Typology of Religious Characteristics," 109–134.
[129] Schneider, "Comparing Stewardship across Faith-Based Organizations," 517–39.
[130] Richard K. Caputo, "Religious Capital and Intergenerational Transmission of Volunteering as Correlates of Civic Engagement," *Nonprofit and Voluntary Sector Quarterly* 38, no. 6 (2009): 983–1002.

tions that embrace the institutionalized system, members of the organization are recruited and trained centrally. These can include volunteers, or staff of such organizations. For faith-based organizations from a background of congregational systems, the congregations involved tend to be influential in deciding on key members in the organization, as well as being a ready source of volunteers for such organizations. Congregations often will specify their preference for a certain percentage of the board to come from a particular denomination or congregation. While fastidious about the composition of the organization, they rarely get involved with training and setting of qualifications. Finally, network systems transcend congregations where individuals associate themselves with the organization because of the specific ministry of the organization. They are dependent on individual social networks of members in the organization, with the founding faith approach a key reason to join the organization. One key element for organizations that function from the network system is the bonding social capital based on shared theological values.[131] This draws people to such an organization, where these organizations become a faith community for its members.

One organizational variable, organizational power,[132] looks closely at boundary maintenance, including development, distribution and use of power within the organization. This variable, focuses on the different stakeholders and what they get, when and how. The extent that the organization's power is derived from explicitly religious sources, or distributed depending on explicitly religious value is dependent on the extent of importance this religion has in society. Organizational participants and their inclusion is another variable which looks closely at the internal stakeholders involved in an organization. To what extent are these stakeholders chosen based on their religious affiliation? And to what extent do they share the same religious beliefs? Key to this variable is the question how they became a part of the organization. They are thus sometimes described as constituencies related to the organization. The constituency constitutes the connection of the organization to a specific group of people or a denomination that can impact the way the organization evolves.[133]

---

[131] See Robert D. Putnam, *Bowling Alone: The Collapse and Revival of American Community* (New York: Simon & Schuster, 2000).
[132] Jeavons, "Identifying Characteristics of 'Religious' Organizations," 79–95.
[133] Westerveld, "Moved by God's Compassion with this World," 22.

3.2.4 Environment

The final aspect presented is the operational environment of the organization. While not directly a characteristic of the organization, it is integral to the kind of organization set up. In the previous chapter, the different theories related to religious organization and their interaction in society has been explored. This included the discussion of bureaucratization and neo-institutional theory. In this section, the neo-institutional theory is further explored with the focus on the external organizational field experienced by Christian faith-based organizations.

As outlined, the neo-institutional theory focuses on the external pressures faced by the religious organization. One way that this external pressures can be further categorized is through the discussion of organizational fields. The organizational field looks at different external stakeholders involved with the organization. These can include key suppliers, resource and product consumers, regulatory agencies and other organizations that produce similar services and products. Relationships within the organizational field can exist both vertically and horizontally.[134]

Faith-based organizations develop relationships with different parties who might have different notions about the Christian faith, and with differing impact upon the organization. On the one hand, faith-based organizations have relations to their founding faith traditions. These can include church congregations, affiliates, organizations and individuals. As seen earlier, these faith communities have an impact on support structures of the organization as well as on people who are part of the community. Support of these faith communities is dependent on the extent to which these organizations reflect their values.[135] On the other hand, these organizations exist within society and might consciously seek validation as legitimate members within their area of expertise. There is a need for these faith-based organizations to connect to higher levels of decision-making as well as share information with other established organizations. This has been considered a key reason why many religious organizations try to seek formal recognition as "NGOs." Being

---

[134] Harry S. Stout and D. Scott Cormode, "Institution and the Story of American Religion," in *Sacred Companies Organizational Aspects of Religion and Religious Aspects of Organizations*, ed. N.J. Demerath III et al. (New York: Oxford University Press, 1998), 62–78.

[135] Schneider, "Comparing Stewardship across Faith-Based Organizations," 517–39.

too explicitly religious can result in legal obstacles when applying for public funding.[136]

The impact of these relationships on the organization can lead to isomorphism. Organizational isomorphism is the process by which institutions lose their distinctive features and come to resemble one another.[137] For Christian organizations, there is a real danger of disregarding one's own Christian understanding in a regular relation with organizations that do not share their faith. Three different mechanisms for isomorphism have been listed which result in organizations resembling each other. In coercive isomorphism, organizations resemble each other through the welding of political influence of some institutions by an explicit show of power and authority. In mimetic isomorphism, organizations resemble each other by mimicking strategies of other similar organizations as they seek to further legitimize themselves. The third kind of isomorphism, normative, takes place when organizations are expected to conform to external standards. Normative pressures of professionalization can push religious organizations into a certain mold to conform to external standards related to what their organizations seek to do. Depending on the context and organizational field of a Christian organization, different kinds of isomorphism may take place.

One such example is Harvard University. Established as an educational institutional, located in New England, it has gradually lost its Christian basis. At the start, the motto of the university was *Veritas Christo et Ecclesiae* ("Truth for Christ and the Church"). Today, this motto has simply been reduced to *Veritas*. To take another example, the Christian Children Fund started in 1938 by a missionary as a charity to help alleviate global poverty among children. It has since lost its Christian roots, and in 2009 changed its name to Childfund International.[138]

In this section, we have looked in detail at the second way that the Christian understanding of the organization can be uncovered. Character-

---

[136] Julia Berger, "Religious Nongovernmental Organizations: An Exploratory Analysis," *Voluntas: International Journal of Voluntary and Nonprofit Organizations* 14, no. 1 (March 2003): 17, 20.

[137] The original theory of isomorphism was elaborated by Paul J. DiMaggio and Walter W. Powell in "The Iron Cage Revisited: Institutional Isomorphism and Collective Rationality in Organizational Fields," *American Sociological Review* 48, no. 2 (1983): 147–60. This write up focuses on the description written by Stout and Cormode, "Institution and the Story of American Religion," 69–70.

[138] Peter Greer and Chris Horst, *Mission Drift* (Bloomington, MS: Bethany House, 2014), 15–22.

istics of the organization that can be related to the Christian understanding have been briefly discussed with the variables listed. This method, describing the religiosity of different organizational variable, reflects a modern approach to the organization. It gives a fuller picture of the organization's Christian understanding compared to the use of typologies. One main limitation of this approach is the static picture of religious understanding of the organization. Information from this method is drawn from the formal identity as described in symbols or policies of the organization. This information can be useful content sources for identity formation. This however does not take into account the "lived" identity, perceptions held by the current members of the organization, or actual activities undertaken by the organization. To have a fuller understanding of religion in the organization, it is important to make space to understand the social processes within the organization that are related to the religious content of the organization. A socio-interpretative approach to the organization is taken up in the third method. It considers how religion can have an impact on creation of meaning in the organization through the study of organizational culture.

3.3 Third Way: Studying the Impact of Christian Values in the Organization's Culture

Moving beyond established methods of studying religion in the organization, the third way focuses on the impact of Christian values on the organizational culture of the organization. To study organizational culture is to take seriously the people of the organization as they work together as a group. This goes beyond prescribed management that influences the organization. Instead, it considers how members of the organization with their own particularity can influence Christian understanding of the organization, focusing on a socio-interpretative approach to the organization.

Study of the organizational culture gives importance to the combined reality experienced in the organization. It focuses on the meaning making process as well as taking seriously the role of organizational members in determining the resulting role of Christian understanding in the organization. This goes beyond explicit measurements and typologies of organizations and seeks to understand meanings and beliefs members assign to organizational behavior, as well as how these assigned meanings influence the ways in which these members behave.[139] To study the organizational

---

[139] David A. Buchanan and Andrzej Huczynski, *Organizational Behaviour* (New Jersey: Prentice Hall, 2007), 624.

culture is to take seriously the subconscious self-salient knowledge of members of the organization.

In the study of organizational culture, the work of organizational culture scientist, Edgar Schein is largely referred to. As defined by him, organizational culture is as a "pattern of shared basic assumptions learned by a group as it solved its problems of external adaptation and internal integration, which has been considered valid, and therefore to be taught to new members as the correct way to perceive, think, and feel in relation to those problems."[140] Recognizing the potential of organizational culture to provide more insight to the organization, the following section presents a detailed introduction to organizational culture, focusing on a) the organization as a group, b) meaning in the organization, c) the role of the external environment in influencing the group, and d) management as mechanisms that regulate meaning creation.

3.3.1 The Organization Comprising a Group of Individuals

This focus on organizational culture turns the focus to the people in the organization. Looking at the cultural perspective provides an alternative to the rational-mechanistic view of organization that considers its people as tools for achieving the organization's goals. This cultural perspective emphasizes non-rational aspects of people, such as their values, beliefs and feelings.[141] In this instance, the organization is looked at as a social unit, an entity made up of a group of individuals. Organizational culture is the result of a set of social constructs within an organization mediated by different organizational members as they seek to develop a system of meaning.[142] This study of the organization's culture is particularly useful in understanding the people's interpretation of the office values.

The organization as a social unit can be studied as a collective group, as well as through the different networks within the organization. The first approach emphasizes the group's unified accumulated learning. What matters is looking at the social unit as a collective in its striving towards patterning and integration. In this instance, organizational culture arises because of humans' need for stability, consistency and meaning. As a social unit, the organization would have developed some kind of shared history

---

[140] Edgar Schein, *Organizational Culture and Leadership* (San Francisco: Jossey-Bass, 2010), 18.
[141] Buchanan and Huczynski, *Organizational Behaviour*, 624.
[142] Martin Kilduff and David Krackhardt, *Interpersonal Networks in Organizations: Cognitive, Personality, Dynamics, and Culture* (New York: Cambridge University Press, 2008), 237.

that would have evolved into a culture.¹⁴³ At the same time, focusing only on the collective nature of the social group can be too simplistic since nuances within the group have an impact on the organizational culture. Therefore, networks present in the organization form an alternative way of looking at the group. Group dynamics are important as the informal network of coworkers determines knowledge of the organization. Because of similarities within a group, they may have the same interpretation of the situation, hence arriving at the same meaning, which can differ from the general meaning held by the entire organization.

Both understanding of the organization is taken seriously here. The organization is understood a social entity made up of people who may all agree on some things, and at the same time, disagree on others, defaulting to an agreement with a smaller group within the organization. Some meanings seem to be agreed on collectively, with others less so, depending on the network to which certain individuals belong. The discussion of meaning in an organizational context is described next.

3.3.2 Meaning Held by Organizations

We have looked at the organization as a group of people that sometimes hold collective views and at other times, differing views. In this section, we focus on what these views are, described as the meaning of the organization. It is this meaning embraced by people in the organization that make up the organization's culture. This system of meaning that the organization embraces is mediated by different factors. The following section examines further the understanding of meaning, followed by a discussion of mediating factors such as networks, power, internalization of meaning as well as the social processes involved. Finally, a separate section on how the environment can impact the overall meaning mediation is discussed, given its importance.

3.3.2.1 The Kind of Meaning in the Organization

An organization exist in society for a particular reason. The meaning embodied in the organization should also be linked to the role of the organization within society. At the same time, the meaning that results in an organization is dependent on the interpretation that staff members have on the way the organization handles two sets of problem related to their role: survival, growth and adaptation within their environment, integration of

---

¹⁴³ Schein, *Organizational Culture and Leadership*, 18.

the internal processes to ensure the capacity to continue to survive and adapt.[144] It cannot be assumed that that the meaning embraced by staff members are primarily influenced by the role of the organization.

Table 3.2 illustrates a comprehensive list of different problems and resultant categories of meaning drawn up by organizational culture scientist Schein. These different categories of meaning develop as an organization solves problems related to the external adaptation and internal integration. These meanings are expressed in society through organizational culture dimensions, existing in the form of thoughts, belief feelings and values of staff members.[145]

Problems of External Adaptation and Survival	Resultant Categories of Meaning
Mission and Strategy	Obtaining a shared understanding of core mission, primary task, manifest functions and latent functions
Goals	Developing consensus on goals, as derived from the core mission
Means	Developing consensus on the means to be used to attain the goal, such as the organization structure, division of labor, reward system and authority system.
Measurement	Developing consensus on the criteria to be used in measuring how well the group is doing in fulfilling its goals, such as the information and control system.
Correction	Developing consensus on the appropriate or repair strategies to be use if goals are not met.
The problems of Internal Integration	**Resultant Categories of Meaning**
Creating a common language and conceptual categories	If members cannot communicate with and understand each other, a group is impossible by definition.

---

[144] Schein, *Organizational Culture and Leadership*, 73.
[145] Ibid., 74.

Defining group boundaries and criteria for inclusion and exclusion	The group must be able to define itself. Who is in and who is out, and by what criteria is membership determined?
Distributing power, authority and status	Every group must work out its pecking order, its criteria and rules for how someone gets, maintains and loses power and authority. Consensus in this area is crucial to help members manage feelings of aggression.
Developing norms of trust, intimacy, friendship and love	Every group must work out its rules of the game for peer relationships, for relationships between the sexes and for the manner in which openness and intimacy are to be handled in the context of managing the organization's tasks. Consensus in this area is crucial to help members define trust and manage feelings of affection and love.
Defining and allocating of rewards and punishment	Every group must know what is heroic and sinful behaviors are and must achieve consensus on what is a reward and what is a punishment.
Explaining the unexplainable	Every group, like every society faces unexplainable events that must be given meaning so that members can respond to them and avoid the anxiety of dealing with the unexplainable and uncontrollable.

Table 3.2 Categories of Meaning in an Organization Related to External Adaptation and Survival and Internal Integration

Source: Edgar Schein, *Organizational Culture and Leadership* (San Francisco: Jossey-Bass, 2010), 74 & 94.

For a faith-based organization, religion can influence the meaning firstly through the external adaptation – where the specific content of faith can assist in the solving of these problems. In addition, the networks and other societal function that this faith has can also influence the meaning in the organization. In the next section, the discussion of networks is further explicated.

3.3.2.2 Importance of Networks in Meaning Creation

The social unit of an organization has been described as the collective group of people in the organization. While the collective group may have similar ideas, there are also instances that the group do not agree with each other. One way that this has been described is through the discussion of subcultures. Schein described the organization as having subcultures that share many assumptions of the total organization, but yet individually hold assumptions beyond those of the total organization, reflecting their functional tasks, their unique experiences. He listed three generic types of subcultures based on their role within the organization. These include the operator subculture, the engineering/design subculture, and the executive subculture. Depending on the subculture, each holds to distinct assumptions due to the shared experiences of the smaller group.[146]

With the description of subculture, organizational culture then is a result of different meanings created and ascribed to organizational events by various groups and interests in pursuit of their aims, a result of different networks and their understanding of organizational events.[147] These networks are key to the final organizational culture that is expressed in the organization. Instead of thinking of them as fixed and quickly decided subcultures, these networks can also be potentially dynamic, continuously forming, and reaffirming. Networks are formed when members share enough in common that there are sets of values and beliefs more or less ambiguously delineating group identity within a subculture.[148] Schein categorized networks based on an individual's functional tasks or experience given his or her level in a hierarchy.[149] Besides an individual's role, another key aspect in networking is the strength of relationships that one has. The stronger the relationships, the stronger the influence the network might have on the individual's beliefs and values. Interpersonal networks influence individual interpretations of experience, and these networks help control the diversity of possible interpretations that occurs within the group.[150] One key implication related to faith-based organizations is the understanding that faith can have differing importance to the organiza-

---

[146] Schein, *Organizational Culture and Leadership*, 55–57.
[147] Ed Young, "On the Naming of the Rose: Interests and Multiple Meanings as Elements of Organizational Culture," *Organizational Studies* 10, no. 2 (1989): 190.
[148] Ibid., 201–202.
[149] Schein, *Organizational Culture and Leadership*, 56–57.
[150] Kilduff and Krackhardt, *Interpersonal Networks*, 247–249.

tion based on the networks that is questioned. This faith impact is dependent on the networks involved which influences the social processes in the organization. Different networks interact with different groups differently resulting in different social processes. Through the interaction of different groups, meaning is created. The social processes involved in creation and transmission of meaning are considered below.

3.3.2.3   Social Processes in Meaning Creation and Transmission

Thus far, we have described the social unit of the organization, the meaning that arises through problem-solving, the networks involved in the organization and now, we discussed the social processes involved in meaning creation and transmission. Meaning in an organizational context is sustained through social processes. There is a process involved before individuals come to embrace the meaning of the organization. A spectrum can be imagined in discussing meaning in the organization. At one end of the spectrum, each individual has his or her own idiosyncratic meaning. At the other end of the spectrum, most organizational individuals have internalized meaning such that it is no longer questioned.[151] The question that this section then answers is, how can meaning be internalized for the group?

At a basic level, meaning is embraced when similar experiences are categorized. Interpretation of these similar experiences through social interactions and group communication creates, transmits and sustains meaning. By use of a certain label for interpretation of these similar events, the group establishes a coincident value of the event, which becomes the basis for communication and regularity within the community. Repeated reciprocity of action reinforces the expected meaning attached to a certain behavior.[152]

One way that the group meaning can be derived is through reflecting on events that take place within the group. This reflection focuses on shared experiences and reactions, as well as a collective understanding of the experiences. Depending on the stage of the group, it will be preoccupied with certain questions before successfully moving on to the next stage. As an example, the group stage of formation sees the group wrestle with the question of authority. The final reflection of the group reinforced by action can then become shared meaning regarding authority. This will then be shared with other members of the group, and possibly to new

---

[151] Barbara Gray, Michel G. Bougon and Anne Donnellon, "Organizations as Constructions and Destructions of Meaning," *Journal of Management* 11, no. 2 (1985): 83.
[152] Ibid., 88.

members through the process of socialization. Questions in the group change as the organization evolves.[153] This is important to note for faith-based organizations. An organization's Christian understanding needs to be part of the narrative in the interpretation of organizational events. In addition, it is also important for the Christian narrative to stay relevant as the organization evolve.

As a socially constructed entity, an organization does not happen naturally but rather within a context of power and intentional management control. Before looking at management control, the next section focuses on an understanding of power, key in the different stages of group dynamics.

3.3.2.4 Power in Meaning Transmission

The final meaning transmitted in an organization is a result of power dynamics of the group. Needless to say, power is crucial in the shaping of meaning for the members.[154] This section provides an introduction to the power dynamics within the group.

Power is instrumental in bringing a group together despite possible differences among its members. It influences and structures rules and procedures that determine the organization in different ways, including "different forms of knowledge, definition of distinct fields of understanding within an organization, the relationships within repertoires of concepts; the establishment of 'truth'; the delimitation of what can and what cannot be said; the emergence and presentation of 'subject-positions' which distributes and hierarchies the field of 'unequal relations.'"[155] This results in a fixed dominant meaning at any one time, not open to question.

Power, rather than being permanent, takes place within a specific situation and needs to be continually reproduced and sustained. Because power is held together by power relations, it is important to understand the power relations present in the organization, which facilitates an understanding of how final meaning is derived.[156]

---

[153] Schein, *Organizational Culture and Leadership*, 198–204.
[154] Gray, Bougon and Donnellon, "Organization as Constructions and Destructions of Meaning," 89.
[155] Gray, Bougon and Donnellon, "Organization as Constructions and Destructions of Meaning," 89.
[156] Stephen Linstead and Robert Grafton-Small, "On Reading Organizational Culture," *Organizational Studies* 13, no. 3 (1992): 339.

3.3.2.5 Internalization of Meaning for Sustainability

So far, the social processes related to how meaning becomes mainstream in the organization, with importance given to power relations has been described. Once meanings within the organization are established, these meanings undergo a process of internalization for these meanings to be sustained in the organization. Internalization is the process of ascribing meaning to an event because it is meaningful to the individual. This means more than understanding the event within the organization. It considers the extent to which individuals agree with the meaning. As the meaning is repeated within the organization, in tune with individuals' preferences, interpretive schemes in the organization can then become crystalized and internalized.[157] The extent to which this meaning is internalized depends on how the meaning of the organization connects to the individual, if he/she agrees to the meaning of the organization.

Many factors are involved in internalization. One factor that influences the strength and substance of what is internalized is the significance of the communicators to the individual. This communicator can be in the form of the modeling and training provided by the organization where individuals acquire meanings associated with specific role-related behavior.[158] In addition, it is dependent on the relationship that the communicator has to the individual, which may seem to be like a 'natural fit' or intentionally constructed. Research shows that organizational identity of organizational members is positively influenced through positive manager-subordinate interactions.[159] Finally, a big factor that influences the extent to which meaning is internalized is the external environment of the meaning. An individual is not only part of the organization, but also part of the broader society that the organization is in. It is therefore understandable that the larger external environment plays a large role in the extent of internalization by the individual. The environment influences the individual to different degrees as these societal values and meaning have an impact on preexisting values and meanings of individuals. It can influence the individual's worldview as well as preferred management style.

---

[157] Gray, Bougon and Donnellon "Organization as Constructions and Destructions of Meaning," 85, 89.
[158] Ibid., 86.
[159] For example, L. Melita Prati, Amy McMillan-Capehart, and Joy H. Karriker, "Affecting Organizational Identity: A Manager's Influence," *Journal of Leadership and Organizational Studies* 15, no. 4 (2009): 404–415.

The deeper the organization meaning is internalized, the deeper it influences the organizational culture of the organization. Organization culture can be studied at different layers, from the outer layer of practice, to the middle layer of values, to the inner layer of basic assumptions.[160] Different scholars have different views on the possible depth of organizational culture. On the one hand, some scholars believe that meaning cannot be fully internalized as individuals would have developed their value system by the time they join an organization. This would result in organizational culture being held at a more superficial level, that of practices. Scholars who hold this view believe that little can influence individuals at the workplace. Operating at the level of practices, people complete the task at hand without subscribing to the cultural meaning to which the task is attached.[161] On the other hand, other scholars believe that organizational culture may become very deep, getting to the point of basic assumptions. As individuals of the organization collectively work through problems confronting the organization, they arrive at a reliable set of beliefs and values for solving the group's problems. These beliefs and values become implicit assumptions to guide behavior, informing group members how to perceive, think about and feel about things. These assumptions tend to be non-confrontable and non-debatable.[162]

In this chapter, the potential and possibility of organizational culture to arrive at the point of basic assumptions is affirmed. As meaning is created and transmitted through social processes, the extent to which people can contribute to and participate in problem solving of the organization influences the degree to which organizational values and beliefs are held. Organizational members can either be actively involved in solving group problems at the organizational level or be passively participating in the organization. It is therefore important to ensure a high level of participation of organizational members in solving organizational problems particularly in different environmental context.

In this section, meaning creation of meaning has been discussed in some detail. The next section focuses on the external environment of the organization, before turning to management control, or how management seeks to influence meaning and its internalization.

---

[160] Schein, *Organizational Culture and Leadership*, 23–24.
[161] Geert Hofstede, Gert Jan Hofstede, and Michael Minkow, *Cultures and Organizations Software of the Mind* (New York: Mc Graw Hill, 2011), 10.
[162] Schein, *Organizational Culture and Leadership*, 28–33.

3.3.3 Influences of External Environment in Organizational Culture

The external environment is the societal operational context of the organization. To look at the external environment is to take culture seriously. As an abstract concept, culture promises to provide better understanding of behavioral norms, practices and values shared among a group of people. To look at the cultural impact of society is to acknowledge the uniqueness of different societies because of the collective learning history shared by people within the society. Having described the impact of the environment on the organization at different points of this chapter and the previous, this section focuses on two main ways that the external environment can affect the organizational culture, firstly through the values and practices embedded in culture, and secondly, through the practices held by those in the similar sector.

3.3.3.1 Values and Practices in Culture

As a means to understand the different depths of culture in society, management scholar Hofstede, Hofstede and Minkow differentiated culture into two different layers: values and practices. Values are broad preferences within the culture of one form over the other, while practices in a culture include rituals, heroes and symbols. These practices are the expression of culture. Because values are well established by individuals from an early age, there is less chance of changing values in the culture once they are formed compared to practices. Such an understanding of culture has an impact on organizations. As individuals enter the organization at an adult age, these individuals do not pick up or form new values from the organization as they have already developed their own.[163]

In addition, longstanding values from each culture results in different preferences of management practices found in different national cultures. These different preferences in national management practices have been a keen topic of interest in international management.[164] One established research of Hofstede was related to his study of IBM, a large multinational company that has worked with computers in 72 countries. He looked at the

---

[163] Hofstede, Hofstede, and Minkow, *Cultures and Organizations Software of the Mind*, 7–10.
[164] This chapter mentions two tools used to look at the impact of National Culture. There are other tools researched as well. To find out more, refer to Sabine Scheffknecht, "Multinational Enterprises: Organizational Culture vs National Culture," *International Journal of Management Cases* 6 (2011): 73–78.

effects of cultural differences and developed four dimensions of cultural differences, including power distance, uncertainty avoidance, individualism and masculinity. Understanding different country values is useful for managers and leaders of the organization as they became aware of working preferences of individuals working in each culture, and can therefore tailor their management controls and leadership styles accordingly. This research on preferred management practices in different countries was also taken by the GLOBE study. GLOBE is a worldwide, multiphase, multi method research project that seeks to investigate how cultural values are related to organizational practices, conceptions of leadership, the economic competitiveness of societies, and the human condition of their members.[165] This project considered nine cultural dimensions for each country studied: performance orientation, uncertainty avoidance, humane orientation, institutional collectivism, in group collectivism, assertiveness, gender egalitarianism, future orientation and power distance.

In these research methods, the key for success in organizations is widely correlated to the ability to be sensitive to identified cultural differences and to accommodate them within management practices in organizations. This correlation however does not take into account the goals of the organization. As faith-based organizations have been described as having a purpose in society, the management practices of the organization cannot be the only factor for success. The values of the country are important, but they cannot be the most decisive for its success. In the next section, the other leading environmental factor that influences the organizational culture, the sector that the organization is in, is described.

3.3.3.2 Organization as Part of a Particular Sector within Civil Society

Besides having an impact on management practices, the particular sector that the organization is working in can also impact the organizational culture. This includes amongst the other factors the level and degree of government regulation, development of the industry within a society, and national economic systems.[166] These factors influence the way that meaning is created in the organization.

---

[165] Globe Project, accessed February 1 2015, http://www.tlu.ee/~sirvir/IKM/Leadership%20Dimensions/globe_project.html. See also Robert J. House, *Culture, Leadership and Organizations: The GLOBE Study of 62 Societies* (Thousand Oaks, Calif: Sage Publications, 2004)

[166] Marcus Dickson, Renee S. Beshears, and Vipin Gupta, "The Impact of Societal Culture and Industry on Organizational Culture," in *Culture Leadership and*

In the previous chapter, the civil society was described as the domain where faith-based organizations operate in. In the role that it plays, the organization may be bound by certain legal constraints that can include non-distribution constraints, voluntary governance or adherence to certain tax rules.[167] These legal constraints can influence the organization depending on the understanding and acceptance of these rules by its staff members. In addition, there are individuals who do not understand or accept the civil society as a "space" for citizens to engage with each other, where conditions of this sphere should be respected and not controlled by the state.[168] This can lead to different expressions of organizational culture because of the different interpretations and subsequent actions held by the staff members.

Finally, real pressure can be exerted on the organization to succumb to isomorphic pressures in some industries, especially when the government has a vested interest in the industry. As an example, with the prerequisite of public funding of social enterprises in the UK comes the expectation that these organizations are managed more professionally and become more self-sufficient. This means that organizations have to exhibit their abilities in areas like performance management, marketing and governance. They should also prove how their organization is becoming more self-sustaining through trade.[169] This can invariably lead such organizations to experience isomorphism, moving resources away from their original intentions, as well as blurring their identity in such industries.

While these external pressures impact the overall organizational culture, this process of creating and transmitting meaning within the organization is not passive, but rather can be intentionally steered through management control. This final section of the chapter looks at how intentional control impacts organizational culture.

Organizations the Globe Study of 62 Societies, ed. Robert J. House et al. (California: SAGE Publications, 2004), 76.

[167] Paige Hull Teegarden, Denice Rothman Hinden, and Paul Sturm, *The Nonprofit Organizational Culture Guide: Revealing the Hidden Truths that Impact Performance* (San Francisco: Jossey-Bass, 2011), 13–19.

[168] Helmut K. Anheier, *Nonprofit Organizations: Theory, Management, Policy* (New York: Routledge, 2005), 56.

[169] Chris Mason, "Isomorphism, Social Enterprise and the Pressure to Maximize Social Benefits," *Journal of Social Entrepreneurship* 3, no. 1 (2012): 76.

3.3.4 Intentional Control in Organizational Culture

Management control is a large mediating factor that influences the culture of the organization. This has otherwise been termed the rationalizing and legitimatizing tasks of management.[170] Management as a study has emerged with the rise of the industrialized society.[171] These tasks of management can include any part of the sense making process, for example introducing concepts, developing cause/effect relationships or imparting values. The goal of management control is to define organizational reality and to construct its consensual acceptance.[172] Some primary functions of the management have been listed as "planning, organizing, staffing and controlling."[173]

Management control provides justification to the actions of the organization, influencing the sense making process through intentionally developing a common understanding and meaning. This management control has an impact both on members of the organization and on the wider external environment, seeking to clarify how organizational activities are consistent with the purposes of the organization, yet play a pertinent role in the larger social system.

Management control involves more than the people involved. It takes place within a process and requires a subsequent system necessary for follow up. It is viewed as making what is going on in the organizational meaningful and sensible to the organizational participants, and furthermore developing a social consensus and social definition around the activities being undertaken. Involving more than labelling or sense making—it involves the development of a social consensus around those labels the definition of activity.[174] Decisions made in management relate to good leadership. Rather than functioning merely as a channel for routine work, management is involved in setting the direction for sense making in the organization. In the following section, two different factors that are highlighted as having a profound impact on the choice of management control of the organization is outlined. These include the operational context of the organization, and the particular stage in which the organization finds itself.

---

[170] Jeffrey Pfeffer, "Management as Symbolic Action: The Creation and Maintenance of Organizational Paradigms," *Research in Organizational Behavior* 3 (1981): 5.
[171] Peter G. Northouse, *Leadership: Theory and Practice*, 6th ed. (Los Angeles: SAGE Publications, 2013), 12.
[172] Gray, Bougon and Donnellon, "Organization as Constructions and Destructions of Meaning," 89.
[173] See Henri Fayol, *General and Industrial Management*, trans. Constance Storrs (London: Pitman and Sons, 1916).
[174] Pfeffer, "Management as Symbolic Action," 21.

3.3.4.1 Impact of Country Context

The environment that the organization is in continues to be important. It has an impact on the kind of management seen as desirable in the operational context of the organization. As an example of how the country context is taken seriously, management scientists focused on two cultural dimensions as described by Hofstede: power distance and uncertainty avoidance. These dimensions are chosen due to their relation to two questions central in organizing: who has the power to decide what as well as what rules or procedures will be followed to attain the desired ends?[175] The first question is related to how power distance is perceived, and the second, to uncertainty avoidance. Power distance is related to the "emotional distance that separates subordinates from their bosses, defined as the "extent to which less powerful members of institutions and organizations within a country expect and accept that power is distributed unequally".[176] Uncertainty avoidance is the cultural dimension within cultures that considers "the extent to which members of a culture feel threatened by ambiguous and unknown situations."[177]

To make research results more useful for organizations, Hofstede juxtaposed his work with that of organizational theorist, Mintzberg, who studied the different aspects of the organization, different mechanisms, and a typical configuration of an organization. This is illustrated in the figure 3.1. This can be a good guide for managers as they navigate the different cultural contexts in different countries. With the goal of social consensus by the group members, the appropriate coordinating mechanisms should either be appropriated, or actively promoted as necessary for problem solving in the organization.

---

[175] Hofstede, Hofstede, and Minkow, *Cultures and Organizations Software of the Mind*, 302.
[176] Ibid., 61.
[177] Ibid., 191.

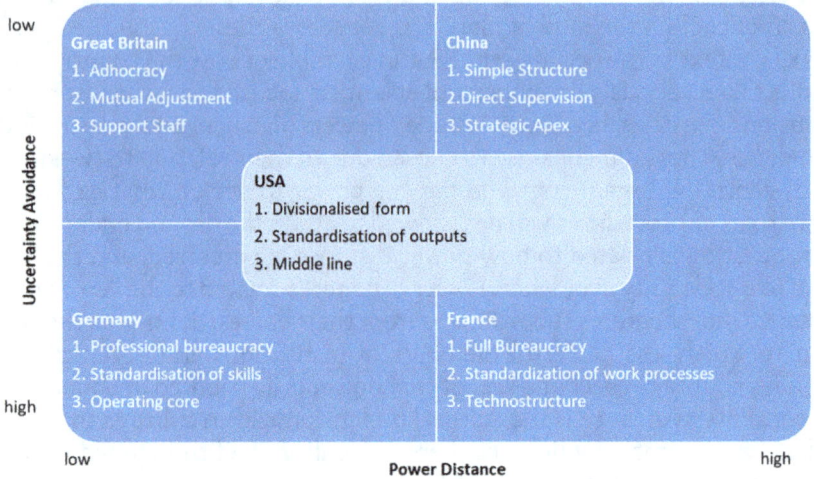

Figure 3.1 Mintzberg's Five Preferred Configuration of Organizations Projected onto a Power Distance x Uncertainty-avoidance Matrix

Source: Hofstede, Hofstede, and Minkow, *Cultures and Organizations Software of the Mind*, 314

3.3.4.2 The Stage of the Organization

Another factor for management to consider is the current stage of the organization. Depending on this stage of the organization, overall management may adopt different emphases for the organization. For example, at the founding stage of the organization, there is the need to intentionally learn together as a group. However, as the organization progresses, some diversity within the culture might be appreciated. As such, management decisions regarding the culture made at the founding of the organization are different from those of a midlife, matured or declining organization.

The need to create a strong organizational culture often occurs at the founding of the organization, with a need to reinforce adoption of the founder's beliefs, values and assumptions within the group. Schein describes two categories of embedding mechanisms available to leaders: Primary embedding mechanisms as well as secondary articulation and reinforcement mechanisms.[178] These different mechanisms as described by

---

[178] Schein, *Organizational Culture and Leadership*, 235.

Schein is illustrated in table 3.3 below. It illustrates the different mechanisms that is available for the leader to reflected on when driving the culture of the organization.

Primary Embedding Mechanisms
• What leaders pay attention to, measure and control on a regular basis
• How leaders react to critical incidents and organizational crisis
• How leaders allocate resources
• Deliberate role modeling, teaching and coaching
• How leaders allocate rewards and status
• How leaders recruit, select, promote and excommunicate
Secondary Articulation and Reinforcement Mechanisms
• Organizational design and structure
• Organizational systems and procedures
• Rites and rituals of the organization
• Design of physical space, facades and buildings
• Stories about important events and people
• Formal statements of organizational philosophy, creeds and charters

Table 3.3 Mechanisms Available to Leaders

Source: Edgar Schein, *Organizational Culture and Leadership* (San Francisco: Jossey-Bass, 2010), 74 & 94.

During the midlife of the organization, differentiation in the organization becomes more pronounced with the strengthening of networks. These networks can originate a result of different reasons, such as functional/occupational, location, the difference in output, market realities or technology, divisionalization or hierarchy level.[179] For an organization in midlife, what is necessary is the insight and skill to help the organization evolve into whatever will make it more effective in the future. In some cases, this might mean increasing cultural diversity, or in other cases to consider how to pull together diverse subcultures and impose new common assumptions

---

[179] Schein, *Organizational Culture and Leadership*, 260.

on them.[180] Such responses involve looking for ways to coordinate, align or integrate different networks. Management needs to think about creating space for mutual respect and dialogue that leads to coordinated action[181]. Finally, for a mature or declining organization, leaders are required to reflect on changes necessary for the organization, deliberating over cultural dimensions that should be changed and aligned. This could lead to a deliberate process of intentional cultural change, a process that needs to be carefully managed.

This section underscores the importance for organizational culture to be intentionally managed instead of being left to freely evolve. Two factors that were discussed include the impact of the environment on the management practice, as well as the current stage of the organization.

In summary, the organizational culture, a socio-interpretative organizational approach enables the subconscious assumptions of staff members to be included as a way to understand the overall religious identity of the organization.

3.4 Concluding Design Phase

This chapter has outlined three different ways to study the Christian understanding of an organization. Each of these methods with its different emphases focuses on a different organizational approach. The first method uses typologies to categorize different faith-based organizations based on a fixed criterion. This reflects a classical approach to organizations. The second method outlines different organizational variables affected by religious variables. With its use of descriptive measures, this method reflects the modern approach. Finally, the third method focuses on the possibility of uncovering Christian values from the organization's culture. To study organizational culture is to take seriously the people of the organization as they work together as a group. This goes beyond the prescribed management that influences the organization. Instead, it considers how members of the organization with their own particularity can influence the Christian understanding of the organization. This method focuses on the symbolic/interpretative approach to organizations.

These different ways broaden the availability of sources through which the organizational selves can be investigated to understand the tacit religious identity of the organization. These different ways form the basis for collection of data as executed in the next phase.

---

[180] Schein, *Organizational Culture and Leadership*, 374–375.
[181] Ibid., 271.

PART B: COLLECTION PHASE

CHAPTER FOUR

Introducing World Vision as Organization in Case Study

In this chapter, we begin with the collection phase. This builds on the theories discussed during the design phase. As introduced, the case study forms the research strategy used in this dissertation. In this chapter, we explicate the methodology used for the empirical field research of this case study. As mentioned, case studies are useful as it provides deep insight to reality. In the collection phase, comprehensive empirical information regarding World Vision is collected. The particular type of case study used is the single case, embedded. This implies the focus on just one organization, World Vision. At the same time, it also includes two units of analysis through the sample of two countries with different contexts, Nepal and Papua New Guinea.

Taking into account that the research question seeks to strengthen the Christian identity, the main purpose of this collective phase is to first clarify the extent of the Christian identity of World Vision in these two different locations. It does this through the following sub-questions:

1) Looking at World Vision collectively, how has World Vision's Christian understanding been expressed in its organizational variables and how has this Christian understanding evolved in the development of the organization?
2) Using the framework of organizational culture dimensions, what Christian values and assumptions are espoused by World Vision based on its core documents?
3) Focusing on two different offices of World Vision, what actual values and assumptions are held by members in each office based on the dimensions as determined in the first question?
4) Focusing on two different offices of World Vision, what is the state of relationships held by different internal stakeholders of the organization?

Figure 4.1 illustrates how the different sub questions fit within the organizational identity model. Through answering the first question, the organization as an object as well as subject are further investigated. This question focuses on World Vision as one single entity, not differentiating the actual religious identity experienced in different World Vision offices. Sub-questions two and three taking seriously the experiences of different offices through the uncovering of the organizational culture in these locations. It recognizes the experiences and interpretation of staff members as valid in the understanding of the overall religious identity of the organization. Finally question four takes seriously the relationships within the office. These relationships mediate the overall dialectic process in the identity formation model between the process and content within the organization.

Figure 4.1 *Collecting Information about the Organizational Identity*

Having looked at the big picture of the methodology, the next section details the two levels of data collection.

4.1 Collecting Data at Two Levels

There are two main levels to this collection phase: study of the organization as a whole and study of the organization at two different locations.

4.1.1 Level of World Vision as a Partnership

The first level focuses on World Vision as an entire partnership. At this level, the question that is asked is "How has World Vision's Christian understanding been expressed in its organizational variables and how has this Christian understanding evolved in the development of the organization?" This question sheds further light on the different understanding of religious selves in the organization, including story, content and even existing processes.[182]

To narrate the story of the organization, the changing nature of the organization is described alongside the organizational theory "organizational life cycle." The organizational life cycle theory provides a structured framework to understand when and how different organizational policies originated in the life of the organization. It focuses on how the organization's Christian identity developed as the organization evolved. Instead of evaluating the theological claims of World Vision, what is important at this point of study is the development of World Vision's understanding of its Christian identity.

To further determine the influence of the Christian understanding on the content and processes of the organization, the religiosity of the three organizational characteristics, defined as goal oriented, boundary maintenance and possessing activity systems are outlined. This introduces the overall religiosity of the organization. This approach recalls the second way of ascertaining Christian understanding as described in chapter three.[183]

4.1.2 Level of World Vision at its Branch Offices

The second level of the case study focuses on an analysis of two branch offices of World Vision, World Vision Nepal and World Vision Papua New Guinea for an in-depth study of the experiences of World Vision offices. These two offices, representing branch offices in World Vision are both situated in the Asia Pacific region. They are chosen because of their similar size yet different external contexts.

The focus on different branch offices of an organization was first established by Geert Hofstede as he sought to understand cultural differences

---

[182] For more details on this theory, refer to chapter 2, section 2.3.2 Religious Identity in Organizations.
[183] For information about the theory, refer to chapter 3, section 3.2.

among different subsidiaries of IBM.[184] Since then, this choice of focusing on one organization has been replicated through the years by different researchers seeking to understand differences in national cultural values.[185] In this case study, instead of emphasizing on national values, we concentrate on the possible impact of a country's particular context to an organization's religious identity. What is studied is the extent to which members of the organization in different locations embraced the Christian identity of World Vision. This second level investigates the extent to which different branch offices of World Vision adopt this Christian Identity through measuring the organizational culture. Doing this deliberately broadens the organizational approach to a socio-interpretative approach, where views of staff members are taken seriously.

4.1.2.1 *Organizational Culture and its Relation to World Vision's Christian Identity*

Organizational culture provides insight into the resulting religious identity of different branch offices. Rather than focusing on the individual organizational selves, it focuses on the result of the interaction among different organizational selves.

As previously described, organizational culture is related to shared meaning held by organizational members. The focus in this collective phase is the extent World Vision's Christian understanding forms part of the shared meaning horizon of its members. Measuring the organizational culture gives insight into the tacit religious identity embraced by the organization. This is done by determining the extent to which an organization's cultural dimensions are influenced by World Vision's Christian understanding.[186]

4.1.2.2 *Determining Christian Values in Organizational Culture Dimensions*

The first step in measuring organizational culture is to first determine how cultural dimensions are influenced by the Christian understanding of the

---

[184] Geert Hofstede, Gert Jan Hofstede, and Michael Minkow, *Cultures and Organizations Software of the Mind* (New York: Mc Graw Hill, 2011), 30.
[185] Ibid., 35.
[186] The theory of this third way of understanding is documented in chapter 3, section 3.3.

Introducing World Vision as Organization in Case Study

organization.[187] A deeper understanding of how the organization performs in each organization cultural dimension can provide further insight into the tacit religious identity embraced by the organization. To determine how World Vision's existing Christian understanding can influence the different dimensions in organizational culture, this project adopts the empirical research method developed by management researchers who sought to link organizational culture with improvement initiatives in organizations.[188] This method relates organizational culture dimensions to members' basic assumptions on a myriad of issues regarding total quality management (TQM) of the organization.[189]

This research established eight cultural dimensions based on a literature review of existing frameworks in organizational cultural studies. This content analysis done by management scholars covered key works done in the area of organizational culture since the late 20th century. It looked for commonalities in different existing frameworks and compiled them into eight dimensions. These dimensions were grouped together, leading to overarching descriptive culture dimensions that could then be used to relate to initiatives of the organization. In this research, these cultural dimensions were described in their relation to TQM. It describes the organizational cultural expressions, particularly the values and beliefs related to each cultural dimension that should be present for successful TQM adoption. This methodology is adopted in this project because it is argued to be comprehensive and practical.

Table 4.1 is a summary of the eight cultural dimensions and the general understanding of each category as proposed by the researchers. These eight dimensions are used in this empirical research and linked to World Vision's religiosity. This is done through reviewing key documents and policies that World Vision has approved and considered core to its existence. Linking Christian values to the organizational cultural dimension an-

---

[187] Organizational culture dimensions are categories that reveal the content of the culture of the organization.

[188] J.R., Detert, R.G., Schroeder, and J.J Mauriel, A Framework for Linking Culture and Improvement Initiatives in Organizations," *Academy of Management Review* 25 (2000): 850–862.

[189] TQM (Total Quality Management) is the general term used in business circles for improving initiatives. See Introduction and Implementation of Total Quality Management https://www.isixsigma.com/methodology/total-quality-management-tqm/introduction-and-implementation-total-quality-management-tqm/ (Accessed 16 June 2016) for more details.

swers the first of the three sub questions of the second level, namely, "dimensions, what Christian values and assumptions are espoused by World Vision based on its core documents?"

Organizational Cultural Dimensions	General Understanding
The basis of truth and rationality in the organization	This dimension focuses on the ultimate reality for the organization. What is considered real and truth affects different characteristics of the organization.
The nature of time and time horizon	This dimension focuses on the understanding of time. Questions that are asked include: Should the organization focus on the long run or short run? How important is time?
Motivation	This dimension focuses on understanding what motivates people fundamentally.
Stability versus change/ innovation/personal growth	This dimension focuses on understanding people's desire for change and stability. To what extent does the organization promote stability or change?
Orientation to work, task and coworkers	This dimension considers how the organization understands work, either as a 'task' or as a social activity.
Isolation versus collaboration/cooperation	This dimension looks at the organization's assumptions about how work is best accomplished, alone or with others.
Control, coordination and responsibility	This dimension focuses on the understanding of control considered necessary by the organization.
Orientation and focus – internal and/or external	This dimension considers the assumption on overall orientation of the organization as either internal or external.

Table 4.1 Description of Organizational Culture Dimensions

Source: J.R., Detert, R.G., Schroeder, and J.J Mauriel, A Framework for Linking Culture and Improvement Initiatives in Organizations," *Academy of Management Review 25* (2000): 850-862.

4.1.2.3 Measuring the Organizational Culture Through the Use of "Clinical Research"

Once the Christian values that impact the different organizational culture dimensions are determined, the next step involves measuring the organizational culture in the two separate country locations. This is done through the use of both qualitative and quantitative research tools, to be discussed in detail in the later section.

In measuring this organization culture, the dynamic and evolving nature of organizational culture is recognized. Staff members may respond to the measurement depending on how the staff members in the organization perceive the act of researching. The staff members of the organization might believe the researcher as spying on them, or as an avenue for release. These perspectives can affect the behavior and responses of different employees.[190]

In light of this, the approach followed in this empirical research is done through "clinical research."[191] The term "clinical research" refers to the deciphering of the culture in a consultant/helper role. Instead of being an independent bystander, the researcher should be seen by staff members to intentionally support the organization. This can lead to active participation by members of the organization, where deeper level of cultural patterns can be uncovered. In this method, the researcher, I, actively worked with members of the organization as they voluntarily provide data, believing that the information will be constructively used.[192] This method may seem unacceptable from a modernist perspective. However, this is acceptable and often appropriated in the study of culture.[193]

For this empirical research, I worked together with the Christian commitments department in World Vision at the Asia Pacific region.[194] The case study research methodology was determined together with a select group of staff members at World Vision known as panel members. This panel is described in more detail below. Together, a shortlist of countries to be surveyed was determined based on their similar sized operations.

---

[190] Edgar Schein, *Organizational Culture and Leadership* (San Francisco: Jossey-Bass, 2010), 180.
[191] Ibid., 183.
[192] Ibid.
[193] See for example section on ethnographic studies in Colin Robson, *Real World Research*, (West Sussex: John Wiley & Sons, 2011), 186.
[194] I worked with the Christian Commitments department in the Asia Pacific Region from 2010–2014 for the purposes of this project.

With support from the Christian commitments department, contact was made with the respective offices and meetings with the management team as well as the staff members arranged. Senior leadership teams of Nepal and Papua New Guinea voluntarily agreed to the research. In this planning phase of the field research, it was repeated at separate occasions the intentional support this research is supposed to provide for the office.

In implementing this empirical research, each step of the data collection and documentation was shared with the senior leadership team of the department. This measuring of the organizational culture answered the second sub-question of this level, namely, "what actual values and assumptions are held by members in each office based on the dimensions as determined in the first question?"

4.1.2.4 Relationships in the Organization as Mediating Content and Process

The final question is related to relationships between stakeholders in the organization. The state of relationships is important as social interactions play an important role in the meaning making of the office. As previously described, meaning making in the organization occurs through social interactions and communication of the group. A closer relationship enables increased frequency of social interactions. It is through relationships that the process and content of an organization are further mediated.[195]

In this case study, relationships are measured through the analysis of the relational proximity. Relational proximity is a heuristic tool that studies interaction between different stakeholders through five different domains: directness, continuity, multiplexity, parity, commonality.[196] The discussion of relational proximity enables one to describe the relationship

---

[195] See section 2.4.2.2, "Importance of Networks in Meaning Creation."
[196] This approach has been developed by the Relationships Foundation. This foundation considers relationships as central in pursuing a biblical vision in society. Since then, the Relationships Foundation has actively developed tools and consultancies with organizations to do a "relational health audit." In this field research, questions are designed to understand the state of relationships based on the five domains of relationships. To learn more about the Relationships Foundation http://www.relationshipsfoundation.org. An example of how this is used in organizations http://www.kpmg.com/UK/en/IssuesAnd Insights/ArticlesPublications/Documents/PDF/Audit/relational-proximity-frame work.pdf (accessed 16 June 2016.)

in factors external to the relationship itself.[197] It broadens the conversation of relationships to more than compatibility, something that is difficult to measure. Speaking in such terms can be useful for subsequent recommendations.

In the first domain, *directness*, proximity is measured in terms of nearness of contact. The closer one is to another stakeholder physically, the closer the relationship in terms of directness. Directness creates encounter, encouraging connectedness and produces effective communication. In *continuity*, proximity is measured in terms of time. Increased frequency and time spent in a relationship deepen the continuity aspect of the relationship. In this instance, continuity creates storyline, which results in a sense of belonging, resulting in momentum in relationship. *Multiplexity* focuses on different spheres of activity where the relationship occurs. How greater the number of spheres of rencontre, how deeper the knowledge of the other, which can then result in mutual understanding, leading to transparency for the organization. *Parity* looks at proximity in terms of levels of power. This considers the extent to which a latent balance of power exists in the relationship. Does one party have all the power, or is there a balance of power? To what extent is this relationship fair, resulting in mutual respect and participation? The final domain, *commonality*, measures the relationship by the degree to which two different parties have similar purposes. This results in shared identity and synergy.[198]

Together, the five domains of relational proximity as outlined above provide answers to the last of the three sub-question asked at this level, "focusing on two different offices of World Vision, what is the state of relationships held by different internal stakeholders of the organization?"

4.2 Data Collection Used in the Case Study

Thus far, the two levels of data collection in the organization have been described. In this section, the data collection used in this field research is elaborated. In theory, a good case study should use multiple sources of data.[199] Accordingly this section reports a mixed method used in data collection, where both qualitative and quantitative research tools were employed.

---

[197] Michael Schulter and David Lee, *The R Factor* (London: Hodder & Stoughton, 1993), 70.
[198] For more information about the relational proximity, see Schulter and Lee, *The R Factor*, 70-91 and *The Relational Manager* (Oxford: Lion Hudson, 2009), 36.
[199] David E. Gray, *Doing Research in the Real World* (London: SAGE Publications, 2004), 134.

This mixed method strategy, with a combination of both qualitative and quantitative research tools, is useful in enhancing the validity of the data. It complements the strengths of both to attain a more comprehensive picture. Qualitative data can help illustrate the empirical findings of quantitative analysis, and together they provide a more complete explanation of the studied phenomenon.[200] Using both qualitative and quantitative research enables different levels of the organizational culture to be queried. This allows for data triangulation of data, therefore increasing the factual accuracy as more than one source is being used in determining organizational culture.[201] Below, the role of the panel, central to the overall field research design is described, thereafter, a description of qualitative and quantitative research tools is employed.

4.2.1 Role of Panel in Determining Data Collection

A panel was set up in this case study to engage members from World Vision as the start of this field research. This panel included members from different functional units across World Vision which included functions such as Operations, Christian Commitments, Administration and People and Culture. It also included members from different levels of the organization.

Besides increasing participation of organizational members in this case study, a key element to the "critical research" method employed in this case study was the setting up of the panel as the panel helped achieved integrity in the field research through increasing reliability of its results.

Key discussion points between the panel members and I included 1) determining World Vision's Christian values and practices based on its core documents alongside the organizational cultural dimensions, 2) reviewing research tools, namely the questionnaire, focus group discussions and interviews. Together with the panel members, the research sub-question "dimensions, what Christian values and assumptions are espoused by World Vision based on its core documents?" was answered.

4.2.2 Qualitative Research: Review of Core Documents, Focus Group Discussions and Interviews

Qualitative research was executed to answer the first sub-question focused on the level of World Vision at its entirety, namely, "How has World Vision evolved as an organization and how is the stated Christian understanding

---

[200] Robson, *Real World Research*, 167.
[201] Schein, *Organizational Culture and Leadership*, 185.

of World Vision expressed in organizational variables?" This question was answered through the review of archival records and policy documents of World Vision.

In addition, qualitative research was also used to further validate the measurement of the organizational culture in the two separate locations as per the sub-question "Focusing on two different offices of World Vision, what actual values and assumptions are held by members in each office based on the dimensions as determined in the first question?" Focus group discussions and interviews were conducted to supplement the information of the questionnaire that was used. This use of qualitative research enabled open and deep discussion on specific cultural dimensions, thereby further confirming and deepening the information received. These focus group discussions were centered on trying to validate the findings of the questionnaire, focusing mainly on organizational culture dimensions.

4.2.3 Quantitative Research: Questionnaire

The main quantitative research tool, the questionnaire, was designed to answer the following sub-questions:

1) Focusing on two different offices of World Vision, what actual values and assumptions are held by members in each office based on the dimensions as determined in the first question?
2) Focusing on two different offices of World Vision, what is the state of relationships held by different internal stakeholders of the organization?

The questionnaire was chosen for its replicability as it can be used to measure the organizational culture in different locations. It is a simple straightforward approach to study attitudes, values, beliefs and motives. It allows for high amounts of data standardization with a level of anonymity, where respondents can be honest when sensitive questions are posed[202]. The questions posed in this questionnaire include organizational cultural dimensions as well as relational proximity to understand the state of relationships in offices. This questionnaire was developed in consultation with the panel members. Besides reviewing the questionnaire, they also tested it and reflected on the interpretative accuracy.

---

[202] Robson, *Real World Research*, 233–234.

4.3 From Methodology to Documentation

In this chapter, the initiation of the collection phase of the dissertation was described with the introduction of the empirical field research of World Vision. This included outlining the sub-research questions that the field research was set out to answer, the two levels that the case study was approached as well as the actual methodology used in the field research were described. Moving forward chapter five begins with documenting the field research done on World Vision in at the partnership level. This includes the focus on the religious variables of the different organizational characteristics, as well as the evolution of the organization through time.

CHAPTER FIVE

Uncovering World Vision Partnership's Christian Understanding

This chapter continues with the collection phase, focusing on World Vision in its entirety. While many offices make up the World Vision partnership, this chapter focuses on the organization as a single entity, with it's own official understanding and development. It answers the first sub-question "How is World Vision's Christian understanding expressed in its organizational variables and how has this Christian understanding evolved through the development of the organization?"

In the first part of this chapter, the Christian understanding is described through organizational characteristics. Organizational characteristics of World Vision are reviewed with an outline of evident religiosity in the different characteristics. In the next part of the chapter, the way the Christian understanding has evolved in the narrative of the organization is outlined using the organizational life cycle theory.

5.1 Reviewing the Religiosity of the Organizational Characteristics

One way that the Christian understanding of an organization can be understood is through outlining the religiosity of different organizational characteristics.[203] In the following section, policy documents of World Vision are used to describe the religiosity of the different organizational characteristics.

5.1.1 Goal Oriented

The impact of religiosity on the goal oriented aspect of the organization includes the organization's goals, products and services, its self-identity, sources of material resources, program characteristics and the religious

---

[203] This has been outlined in Chapter 3, section 3.2.

environment with which it chooses to interact. The following section discusses the impact of religiosity on the goal oriented characteristics of World Vision.

World Vision has a clear public message regarding its self-identity. In its websites and public documents, it often introduces itself as a "Christian relief, development and advocacy organization dedicated to working with children, families and communities to overcome poverty and injustice. Inspired by its Christian values, World Vision is "dedicated to working with the world's most vulnerable people; serving all people regardless of religion, race, ethnicity or gender."[204] The Christian identity of World Vision is communicated as the motivation for World Vision to work with all people.

As an international development organization, World Vision is a member of the INGO Charter, which represents its commitment to the standards of accountability in the INGO scene. Accountability for World Vision is based on "its Christian identity, calling us to be good stewards of what the Lord entrusts to the organization."[205] As an organization, it/they "aspire to the highest levels of best practice and accountability in all that we do." These include observing external standards such as the Red Cross Code of Conduct.

Besides being part of the public image of World Vision, this Christian understanding is also imbued in the core purpose of the organization. Several core documents described the purpose of the organization in terms of its Christian understanding. These include the Mission Statement, Witness to Jesus Christ policy, and Vision Statement and Core Values. The Mission Statement clearly states the Christian purpose of the work World Vision does. It states, "World Vision sees itself as an international partnership of Christians whose mission is to follow our Lord and Savior Jesus Christ in working with the poor and oppressed to promote human transformation, seek justice and bear witness to the good news of the Kingdom of God." This mission statement clearly states the motivation as well as the direction of World Vision's work.[206] As a follow-up to the Mission Statement, World Vision also developed the policy, 'Witness to Jesus Christ' policy to further define what "bearing witness to the Kingdom of God meant" in an organizational setting. Clearly related to the purpose of the organization, this 'Witness to Jesus Christ' policy describes what bearing witness means

---

[204] World Vision International, accessed June 28, 2015, http://www.wvi.org.
[205] World Vision International, "Accountability," accessed June 29, 2015, http://www.wvi.org/accountability.
[206] World Vision, "Mission Statement," Partnership Core Documents (1992).

for different functions of the organization, including funding possibilities, staff management as well as the criteria for when World Vision should enter different contexts.[207]

In addition, the Vision Statement, commissioned in 2003, which states "Our vision for every child, life in all its fullness; Our prayer for every heart, the will to make it so" was a succinct statement meant to be inspirational and "express what God wants for World Vision." Based on John 10:10, it "centers on Christ, focuses on children, challenges the donor and embraces the fullness of life."[208] This clear Christian aspiration was also stated as the first core value of World Vision, indicating the deep understanding of the Christian purpose of the organization.[209]

As World Vision grew from a purely evangelical organization to an ecumenical one embracing different Christian traditions, it developed the guiding beliefs document to explicate the beliefs of World Vision, as well as to affirm the calling of World Vision as "part of the one universal Church with a particular calling and ministry to serve the poor in the name of Christ."[210] This policy document reinforces the central position Christian faith has for the purpose of the organization.

Operationally, World Vision designs its program based on the development program approach. Its main goal is "sustained well-being of children within families and communities, especially the most vulnerable'. There are four main aspects in this approach. These include 1) contributing towards child well-being, 2) working with communities and partners, 3) Equipping local level staff and 4) Basic program parameters.[211] These different aspects are influenced by Christian thinking intentionally. Examples are briefly described below.

---

[207] World Vision, "Witness to Jesus Christ Policy," Partnership Policy and Decision Manual (16 September 1995).
[208] World Vision, "Vision Statement," Partnership Core Documents (August 2004).
[209] World Vision, "Core Values," Partnership Core Documents (March 1990).
[210] In this document, the four key gospel affirmations that unite Christians as followers of Jesus as they serve the poor includes the following a) Uniqueness of Christ, b) Authority of Scripture, c) Personal faith within Christian community and d) Commitment to mission. See World Vision, "Guiding Beliefs," Partnership Core Documents (19 September 1992).
[211] World Vision, "The Handbook for Development Programs: The Essentials," (2011), 7, accessed June 15, 2015, http://www.wvi.org/sites/default/files/ Handbook_for_Development_Programmes.pdf.

The understanding of child well-being includes as one key aspiration "experience love of God."[212] Following this aspiration, World Vision developed the "Spiritual Nurture of Children" as a guide to its programming.

Regarding working with communities and partners, World Vision's "preferred local role is to serve as a catalyst and builder of the capacity of local partners and partnerships for child well-being." To accomplish this, it seeks to work effectively with a wide range of groups and organizations in ways that strengthen and empower them. Committed to working with other faith partners, World Vision has clearly listed churches and other faith-based organizations (FBOs) as partners with whom they will work. The working relationship between World Vision and other partners should be based on equity, transparency and mutual benefit.[213]

About equipping local level staff, World Vision has listed the importance of "incarnational living for key program staff" among the people they serve.[214] As listed in the ministry framework, "the most important key to our relationship with God is incarnational living, which implies humility and grace, recognition of the equality of all human beings, identification with the poor and vulnerable, and recognition of their right to life with dignity. This is the responsibility for which, as individuals, we answer to God, seeking God's transformation of our lives as we affirm God' power to transform others and every aspect of life."[215] Besides incarnational living, staff are also encouraged to engage in regular, intentional reflection and learning which lead to improvements.

Besides the influence of Christian understanding on individual aspects, World Vision clearly values spiritual discernment in the overall program implementation. The "Critical Path" is a process of putting the development program approach into action through working alongside communities and local stakeholders towards the sustained well-being of children – especially the most vulnerable.[216] This represents a joint endeavor between World Vision staff and the community. While working in a community, World Vision "recognizes in humility, that God is already at work in a community. "The Critical Path is a process of seeking to discern how to join in God's work. Prayer and reflection based on a study of scripture and

---

[212] World Vision, "Children's Well-Being," World Vision Partnership Policy and Decision Manual (17 September 2009).
[213] World Vision, "The Handbook for Development Programs: The Essentials," 14.
[214] Ibid., 8.
[215] World Vision, "Ministry Framework Revised – Summary," (November 2010), 5.
[216] World Vision, "The Handbook for Development Programs, The Essentials," 25.

listening to children, the poor and partners are key parts of this discernment."²¹⁷

From this introduction of the goal oriented characteristic of the organization, we have looked at how World Vision mainstreamed its Christian understanding in its goals. We turn our attention now to the boundary maintenance characteristic.

5.1.2 Boundary Maintenance

The boundary maintenance aspect of the organization focuses on organizational power, participants and their inclusion, organizational fields, and partnerships. It focuses on the different stakeholders and their impact to the organization. Before looking at individual aspects of boundary maintenance, it is appropriate to highlight that one core value of World Vision includes valuing people. "We give priority to people before money, structure, systems, and other institutional machinery. We act in ways that respect dignity, uniqueness, and intrinsic worth of every person—the poor, the donors, our staff and their families, boards, and volunteers. We celebrate the richness of diversity in human personality, culture and contribution."²¹⁸ People are understood as having inherent value at World Vision.

Within World Vision, a specialized Christian Commitments department is responsible for "reinforcing Christian foundations, identity and witness." Within this department, different ministry leaders focus on specifics such as "Christian Formation and Leadership Development," "Interfaith Engagement," "Ministry Integration," "Supporter and Church Engagement" etc.²¹⁹ However, the extent of power of this department and of its ability to contribute depend on the overall composition, particularly office leadership.

Office participants may include board members, staff members, or volunteers. In the next few paragraphs, the extent to which the religious identity of each category of participants in the organization is deliberately considered is examined, based on existing organizational documents.

Depending on the status of the World Vision office in the broader partnership, board members or advisory council members form an integral

---

[217] Ibid., 26.
[218] World Vision, "Core Values," Partnership Core Documents (March 1990).
[219] This is related to the global Christian commitments strategic outcomes and objectives for 2011-2014.

part of the office.[220] In general, board members or advisory council members are present to ensure that the work done in the office is in accordance with the ethos, mission and vision of World Vision based on existing policies. One key criterion for choosing a board member is related to his/her faith. Based on documents, the member should be a "professing and practicing Christian, participating in the worship and life of a local church."[221]

The next category of participants is staff. As far as legally possible, World Vision seeks to employ individuals who are committed followers of Jesus Christ. This preference is reflected in the recruitment guidelines of World Vision. Based on the Witness to Jesus policy, staff should "embody a vibrant Christian spirituality, subscribe to our Core Documents and fulfill the individual indicators for Christ-centered life and work in the Core Capabilities Frame. They participate in local churches and are respectful of the diversity in church traditions." While preferring a Christian, this policy is also realistic about contexts where this is not possible. It allows for exceptions, stating that "When a National Office or other partnership entity determines that hiring adherents of other world religions for non-management positions will not prevent the fulfillment of World Vision's total mission, exceptions are permitted, subject to the approval by the National Director or CEO."[222]

With regard to volunteer members of the community, nothing explicit is mentioned about the religious affiliation of these volunteers. As they are often chosen during operational processes, the choice of volunteers as well as overall volunteer administration are often left with the operations department.

Finally, in the discussion of organizational fields, the primarily field to which World Vision belongs to are organizations that claim to do development work. As indicated in their website, "World Vision work[s] with all others who share our passion to help children flourish. These include individuals, institutions, governments, corporations, faith communities and more."[223] At the same time, World Vision has in its policies indicated it prefers to partner with churches. A key ministry policy of World Vision is the

---

[220] There are four different categories that a World Vision office can be depending on its development. This includes National Office, Branch Office, Interdependent office and independent office.

[221] World Vision International, "Board Policy on Boards and Advisory Councils of World Vision National Offices" (Amended November 2014).

[222] World Vision, "Witness to Jesus Christ Policy," Partnership Policy and Decision Manual (16 September 1995).

[223] World Vision, "Good Partners and Best Practice." Accessed June 29, 2015, http://www.wvi.org/accountability/structure-and-funding

'Partnership with Churches' policy. This policy originated from the belief that spiritual transformation is integral to transformational development and the church as God's sustaining instrument in the world, as such, World Vision considers this relationship as "indispensable."[224]

5.1.3 Activity Systems

Activity Systems are intentionally designed systems within an organization for the achievement of goals. These include rules, procedures, strategies, or technologies in the organization. These processes can be affected or shaped by religious beliefs. In its approach, the organization may also take into account the driving motivations of founders, members and employees. Focusing on the organization as an entirety, the main activity system that this section discusses is the organizational structure of World Vision. The structure of the organization provides insights into transfer of information or power centers within the organization.

One of the first documents that sought to make sense of World Vision's organizational structure was the Covenant of Partnership. This document sought to clarify the different organizational entities and the different things that different branch offices of World Vision covenanted on in the World Vision partnership. These included clauses on World Vision's identity and purpose, contributing to the enrichment of partnership life and entity; working within the accountability structures by which the partnership function; observing agreed financial principles and procedures as well as presenting consistent communication messages.[225] This covenant was supplemented when World Vision formally organized itself as a federal partnership of different national entities with a Global Centre in 1992, as suggested by organizational scientist Charles Handy. This federal model was adopted in 1992 alongside the Covenant of Partnership as the guiding document to the ever-growing organization. Instead of thinking of this merely as an organizational process, the partnership president while describing the federal model reinforced the importance of the relationship to be in "Jesus Christ and the commitment we make to each other that will make a new partnership work."[226]

---

[224] World Vision, "Partnership with Churches," Partnership Policy and Decision Manual (16 September 1995, revised 13 March 2003).
[225] World Vision, "Covenant of Partnership," Partnership Core Documents (1978).
[226] Graeme Irvine, "A New Partnership," (address at a combined WVUS/WVI Chapel, February 22, 1989).

With its adoption of the federal model, World Vision also adopted the following principles as standard modes of operation for different entities of World Vision. They are 1) Empowerment – where decision-making and its related accountability are moved as close as possible to those affected by the decision, 2) Interdependence -where units can only accomplish their shared mission by working with each other, 3) Twin- Citizenship – which involves an individual or group being committed to both a local and a global organization, and 4) Accountability – where individuals, groups and units are held responsible for behaving in a manner consistent with an organization's shared values and common mission. At the center of this model was the Global Centre that contains certain reserve powers. Decisions deemed as both high risk and broad in scope are to be the reserve powers of the Global Centre. At the same time, the Global Centre is responsible for the intentional stating of the "common mission" or "providing spiritual leadership."[227]

Besides the Global Centre, the International Board is the guardian of WV's purpose and governs World Vision. This board meets every three years, called the triennial council, with two main responsibilities: Fiduciary oversight of management and operations to ensure overall health and well-being of the Partnership as well as ensuring alignment of partners through developing Partnership-wide policies and exercising reserve powers.[228] This board can also vote to suspend the rights of a national office if it is not in compliance with membership criteria[229] as well as amend core documents of World Vision. These core documents include the vision statement, mission statement, core values, statement of faith, covenant of partnership. It is interesting to note that of these five documents, four are directly related to the Christian identity of the organization. Looking at the existing composition of the board, there are currently 24 people in the international board representing 18 different countries. 3 members of this group explicitly work for Christian ministries.[230]

---

[227] World Vision, "Partnership Principles in Action, World Vision's Governance, Decision Making and Accountability Principles," (December 2007).
[228] World Vision, "How is World Vision Governed?" World Vision Partnership Orientation.
[229] World Vision International, "Bylaws," amended August 2010.
[230] The list of the board is found on "Board of Directors," World Vision International, accessed April 2015, http://www.wvi.org/board-directors. The following occupation of the board members found was found from an external website listing the board members of World Vision International, accessed April 2015, https://www.aihitdata.com/company/002D072C/WORLD-VISION-INTER NATION AL-GLOBAL-CENTRE/people.

5.1.4 Organizational Characteristics Marked by Rich Christian Religiosity

Thus far, the Christian understanding of different characteristics of the organization have been surveyed. Based on this survey, it can be concluded that a rich inclusion of religiosity in the different organizational characteristics is evident. Looking at the organization as an object, it is rich in Christian understanding. This information however is limited. It does not look at the different 'selves' of the organization such as the development of the organization over time. An organization does not stay static but evolves over time. In the same way, the Christian understanding of World Vision is not stagnant but changes. To supplement this information, the following section presents the narrative of World Vision focusing on the focus on the organization's Christian understanding through the appropriation of the organizational life cycle model.

5.2 Mapping the Evolution of World Vision

This section describes World Vision's evolution focusing on the Christian understanding using the organizational life cycle theory. The five-stage model of the organizational life cycle is one way of describing the narrative of the organization in specific stages. These stages include: Birth, Survival, Success (Maturity), Renewal, and Decline.[231]

This model was created initially as organizations were deemed to mimic the life cycle, passing strictly from one phase to the other. This organizational life cycle model was tested empirically in different organizations. Similar phenomena of different organizations were categorized and structured into a framework to interpret existing activities and structures.[232] While the model has proven useful, its strict causal sequencing has since been relaxed due to its questionable validity.

Recognizing the potential as well as the weakness of this model, this model is appropriated in this chapter to facilitate understanding of the narrative of World Vision. In using this model, I do not intend to describe a causal effect between one stage and another, but rather a roadmap to

---

[231] Donald L. Lester, John A. Parnell, and Shawn Carraher, "Organizational Life Cycle: A Five Stage Empirical Scale," *The International Journal of Organizational Analysis* 11, no. 4 (2003): 339–354.

[232] For an example as well as the main literature used for Organizational Life Cycle, see Danny Miller and Peter H. Friesen, "A Longitudinal Study of the Corporate Life Cycle," *Management Science* 30, no. 10 (October 1984): 1161–1183.

understand how the organization has evolved. Describing the organization in the different stages is useful for understanding how activities and structures change over time, and if possible, for identifying critical transitions, as well as pitfalls that the organization should seek to avoid as it grows in size and complexity. It is used in this chapter to first understand the evolution of the organization over time, before describing the evolution of the Christian understanding over time.

We will in the following section first look at a brief introduction of each phase. We will then move on to focus on World Vision, describing separately the different components of this phase in the form of situation, structure, decision making style, and strategy.[233] Table 5.1 shows the way the different components are characterized in each different life cycle stage. In the following section, information from World Vision's internal database is used to flesh out each phase. These sources include speeches, policies, and figures, as well as other historical information at different points in time in the organization's existence.

Life Cycle Stage	Situation	Structure	Decision Making Style	Strategy
Existence	Small Young Homogenous	Informal Simple Owner-Dominated	Centralized Trial and Error	Prospector/First Mover
Survival	Medium Sized Environment More Competitive	Functional Some formality	Some delegation Begin formal processing	Analyzer/Second Mover/Differentiation
Success	Heterogeneous Environment Larger size	Formal Bureaucratic Functional Divisional	Reliance in internal information Information processing Reliance on	Defender/Segment Control

---

[233] These categories were described in the study of Miller and Friesen, "A Longitudinal Study of the Corporate Life Cycle," 1164.

			Internal Information processing	
Renewal	Very Heterogeneous Very Large	Some Matrix	Sophisticated controls Formal Analysis in Decision Making	Analyser/ Combination Differentiation
Decline	Homogenous and Competitive Environment	Formal Bureaucratic Mostly functional	Moderate Centralization Less Sophisticated Information Processing	Low Cost Reactor/Product service Low Cost

Table 5.1 Life Cycle Stage Characteristics

Source: Donald L. Lester, John A. Parnell, and Shawn Carraher, "Organizational Life Cycle: A Five Stage Empirical Scale," *The International Journal of Organizational Analysis* 11, no. 4 (2003): 339–354.

5.2.1 Birth Phase

The birth phase of an organization relates to its recent founding and relatively small size. At this stage, organizational functioning is largely dependent on its leader, where power tends to be highly centralized and informal. Information processing and decision-making methods tend to be used. At the same time, considerable innovation tends to occur in the organization. Risk taking is considered normal at this stage.[234]

5.2.1.1 Situation

In September 1950, World Vision was inaugurated by an American, Bob Pierce as president, together with Paul Meyers as vice president and Frank Philoopis as executive secretary.[235] This birth phase covered the span of

---

[234] Miller and Friesen, "A Longitudinal Study of the Corporate Life Cycle," 1162.
[235] Marilee Pierce Dunker, *Man of Vision* (Waynesboro, GA: Authentic Media, 2010), 100.

time from the founding in 1950 to 1967, when Pierce, the founder of World Vision stepped down. During this period, the organization was relatively small. As a missionary aid organization, its goal was to meet critical needs of the Orient as well as support local missionaries. It was officially inaugurated as a missionary service organization meeting emergency needs in crisis areas of the world through existing evangelical agencies.[236]

5.2.1.2 Strategy

Bob Pierce had been a travelling evangelical speaker for Youth for Christ, an evangelical organization, who became passionate about the suffering in the Orient during his first visit to China. He was convinced that spiritual needs and physical needs both needed to be met for the poor.[237] He started thinking about ways to raise money for physical needs of people in the Far East. Upon returning from his travels, he made videos to raise awareness and money for emergency aid for people suffering in Korea. These videos were largely successful and a large amount of money was raised. This marked the start of World Vision. Bob Pierce continued to share about human needs as well as the work of World Vision through radio broadcasts and TV shows.

Once funds were received, the work of World Vision began to develop. In 1953, the Child Sponsorship Program began to support orphans of the conflict in the Korean War during the ceasefire. Some of these children were in orphanages built by World Vision; others were in orphanages managed by churches partnered with World Vision. In time, this Child Sponsorship Program expanded to other countries such as Taiwan, India, Myanmar, India etc. By 1959, more than 13,000 children in 152 havens were supported in the Far East.[238]

Besides World Vision's work of child sponsorship, Bob Pierce also held pastoral conferences for local pastors, bringing together renowned speakers beginning in 1953 as well as evangelical crusades for locals in different countries where he travelled, first in 1957 and thereafter in 1959.[239]

---

[236] Graeme Irvine, "Our Pilgrimage: An Historical Perspective WV Field Directors' Conference" (Address to the WV Field Directors' Conference, Melbourne Australia, October 18, 1982).
[237] World Vision, "World Vision in the 1960s," accessed March 10, 2015, https://youtu.be/g_lSI-QAMAo.
[238] World Vision, "Understanding Child Sponsorship: A Historical Perspective" (August 1996).
[239] Dunker, *Man of Vision*, 127, 139, 141, 147.

5.2.1.3 Structure

This was an entrepreneurial time with fast development of the organization and a myriad of activities. Decision-making was fast. One of the first core documents developed in 1950 was the "Statement of Faith."[240] This document outlined the common beliefs integral to the organization's existence. However, at this stage, there was little focus and guidelines for projected activities the organization.

5.2.1.4 Decision-Making

For the most part, World Vision was synonymous with Bob Pierce during this phase. Other members of the organization saw their role as supporting him as he went about accomplishing his goals.

He travelled and met with other missionaries and local pastors and committed money based on what he saw as perceived needs. He raised money and worked through existing church communities and networks primarily in the US. Major decision making was made by him with little or no participation by others. There was a lack of accountability and planning. This lack brought World Vision almost to the brink of bankruptcy.[241] By 1967, Bob Pierce resigned from World Vision, officially due to ill health. With this change of leadership, a new era of World Vision began.

5.2.2 Survival Phase

During the survival phase, the organization grows and increases in number of stakeholders. Formalization of the structure begins to develop, where decisions become less centralized, with initial development of formal information processing and decision-making methods. During this period, the organization develops its own distinctive competencies with a broadening of its offer in closely related areas.[242]

At World Vision the survival phase took place from 1967–1984. It began with the resignation of Bob Pierce, stretching throughout the tenure of Stanley Mooneyham as president as well as the presidency of Ted Engstrom. During this period of time, World Vision expanded its operations, established its role in development, decentralized by setting up regional

---

[240] World Vision, "Statement of Faith" (1950).
[241] Graeme Irvine, "Our Pilgrimage."
[242] Miller and Friesen, "A Longitudinal Study of the Corporate Life Cycle," 1162.

offices, and increased formalization of structure through its "Declaration of internationalization."

5.2.2.1 Situation

During this period, the annual operating budget of World Vision grew from $5.1 million in 1969 to an income of $143.9 million in 1982. It continued to work with children around the world and conduct pastors' conferences. The work that World Vision did with children evolved from being focused on the individual child to becoming community based. During this time, World Vision began emergency work with relief goods sent to East Pakistan, war torn Cambodia and Laos. In 1974, World Vision began work in Africa with its first office in Kenya. In 1979, a total of 88 World Vision relief projects aided 446,000 people worldwide. The agency provided funds for evangelistic activities in 22 countries.[243]

5.2.2.2 Strategy

World Vision actively advertised its work using television programming. This medium allowed World Vision to show what it was doing, increase brand recognition around the US as shows were distributed to many different TV stations, and raise funds. To illustrate, in May of 1975, World Vision aired its first five-hour telethon. Results of the June-September broadcasts were just under $700,000 in one-time and first pledge gifts.[244]

With this increase in the magnitude and complexity of work completed, World Vision saw the need to consider its work as part of development and formally created a ministry of development in 1973. Aims of development were to include:

1) Caring for children and families
2) Strengthening leadership
3) Reaching the unreached
4) Developing self-reliance
5) Challenging to mission
6) Providing emergency aid

---

[243] World Vision, "WV History Briefs" (29 August 1996).
[244] World Vision, "Understanding Child Sponsorship: A Historical Perspective" (August 1996).

In 1979, World Vision continued to strengthen its understanding of this ministry and became further committed to an integrated, holistic approach to ministry, formally considering a development approach for all child sponsor funded programs. This understanding was further reinforced in the declaration of internationalization, where the aims of World Vision holistic development were formally introduced as:

1) Ministry to Children and Families
2) Providing Emergency Aid
3) Developing Self-Reliance
4) Reaching the Unreached
5) Strengthening Leadership
6) Challenging Mission[245]

These aims further clarified the understanding of holistic development of World Vision. As a key part of the evangelical movement, the aims of challenging mission saw the cooperation of World Vision with Evangelical movement, the Lausanne Committee for World Evangelization, in the setting up of the *Mission Advanced Research and Communication Center (MARC)* in 1967. This center collected and published data evangelism. These included publications about "unreached people," as well as the "Mission Handbook: North American Protestant Ministries Overseas."[246]

5.2.2.3 Structure

During this stage, the organization demonstrated a clear intention to standardize activity systems for the smooth running of the organization.

Setting up of regional offices provided the structure necessary for standardization of financial reports, required of field offices as spelled out in the new Standard Operating Procedures Manual for Field Offices. By 1975, a new field budgeting system was implemented which included a formalized field accounting system.[247]

At the same time, the declaration of internalization resulted in the restructuring of World Vision, particularly in the setting up of an independent World Vision International Office in 1978. This office was separated

---

[245] Graeme Irvine, "Our Pilgrimage."
[246] Steve W. Haas, "MARC to Make Transition, Retain Its Mission" MARC Newsletter 03-4, World Vision Publications, Nov. 2003.
[247] World Vision, "Understanding Child Sponsorship: A Historical Perspective" (August 1996).

from other offices with its own international board and council.²⁴⁸ Describing this international office, Stan Mooneyham said that "it is a legal entity that exists in its own right, yet it has no constituency except its founding members. It deals with huge amounts of money, yet raises none of these funds itself. It has awesome leadership and stewardship responsibility, yet as an organization it has no power to command the Partnership."²⁴⁹

5.2.2.4 Decision-Making

At this phase of the organization, more people became involved in the activities of the organization. This led to an increasing need to clarify their participation in World Vision. This need led to a process of internationalization. In May 1978, the declaration of internationalization was signed. This declaration was meant to foster a deeper sense of identity among the different stakeholders, where different members could truly broaden their participation through partnership. In this declaration of internalization, offices committed to abide by World Vision's statement of faith.²⁵⁰ In addition, the declaration supported the common mission that all would actively support. Internationalization representatives of different countries where World Vision was active signed this declaration of internalization.²⁵¹

Regional offices were also set up in different parts of the world to support the field operations of the work. The first office was opened in Central Asia in 1977 and in time, Latin America, Africa as well as the Asia regional offices opened. The regional offices were an extension of the International office with the intention to provide leadership and management for each of the field offices located closer to the field. In addition, it was envisioned that the regional office could strengthen participation of field offices. These provided a way for broader field participation in key decisions and key planning. The regional director was then considered the person who represented the field, he/she was in touch with the realities in the field and could contribute that unique perspective in the planning function.²⁵²

---

[248] Graeme Irvine, "Our Pilgrimage."
[249] Graeme Irvine, "The Internationalization Journey" (Prepared at the request of the chair of the Partnership Task Force).
[250] World Vision, "A Declaration of Internationalization" (31 May 1978).
[251] Graeme Irvine, "The Internationalization Journey."
[252] Graeme Irvine, "Our Pilgrimage."

5.2.3 Growth Phase

During the growth phase, the organization continues to grow rapidly in different markets to form a medium sized firm with multiple stakeholders. During this period of time, there tends to be incremental innovation in business strategy. With regard to the organizational structure, formal information processing and decision-making methods experience an initial development.[253] Often formalization and control through bureaucracy become the norm of the organization in this phase.[254]

The growth phase lasted approximately 20 years. This started with the beginning of the tenure of World Vision's fourth President Tom Houston in 1984 and lasted up till the early 2000s during the tenure of Dean Hirsch, sixth President of World Vision. This sentiment of transition is echoed in Tom Houston's council address in 1986, with "a partnership in transition."[255] During this phase of the organization, World Vision grew exponentially; new policies were developed for the increased number of stakeholders as well as to clarify the direction and systems of World Vision.

5.2.3.1 Situation

World Vision grew rapidly between the early 1980s to the early 2000s. In 1983, the gross income of World Vision was about $153 million; in 2003, the gross income of World Vision reached $1.25 billion.[256] At the same time, World Vision supported approximately 300,000 children in 1982[257] and by the end of the fiscal year 2004, World Vision was supporting approximately 2.5 million children.[258]

---

[253] Miller and Friesen, "A Longitudinal Study of the Corporate Life Cycle," 1162.
[254] Lester, Parnell, and Carraher, "Organizational Life Cycle," 339–354.
[255] Tom Houston, "Address to WVI Council 1986; Partnership in Transition," prepared for WVI Council September 16, 1986.
[256] Tom Houston, "Address to WVI Council 1986; Partnership in Transition," (Prepared for WVI Council September 16 1986); World Vision International, "Annual Review 2012," accessed March 3, 2015, http://www.wvi.org/ international/publication/world-vision-international-annual-review-2012.
[257] World Vision, "Understanding Child Sponsorship: A Historical Perspective" (August 1996).
[258] World Vision, "Child Sponsorship Operations and Global Services FY 2004".

5.2.3.2 Strategy

During this period, the child sponsorship model evolved again. International Childcare standards were developed in 1988 to detail specific standards for sponsorship projects. These included decisions for each area development project to be funded by a single support office, improved relationships between the child and its sponsor as well as increased focus on Christian values and the human centeredness of Child Sponsorship[259]. As a way to reemphasize the importance of child sponsorship, the vision statement was developed and adopted partnership wide.[260]

In 1992, the Mission Statement was created to clarify the purpose of World Vision's work. This included: Transformational Development, Emergency Relief, Promotion of Justice, Partnership with Churches, Public Awareness as well as Witness to Jesus Christ.[261] What seems to be omitted is the challenging mission that was part of its previous strategy. In 1995, the Witness to Jesus Christ policy was developed, expanding on the mission statement, recognizing witness to Jesus Christ as an integrating principle in the work of World Vision, expressed in holistic ways through its ministries of relief, development, advocacy and public awareness.[262] During this phase, the guiding beliefs document was developed marking the shift of World Vision from an evangelical organization to "an international partnership of Christians." This document clarified the ecumenical identity of World Vision, its understanding of the church, as well as its understanding of how World Vision related to the church.[263]

5.2.3.3 Structure

It was important for the organization in this phase that members of the organization truly identified with the mission, vision and values of the organization.

While the declaration of internationalization developed in 1978 was considered a step forward, it was inadequate in providing guidelines for

---

[259] World Vision, "Understanding Child Sponsorship: A Historical Perspective" (August 1996).
[260] The vision statement of World Vision reads "Our Vision for every child, life in all its fullness; Our prayer for every heart; the will to make it so."
[261] World Vision, "Mission Statement," Partnership Core Documents (1992).
[262] World Vision, "Witness to Jesus Christ Policy," Partnership Policy and Decision Manual (16 September 1995).
[263] World Vision, "Guiding Beliefs: The Church and World Vision," Partnership Policy Manual (19 September 2002).

Uncovering World Vision Partnership's Christian Understanding

actual implementation. In 1992, a new Covenant of Partnership was formulated as a response to the increasing number of members within World Vision. This was the next step following upon the declaration of internationalization. This covenant was "essentially a statement of accountability between national member-entities within the WV partnership, setting out the privileges and responsibilities between them."[264] The Covenant of Partnership had sections of agreement which included: 1) Uphold WV identity and purpose, 2) Enrichment of partnership life and unity, 3) Work with Accountability structures by which the partnership functions, 4) Observe Financial Principles and Process, 5) Present Consistent Communication messaging.[265] While claiming to be a voluntary commitment rather than legal contract, the Covenant of Partnership is part of the bylaws which World Vision operates under. As far as possible, the spirit of this Covenant of Partnership was for controls to be decentralized and exercised as close as possible to the point of operation within an agreed framework.[266]

5.2.3.4 Decision-Making

During this phase, decision-making priorities were once again reinforced. Firstly, the understanding of partnership was further developed. Task forces were set up to determine how partnership can truly be made a verb. At the same time, policies and processes were developed and intentionally aligned with activities listed in the mission statement.[267]

One key document developed during this time was the "Core Values" document. In the middle of the 1980s, the sentiment arose that partnership was not truly happening in practice.[268] In 1989, the Core Values document

---

[264] World Vision, "Covenant of Partnership," Bylaws of World Vision (1992).
[265] Ibid.
[266] World Vision, "Understanding Child Sponsorship: A Historical Perspective" (August 1996).
[267] Dean Hirsch, "The Last Three Years in Perspective" (September 1998).
[268] This was expressed during the field directors conference in 1987, where field directors perceived that in reality, partnership did not happen. Instead, they voiced tensions, frustrations and contradictions that they saw happening. Their perceived reality was one characterized by an imbalance of power, the imposition of systems over ministry, a bureaucratic mind-set instead of responsiveness to the needs of people, and dominance of the West in determining the identity of the organization. This conference highlighted the need to rethink their common identity. See World Vision, August 1996; Graeme Irvine, "The Core Values Process" (Address to the WV Field Directors' Conference, October 1988).

was created composed of "underlying beliefs; fundamental principles, hidden attitudes that determine action."[269] At the conclusion of this process, the core values included were: "We Value People, We are Responsive, We are Christian, We are committed to the Poor, We are Stewards and We are Responsive."[270]

5.2.4 Revival Phase

During the revival phase, the organization expands and becomes very large. Because of its size and increased heterogeneity, the organization tends to be more susceptible to environmental changes compared to other phases. During this phase, the organization normally starts establishing sophisticated controls with a more formal analysis in decision-making. Divisional structures are adopted to deal with the growth of the organization. Increased planning as well as substantial innovation in its business strategy often marks this phase. In dealing with challenging situations, the organization tends to rely on sophisticated structural and decision-making processes.[271]

World Vision has been in the revival phase since the early 2000s.[272] Signs of transition began as World Vision began to experience large growth in the middle of the presidency of Dean Hirsch.

5.2.4.1   Situation

Since the 2000s, World Vision has experienced significant growth. While operating with a budget of $1.25 billion in 2003, this number increased to $2.58 billion in 2009. This rapid growth saw World Vision active during relief efforts in Pakistan as well as the Asian Tsunami, working in development projects in more than 1300 areas. In 2012, the annual income was estimated at $2.67 billion.[273]

This growth led the organization to initiate an organization wide change process – Our Future. In the 2003 National Directors Conference,

---

[269] Graeme Irvine, "The Core Values Process" (Address to the WV Field Directors' Conference, October 1988).
[270] World Vision, "Core Values," Partnership Core Documents (March 1990).
[271] Miller and Friesen, "A Longitudinal Study of the Corporate Life Cycle," 1162.
[272] Information about the organization is given until 2012 as it is up until that point that the empirical research was conducted.
[273] World Vision International, "Annual Review 2012," accessed March 3, 2015, http://wvi.org/sites/default/files/2012worldvisionar/index.html.

there was a consensus that growth strained existing systems, infrastructures and capacities of World Vision. There was increasing frustration that more time was "spent serving our organization and less on working for transformation among the poor." What initially started off as clarifying the organization's "Big Goals" gradually evolved into an extensive change initiative, Our Future. This change initiative was taken up with participation of external consultants who helped support the change process. Its overarching goal was to help "staff fulfill their calling and to free up resources for children and communities." It was envisaged that this could be done through: "Learning from and replicating successes; focusing more resources (time, talent and money) on transforming lives; and improving board governance and management decision-making."[274]

5.2.4.2 Strategy

The 'Our Future' initiative had an intentional focus on developing a partnership strategy. One of its first steps was developing a consensus regarding principle level choices. This included "tackle the causes of poverty, empowerment, driven by field needs and ministry channels to be 'relief, development and advocacy'." This led subsequently to the formulation of the five strategic mandates, intended to set the management agenda of the organization for a period of three years. The five strategic mandates included

1) Reinforce our Christian foundations, identity and witness
2) Strengthen our grassroots field capacity and ministry
3) Grow resources and influence to increase our impact
4) Be an authoritative voice at all levels driving change
5) Build the organization and its sustainability

In 2011, a partnership strategic goal was approved for World Vision to reach 150 million of the world's most vulnerable children. To accomplish this, five strategic measures were identified: a) Contribution to Child Wellbeing Aspirations based on Global Targets, b) Number of children participating in programs, and number of children impacted by World Vision, c) Number of advocates for transformation, d) Partnership Average Growth Rate (PAGR) and number of donors and e) Amplifying voices for change: Global brand and trusted reputation.[275]

---

[274] World Vision, "From Genesis to Exodus: Our Future's Legacy" (April 2008).
[275] Ibid.

During this period, key strategic documents regarding the ministry were also approved for use. Children's well-being was further defined and set out partnership standards of World Vision in the areas of their work. Key in this document are the aspirations that World Vision has for the children, which include 1) enjoy good health, 2) are educated for life, 3) experience love of God and their neighbors and 4) are cared for, protected and participating.[276] An additional policy 'principles to guide the spiritual nurture of children' was also approved in 2010 to "inform contextually appropriate national policies on the spiritual nurture of children in light of the World Vision's Christian Commitments."[277]

In light of these policies, revisions also were made to the model of development. This model detailed the path taken during development, emphasizing the partnership between World Vision and local partners and communities. It also clarified the overarching goal of child well-being and the spirit of learning and God's presence during this process. A pictorial representation of the model of development is seen below in figure 1.[278]

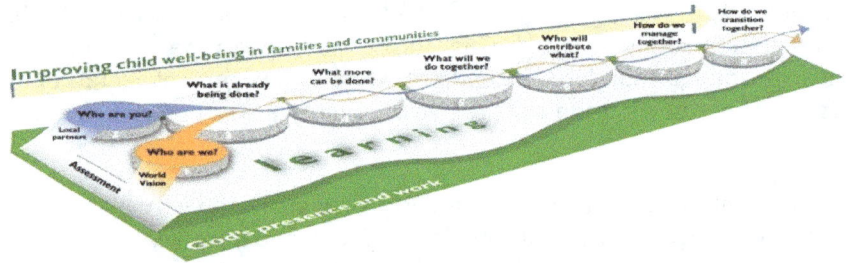

Figure 5.1 Critical Path in World Vision Development Program Approach

Source: World Vision International, "World Vision Development Program Approach," accessed May 15, 2015, http://www.wvi.org/development/publication/brief-overview-development-programmes-approach.

---

[276] World Vision, "Children's Well-Being 17 September 2009 World Vision Partnership Policy and Decision Manual
[277] World Vision, "Principles to Guide Formation of National Policies on Spiritual Nurture of Children," Partnership Ministry Policy (19 April 2010).
[278] For more information, see World Vision International, "World Vision Development Program Approach," accessed May 15, 2015, http://www.wvi.org/development/publication/brief-overview-development-programmes-approach.

Amid these changes came a reaffirmation of World Vision's Christian witness. This was done in a meeting of the partnership representative committee, which included leaders of World Vision at different levels. This reaffirmation was made in the midst of diversity and changes and sought to clarify what was meant in the mission statement "witness to Jesus Christ by life, deed, word and sign that encourages people to the Gospel."[279] A subsequent document was developed for leaders to understand the stand of World Vision.[280]

At the same time, the ministry framework was designed to articulate the common goal for World Vision. In this document, this common goal was described as the "sustained well-being of children, within families and communities, especially the most vulnerable."[281] This document was designed as a means to bring together strategy and vision from the three different pillars of the organization—development, relief and advocacy, as well as Children in Ministry and Christian Commitment in an integrated way. Different approaches, principles, aspirations and outcomes and the way they link to the goal of sustained well-being of children were described.[282] In this strategic document describing the ministry operations of World Vision, the Christian Commitments of World Vision was relegated to specific approaches, instead of the overarching goal, as described in the mission statement.[283]

5.2.4.3 Structure

At this stage, the federal model was re-examined for the World Vision context with the development of common definitions for the partnership principles "Empowerment, Accountability, Twin citizenship and Interdependency." At the same time, there was also the rebranding of the old partnership office to the Global Centre, with a clear mandate of supporting the

---

[279] World Vision, "Mission Statement," Partnership Core Documents (1992).
[280] World Vision, "Partnership Affirmation of Christian Witness" (May 2011).
[281] See World Vision International, "The Ministry Framework", accessed May 15, 2015, http://www.wvi.org/development/publication/ministry-framework-0.
[282] Ibid.
[283] As described in the Mission Statement, "World Vision is an international partnership of Christians whose mission is to follow our Lord and Savior Jesus Christ in working with the poor and oppressed to promote human transformation, seek justice and bear witness to the good news of the Kingdom of God." The way that following our Lord and Savior Jesus Christ was not in any way described in this new ministry framework.

partnership and the field as well as clearly detailed 'reserve powers'. These reserve powers are:[284]

- *Set strategic priorities* means providing vision, direction and purpose for the entire Partnership
- *Ensure accountability* over financial, operational, strategic and mission alignment
- *Provide global stewardship* includes managing global cash flow and the financial strategy for the Partnership
- *Promote the World Vision Way* entails the formalization of a shared vision and values, to be manifested both internally and externally
- *Develop capabilities* and transfer throughout the Partnership so that all are properly equipped.

5.2.4.4   Decision-Making

If the growth phase was about clarifying the relationships, allowing more decisions to be made at the field level, this phase can arguably be seen as consolidating and further explicating power.

Along with reviewing the federal model and clarifying the definition of the partnership principles, the decision-making and accountability team outlined a decision-making map as well as frameworks on how decisions should be (see figure 5.2 below). They also attempted to clarify the roles of the WVI Board, WVI President, regional offices and Regional Vice Presidents, management groups and local boards in their strategic and operational decisions. Clear objectives and scorecards were also developed for the Senior Leadership Team within World Vision as they would lead the organization forward.[285]

---

[284] World Vision, "Partnership Principles in Action: World Vision's Governance, Decision Making and Accountability Principles" (December 2007).
[285] Ibid.

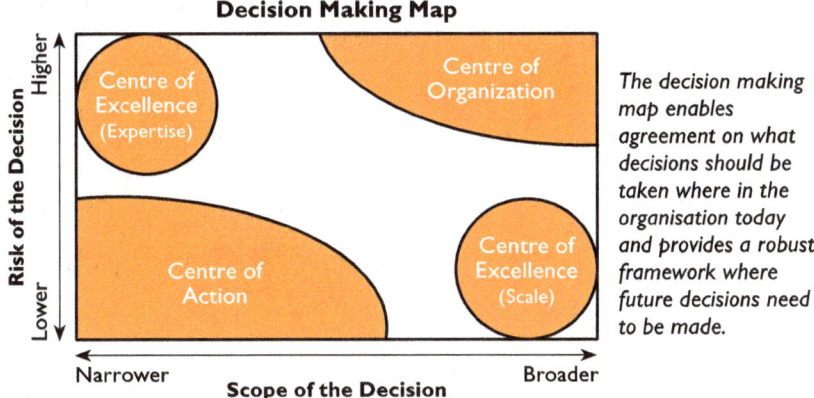

Figure 5.2 Decision Makers in World Vision

Source: World Vision, "Partnership Principles in Action: World Vision's Governance, Decision Making and Accountability Principles" (December 2007).

5.2.5 Evolution of the Christian Understanding in World Vision

The evolution of World Vision has been marked by four main attributes as per the organizational life cycle theory. These attributes include situation, strategy, structure and decision-making. In studying the development of the organization, we ended our discussion of World Vision in the revival phase. In outlining the actions of World Vision, it is not my intention to predict the future of World Vision. What is rather emphasized is the narrative of World Vision alongside an established organizational theory. The organizational life cycle is particularly helpful because of the existing theory attached to it, as well as its description of the organization in terms of situation, strategy, structure and decision making. A summary of the different attributes at World Vision are described below.

From a situational point of view, the organization has evolved from a clearly American evangelical missionary organization to one of the largest Christian international relief, development and advocacy organization with a portfolio of $2.67 billion. The work of World Vision has also increased significantly in scope and breadth. At time of research, it includes projects in Africa, Asia, the Middle East and South America. Instead of being a straight forward missionary organization, for World Vision, being Christian has become an adjective describing the kind of development relief and advocacy organization it is.

The strategy of the organization has also clearly evolved. Where the organization's activities were initially dictated mainly by the founder, Bob Pierce who saw himself as a missionary, it has since evolved to being an established member in the development, relief and advocacy sectors. The strategy related to the organization's Christian understanding has also evolved through the years. In the initial phases of World Vision, the Christian understanding was seen to dominate all of the purpose of the organization. The organization was clearly described as involved in challenging mission, even in church growth and leadership. This clear attention to challenging mission was replaced by policy documents such as the Mission Statement, Guiding Beliefs, Partnership with the Churches, Witness to Jesus Christ amongst others during the growth phase. During this time, World Vision widened its understanding of Christianity to include other Christian traditions besides the evangelical tradition. It was clear that the work that World Vision does was understood as holistic witness in "life, word, deed and sign."[286]

In the revival phase, there seems to be a diminished Christian influence on the overall ministry and strategy of the organization. While there is an awareness of the lack of the holistic witness because of the organization's call to "reinforce Christian foundations, identity and witness"[287] by the organization, this awareness was not explicitly included in the partnership goal. The approved partnership goal was concerned with reaching 150 million of the world's most vulnerable. It was a clearly stated numerical goal with numerical targets clearly listed, measuring indicators like growth rates, number of donors, advocates, etc. These measures seem to focus on quantitative targets instead of qualitative ones which focus on actual content. This goal does not give any indication that the organization's Christian foundations, identity and witness was important. This impression is further cemented by the ministry framework strategy document for the partnership, where there is reduced attention given to the Christian aspect of development. Instead of Christian witness setting the overall purpose of the organization, Christian understanding is mentioned in specific aspects of approaches, principles and outcomes, such as "love of God and their neighbors" or "incarnational living."[288]

---

[286] World Vision, "Witness to Jesus Christ Policy," Partnership Policy and Decision Manual (16 September 1995).
[287] World Vision, "From Genesis to Exodus: Our Future Legacy" (April 2008).
[288] World Vision International, "The Ministry Framework," accessed May 15, 2015, http://www.wvi.org/development/publication/ministry-framework-0.

In terms of structure, the organization evolved from a predominantly American organization into an international partnership adopting the federal model. This federal model was initially developed to help determine what was necessary to include in each office as part of the covenant of partnership. The intention of embracing this model was to allow the greatest amount of decentralization possible, where controls could happen as close to the field as possible. In fact, this covenant of partnership was claimed to be voluntary instead of legally binding. This decentralization was reversed in the revival phase when this federal model was revisited. At this point, centralization of "reserve powers" of the Global Centre was emphasized. One of the key powers mentioned was the ability to "set strategic priorities."[289] This resulted in the Global Centre having more authority to lead the organization which increased the influence of the Global Centre in terms of promoting the importance of World Vision's Christian understanding. This is perhaps aptly illustrated in the example of the partnership goal as determined by the Global Centre, where the focus was on a quantitative target with a distant relationship to the organization's Christian understanding.

Closely linked to the structure is the nature of decision-making in World Vision. As an organization, World Vision evolved from decisions made by one individual, to the development of a 'loose' partnership where field leadership were given more autonomy to eventually evolving into a 'tighter' partnership where key decisions are made centrally. It is also interesting to note the role of faith in decision making.

During the earlier declaration of internationalization where more participation was granted to field leaders, these leaders were committed to abide by the statement of faith as well as the common mission of World Vision. As the organization evolved, Core Values were developed as values that the partnership should strive for in the decisions they make. One of the core values was "we are Christian". Being Christian continues to be deemed to be central for decision making. During the revival phase, the system was set up to systematically determine the decision makers involved did not include any consideration for the Christian understanding of the organization. The decision-making map evaluated decisions based on "risk" and "scope." Roles of different leaders in the organization were articulated based on the same markers. These documents showed little evidence of reflection on what this meant for the Christian understanding of

---

[289] World Vision, "Partnership Principles in Action: World Vision's Governance, Decision Making and Accountability Principles" (December 2007).

the organization. Instead of being core to the existence to the organization, being 'Christian' was no longer part of the thinking in the decision-making systems.

5.3 Collecting Information on World Vision as a Partnership: Concluding Thoughts

This chapter address the first level of the case study, written to answer the first sub-question: "How is World Vision Christian understanding expressed in its organizational variables and how has this Christian understanding evolved through development of the organization?" It focuses on the development of World Vision as a partnership.

In the first part of this chapter, the religiosity of the different organizational characteristics of World Vision were surveyed. Based on the findings, it was evident that rich Christian religiosity was present in the different organizational characteristics.

In the next part, the dynamic nature of the organization is captured through outlining the narrative of the organization using the organizational theory "organizational life cycle." This organizational life cycle approach focuses on the change of the organization based on structure, situation, strategy and decision making. Based on the survey, the organization's changes have been documented. What is clear is the diminished role in the Christian understanding of the organization.

In the next chapter, the study of two branch offices of World Vision are further studied to give a deeper understanding of the inner workings of the organization.

CHAPTER SIX

Measuring World Vision's Organizational Culture in Two Different Locations

The previous chapter described the Christian understanding of World Vision as a partnership, this chapter continues the collection phase by focusing on the second level, the branch offices of World Vision where work is done. It focuses on capturing the extent staff members in different branch offices embrace the Christian identity of World Vision. As described earlier, this is done primarily through the study of the organizational culture.

The study of the organizational culture broadens the organizational approach to include the socio-interpretative approach, where views of staff members are included. This gives of the tacit identity of the organization.[290] Figure 6.1 illustrates the relevant schematic framework to understand the basic flow of this chapter.

Figure 6.1. Schematic Framework of Measuring Organizational Culture

The first section, *Uncovering Christian values of World Vision*, describes Christian values espoused by World Vision. This section answers the sub-question: "What Christian values and assumptions are espoused by World Vision based on its core documents according to the organizational culture dimensions?" The second section, *Developing the research tool*, presents the

---

[290] See Chapter 2, section 2.3.3.1 Tacit Religious Identity in Organizations

questionnaire, focus group discussion and one to one interviews conducted during the field research in detail. This section supplements the general methodological description in chapter 3, communicating the methodology of the field research. The final section, *Implementing the research tool,* describes research findings. It answers the second sub-question "Looking at two different offices of World Vision, what are the findings of actual values and assumptions held by members in each office based on the dimensions as determined in the first question?" as well as the third sub-question: "What is the state of relationships held by different internal stakeholders of the organization?" In answering these questions, we develop a deeper understanding of the meaning held and mediated by the staff members in both branch offices. This contributes to the overall Christian understanding of the organization.

6.1 Uncovering Christian Values of World Vision Based on Organizational Culture Dimensions

The organizational culture measured in this dissertation is expressed in terms of organizational culture dimensions. The eight organizational cultural dimensions used in this case study are derived from the literature review, which consolidated different organization cultural dimensions used by different management specialists in the past. Organizational culture values are dependent on the interpretation of staff members. To determine the Christian values espoused by World Vision, a panel was brought together to identify Christian values relevant to each organizational cultural dimension. As previously described, this panel consisted of different staff members in World Vision as well as me. This panel sought representatives from different sectors of the organization. This section details the joint interpretation of the panel on the ideal Christian values for each dimension based on the existing core documents of World Vision. These Christian values described in this section have been interpreted to be applicable to the entire World Vision partnership.

6.1.1 Ideas about the Basis of Truth and Rationality in the Organization

This dimension explicates different viewpoints different Organizations have regarding truth and how it is discovered. These different opinions regarding truth and rationality in turn impact the organization as it determines the degree to which an organization adopts either normative or pragmatic ideals.[291]

For World Vision, ultimate truth is found in Christ. It is by "follow(ing) our Lord and Savior Jesus Christ in working with the poor and oppressed"[292] that World Vision finds its collective mission as an organization.[293] Bearing witness to Christ is "an integrating principle" that World Vision intends to express in holistic ways through its ministries of relief, development, advocacy and public awareness.[294] Stating truth as found in Christ, World Vision's goals are normative in nature. The Christian Scriptures are considered the "authority" in discerning these normative goals as they represent the "inspired, the only infallible, authoritative Word of God."[295]

Therefore, for World Vision the basis of truth and rationality is found in the Bible as it provides one with an increased understanding of Christ in his identification with the poor and oppressed.

6.1.2 Ideas of Nature of Time and Time Horizon

This dimension focuses an organization's understanding of time. This can be related to the definition and measurement of time, the understanding of the importance of time in the organization, or on the issue of time horizon. The impact of an understanding of time horizon differs whether an organization focuses on long term planning and goal setting or primarily on the here and now.[296]

One way to understand World Vision's understanding of time is found in its understanding of the Kingdom of God. World Vision sees its mission to bear witness to the good news of the kingdom of God.[297]

---

[291] James R. Detert, Roger G. Schroeder, and John J. Mauriel, "A Framework for Linking Culture and Improvement Initiatives in Organizations," *Academy of Management Review* 25 (2000): 853.
[292] World Vision, "Mission Statement," Partnership Core Documents (1992).
[293] World Vision, "Guiding Beliefs: The Church and World Vision," Partnership Policy Manual (19 September 2002).
[294] World Vision, "Witness to Jesus Christ Policy," Partnership Policy and Decision Manual (16 September 1995).
[295] World Vision, "Statement of Faith" (1950).
[296] Detert, Schroeder, and Mauriel, "A Framework for Linking Culture and Improvement Initiatives in Organizations," 854.
[297] World Vision, "Mission Statement," Partnership Core Documents (1992).

According to World Vision's understanding of the Kingdom of God, glimpses of this kingdom can be experienced in the present through the work of Christ and the presence of the Holy Spirit. Yet the full expression of this kingdom is still to come. It is a future where all creation is restored and suffering and evil defeated.[298] Operating in this 'already' and 'not yet' tension, World Vision sees its role as sharing in the suffering of the world, bearing witness to God's reign through showing compassion to those who suffer, reconciling relationships and working towards people live with dignity, justice, peace and hope.[299]

Responsiveness is key in World Vision's understanding of time as World Vision seeks to be responsive to God's direction in the diverse contexts where it operates, bearing witness to God's reign in the present. In addition, this understanding of responsiveness is also a core value of World Vision.[300] To be responsive is to have an eye on long term commitment, especially in areas, for sustainable long-term development, yet at the same time to be prepared for sudden emergencies.

6.1.3 Motivation

The concept of motivation is central in the very nature of what it means to be human. This encompasses ideas about whether people are motivated from within or by external forces, whether people are inherently good or bad, whether people should be rewarded or punished, and whether people's effort or "output" can be changed by manipulating their motivation.[301]

World Vision clearly states that it is motivated to witness because of the God of love who first loved. Inspired by Christ, employees of World Vision are empowered to love their neighbors. Generously loving one's neighbors is the best witness to God. This act is free and not practiced as a way of achieving other ends.[302]

It can therefore be said that World Vision is intrinsically motivated to do a good work as the love of God compels it. The work is an expression of loving the neighbor. As such, employees are primarily motivated intrinsically, so outputs should not change regardless of the beneficiary's response.

---

[298] World Vision, "Witness to Jesus Christ Policy."
[299] Ibid.
[300] World Vision, "Core Values," Partnership Core Documents, March 1990.
[301] Detert, Schroeder, and Mauriel, "A Framework for Linking Culture and Improvement Initiatives in Organizations," 855.
[302] World Vision, "Witness to Jesus Christ Policy."

6.1.4 Stability versus Change/Innovation/Personal Growth

This dimension focuses on propensity for change. Some individuals are considered risk takers, while others have a higher need for security. This same logic is applied to organizations. Some organizations generally promote risk taking where organizational innovation takes center stage, with a push for constant continuous improvement. Such organizations tend to hold to an institutionalized belief that they can always be better. At the other end of the spectrum, risk averse organizations focus on "not rocking the boat" and conceptions about doing or being "good enough" abound.[303]

As an organization, World Vision tends towards risk taking. The core value "we are responsive" reflects World Vision's desire to be responsive to new and unusual opportunities as it openly encourages innovation, creativity and flexibility. In addition, staff are encouraged to maintain an attitude of learning, reflection and discovery in order to grow in understanding and skill.[304] At the same time, World Vision recognizes 'human fallibility' and in turn relies on the "Holy Spirit as enabling the creativity and discernment of World Vision staff, such that WV witnesses to Jesus Christ and the reign of God to the fullest extent possible in each context."[305]

As such, with regard to this organizational dimension, it has been inferred that World Vision is open to change and innovation, understanding the importance of intentionally discerning the Holy Spirit's guidance as it also understands its own limitations and dependence on God.

6.1.5 Orientation to Work/Task/Coworkers

Orientation to work/task/coworkers considers the centrality of work in an individual's life and the balance between work as a production activity and a social activity. Some view work as an end in itself, where work is seen primarily as a set of tasks to be completed, whereas others view work as a means to an end, such as a comfortable life, where social relationships formed at work are deemed a more important goal.[306]

---

[303] Detert, Schroeder, and Mauriel, "A Framework for Linking Culture and Improvement Initiatives in Organizations," 854.
[304] World Vision, "Core Values," Partnership Core Documents, March 1990.
[305] World Vision, "Witness to Jesus Christ Policy."
[306] Detert, Schroeder, and Mauriel, "A Framework for Linking Culture and Improvement Initiatives in Organizations," 856.

Key to the mission of World Vision is to "witness God's love for the poor and the oppressed."[307] The work that is done should ultimately point to the love of God. Besides the tasks involved, staff should have the "hearts and minds" to witness God's love for the poor and oppressed.[308] The process of how work is completed is as important to illustrate to different stakeholders the love of God. This focus on relationship is also emphasized in World Vision's core value "We value People." This core value clearly elaborates the priority given to people before money, structure, systems and other institutional machinery. Another basis for this value of people can also be seen in the Covenant of Partnership, a document created to affirm the principle of relationships based on "commonly held mission, values and commitments."[309]

It can be concluded that World Vision prioritizes its people as they are considered key to executing the work of World Vision.

6.1.6 Isolation versus Collaboration/Cooperation

This cultural dimension deals with the best way that work should be done in the organization, particularly the role of relationships in accomplishing work. Some organizations prefer that individuals accomplish work separately. Working together in this context is considered to be inefficient. In contrast, other organizations place a premium on collaboration as a means to better decision making and overall output. These organizations are likely to foster team work and organize tasks around groups of people rather than individuals.[310]

From its core documents, it can be concluded that World Vision considers collaboration and cooperation as central to its work. Clearly stated in the mission statement is World Vision's mission to "work with the poor."[311] This suggests the importance of collaboration, which is also reinforced in its core value "We are Partners." This core value highlights the importance of the World Vision partnership with the poor, donors, and the church in shared ministry, as well as with other humanitarian organizations.[312]

---

[307] World Vision, "Mission Statement," Partnership Core Documents (1992).
[308] Ibid.
[309] World Vision, "Covenant of Partnership," Bylaws of World Vision (1992).
[310] Detert, Schroeder, and Mauriel, "A Framework for Linking Culture and Improvement Initiatives in Organizations," 856.
[311] World Vision, "Mission Statement," Partnership Core Documents (1992).
[312] World Vision, "Core Values", Partnership Core Documents (March 1990).

World Vision considers relationships key to the success of its work. It is through relationships formed that World Vision will be able to attain its goals.

6.1.7 Control/Coordination/Responsibility

This dimension considers how control is concentrated in the organization, whether at the top or shared. When control is concentrated or "tight," formalized rules and procedures are set by a few persons. These rules and procedures are intended to guide the behavior of the majority. Decision-making in tight organizations tend to be centralized. In contrast, organizations in which work is loosely controlled, cherish flexibility and autonomy of the workers. Decision-making within the loosely controlled organization tends to be shared throughout the organization.[313]

Based on the core documents, it can be said that individuals are valued as they are central to the witness that World Vision seeks to give. This leads World Vision to "act in ways that respect the dignity, uniqueness and intrinsic worth of every person." This includes "celebrating the richness of diversity in human personality, culture and contribution" and particularly for staff, the practice of "a participative, open, enabling style in working relationships." People are accepted for their fallibility, making it all that more important to prayerfully rely on the Holy Spirit to inspire the "creativity and discernment of staff."[314]

People are not only valued separately as individuals, but also collectively as partners. World Vision accepts "the obligations of joint participation, shared goals and mutual accountability that true partnership requires. They affirm their inter-dependence and willingness to yield autonomy as necessary for the common good. They commit themselves to know, understand and love each other."[315] These points are also echoed in the internal Covenant of Partnership, a document affirming the principle of relationships based on commonly held mission, values and commitments. Rather than being legally binding, which might give the impression of a tight centralized organization, this document intentionally states that this covenant of partnership is based on the principle of interdependent national entities held together under God, by voluntary commitment rather than legal contract.[316]

---

[313] Detert, Schroeder, and Mauriel, "A Framework for Linking Culture and Improvement Initiatives in Organizations," 857.
[314] World Vision, "Witness to Jesus Christ Policy."
[315] World Vision, "Core Values", Partnership Core Documents (March 1990).
[316] World Vision, "Covenant of Partnership", Bylaws of World Vision (1992).

From the core documents, it can be concluded that World Vision as an organization seeks to be loosely controlled with an open, enabling style where staff are seen to be key to the witness that being undertaken. This provides for autonomy for staff. Decision-making is shared and involves different members of the organization as it corporately seeks to rely on the Holy Spirit for inspiration and guidance.

6.1.8 Orientation and Focus

This dimension reviews the relationship between an organization and its environment. In the extreme, either the organization itself assumes control, or else is controlled by its external environment. In addition, this dimension also considers the fundamental orientation of the organization as either internal or external.[317]

The work of World Vision is done with the intention to honor God, in ways that point people to the activity and character of God.[318] This intention indicates a clear internal orientation that the organization needs to preserve. However, this does not mean that the organization works alone. In the core value "we are partners," World Vision sees itself as a partner with the poor and with donors in shared ministry, it seeks to pursue relationships with all churches and desires mutual participation in ministry. It maintains a co-operative stance and a spirit of openness towards other humanitarian organizations.[319]

It can be said that World Vision actively engages in external partnerships while maintaining its internal orientation as it seeks to honor God and respond to God's direction in diverse contexts.

6.1.9 Summary of Values Required to Maintain Christian Identity

Thus far, World Vision Christian values have been described according to eight different organizational culture dimensions. This answers the sub question: "What Christian values are espoused by World Vision based on its core documents according to the organizational culture dimensions?" These values form the basis of the questions posed to the staff members.

---

[317] Detert, Schroeder, and Mauriel, "A Framework for Linking Culture and Improvement Initiatives in Organizations," 857.
[318] World Vision, "Witness to Jesus Christ Policy."
[319] World Vision, "Core Values," Partnership Core Documents (March 1990).

Table 6.1 provides a summary of these World Vision Christian values compared according to the eight different dimensions. In addition, the expected practices of each Christian value that was interpreted by the panel are mentioned **in bold** in the table. The practices show the presence of these values within the organization.

Organizational Cultural Dimensions	World Vision Values and practices
Basis of truth and rationality in the organization	World Vision takes the Bible seriously as it provides the organization an increased understanding of Christ in his identification with the poor and the oppressed. • **Staff members understand Christ's identification with the poor and oppressed as described in the Bible.** • **Decision-making Processes in the organization incorporate the biblical understanding**
Nature of time and time horizon	World Vision seeks to be responsive to God's direction in diverse contexts, as it seeks to bring God's reign in the present. • **Staff members earnestly seek God's direction in decision making** • **Decisions are made in a timely manner, responding to current issues while making room for emergencies**
Motivation	World Vision is intrinsically motivated to do good work as the love of God compels it. • **Religious Orientation of World Vision is a key factor in the quality of work that World Vision produces** • **Staff choose to work for World Vision because of the religious orientation of World Vision**

Stability vs change/innovation/personal growth	World Vision is open to change and innovation, understands the importance of intentionally discerning the Holy Spirit's guidance as it understands it own limitations and its ultimate dependence on God. • **World Vision is open and positive to change** • **Organizational systems are put in place for reliance on the Holy Spirit during change and innovation**
Orientation to work/task/coworkers	World Vision sees people as a priority before money, structure, systems and other institutional machinery • **People and Culture (Human Resources) practices consider the value of staff above other constraints** • **Time is provided for staff fellowship as well as other staff spiritual nurture activities**
Isolation vs collaboration/cooperation	World Vision considers relationships key to the success of its work. • **There is an understanding that relationships with internal stakeholders are key for the organization's success** • **The working environment should be supportive for the building of work relationships**
Control/coordination/responsibility	World Vision makes decisions with different members of the organization as the organization corporately seeks to rely on the Holy Spirit for inspiration and guidance. • **Staff seek for the Holy Spirit's inspiration and guidance collectively** • **Staff views are represented in the decision-making process**

Orientation and Focus	World Vision actively engages in external partnerships as it seeks to honor God and respond to God's direction in diverse contexts. • External partners of World Vision are clearly identified keeping in mind mutual participation in ministry • Clear strategy and work plans are created to articulate how World Vision intends to work with external partnerships

6.2 Outlining the Field Research Design to Measure Organizational Culture

The previous section described World Vision's Christian values with regard to each organizational cultural dimension. Expected practices related to each value have also been detailed in Table 6.1. To measure these values amongst staff members, a mixed method design is adopted. A questionnaire, interviews, and focus group discussions were used to test the extent to which these Christian values are shared by different organizational staff members. In addition, the questionnaire also included questions pertaining to the relational proximity of different staff members of the organization, a key element in understanding the social processes involved in the mediation of organizational culture. These different tools are described in this section.

6.2.1 Questionnaire

To understand the extent that these values are part of the actual organizational culture in the different locations, the organizational practices that are expressed from these values should first be ascertained. These organizational practices are the expressed layer of the organization's culture, easy to measure through the use of questionnaire. Together with focus group discussions and individual interviews, the extent that the values and practices prevalent in the organization can be determined.

The questionnaire, developed in collaboration with the panel, is a standardized tool to be used in both offices. This can be used as comparative data between the different World Vision offices. This questionnaire included an introductory section, questions about each organizational cultural dimension, and questions about relationship proximity. Because of the length of the questionnaire, the relationship between the questions and the relevant cultural dimensions as well as relational proximity are presented in Appendix 1.

In addition to the questionnaire, focus group discussions and interviews were also implemented in this case study as a means to further verify information provided by the questionnaire. These are presented next.

6.2.2 Focus Group Discussions and Interviews

To validate the information received from the questionnaire, both focus group discussions and interviews were also carried out in this field research.

Individual interviews were carried out with selected members of the senior leadership in each office. In addition, focus group discussions were carried out with various staff members clusters. The introductory questions in the individual interviews as well as the focus group discussions are similar. These questions are presented in Appendix 2.

6.3 Documenting Research Results

Thus far, the World Vision Christian values and practices related to each organizational cultural dimension have been presented. In addition, the field research tools including the questionnaire, focus group discussion, and interview questions have also been outlined. The final section of this chapter presents specific results for each country office. These two offices represent examples of World Vision branch offices implementing the work of World Vision. Taking into account that each country is a separate unit of analysis, the findings of the research are described separately, first for WV (World Vision) Nepal, and then for WV Papua New Guinea. Recognizing that the data collected represents a key part of the overall process involved in this dissertation, a comprehensive report of the data collected is presented in this main text.

6.3.1 Data Collection in WV Nepal

World Vision started in Nepal in 2001. In 2012, fourteen Area Development Programs (ADP)[320] existed all over Nepal, with 167 staff. I visited WV Nepal from 5 – 12 February 2012 to conduct the field research. During this time, a total of 54 respondents completed the questionnaire, 5 different focus

---

[320] Area Development Programs (ADP) are the program areas that World Vision works in. Each ADP typically has a manager and staff to support the work done in the ADP.

groups sessions were conducted, and 3 interviews with senior management team members were conducted.

6.3.1.1 Introductory Portfolio of Respondents[321]

Table 6.2 Length of Service with World Vision Nepal	0-2.9 Years	3-5.9 Years	6-8.9 Years	> or = 9 Years
How many years have you worked in your current role with World Vision? (N=54)	41%	13%	31%	15%
How long have you worked in the current World Vision office? (N=54)	26%	17%	39%	19%

Most staff at World Vision Nepal had been employed for a significant amount of time. However, they had not been doing the same role during their entire tenure. As illustrated in table 6.2, the largest percentage of respondents (41%) worked for World Vision in their current role only between 0-2.9 years. However, more than half of the respondents at World Vision Nepal had worked for World Vision in their current office for more than six years (58%).

Table 6.3 Religion of Respondents at World Vision Nepal	Percentages
Christian	56%
Hindu	41%
Secular	4%

When asked about their religious affiliation, 56% respondents responded that they were Christians whilst 41% responded that they were Hindu and 4% responded that they were secular (See table 6.3). World Vision Nepal had more Christians working for them than the national average of 1.8%. According to the census, the population of Hindus in Nepal was 81.34% on average.[322]

---

[321] To refer to the questions that the tables are based on, refer to appendix 2, section on personal information and introduction of the questionnaire.
[322] As depicted in "National Population and Housing Census 2011, table 8, population by religion and sex, retrieved on October 6, 2015, http://cbs.gov.np/nada/index.php/catalog/54.

Table 6.4 Overall Importance of the Organization's Religious Motivation and Values in Choosing a Job at World Vision Nepal (N=54)			
very important	important	not important	unrelated
38.2%	49.1%	7.3%	5.5%
Importance for Christians of the Organization's Religious Motivation and Values in Choosing a Job at World Vision Nepal (N=31)			
64.5%	32.3%	3.2%	0%
Importance for Non-Christians of the Organization's Religious Motivation and Values in Choosing a Job at World Vision Nepal (N=23)			
4.3%	73.9%	13.0%	8.7%

As an introductory question to the Christian understanding of the office, the importance of an organization's religious affiliation and values in choosing a job was asked. The majority of all respondents (88.9%) responded that it was important or very important (See table 6.4). It was also clear that the religious motivation played a more important role for the Christians compared to the non-Christians. One reason that the Christians emphasized the importance of the religious motivation was the way that recruitment was done in WV Nepal. There was an explicit internship program at WV Nepal with youth in churches that often resulted in new recruits of WV Nepal.

Based on the interviews and focus group discussions, it was also clear that World Vision Nepal had not shied away from its Christian identity. From its job advertisements, it was clear to potential candidates that it was a Christian organization. In addition, the Christian understanding is explicitly communicated to staff during interviews as well as the orientation process. This contributed to the importance that staff members placed on the religious motivations and values in choosing a job as they deemed the Christian identity important for the organization.

6.3.1.2 Organizational Culture Dimensions[323]

After looking at the introductory information, we can turn our attention to the Christian values related to each organizational culture dimensions. In this section, the findings of the relevant questions are first presented,

---

[323] For the questions that the tables are based on, please refer to Appendix 2 section on organizational culture dimensions.

before they are interpreted collectively to derive an understanding of the importance of the Christian value in each organizational culture dimension. This is done by looking at the extent the findings reveal the practices for each organizational culture dimension. These practices have been detailed alongside the Christian value of each dimension in table 6.1. Information from the focus group discussions as well as the interviews are also included for a fuller understanding in the documenting of the findings. Conclusions from the data collection are made for each organizational culture dimension at the end of each subsection. After describing each of the eight organizational culture dimensions, a summary of the values held by World Vision Nepal is documented in 6.3.1.2.9.

6.3.1.2.1 Basis of truth and rationality in the organization

The following tables provide the findings regarding this cultural dimension.

Table 6.5 The Influence of World Vision's Mission Statement at World Vision Nepal for All Staff	Yes	No
Does the Mission Statement influence your work? (N=54)	92.7%	7.3%
Does the Mission Statement influence your office? (N=53)	85.5%	10.9%
The Influence of World Vision's Mission Statement at World Vision Nepal for Christian Staff	Yes	No
Does the Mission Statement influence your work? (N=31)	93.5%	6.5%
Does the Mission Statement influence your office? (N=30)	90%	10%
The Influence of World Vision's Mission Statement at World Vision Nepal for Others	Yes	No
Does the Mission Statement influence your work? (N=23)	91.3%	8.7%
Does the Mission Statement influence your office? (N=23)	87%	13%

One way of understanding whether staff members internalized Christ's identification with the poor and oppressed is by looking at how World Vision's mission statement influenced the respondents in their work and in the office where they work. Most respondents indicated that the mission statement affected both one's work and one's office (table 5.5). However, the perceived influence of the mission statement to the office was less than that of the individual (85.5% instead of 92.7% for all staff). In addition, there was no significant difference in response between Christian and other staff.

When asked for concrete examples of influence, from the mission statement, comments included "works for the poor and marginalized," "it was motivating to follow God's example in loving the poor and oppressed." With those who disagreed that the mission statement influenced their work, individuals considered the difficulty of applying the mission statement to their work. They did not see the difference between the work of World Vision and that of other organizations since the mission statement was not applicable to their "everyday work." There was little perceived difference between World Vision and other organizations.

Table 6.6 The Relative Importance for Decision Making at World Vision Nepal (1 being the most important)

	Global & regional strategies	Donor Expectations	Country Statistics	Relationship with the government and other stakeholders in the community	Field Financial guidelines	Human Resources policies	Biblical perspectives on the decision that is being made	Local cultural practices
Overall (N=50)								
mode	1	4	1	3	5	6	7	8
median	2	4	2	3	5	5	5	5
average	3.4	4.5	2.6	3.6	4.9	4.9	4.8	5.0
rank	2	4	1	3	6	7	5	8
Christians (N=28)								
mode	1	5	1	2	7	4	1	8
median	3	4.5	2	3	5	4	4	6
average	4	4.63	2.83	3.64	5.04	4.7	4.28	5.46
rank	3	5	1	2	7	6	4	8
Non-Christians (N=22)								
mode	1	4	2	3	6	6	7	8
median	2	4	2	3	5	6	6.5	4
average	2.64	4.25	2.24	3.55	4.73	5.09	5.5	4.84
rank	2	4	1	3	5	7	8	6

Table 6.6 indicated key information used in decision making in the office. In WV Nepal, country statistics were unanimously the most important for

all staff, Christians and Non-Christians. In addition, it was also clear that the influence the Non-Christian staff have as there was similar ranking between the Non-Christian staff and the overall staff.

One clear example of the influence of the Non-Christian staff was the diminished importance of the biblical perspectives due to the perceptions of the Non-Christian staff. This led to an average importance of 5.5 for all staff compared to 4.28 for Christian staff. When staff were asked why they thought these biblical perspectives were not as important, staff assumed that that these perspectives had already been incorporated into global or regional strategies and were therefore not explicitly considered in decision making at the country level. In addition, because of the importance of the global and regional strategies perceived by other staff, this ended up becoming the second most important overall factor for decision making after country statistics. This global and regional strategies was clearly more important for Non-Christians with an average score of 2.64 as compared to 4 for Christians.

Table 6.7 Scriptures in Decision-making Process at World Vision Nepal		
Scriptures are consulted as part of the decision-making process	Yes	No
All (N=52)	56%	44%
Christians (N=29)	48.3%	51.7%
Non-Christians (N=23)	65%	35%
Scriptures are considered in the decision-making process in the following manner	Collectively	Individually
All (N=40)	24	16
Christians (N=24)	11	13
Non-Christians (N=16)	13	3

Based on table 6.7, a slight majority (56%) of all respondents agreed that scriptures were consulted as a part of the decision-making process. Comparing the results of Christian staff members and non-Christian staff members, more Non-Christians believed that scriptures were involved in decision making compared to Christian staff members. 65% of Non-Christians said yes to scriptures being consulted while 48.3% of Christians believed that they were used. In addition, more people believed that scriptures were used collectively instead of individually, particularly in the Non-Christian category.

Broaching this further in focus group discussions, what was clear was the recollection of organizational events that depended on scriptures. This included events such as regular devotions, as well as special occasions like World Vision partnership's day of prayer or Christmas and Easter celebrations. At World Vision Nepal, devotions are taken seriously. There was a spiritual nurture coordinator whose role was to decide on the content of devotions as well as coordinate these devotions and prayer requests across the organizations. Devotions were done on a regular basis in the different locations that World Vision Nepal operated in and its content related to the different strategic decisions it needed to make. With regard to the use of scriptures individually, it was clear during the different discussions that this was dependent on individual leaders and their personal views and preference about scriptures. There was no perceived standard with regard to this.

Table 6.8 Obstacles in Using Scriptures in the Decision-making Process at World Vision Nepal

	One needs to be sensitive to the Non Christian country context that we are operating in	Scriptures are not relevant in the decision making process	Use of Scriptures is personal and should not be used in work related decisions	One needs to be sensitive to other staff in the office that are not Christian	Others – please specify
Overall (N=45)	27	3	10	21	4
Christians (N=26)	11	1	4	7	1
Non-Christians (N= 19)	16	2	6	14	3

Table 6.8 showed the results given when asked about the obstacles in using scriptures for decision making. Overall, the key obstacles that were mentioned were related to the non-Christian environment that World Vision operated in (27 responses), as well as to the non-Christian staff working in World Vision (21 responses). This trend was observed for both Christian and Non-Christian staff.

Based on the responses in this section as illustrated in table 6.6 to table 6.8, one can conclude that for World Vision Nepal, there was an understanding that the Bible was important to the organization. Bible verses were particularly used during devotions and other special events at World Vision. However, there was no clear consensus about how the bible was consulted in decision-making as well as the validity of the bible for everyday work. Staff members have explicitly questioned the applicability of scriptures for their day to day work. In addition, staff members assumed that the Biblical perspective have already been worked out at the global and regional level, and as such, were not necessary to be contemplated again at the country level.

6.3.1.2.2 Nature of Time and Time Horizon

The following tables provided the findings with regard to this cultural dimension.

Table 6.9 Extent of Importance in Goal Setting at World Vision Nepal							
		Compliance to pre-discussed strategy and objectives for the office	Consideration of operational challenges as they arise at the current moment	Planning for future objectives and direction of the office	Consideration of emergencies in the country context and the response of the office to the emergency	The following of God's direction in the completion of the goal
Overall	Mode	1	3	2	4	5

(N=48)	Median	2	3	2	4	3
	Average	2.23	2.83	2.33	3.27	3.04
	Ranking	1	3	2	5	4
Christians (N=27)	Mode	1	3	2	4	1
	Median	2	3	2	4	1.5
	Average	2.6	2.8	2.3	3.2	2.6
	Ranking	2	3	1	4	2
Non-Christians (N=21)	Mode	1	3	2	4	5
	Median	1	3	2	4	5
	Average	1.9	2.9	2.4	3.3	3.5
	Ranking	1	3	2	4	5

One way to understand if God's direction was sought in decision-making was to consider how goals were set. As table 6.9 depicted, most respondents overall considered compliance to pre-discussed strategy and objectives as the most important in decision making, followed by planning for future objectives. This compliance to the pre-discussed strategy and objectives was also perceived as the most important for non-Christian staff.

With respect to the particular Christian value, Christian staff members in general believed that following God's direction was important (average of 2.6), this sentiment was not shared by Non-Christians who believed that God's direction was the least important (average of 3.5).

Prodding further through focus group discussions, it was evident that decision making was clearly defined at World Vision Nepal, with clear rules of engagement for different levels of stakeholders. This clear structure of compliance has at times led to discontentment with respondents who mentioned the 'strict, rigid' measures. They mentioned examples of how they were pressured to spend money based on project timelines instead of focusing on quality. In addition, the need to comply to project plans and policies had also led staff members to think that they were "unable to directly help those in need in the field."

When asked specifically about following God's direction, respondents once again raised the assumption that these perspectives had been included in the region or global strategies that they sought to implement. At the same time, the understanding of emergencies impacting decision making was ranked the lowest (fifth) in the decision making of goals in the office.

Table 6.10 Extent that Goals are Time Bound with Timelines Observed (N=46)			
Goals are not time bound, timelines are not observed at all	Goals are seldom time bound, timelines are not observed most of the time	Goals are somewhat time bound, timelines are observed as far as possible	Goals are extremely time bound, timelines are observed strictly
11%	11%	46%	33%

Responses in table 6.10 regarding timelines showed a clear understanding that goals were mostly time bound. 46% of the respondents observed that timelines were observed as far as possible, while 33% respondents considered that goals were extremely time bound.

Table 6.11 World Vision Nepal Seeks God's Direction in the Setting of Goals		
	Yes	No
Overall (N=51)	80%	20%
Christians (N=29)	76%	24%
Non-Christians (N=22)	86%	14%

A large majority of all respondents (80%) said yes when asked directly if God's direction was sought in the setting of goals (Table 6.11). Christians were more critical compared to the non-Christians on whether God's direction was sought in the setting of goals. 76% of Christians believed that God's direction was sought compared to 86% of non-Christians.

Table 6.12 How World Vision Nepal Seeks God's Direction in the Setting of Goals

	Setting aside time for prayer during office hours	Reading the bible	Regular devotions	Personal reflection	Setting aside time for decision makers to reflect on the work issues	Using Christian principles for work practices
Overall (N=48)	14	16	32	11	15	27
Christians (N=27)	7	7	17	5	8	14
Non-Christians (N=21)	7	9	15	6	7	13

When asked how God's direction was sought, majority of the staff considered regular devotions as well as the use of Christian principles for work practices as main ways in which God's direction is considered (Table 6.12). This trend was described by both Christian and non-Christian staff members. During focus group discussions, the kind of Christian principles that were mentioned included principles like "stewardship" as well as "accountability."

	Table 6.13 Obstacles in Seeking God's Direction in the Setting of Goals at World Vision Nepal				
	To be sensitive to the Non-Christian country context that we are operating in	God's direction is not related to the setting of goals of the organization	To be sensitive to staff who are not Christian	I do not know what God's guidance is	Others – please specify
Overall (N=46)	36	3	13	1	5
Christians (N=24)	18	0	8	1	5
Non-Christians (N=22)	18	3	5	0	0

When asked about the obstacles related to seeking God's direction, respondents listed the country context as well as the non-Christian staff as important reasons requiring sensitivity. (Table 5.13). There was no distinct difference in trend between the Christian and Non-Christian staff.

Table 6.9 to table 6.15 revealed the findings regarding the cultural dimension, nature of time and time horizon. It can be said from these findings that staff members believed that God's direction was sought in the goals that they set. However, it was also clear that God's direction was not actively sought, but rather compliance to pre-discussed strategies. Seeking God's direction seemed to be secondary to the pre-discussed strategies. At the same time, emergencies were not directly planned for in the setting of goals.

6.3.1.2.3 Motivation

Tables 6.14 and 6.15 documented the findings with regard to the organizational dimension motivation.

Table 6.14 Reasons for Working with World Vision Nepal

Reasons why an individual works for World Vision Nepal

		Job Description	Sector (INGO, NPO) that World Vision is a part of	Existing staff in the Office	Religious Identity of World Vision	Espoused values and mission of world vision	Conditions offered by World Vision (salary & benefits)	Others – please specify
Overall (N=53)	Mode	1	2	4	1	2	6	1
	Median	2	3	4	3	3	4	1
	Average	2.34	2.95	4.17	3.11	2.95	4.05	2.50
	Ranking	1	2	5	3	2	4	
Christian (N=30)	Mode	3	1	6	1	2	6	
	Median	3	3	4	1	2	4	
	Average	3.08	3.22	4.47	2.07	2.91	4.17	
	Ranking	3	4	6	1	2	5	
Non-Christian (N=23)	Mode	1	3	4	5	1	2	
	Median	1	2.5	4	5	3	3	
	Average	1.5	2.7	3.8	4.7	3	3.9	
	Ranking	1	2	4	5	3		

Reasons why other staff might choose to work World Vision							
Overall (N=53)	mode	1	1	6	5	3	2
	median	3	2	4	5	4	2
	average	2.64	2.30	4.27	3.93	3.87	2.98
	ranking	2	1	6	5	4	3
Christian (N=30)	mode	3	1	6	1	5	2
	median	3	2	5	3.5	5	2
	average	3.08	2.38	4.36	3.42	4.28	2.8
	ranking	3	1	6	4	5	2
Non-Christian (N=23)	mode	1	1	4	5	4	6
	median	2	2	4	5	4	3
	average	2.10	2.19	4.16	4.58	3.38	3.25
	ranking	1	2	5	6	4	3

Based on the responses collated in table 6.14, the overall main reason why an individual would join World Vision was because of the job description. This importance of the job description was echoed by Non-Christian staff. For Christian staff members, the religious identity of the organization was the main reason.

As a means of validating the responses received as well as providing further critical distance to the understanding of motivation, respondents were also asked a slightly different question, "why others choose to work at World Vision." In response to this question, different main reasons were suggested. The overall main reason was the sector that World Vision was part of, that of an International Organization. This reason was also affirmed by the Christian staff. Non-Christian staff however stayed true to the job description as being the most important reason for choosing the job. It was also interesting to note that the religious motivations of the organization ranked fourth for Christian staff, a contrast to the most important reason for personally joining the organization.

Based on this table, it can be concluded that the religious identity of World Vision was not decisive as to why an individual joined World Vision. Instead, the reputation and recognition of World Vision as an International Organization was brought up as a key reason why individuals joined World Vision. Based on the focus group discussions, it was even suggested that as an international organization, staff could join the United Nations after their stint with World Vision.

Table 6.15 Motivating and Demotivating Factors at World Vision Nepal

What are the top three factors that motivate you in your current role?

	Management style of Senior Leadership Team	Work place environment	Job Scope	Career Advancement Opportunities	Learning and Development Activities	Changes in work conditions (Salary and Benefits)	Mission and Purpose of World Vision	Others – please specify
Overall (N=54)	5	40	14	16	33	5	30	1
Christian (N=31)	4	19	7	8	20	2	19	1
Non-Christian (N=23)	1	21	7	8	13	3	11	

What are top 3 factors that demotivate you in your current responsibility?

| Overall (N=54) | 28 | 11 | 14 | 16 | 10 | 29 | 4 | 8 |

Christian (N=31)	15	8	8	8	3	17	2	6
Non-Christian (N=23)	13	3	6	8	7	12	2	2

Based on table 6.15, the top three motivational factors for all staff members included the workplace environment, learning and development activities, and the mission and purpose of World Vision. This was consistent for both Christian and Non-Christian staff. The top three demotivating factors included work conditions (Salary and Benefits), management style of the senior leadership team, and career advancement opportunities. This was also consistent for both Christian and Non-Christian staff. It was worth nothing that while job scope figured as an important factor in choosing a job with World Vision, it was not considered as strongly motivating or demotivating.

From the responses given in both table 6.14 and 6.15 regarding the cultural dimension motivation, it can be concluded that the religious orientation of the organization was clearly not the primary motivation for staff working in the organization or for them to continue in their jobs. Factors like program content or work colleagues were more motivational for respondents to do a good job as compared to the religious orientation.

6.3.1.2.4 Stability vs Change/Innovation/Personal Growth

Table 6.16 to table 6.22 documented the findings with regard to the cultural dimension stability vs change/innovation/personal growth.

Table 6.16 Understanding of Change at World Vision Nepal			
How often do changes in your office takes place? (N=54)			
Very often	Often	Sometimes	Seldom
13%	24%	44%	19%
How does your office consider change? (N=53)			
Change is extremely undesirable	Change is somewhat undesirable	Change is somewhat desirable	Change is extremely desirable
4%	17%	60%	19%

From table 6.16, a majority of respondents described changes in the organization to take place fairly frequently within the organization (often and sometimes). For most respondents, change was seen positively with it being considered somewhat desirable (60%) or extremely desirable (19%).

Table 6.17 Changes that Take Place Most Often at World Vision Nepal (N=47)								
	Organizational Processes	Field Financial Manual	Human Resources Policies	Organizational Structure	Long Term Organizational Strategy and Objectives	Project Log frames	Staff Turnover	Available Funding
median	3	3	4	4	5	6	1	6
average	3.4	3.6	4.0	3.9	4.9	5.5	2.7	5.4
ranking	2	3	5	4	6	8	1	7

Based on table 6.17, the highest noted change in the organization was staff turnover, followed by organizational processes and the field financial manual.

Table 6.18 Main Reasons for Changes in the Office at World Vision Nepal (N=48)				
Sudden change in environmental conditions in country context	Management style of Senior Leadership within the office	Change in Partnership direction	Desire for continuous improvement and progress in office	Others – please specify
12	22	14	20	3

As reported by respondents as outlined in table 6.18, the main reasons for changes in the office were the management style of senior leadership as well as the organization's desire for continuous improvement and progress in the office.

Table 6.19 God's Guidance Sought in the Consideration of Changes at World Vision Nepal		
	Yes	No
Overall (N=52)	65%	35%
Christians (N=30)	50%	50%
Non-Christians (N=22)	86.4%	13.6%

Based on table 6.19, the overall majority (65%) of the respondents believed that God's guidance was considered in the changes in the office. Non-Christians were more certain about God's guidance being sought after compared to Christians.

Table 6.20 When God's Guidance is Considered in the Change Process at World Vision Nepal				
	In the evaluation of need for change	Planning process for change	During change process	After change process, as means of reflection
Overall (N=45)	22	27	18	21
Christians (N=24)	10	14	11	12
Non-Christians (N=21)	12	13	7	9

With respect to where in the change process God's guidance was sought, most of the respondents believed God's guidance was considered in the planning process (see table 6.20). This was followed by the period of evaluation of need for change, after the change process and during the change process. This trend was consistent for both Christian and Non-Christian staff members.

Table 6.21 How God's Guidance is Considered in the Changes Experienced by World Vision Nepal

	Setting aside time for prayer during office hours	Reading the bible	Regular devotions	personal reflection	Setting aside time for decision makers to reflect on the work issues	Using Christian principles to understand change
Overall (N=46)	15	14	28	9	12	17
Christians (N=26)	8	7	15	5	6	7
Non-Christians (N=20)	7	7	13	4	6	10

When asked how God's guidance was considered in the decision-making process, the most frequented response was through regular devotions (Table 6.21). This trend was seen in both Christian and non-Christian staff. Other options of how God's direction was sought were the use of Christian principles to understand change, setting aside time aside for prayer during office hours and reading the bible. What was mentioned during the focus group discussions was also the importance of the individual leader on relying on God's dependence. Different leaders had different views about the role of God in decisions made at World Vision.

Table 6.22 Obstacles in Seeking God's Guidance in Changes that Take Place at World Vision Nepal

	To be sensitive of the Non-Christian country context that we are operating in	The Holy Spirit speaks to individuals and not corporately to the organization	To be sensitive to staff who are not Christian	God's guidance is not required to assist in changes in the Organization	I do not know what God's guidance is	Others - Please specify
Overall (N=45)	24	9	13	4	4	24
Christians (N=27)	11	6	8	3	1	11
Non-Christians (N=18)	13	3	5	1	2	13

The main obstacle in seeking God's guidance perceived by majority of the respondents was the non-Christian context that World Vision was operating in (table 6.22). This was echoed by both Christian and Non-Christian staff. This obstacle of the Non-Christian context was also repeated in the use of scripture as well as God's guidance in goal setting as depicted in tables 6.8 and 6.13.

With regard to this cultural dimension, stability vs change/innovation/personal growth, respondents indicated that the office had a positive outlook toward change. God's direction was most sought after during the planning for change. Main reasons for change in the office included the management style of the senior leadership team, and the desire for innovation. As for the nature of these changes, the majority were related to people, organizational systems, and policies. Based on these responses given, it can be concluded that while change is embraced, the relationship of change to God's dependence was not clearly expressed and embraced by members of the office.

6.3.1.2.5 Orientation to Work/Task/Co-workers

Tables 6.23 provided findings to the organizational dimension, orientation to work/task/co-workers.

Table 6.23 Priority for World Vision Nepal from the Most Important to the Least important

Overall (N=49)	Completion of pre-agreed tasks as determined by formal documents of World Vision	Observation of organizational structures and the relevant levels of authority	Observation of field financial manual	Observation of P&C (People and Culture) policies (Human Resources)	Relationships between individuals within and outside of organization
mode	1	1	3	4	5
median	1	2	3	4	4
average	2.11	2.48	2.90	3.29	3.31
rank	1	2	3	5	4

As detailed in table 6.23, task completion was considered to be of utmost priority for the office. This was followed by the observation of organizational structures and the observation of the field financial manual. People & Culture policies held the least important priority for their office. This focus on work tasks or structures above people was reinforced during focus group discussions. Staff members recounted the rigidity of structures in the office, such as the inability to use office vehicles or the difficulty of having only one computer in the field office. They also considered how project implementation prioritized policies, systems and structures instead of the target people.

In defense to World Vision being people oriented, staff members recognized World Vision as one of the few organizations in Nepal that paid the full medical claim, and provided staff care, maternity leave, social security and family leave. One member of the leadership team emphasized the equality of the People and Culture policies. Regardless of an individual's position in the office, people were treated equally. As an example, they were provided with the same travelling benefits. This response differed starkly from the response of the questionnaire where respondents felt that human resources policy had low priority. One plausible reason why respondents might have considered people and culture policies to have the lowest priority could be the perceived differential treatment between staff from field offices and those in the central office at the capital. During focus group discussions, staff members brought up the inequality of salary or staff development opportunities where staff in the central office were given priority.

Another aspect related to valuing people was the resources spent on staff's spiritual nurture. Apart from regular devotions, World Vision gave out long service awards to their long serving staff, celebrated Christmas and Easter and observed the partnership Day of Prayer. They also sent regular emails encouraging staff with Bible verses. These activities were considered key to the staff's spiritual nurture. In addition, each field office had a spiritual point person who was responsible for the implementation of spiritual nurture activities such as devotions, compiling prayer requests as well as active care for staff.

Based on the findings, it was clear that World Vision did seem to value their staff members. However, respondents did not believe that World Vision prioritized them before money, structure, systems and other institutional machinery.

6.3.1.2.6 Isolation vs Collaboration/Cooperation

Tables 6.24 to 6.26 documented the findings with regard to this cultural dimension.

Table 6.24 World Vision Nepal's Views on Relationships with Internal Stakeholders (N=52)			
Relationships are very important and are considered to be key to success to the office	Relationships are important and are considered to be a useful component in the office	Relationships are somewhat important and are considered good to have important in the office	Relationships are not important to the success of the office
56%	34%	10%	0%

There was a clear understanding among the respondents that relationships with internal stakeholders were very important or important. In table 6.24, more than half of the respondents considered relationships to be key to the success of the office (56%).

Table 6.25 The Role of Relationships for Internal Stakeholders at World Vision Nepal							
Relationships do not have a role. Work tasks should be completed independent of relationships	Relationships are able to provide new networks that might be useful in work context	Relationships are important in current cultural contexts as basis for working in said context	Relationships lead to trust, which is effective for accomplishing work	Relationships provide opportunities to witness to God's love	Relationships enable diversity of people to work together	Others – please specify
Overall (N=52)							
3	28	25	31	29	26	1
Christians (N=31)							
3	15	15	19	22	17	
Non-Christians (N=21)							
0	13	10	12	7	8	0

When asked about the role of relationships (table 6.25), more than half of the respondents linked this to the accomplishment of work. Other key roles for relationships included opportunities to witness to God's love as well as to provide new networks that might be useful in the work context. The witness to God's love was the most important reason for relationships for Christians but did not play an important for Non-Christians. The new networks that might be useful in the work context were seen to be more important for Non-Christians.

Table 6.26 How Work is Accomplished at World Vision Nepal (N=49)	
Work is done individually with individuals responsible for work outputs	Work is done collectively with team collectively responsible for work outputs
32%	68%

This understanding of relationships as important for the accomplishment of work made sense in light of the responses given to the question regarding how work was accomplished in the office. As depicted in table 6.26, 68% of the respondents considered work as done collectively with the team responsible for work outputs.

In general, the positive working environment was mentioned in different focus group discussions. This included comments like "friendly' environment" or "team building approach." One leader remarked that he intentionally cared for his people, washed their feet, respected and shared with them. He encouraged his staff to be involved. In conclusion, it can be said that the leadership of World Vision did encourage a positive working environment, where relationships were considered important for the success of the office.

6.3.1.2.7 Control/Coordination/Responsibility

The findings of this cultural dimension were documented in table 6.27 to table 6.29.

Table 6.27 Decision Making at World Vision Nepal			
How are decisions generally made in the office? (N=51)			
Decisions are made mainly by the National Director with little or no consultation with others	Decisions are made mainly by the Senior Leadership Team with little or no consultation with others	Decisions are made by the Senior Leadership Team in consultation with some managers	Decisions are made collectively by the Senior Leadership in consultation with different levels of staff
6	15	28	16

How are decisions communicated to different members of the office? (N=53)			
Through email	1 to 1 meetings with direct managers	Corporate staff meetings	Others – Please Specify
47	9	18	4

As shown in table 6.27, decisions are perceived to be made by the Senior Leadership Team in consultation with the managers. When asked during interviews and focus group discussions, individuals commented that there was a set procedure depending on the decision made. This procedure ranged from being participatory to consulting with relevant stakeholders, to discussing with specific function directors, to discussing amongst the senior management team and the National Director. Ultimately the decision maker decides the procedure depending on the decision. With regard to decisions made by the senior leadership team, the department director of the decision will be responsible for collecting relevant information. This information will form the basis for decision making made by the leadership team. As a follow up, relevant policies as well as organizational processes were drawn up.

When asked about the way that decisions are communicated, it has been reported that most decisions were communicated via emails. The next most common method was through staff meeting. During focus group discussion, there seemed to be a disconnect felt by field staff from the central office. Field staff described feeling detached and discriminated because of the lack of information. In addition, they discussed the barriers caused by hierarchy and fixed job levels. These staff were not made aware of decisions made or staff movement.

Table 6.28 God's Guidance in Decision Making at World Vision Nepal		
	Yes	No
Overall (N=52)	75%	25%
Christians (N=30)	66.7%	33.3%
Non-Christians (N=22)	86.4%	13.6%

As depicted in table 6.28, 75% of the staff believed that God's guidance was sought in the decision-making process. When asked how this guidance was sought, the main response was during regular devotions. It is interesting to note that a bigger percentage of Non-Christians believed that God guided the decisions at World Vision more than Christians (86.4% compared to 66.7%).

Table 6.29 How God's Guidance is Sought in the Decision Making process at World Vision Nepal							
	Setting aside time for prayer during office hours	reading the bible	regular devotions	personal reflection	setting aside time for decision makers to reflect on the work issues	using Christian principles for work practices	others – please specify
Overall (N=48)	19	12	37	19	11	18	4
Christians (N=26)	12	5	19	12	6	10	
Non-Christians (N=21)	7	7	18	7	5	8	

In understanding how God's guidance was included in the decision-making process, devotions featured as key to seeking God's guidance (Table 6.29). This was consistent for both Christian and Non-Christian staff.

Based on the responses received for this cultural dimension, control/coordination/responsibility, it can be concluded that respondents believed that there were clear procedures made regarding decisions. In general, decisions were made in consultation with some staff members. God's guidance was understood to be sought during regular devotions.

6.3.1.2.8 Orientation and Focus

The final cultural dimension, orientation and focus, is presented in tables 6.30 and 6.31.

Table 6.30 Views on Relationships with External Stakeholders at World Vision Nepal (N=52)			
Relationships are very important and are considered to be key to success to the office	Relationships are important and are considered to be a useful component in the office	Relationships are somewhat important and are considered good to have important in the office	Relationships are not important to the success of the office
31	23	8	0

In general, relationships with external stakeholders were considered to be important. As depicted in table 6.30, 31 respondents, more than half of the respondents considered relationships to be very important while 23 of the respondents considered relationships to be important. One reason why external partners were so important was because, as an international NGO in Nepal, World Vision was unable to legally implement activities alone. Legally, only local organizations are able to implement agencies of development projects. As such, World Vision Nepal had clear strategies for partnerships such as knowledge and resource sharing, legal purposes and support.

Some external partnerships described by respondents included government ministries at different levels (district, local), cooperatives, community based organizations (CBOs) local NGOs, other INGOS and the UN. Working with the government enables sustainability of a project with deeper collaboration and resource sharing, while working with local NGOs and CBOs is necessary due to government restriction regarding INGOs directly implementing activities. An established NGO selection process was developed centrally by the National Office and used by the different field offices.

Another point regarding external partnerships that was brought up during focus group discussions was the relationship between World Vision and local churches. At time of the field visit, World Vision did not partner with Nepali churches regularly but instead worked with them occasionally depending on the subject. Some examples provided included providing development training to pastors and congregational members on an ad hoc basis, donating furniture to churches; sending their prayer requests to some pastors, publishing internship opportunities in churches and involving church pastors in events like Christian, Easter and Day of Prayer celebrations.

Table 6.31 The Role of Relationships in the office with External stakeholders at World Vision Nepal (N=53)					
Relationships do not have a role. Work tasks should be completed independent of relationships	Relationships are able to provide new networks that might be useful in work context	Relationships are important in current cultural contexts as basis for working in said context	Relationships lead to trust, which is effective for accomplishing work	Relationships provide opportunities to witness to God's love	Relationships enable diversity of people to work together
1	35	31	26	22	21

When asked about the role of relationships with external stakeholders, a majority of the respondents considered relationships as key to providing new networks that might be useful in the work context. The importance of relationships in the cultural context was also an important reason for relationships (Table 6.31).

Based on the different questions and answers related to this cultural dimension, responses showed a clear understanding from the respondents of who the external partners were, how these partners were involved as well as a clear strategy for sustainability and collaboration in their work. There were clear strategies and work plans in place showing how World Vision would work with external partners. What was not evident was how these relationships related to the understanding of God. It was also important to note that WV Nepal worked with churches on an ad hoc basis instead of the churches being a regular partner.

6.3.1.2.9 Summarized Values held by World Vision Nepal

Thus far, we have looked at individual cultural dimensions and the detailed findings from World Vision Nepal. For ease of reference, Table 6.32 summarizes World Vision Nepal's Christian values according to organizational cultural dimensions.

Table 6.32 Summary of World Vision Nepal Values	
Basis of truth and rationality in the organization	While understanding that scriptures were key to the organization, members had questioned the explicit applicability of scriptures to their day to day work. In addition, staff had an assumption that the scriptures and Christian worldview were worked out at the global and regional level, and as such, were not necessary to be thought through at the country level.
Nature of time and time horizon	While it was clear that goals were time bound, it was not clear that emergencies were planned for and that God's direction was actively sought in decision making of WV Nepal.
Motivation	The religious orientation of the organization could not be seen to be the primary motivation for staff working in the organization or for them to continue in their jobs.
Stability vs change/ innovation/personal growth	Change was embraced in World Vision Nepal. However, the relationship to God's dependence was not as clearly expressed and embraced by members of the office.
Orientation to work/ task/coworkers	While World Vision did seem to have organizational processes in place that seem to value their staff, respondents still did not believe that World Vision valued people as a priority before money, structure, systems and other institutional machinery.
Isolation vs collaboration/cooperation	World Vision encouraged a positive working environment, where relationships are considered important for the success of the office.

Control/coordination/responsibility	In general, respondents believed that decisions were made in consultation with at least some staff members. God's guidance was understood to be sought during regular devotions.
Orientation and Focus	There was a clear strategy and openness to work with external partners in Nepal, where partners are involved with the intention of sustainability and collaboration in their work. It was not clear that these relationships were developed with the perspective of honoring God in mind.

In general, it could be concluded that staff members were aware of management efforts to incorporate Christian values in the organizational practices at World Vision Nepal. At the same time, it was also clear that these management efforts seem to be lacking as they did not result in Christian values having a central place in the organization's culture.

6.3.1.3 State of Relationships in WV Nepal

This section reviews the state of relationships in WV Nepal. To find out more about relationships within the office, further questions were asked about the state of relationships. In the questionnaire, a total of 21 field staff, 17 support staff, 11 middle management and 5 senior management staff responded to this section of the questionnaire. This information about relationships is useful to understand the social networks involved in the overall meaning transmission in the organization. Results are presented in this section.

Before these are presented, table 6.33 provide introductory information about external relationships that WV Nepal had with stakeholders outside WV Nepal.

Table 6.33 Ranking of the Stakeholders in the way it Influences the Strategy and Direction at World Vision Nepal (N=42)

	Beneficiaries of the work of World Vision	Other NGOs working in the same country context	Global Centre	Relevant Support Offices	Regional Office	Local churches within area of work in World Vision in country context	Government officials in country context	Direct Donors
mode	1	3	1	5	4	8	2	6
median	1	4.5	3	4	4	7	3	6
average	2.29	4.33	3.716	3.98	3.60	6.06	3.38	5.56
rank	1	6	4	5	3	8	2	7

Based on table 6.33, the beneficiaries, government officials and regional office were considered to be the most influential to the strategy and direction of the office.

Table 6.34 Average Rating on Relationships with Stakeholders at World Vision Nepal (1= very close, 2=somewhat close, 3=somewhat distant, 4=very distant) (N=53)

	Field Staff	Support Staff	Middle Management	Senior Management	External (Global Centre)	External (Regional Office)	External (Support Office)
Senior Management	2.20	1.80	1.40	1.00	3.20	2.80	2.80
Middle Management	1.82	1.73	1.60	2.09	3.22	2.82	2.80

| Support Staff | 1.63 | 1.50 | 1.69 | 2.75 | 3.56 | 3.25 | 3.00 |
| Field Staff | 1.10 | 2.00 | 1.83 | 2.88 | 3.86 | 3.86 | 3.71 |

Regarding relationships with WV, staff reported relationships that they had with their own category the closest relationships (Table 6.34). In addition, closer relationships were also reported among stakeholders in the same office than those outside such as with the Global Centre, Regional Office and Support offices. The relationship with the Global Centre was considered the most distant for all stakeholders.

In the country office, senior management perceived their relationships as furthest away from field staff. Middle management, support and field staff perceived their relationships as furthest from senior management.

Table 6.35 Average Perceived Influence of Different Stakeholders at World Vision Nepal (1=extremely influential, 2= very influential, 3=somewhat influential, 4= little or no influence) (N=53)

	Field Staff	Support Staff	Middle Management	Senior Management	External (GC)	External (RO)	External (SO)
Senior Management	2.60	2.20	1.40	1.20	2.80	2.40	2.80
Middle Management	2.09	2.27	2.27	2.09	3.09	2.73	3.00
Support Staff	2.25	2.13	2.19	2.75	3.56	3.33	3.38
Field Staff	1.43	2.21	2.35	2.90	3.76	3.86	3.71

No stakeholder was unanimously perceived to be the most influential in the office by all stakeholders. Senior management, support staff and field staff considered themselves to be the most influential while middle management considered both senior management and field staff to be equally influential. However, all stakeholders held in consensus that external stakeholders were generally considered to be less influential compared to internal stakeholders (Table 6.35).

In the next section, relationships between the stakeholders are further analyzed through the use of relationship proximity. This focuses on five different domains: directness, continuity, multiplexity, parity and commonality. Relational proximity relates to interaction between different stakeholders, rather than compatibility. Average scores of each domain for each stakeholder are provided in the reporting of relational proximity. For more details about each domain, the full report is provided in Appendix 3.

6.3.1.3.1 Senior Management

Table 6.36 Average Perception Regarding Relational Proximity for Senior Management at World Vision Nepal (N=5) (1= Strongly Agree, 2= Agree, 3= Neutral, 4=Disagree, 5=Strongly Disagree)

	Field Staff	Support Staff	Middle Manage-	Senior Manage-	External (GC)	External (RO)	External (SO)
Directness	2.50	2.15	2.00	1.90	3.65	2.75	2.90
Continuity	2.20	2.19	2.00	1.79	2.95	2.44	3.18
Multiplexity	1.70	1.84	1.76	1.68	2.69	2.31	2.45
Parity	2.19	2.18	2.18	1.76	2.55	2.42	2.32
Commonality	2.14	2.03	2.15	1.69	2.88	2.35	2.46
Overall Average scores for Senior Management	2.14	2.08	2.02	1.76	2.94	2.45	2.66

Table 6.36 depicts the summarized information for senior management according to the five different domains in relational proximity. In general, senior management saw themselves as closest to other senior management members (1.76), ahead of middle management (2.02), support staff (2.08) and finally field staff (2.14). This pattern was repeated in the domains parity, continuity and directness. For commonality and multiplexity, senior management saw itself as closer to field staff than to support staff.

Regarding external stakeholders, senior management saw themselves closest to the regional office, support offices, followed by the Global Centre. This trend is seen in the domains commonality, multiplexity and directness. For continuity, senior management saw itself closer to the Global Centre, then the regional office, followed by support offices and for parity, senior management saw themselves closer to support offices than to regional office and the Global Centre.

6.3.1.3.2 Middle Management

Table 6.37 Perception regarding Relational Proximity for Middle Management at World Vision Nepal (N=8) (1= Strongly Agree, 2= Agree, 3= Neutral, 4=Disagree, 5=Strongly Disagree)							
	Field Staff	Support Staff	Middle Management	Senior Management	External (GC)	External (RO)	External (SO)
Directness	1.80	1.77	1.86	2.31	3.70	3.50	3.80
Continuity	1.69	1.58	1.86	2.36	3.94	3.83	3.89
Multiplexity	1.81	1.84	1.98	2.90	3.62	3.57	3.57
Parity	1.88	1.96	1.71	2.39	2.86	2.74	2.92
Commonality	1.75	1.88	1.89	2.52	3.11	3.06	3.22
Overall Average scores for Middle Management	1.78	1.81	1.86	2.49	3.45	3.34	3.48

Table 6.37 showed the consolidated information for middle management and its perceptions of relationships with other stakeholders. In general, the middle management had the closest relationship with field staff (1.78) before support staff (1.81) and other middle management staff (1.86). This closeness to field staff was also reflected in three of the five domains: multiplexity, parity and commonality.

Compared to other internal stakeholders, middle management had a distinctly distant relationship with senior management. Middle management also perceived a larger distance from external stakeholders, where the regional office (3.34) was perceived as the closest compared to the Global Centre (3.45) and support offices (3.48).

6.3.1.3.3 Support Staff

Table 6.38 Perception regarding Relational Proximity for Support Staff at World Vision Nepal (N=8)
(1= Strongly Agree, 2= Agree, 3= Neutral, 4=Disagree, 5=Strongly Disagree)

	Field Staff	Support Staff	Middle Management	Senior Management	External (GC)	External (RO)	External (SO)
Average on Directness	1.91	1.80	2.23	3.27	4.25	4.11	3.82
Average on Continuity	1.89	1.77	2.43	2.84	4.20	4.18	3.93
Average on Multiplexity	2.09	2.07	2.44	2.77	3.94	3.95	4.08
Average on Parity	2.29	2.30	2.46	2.90	3.25	3.25	3.25
Average on Commonality	2.38	2.25	2.63	3.08	3.50	3.52	3.60
Overall Average Scores for Support Staff	2.11	2.04	2.44	2.97	3.83	3.80	3.74

Table 6.38 illustrated the perception of support staff on their relationship with other stakeholders based on the five different domains of relational proximity.

On average, the support staff perceived themselves to be closest to other support staff (2.04) before field staff (2.11) and middle management (2.44). This table also showed evidently that support staff felt most distant from senior management. This trend was repeated for each of the relationship domains.

With regard to external relationships, support offices were reported to be slightly closer compared to the regional office and the Global Centre.

6.3.1.3.4 Field Staff

Table 6.39 Perception Regarding Relational Proximity for Field Staff at World Vision Nepal (N=32) (1= Strongly Agree, 2= Agree, 3= Neutral, 4=Disagree, 5=Strongly Disagree)							
	Field Staff	Support Staff	Middle Management	Senior Management	External (GC)	External (RO)	External (SO)
Average on Directness	1.14	1.79	2.26	3.24	4.27	4.28	4.14
Average on Continuity	1.30	1.91	2.27	3.08	4.09	4.11	4.04
Average on Multiplexity	1.65	2.13	2.47	3.46	4.05	4.13	4.10
Average on Parity	1.73	2.03	2.54	3.05	3.54	3.58	3.51
Average on Commonality	1.67	1.98	2.51	3.17	3.64	3.65	3.62
Average scores for Field Staff	1.50	1.97	2.41	3.20	3.92	3.95	3.88

Table 6.39 consolidated the perception of field staff of their relationship with other stakeholders based on the domains of relational proximity.

On average, field staff considered themselves closest to other field staff (1.5). They were next closest to support staff (1.97), followed by middle management (2.41) and then senior management (3.2). This trend was consistently repeated for each of the five domains. With regard to external stakeholders, the results indicated more distance than for internal stakeholders, though with little variation in the perceived distance from each of the three stakeholders.

6.3.1.3.5 Relationships in WV Nepal

This section summarizes the relationships at WV Nepal. This focus on relationships provide deeper insight into social networks present in the organization. It is also useful for understanding processes involved in group learning, an integral process in organizational culture. Relationship proximity was used to further clarify interaction among different stakeholders based on the five different domains.

Based on the results, the domain receiving the widest range of responses from all different stakeholders was directness. As previously mentioned, directness considers the nearness of contact that the stakeholder has with other stakeholders. This wide range of responses may be explained in part by the varying spatial distance of different stakeholders. Some stakeholders are situated in the field office, some in the capital city, and others elsewhere around the globe in different support offices, regional offices and Global Centre.

Another notable finding of this field research is the unanimous distance that the field staff, support staff and middle management felt from senior management. Contrary to sentiments of these staff, senior management did not report the same distance from these stakeholders. This distant relationship was also described during focus group discussions, where staff members described the organization's tendency to work within the hierarchy leaving little contact with senior management staff.

Generally, more distant scores were given to stakeholders outside WV Nepal. This may be a reason why Christian values were not central to the organization. As seen in chapter four, World Vision Christian values were developed as partnership policies, made at a global level. Lack of a deep relationship with external stakeholders who were ambassadors of these policies might have led to the reduction of impact in the transmission of these values to the national office.

Having finished describing the state of relationships, we complete our survey of World Vision Nepal. We next turn our attention to the findings of the next office, World Vision Papua New Guinea.

6.3.2 Data Collection in WV Papua New Guinea

From 12–16 March 2012, I visited WV Papua New Guinea (PNG). World Vision started Papua New Guinea in 1974 and in 2012 had only grant projects operating in different areas, with the biggest project being TBDots, the treatment of tuberculosis. This was a joint effort with the global fund,[324] as well as the Ministry of Health in Papua New Guinea. During that time, WV PNG had a combined staff of 186 persons. During time spent in the office,

---

[324] The Global Fund is a financing institution, providing support to countries in the response to the three diseases: AIDS, tuberculosis and malaria. See http://www.theglobalfund.org/en/

a total of 53 respondents completed the questionnaire, 5 different focus groups sessions were conducted and 3 interviews held with different staff members.

6.3.2.1 Introductory Portfolio of Respondents

Table 6.40 Length of Service at World Vision Papua New Guinea	0-2.9 Years	3-5.9 Years	6-8.9 Years	> or = 9 Years
How many years have you worked in your current role with World Vision? (N=51)	31	15	3	2
	61%	29%	6%	4%
How long have you worked in the current World Vision office? (N=50)	29	13	3	5
	58%	26%	6%	10%

In general, staff members have worked at World Vision Papua New Guinea (WV PNG) for a relatively short time. As illustrated in table 6.40, more than half of the respondents had been with World Vision for fewer than three years and in their current role for less than three years. One key reason for this short length of service was the grant nature of the office, which resulted in a high turnover.

Table 6.41 Religion of Respondents at World Vision Papua New Guinea (N=53)	Percentages
Christian	92%
No Comment	8%

When asked about their religious affiliation, 92% respondents responded that they were Christians while 8% did not indicate their religious affiliation (See table 6.41). This is comparable to the predominant Christian country context where the office was located.[325]

---

[325] According to the 2010 census, 95.6% of the population consider themselves Christian. Of these, 26% consider themselves Catholic and 69.6% Protestants. See "Papua New Guinea 2011 National Report," accessed May 15, 2015, http://sdd.spc.int/en/resources/document-library?view=preview&format=raw&fileId=218.

Table 6.42 Importance of World Vision Papua New Guinea's Religious Motivation and Values in Choosing a Job (N=57)			
very important	important	not important	unrelated
68%	26%	5%	0%

As an introductory question to Christian understanding of the office, the importance of an organization's religious affiliation and values in choosing a job was asked. A significant majority of respondents (94%) responded that it was important or very important (See table 6.42).

After this presentation of an introductory profile of the respondents, this section describes the responses on each organizational cultural dimension.

6.3.2.2 Organizational Culture Dimensions

The findings of organizational cultural dimensions of WV PNG is reported below. This includes information from the questionnaire as well as appropriate information from focus group discussions and interviews. Similar to data collection in WV Nepal, the summarized understanding of each value is given at the end of each dimension. For a list of the Christian values for all the eight dimensions, refer to 6.3.2.2.9 Summarized Values held by WV PNG.

6.3.2.2.1 Basis of truth and rationality in the organization

The findings of the organizational cultural dimension, basis of truth and rationality in the organization are documented in tables 6.43 – 6.46.

Table 6.43 The influence of World Vision's Mission Statement on World Vision Papua New Guinea	Yes	No
Does the Mission Statement influence your work? (N=56)	95%	5%
Does the Mission Statement influence your office? (N=53)	91%	9%

Most of the respondents indicated that the mission statement affected both one's work and one's office (table 6.43). This perceived influence on the office was less than for the individual (95% instead of 91%). When asked for concrete examples of influence during focus group discussions, members gave range of answers. This included those who explicitly mentioned following the example of Christ. This means: to be fair minded, to "not get involved in the communities and partner political agendas." For respondents who did not agree that the mission statement was influencing work/office, a variety of reasons was also given. As an example, respondents considered the evident lack of accountability and decision-making that neglected the mission statement.

Table 6.44 Extent of Importance for Decision Making at World Vision Papua New Guinea (1 being most important)									
	Global & regional strategies	Donor Expectations	Country Statistics	Relationship with the government and other stakeholders in the community	Field Financial guidelines	Human Resources policies	Biblical perspectives on the decision that is being made	Local cultural practices	Others
mode	7	1	5	4	4	2	1	8	
median	4	3	5	4	4	4	5	7	
average	4.40	3.56	4.96	4.10	4.06	4.21	4.27	6.05	
rank	6	1	7	3	2	4	5	8	

Table 6.44 indicated key information used in decision making. At WV PNG, this included donor expectations as well as field financial guidelines. This was not surprising since WV PNG was 100% funded by external grants. In focus group discussions held with staff members, staff members reinforced their perceptions of limitations set by the grant funding nature of the office. Decisions were dependent on the project plan. The senior management team described a charter that was used for decision making. One key aspect of this charter was the importance of managing resources as well as possible.

Table 6.45 Scriptures in Decision Making Process at World Vision Papua New Guinea

Are scriptures consulted as part of the decision-making process? (N=52)	Yes	No
	35%	65%
How are scriptures considered in the decision-making process? (N=40)	Collectively	Individually
	33%	67%

In looking specifically at how Scriptures was part of the decision-making process, results showed that a majority of the staff (65%) did not believe that Scriptures were considered as part of the decision-making process (table 6.45). For those who considered scriptures as part of the decision-making process, a majority of the staff believed that this was an individual endeavor (67%).

During focus group discussions, respondents described the limited possibility for Christian activities due to the funding nature of the work at WV PNG. For respondents who described the presence of scriptures in decision making, this was because of the "servant leadership of leaders," where some leaders sought to be Christ like in their personal, spiritual and work lives.

When Scriptures were used, this was done mostly during devotions, as well as special occasions like World Vision's partnership day of prayer. World Vision PNG has a volunteer pastor who organized special occasions as well as devotions.

Table 6.46 Obstacles in Using Scriptures in the Decision-making Process at World Vision Papua New Guinea (N=46)

One needs to be sensitive to the Non-Christian country context that we are operating in	Scriptures are not relevant in the decision-making process	Use of Scriptures is personal and should not be used in work related decisions	One needs to be sensitive to other staff in the office that are not Christian	Others – please specify
18	12	13	13	12

When asked about obstacles to using Scriptures for decision making, staff named the non-Christian country context where World Vision operated, the irrelevance of Scriptures at work due to its personal nature, and sensitivity to other non-Christian staff members (table 5.46). This response was curious as Papua New Guinea was not a non-Christian context. During focus group discussions, respondents clarified that what was meant was the non-Christian nature of the projects that made it difficult to use scriptures in the decision-making of the office. This was particularly problematic because of the perceived restrictions from the donors. Therefore, instead of the country context, it seemed that it was the donors that seemed to be the biggest obstacle.

Based on the responses, one can conclude that for the culture dimension basis of truth and rationality, World Vision PNG had no clear view that scriptures were key to decision making in the organization. The use of scriptures was instead left to the discretion of individual leaders who may or may not use them.

6.3.2.2.2 Nature of Time and Time Horizon

The findings for this organizational culture dimensions are documented in tables 6.47-6.51.

	Level 6.47 Extent of Importance in Goal Setting at World Vision Papua New Guinea (N=48)				
	Compliance to pre discussed strategy and objectives for the office	Consideration of operational challenges as they arise at the current moment	Planning for future objectives and direction of the office	Consideration of emergencies in the country context and the response of the office to the emergency	The following of God's direction in the completion of the goal
Mode	2	3	2	4	1
Median	3	3	2	4	2
Average	2.78	2.89	2.57	3.70	2.83
Ranking	2	4	1	5	3

One way of understanding if God's direction was sought in decision-making was to consider the goal setting in the office. As explicated in table 6.47, it was evident that most respondents considered planning for future objectives and direction of the office as most important for the office, followed by compliance to pre-discussed strategy and objectives for the office.

One reason for this answer could be that at the time of this field research, the WV PNG office was in the process of reviewing its strategy since the current one was coming to an end. This could explain the perception of linking decisions to planning for future objectives and direction. In general, staff members noted the challenge of setting long term goals in light of the grant funding nature of the office, as well as yearly contracts given to staff. Project planning was very much dependent on the project framework, which in their opinion was developed at a partnership level, and adapted based on donors. At the same time, management described the tension of moving the office in a certain direction yet receiving projects that moved the organization in a different direction. Coordination seemed to be particularly complicated especially as staff members were offered short term contracts.

Table 6.48 Extent that Goals are Time Bound with Timelines Observed at World Vision Papua New Guinea (N=45)			
Goals are not time bound, timelines are not observed at all	Goals are seldom time bound, timelines are not observed most of the time	Goals are somewhat time bound, timelines are observed as far as possible	Goals are extremely time bound, timelines are observed strictly
2%	10%	60%	28%

Responses shown in table 6.48 regarding timelines indicated a clear understanding that goals were mostly time bound. 60% of the respondents observed that timelines were observed as far as possible, while 28% respondents considered that goals were extremely time bound.

Table 6.49 World Vision Papua New Guinea Seeks God's Direction in the Setting of Goals (N=49)	
Yes	No
82%	18%

When asked if God's direction was sought in the setting of goals, a large majority (82%) said yes (Table 6.49). When asked how they saw the organization as following God's direction, respondents offered during the focus group discussion examples where they had seen God's direction was directly sought. This included the area leader leading the office in prayer before responding when a World Vision driver accidentally killed a child in a village. Other respondents described God's direction sought through the good that the projects had done in communities where World Vision worked. For these respondents, World Vision was responsive to God's direction when project designs took into consideration different stakeholders in community.

Table 6.50 Seeking God's Direction in the Setting of Goals at World Vision Papua New Guinea (N=50)					
Setting aside time for prayer during office hours	Reading the Bible	Regular devotions	Personal reflection	Setting aside time for decision makers to reflect on the work issues	using Christian principles for work practices
21	13	32	15	13	18

When asked how God's direction was sought, majority of the staff considered regular devotions as well as setting aside time for prayer during office hours as main ways where God's direction was considered (Table 6.50). Christian principles named included openness and transparency.

Table 6.51 Obstacles in Seeking God's Direction in the Setting of Goals at World Vision Papua New Guinea (N= 46)				
To be sensitive to the Non-Christian country context that we are operating in	God's direction is not related to the setting of goals of the organization	To be sensitive to staff who are not Christian	I do not know what God's guidance is	Others – please specify
14	7	9	4	9

Not everyone responded to questions regarding obstacles. For those who responded, the key obstacles included being sensitive to the Non-Christian context (Table 6.51). This was interesting as Papua New Guinea was in fact predominantly Christian. In closer dialogue with the staff members, one possible suggestion found was the non-church environment out of which members operated. They perceived a difference in what World Vision was doing, compared to the church environment, which they associated with God's direction.

Based on this cultural dimension, responses indicated that staff members' did not agree that God's direction was intentionally sought in the decision making of WV PNG. As goals set by the organization were linked to project plans pre-agreed, the organization did not pre-plan for emergencies.

6.3.2.2.3 Motivation

Findings for this dimension on motivation is documented in tables 6.52 and 6.53.

Table 6.52 Reasons for Working with World Vision Papua New Guinea							
	Job Description	Sector (INGO, NPO) that World Vision is a part of	Existing staff in the Office	Religious Identity of World Vision	Espoused values and mission of world vision	Conditions offered by World Vision (salary & benefits)	Others – please specify
Reasons why an individual works for World Vision Papua New Guinea (N=51)							
Mode	1	1	6	1	2	6	7
median	3	3	5	2	3	5	7
average	2.89	2.78	4.43	2.38	3.30	4.32	6.83
ranking	3	2	6	1	4	5	7
Reasons why other staff might choose to work for World Vision Papua New Guinea (N=52)							
Mode	1	3	6	1	2	6	7
median	2.5	3	5	3	4	3	7
average	2.85	3.17	4.60	2.98	3.52	3.46	6.57
ranking	1	3	6	2	5	4	7

Responses summarized in table 6.52 showed that the main reason individuals joined World Vision was the religious identity of the organization. The sector where World Vision worked as well as the job description were other important reasons highlighted. In providing some distance to this question, the next question asked why others would join the organization. In answering this question, the job description became the most important reason, followed by religious identity and the sector that World Vision was in.

During focus group discussions, bettering the needs of the community was repeated as an important motivation for individuals to work for an organization that improved lives in the community. Another important motivation was the necessity of finding a job. The actual organization was secondary to the eventuality of finding a job. It is notable that there was little mention of religious identity of the organization as key to the respondents during the focus group discussions, despite it being considered in the questionnaire as the most important reason for choosing to work for World Vision.

Table 6.53 Motivating and Demotivating Factors at World Vision Papua New Guinea (N=53)								
	Management style of Senior Leadership Team	Workplace environment	Job Scope	Career Advancement Opportunities	Learning and Development Activities	Changes in work conditions (Salary and Benefits)	Mission and Purpose of World Vision	Others – please specify
What are the top three factors that motivate you in your current role?								
Rank	5	1	4	2	2	6	3	
What are top 3 factors that demotivate you in your current responsibility?								
Rank	3	6	2	5	4	1	8	7

When asked to identify factors that motivated and demotivated the individual, the top three motivational factors as seen in table 6.53 included the workplace environment, the learning and development activities, and career advancement opportunities. The top three demotivating factors included work conditions (salary and benefits), job scope, and the management type of the senior leadership team. During focus group discussions, the pay system of World Vision PNG was repeated regularly as a demotivating factor. Instead of being paid fortnightly as staff members wished, they were instead paid twice a month (on the 15th and 30th). This was seen as a big inconvenience in terms of personal financial commitments.

Concluding this organization culture dimension, responses given do not show that the religious orientation of the organization was seen to be the primary motivation for staff working in the organization or for them to continue in their jobs. Factors like needs in the community, and factors related to their employment terms were more influential at motivating/demotivating them to do a good job.

6.3.2.2.4 Stability vs Change/Innovation/Personal Growth

The findings related to this organizational culture dimension include tables 6.54 to 6.60.

Table 6.54 Understanding Change at World Vision Papua New Guinea			
How often do changes in your office takes place? (N=51)			
Very often	Often	Sometimes	Seldom
14%	25%	39%	22%
How does your office consider change? (N=50)			
Change is extremely undesirable	Change is somewhat undesirable	Change is somewhat desirable	Change is extremely desirable
8%	20%	65%	8%

Table 6.54 show that a majority of the respondents (64%) considered changes to take place fairly frequently (often and sometimes) within the organization. In general, changes were considered to be somewhat desirable (65%).

Table 6.55 Changes that Take Place Most Often at World Vision Papua New Guinea (N=48)								
	Organizational Processes	Field Financial Manual	Human Resources Policies	Organizational Structure	Long Term Organizational Strategy and Objectives	Project Log frames	Staff Turnover	Available Funding
median	4	5.5	5	5	5	4	1	3
average	3.87	5.13	4.86	4.57	5.00	4.68	2.53	3.73
ranking	3	8	6	4	7	5	1	2

Table 6.55 indicates that the most frequent change reported in the office was staff turnover. Available funding was the next most frequent. During focus group discussions, staff turnover was again mentioned as the most common change. This was partially attributed to the project nature of the office, as well as yearly contracts given to staff. These contracts increased job insecurity which in turn led to an increase in staff turnover.

Table 6.56 Main Reasons for Changes at World Vision Papua New Guinea (N=48)				
Sudden change in environmental conditions in country context	Management style of Senior Leadership within the office	Change in Partnership direction	Desire for continuous improvement and progress in office	Others – please specify
3	6	19	23	3

As reported by respondents, the main reason for changes in the office was the organization's desire for continuous improvement and progress in the office followed by change in partnership direction (Table 6.56). This idea of change for continuous improvement was confirmed during the focus group discussions as focus group participants described that changes leading to more impact were particularly welcomed.

Table 6.57 Seeking God's Guidance in the Consideration of Changes at World Vision Papua New Guinea (N=49)	
Yes	No
82%	18%

Table 6.57 showed that a majority (82%) of the respondents believed that God's guidance was considered in the changes.

Table 6.58 When God's Guidance is Considered in the Change Process at World Vision Papua New Guineas (N=46)			
In the evaluation of need for change	Planning process for change	During change process	After change process, as means of reflection
20	34	26	13

Table 6.58 indicated that God's guidance was sought mainly during the planning process (34 respondents). During focus group discussions, participants described the openness and frequent communication they experienced during the change process. As an example of how God's guidance was considered during the change process, participants recounted that during the restructuring process, leaders of the organization had been intentional in having a retreat to reflect and pray, and were also open in asking for prayer from the rest of the staff.

Table 6.59 How God's Guidance is Considered in the Changes Experienced by World Vision Papua New Guinea (N=47)						
Setting aside time for prayer during office hours	Reading the Bible	Regular devotions	personal reflection	Setting aside time for decision makers to reflect on the work issues	Using Christian principles to understand change	Others – Please specify
16	13	39	13	13	17	0

When asked how God's guidance was considered in the decision-making process, more than half (39 respondents) responded that God's guidance was considered via regular devotions (Table 6.59). Other options included using Christian principles like 'open communication' to process change, as well as setting aside time aside for prayer during office hours.

Table 6.60 Obstacles in Seeking God's Guidance in Changes Experienced at World Vision Papua New Guinea (N=42)					
To be sensitive of the Non-Christian country context that we are operating in	The Holy Spirit speaks to individuals and not corporately to the organization	To be sensitive to staff who are not Christian	God's guidance is not required to assist in changes in the Organization	I do not know what God's guidance is	Others – Please specify
16%	33%	27%	7%	4%	13%

Table 6.60 presented the main obstacle to seeking God's guidance perceived by 33% of the respondents as the individual nature of faith. The Holy Spirit spoke to individuals and not corporately to the organization. This was also mentioned during different discussions where participants described that the extent to which God's guidance was sought was dependent on the individual leader.

Concluding the findings for this cultural dimension, respondents generally regarded change positively especially for continuous improvement of the office. Most respondents indicated that God's direction was involved in the change process, mostly during planning for change. Devotions were seen as the main tool used in seeking God's direction by the office as other forms are dependent on individual leaders. It can therefore be established that for WV PNG, while change was embraced, the relationship of change to God's dependence was largely dependent on individual leaders.

6.3.2.2.5 Orientation to Work/Task/Co-workers

Table 6.61 details the findings of the cultural dimension, orientation to work/task/co-workers.

Table 6.61 Priority for World Vision Papua New Guinea from the Most Important to the Least Important (N= 49)					
	Completion of pre-agreed tasks as determined by formal documents of World Vision	Observation of organizational structures and the relevant levels of authority	Observation of field financial manual	Observation of P&C (People and Culture) policies (Human Resources)	Relationships between individuals within and outside of organization
mode	5	4	3	2	1
median	3.5	3	2.5	2	3.5
average	3.20	2.89	2.96	2.62	2.96
rank	4	2	3	1	3

As Table 6.61 showed, observation of P&C policies was perceived to be of utmost priority for the office. This was followed closely by observation of organizational structures and observance of the field financial manual. During focus group discussions, it was clarified that priority of P&C policies did not mean a priority for staff. Participants in focus group did not associate the people and culture policies to be related to staff well-being. Instead of valuing staff, these policies represented structures and systems that were put in place to ease administration. The bi-monthly pay system was brought up as an example of how People & Culture policies were not supportive of staff, but needed to be observed as they were part of structural policies. Other examples were also given such as the lack of pick-ups at the airport despite security concerns, or inflexibility of pick-ups of staff to include children.

Despite the frustration with the people and culture policies, staff members affirmed that time was set outside for weekly devotions as well as for prayer during meetings. As part of regular practice, World Vision planned for regular devotions, gave out long service awards to their long serving staff and observed the partnership Day of Prayer.

Concluding this section, staff members did not believe that people were valued above other constraints at World Vision. They did however experience intentional time spent on organizational fellowship events.

6.3.2.2.6 Isolation vs Collaboration/Cooperation

The findings of this organizational cultural dimension are consolidated in tables 6.62 to 6.64.

Table 6.62 Views on Relationships with Internal Stakeholders at World Vision Papua New Guinea (N=51)			
Relationships are very important and are considered to be key to success to the office	Relationships are important and are considered to be a useful component in the office	Relationships are somewhat important and are considered good to have important in the office	Relationships are not important to the success of the office
63%	25%	12%	0%

Table 6.62 revealed a clear understanding among the respondents that relationships with internal stakeholders were either very important or important. More than half of the respondents considered relationships to be key to the success of the office (63%).

Table 6.63 The Role of Relationships for Internal Stakeholders at World Vision Papua New Guinea (N=51)

Relationships do not have a role. Work tasks should be completed independent of relationships	Relationships are able to provide new networks that might be useful in work context	Relationships are important in current cultural contexts as basis for working in said context	Relationships lead to trust, which is effective for accomplishing work	Relationships provide opportunities to witness to God's love	Relationships enable diversity of people to work together	Others – please specify
3	28	19	31	20	27	3

As table 6.63 showed, most respondents linked relationships in their importance to leading to trust, which was effective for accomplishing work tasks. Other key reasons for relationships included providing new networks that might be useful in the work context as well as enabling diversity of people to work together.

Table 6.64 The Accomplishment of Work at World Vision Papua New Guinea (N= 52)

Work is done individually with individuals responsible for work outputs	Work is done collectively with team collectively responsible for work outputs
30%	70%

Table 6.64 indicated that 70% of respondents considered work to be done collectively by a team.

Based on different interviews and focus group discussions, it was clear that a certain camaraderie within colleagues of the office existed, fostered by the senior management team. There was an intentional effort by senior management to be open and transparent, with a clear understanding that good relationships in teams led to successful completion of goals. In concluding the findings regarding this cultural dimension, it can be said that the leadership of World Vision encouraged a positive working environment with a clear understanding that good relationships lead to successful completion of goals.

6.3.2.2.7 Control/Coordination/Responsibility

The findings of this organizational culture dimension for WV PNG can be found in tables 6.65 to 6.67.

Table 6.65 Decisions at World Vision Papua New Guinea			
How are decisions generally made in the office? (N=52)			
Decisions are made mainly by the National Director with little or no consultation with others	Decisions are made mainly by the Senior Leadership Team with little or no consultation with others	Decisions are made by the Senior Leadership Team in consultation with some managers	Decisions are made collectively by the Senior Leadership in consultation with different levels of staff
5%	23%	32%	40%
How are decisions communicated to different members of the office? (N=53)			
Through email	1 to 1 meetings with direct managers	Corporate staff meetings	Others – Please Specify
52%	19%	12%	17%

Table 6.65 showed that a majority of staff agreed that considerable consultation was made with different levels of staff during the decision-making process. 32% responded that consultation was made with some managers and 40% responded that consultation was made with different levels of staff.

In focus group discussions and interviews, staff described strategic and high-level decisions as made by the senior management team. Other decisions were guided by existing policies or project framework. During discussions, it became evident that in the Melanesian culture, Papuans believed that decision making should be made by the 'big man.' This meant that staff members were not used to deciding for themselves, and were content with higher level decisions made by their perceived leaders. This phenomenon has led one senior leader to mention the need to teach staff to make decisions for themselves, and to work within hierarchies instead of going directly to the 'big man.'

In addition, senior management staff mused about the number of decisions that could indeed be made autonomously. More often than not, decisions had been already made by the World Vision partnership or by donor requirements. These senior management staff described themselves as being a 'filter' for local staff, absorbing pressure felt by external forces.

Table 6.66 God's Guidance in Decision Making at World Vision Papua New Guinea (N=50)	
Yes	No
87%	13%

87% of the staff believed that God's guidance was sought in the decision-making process (Table 6.66). However, during interviews and focus group discussions, it was brought up that the extent to which God's guidance was sought depended on different individual leaders.

Table 6.67 How God's Guidance is Sought in the Decision Making Process at World Vision Papua New Guinea							
setting aside time for prayer during office hours	reading the bible	regular devotions	personal reflection	setting aside time for decision makers to reflect on the work issues	setting aside time for decision makers to reflect on the work issues	using Christian principles for work practices	others – please specify
17	8	30	7	8		21	2

As seen in table 6.67, devotions featured as key to seeking God's guidance in decision-making in the questionnaire. In summary for this cultural dimension, respondents believed that decisions were made in consultation with staff members. However, instead of decisions representing staff member's point of view, they were made in response to external realities or pressures of the office.

6.3.2.2.8 Orientation and Focus

For this cultural dimension, tables 6.68-6.69 documented the findings.

Table 6.68 Views on Relationships with External Stakeholders at World Vision Papua New Guinea (N=50)			
Relationships are very important and are considered to be key to success to the office	Relationships are important and are considered to be a useful component in the office	Relationships are somewhat important and are considered good to have important in the office	Relationships are not important to the success of the office
36	26	6	0

Relationships with external stakeholders were considered to be very important to more than half of the respondents (Table 6.68). Based on focus group discussion, key external stakeholders mentioned included the stakeholders from the ministry of health, external donors as well as the wider World Vision partnership.

When members were asked about church partnerships, no clear strategy emerged for WV PNG. Some interviewees discussed the lack of partnership with churches, others mentioned dependence on individual leaders, with some networking with churches in the community in the implementation of a program, and others discussed the need to be sensitive to showing favoritism for one denomination over another.

Table 6.69 Role of Relationships with External Stakeholders at World Vision Papua New Guinea (N=53)

Relationships do not have a role. Work tasks should be completed independent of relationships	Relationships are able to provide new networks that might be useful in work context	Relationships are important in current cultural contexts as basis for working in said context	Relationships lead to trust, which is effective for accomplishing work	Relationships provide opportunities to witness to God's love	Relationships enable diversity of people to work together	Others – please specify
2	36	24	31	20	25	2

Table 6.69 indicated that a majority of respondents considered relationships as key in providing new networks that might be useful in the work context. The importance of relationship leading to trust, which was effective for accomplishing work, was also frequently mentioned. The extent of the role of relationships in contributing as a witness to God's love was one of the least chosen options.

For this cultural dimension, it can be concluded that external stakeholders were taken seriously in WV PNG. The main role for these relationships was for networking purposes or for effective accomplishment of work tasks. It was not evident that these relationships were considered in light of World Vision's ministry.

6.3.2.2.9 Summarized Values held by World Vision PNG

Table 6.70 Summary of World Vision PNG Values	
Basis of truth and rationality in the organization	There was no clarity that scriptures were key to decision making in the organization. Instead, use of Scriptures was left to the discretion of individual leaders.
Nature of time and time horizon	It was not unanimous that God's direction was intentionally sought in decision making of WV PNG. Goals were generally not pre-planned for emergencies.

Motivation	The religious orientation of the organization was not the primary motivation for staff to work for World Vision. Other factors like needs in the community, employment terms were more influential at motivating/demotivating staff to do a good job.
Stability vs change/innovation/personal growth	Change was embraced in the organization. The extent that change was dependent on God was dependent on individual leaders.
Orientation to work/task/coworkers	Staff members did not believe that people were valued above other constraints in the People and Culture policies. They did however experience intentional time spent on organizational fellowship events
Isolation vs collaboration/cooperation	The leadership of World Vision encouraged a positive working environment.
Control/coordination/responsibility	In general, decisions were made in consultation with staff members. However, these decisions were made in response to external realities or pressures instead of representing staff members' point of view.
Orientation and Focus	External stakeholders were taken seriously in WV PNG. The main role for these relationships was for networking purposes. It was not clear that these relationships were considered in light of World Vision's 'ministry'.

Table 6.70 summarized World Vision PNG's values according to organizational cultural dimensions. In general, despite the Christian country context in which World Vision PNG operated, the organizational culture of WV PNG was very much dictated by external forces such as donor requirements, or the wider World Vision partnership. The extent to which Christian values influenced the organizational culture was dependent on individual leaders of each department.

6.3.2.3 *Relational Proximity in WV PNG*

This section documented the state of relationships in WV PNG. Further questions were asked about the state of relationships in the questionnaire.

A total of 18 field staff, 19 support staff, 12 middle management and 4 senior management staff responded to this section of the questionnaire. The results are presented below.

Before this presentation of relationships within World Vision, table 71 provided introductory information about external relationships that WV PNG had with stakeholders outside WV PNG.

Table 6.71 Ranking of the Following Stakeholders in the way it Influences the Strategy and Direction at World Vision Papua New Guinea (N=46)

	Beneficiaries of the work of World Vision	Other NGOs working in the same country context	Global Centre	Relevant Support Offices	Regional Office	Local churches within area of work in World Vision in country context	Government officials in country context	Direct Donors
Mode	1	4	1	3	3	7	5	1
median	2	5	4	4	4.5	6	5	3
average	2.70	4.73	4.56	3.84	4.61	4.98	4.97	3.64
Rank	1	6	4	3	5	8	7	2

Based on table 6.71, the beneficiaries, followed by the direct donors and the support offices were considered the most important stakeholders of WV PNG.

Table 6.72 Average Rating on Relationships with Internal Stakeholders at Papua New Guinea
(1= very close, 2=somewhat close, 3=somewhat distant, 4=very distant) (N=53)

	Field Staff	Support Staff	Middle Management	Senior Management	External (Global Centre)	External (Regional Office)	External (Support Office)
Senior Management	2.25	2	1.25	1	2.75	2.75	2.75
Middle Management	1.85	1.7	1.38	2.18	3.33	3.17	3.08
Support Staff	2.27	1.55	1.91	2.36	3.52	3.52	3.43
Field Staff	1.11	1.47	1.68	2.61	3.67	3.72	3.39

According to table 6.72, staff in the same category reported the closest relationship to each other. Closer relationships were also reported with stakeholders in the same office before stakeholders outside PNG such as the Global Centre, Regional Office and Support offices. Within the country office, senior management considered themselves most distant from field staff, while every other stakeholder in the office, middle management, support and field staff, considered themselves most distant from the senior management.

With regard to external stakeholders, staff members reported a slightly closer relationship compared to that of the Global Centre and Regional Office.

Table 6.73 Average Perceived Influence of Different Stakeholders at World Vision Papua New Guinea (N=53) (1=extremely influential, 2= very influential, 3=somewhat influential, 4= little or no influence)

	Field Staff	Support Staff	Middle Management	Senior Management	External (GC)	External (RO)	External (SO)
Senior Management	2.25	2.25	1.50	1.50	3.25	3.00	2.75

Middle Management	1.77	2.08	1.75	2.33	3.27	3.18	2.64
Support Staff	2.4	1.86	1.86	2.33	3.25	3.1	3
Field Staff	1.32	2.11	2.28	2.76	3.50	3.44	3.19

Table 6.73 showed that all stakeholders perceived themselves to be the most influential in the office. Additionally, middle management was also seen to be rather influential across the board. Looking at individual staff categories, middle management considered middle management as the most influential (1.75) followed by field staff (1.77). The senior management team considered senior management and middle management as equally influential (1.50). Support staff considered support staff and middle management as equally influential (1.86) and finally, field staff considered field staff to be the most influential (1.32). External stakeholders were seemingly less influential compared to internal stakeholders.

The following tables analyzed further the relationships between stakeholders using the relational proximity framework. As per the practice of WV Nepal, only the average scores of each domain are presented in the main text. For more details about each domain, the full report is provided in Appendix 3.

6.3.2.3.1 Senior Management

Table 6.74 Average Perception Regarding Relational Proximity for Senior Management at World Vision Papua New Guinea (N=4) (1= Strongly Agree, 2= Agree, 3= Neutral, 4=Disagree, 5=Strongly Disagree)

	Field Staff	Support Staff	Middle Management	Senior Management	External (GC)	External (RO)	External (SO)
Directness	2.19	1.75	1.50	1.06	3.38	2.63	2.88
Continuity	2.69	2.00	1.81	1.63	3.33	3.27	2.69
Multiplexity	2.44	2.40	2.19	1.88	3.13	2.75	2.75
Parity	2.19	2.18	2.18	1.76	2.55	2.42	2.32
Commonality	2.14	2.03	2.15	1.69	2.88	2.35	2.46
Overall Average scores for Senior Management	2.33	2.07	1.97	1.60	3.05	2.68	2.62

Table 6.74 showed the consolidated information for senior management according to the five different domains of relational proximity. In general, senior management saw themselves as closest to other senior management members (1.60), before middle management (1.97), support staff (2.07) and finally field staff (2.33). This trend was repeated in the domains of directness, continuity and multiplexity. For parity, averages were the same for support staff and middle management (2.18) which was also similar to field staff (2.19). For commonality, senior management saw themselves as closer to support staff (2.03), and even field staff (2.14), before middle management (2.15).

Regarding external stakeholders, senior management saw themselves on average closest to support offices (2.62), before the regional office (2.68), followed by the Global Centre (3.05). This trend is however not regular across the different domains. For directness and commonality, senior management saw themselves as closer to the regional office. For continuity and parity, senior management saw themselves as closer to the support office. What was unanimous was the distance felt from the Global Centre.

6.3.2.3.2 Middle Management

Table 6.75 Perception Regarding Relational Proximity for Middle Management at World Vision Papua New Guinea (N=13) (1= Strongly Agree, 2= Agree, 3= Neutral, 4=Disagree, 5=Strongly Disagree)							
	Field Staff	Support Staff	Middle Management	Senior Management	External (GC)	External (RO)	External (SO)
Directness	1.63	1.63	1.56	2.31	4.28	4.06	3.60
Continuity	1.65	1.67	1.55	2.28	4.04	4.06	3.58
Multiplexity	1.58	1.58	1.68	2.34	3.63	3.54	3.15
Parity	1.85	1.83	1.71	2.29	2.95	3.00	2.86
Commonality	1.56	1.67	1.58	2.35	3.36	3.25	3.14
Overall Average scores for Middle Management	1.66	1.68	1.62	2.31	3.65	3.58	3.26

Table 6.75 showed the consolidated information for middle management and its perceptions of relationships with other stakeholders. In general,

middle management had the closest relationship with other middle management (1.62). It also shared close relationships with field staff (1.66), support staff (1.68), and other middle management staff (1.86). Compared to other internal stakeholders, middle management felt the largest distance from senior management. In general, middle management also perceived a larger distance from external stakeholders, where support offices were perceived as slightly closer (3.26) to middle management compared to the Global Centre and the Regional Office.

6.3.2.3.3 Support Staff

Table 6.76 Perception Regarding Relational Proximity for Support Staff at World Vision Papua New Guinea (N=22)
(1= Strongly Agree, 2= Agree, 3= Neutral, 4=Disagree, 5=Strongly Disagree)

	Field Staff	Support Staff	Middle Management	Senior Management	External (GC)	External (RO)	External (SO)
Average on Directness	2.05	1.90	2.07	2.84	4.22	4.28	4.02
Average on Continuity	1.93	1.99	2.18	2.68	4.15	4.15	3.94
Average on Multiplexity	2.03	2.05	2.37	2.70	3.78	3.74	3.68
Average on Parity	2.20	2.11	2.31	2.54	2.97	2.98	2.78
Average on Commonality	2.36	2.36	2.43	2.85	3.39	3.38	3.28
Overall Average for Support Staff	2.11	2.08	2.27	2.72	3.70	3.71	3.54

Table 6.76 illustrated the perception of the support staff on its relationships to other stakeholders based on the five different domains of relational proximity.

On average, support staff perceived themselves to be closest to other support staff (2.08). It felt closest then to field staff (2.11), middle management (2.27), and senior management (2.72). While the domains in general followed the same trend, for the domains of directness and continuity, support staff reported closer relationship to field staff compared to other support staff.

With regard to external relationships, the support staff perceived closer relationships with the support office compared to other external stakeholders.

6.3.2.3.4 Field Staff

Table 6.77 Perception Regarding Relational Proximity for Field Staff at World Vision Papua New Guinea (N=19)
(1= Strongly Agree, 2= Agree, 3= Neutral, 4=Disagree, 5=Strongly Disagree)

	Field Staff	Support Staff	Middle Management	Senior Management	External (GC)	External (RO)	External (SO)
Directness	1.51	1.91	2.07	2.85	4.15	4.10	3.98
Continuity	1.78	2.00	2.27	3.22	4.45	4.37	4.30
Multiplexity	1.89	2.08	2.42	3.08	4.10	4.10	4.09
Parity	2.11	2.32	2.50	2.92	3.69	3.69	3.66
Commonality	2.05	2.41	2.52	3.23	4.03	3.98	3.93
Overall Average for Field Staff	1.87	2.14	2.35	3.06	4.08	4.05	3.99

Table 6.77 consolidated the perceptions of field staff regarding its relationships to other stakeholders based on the domains of relational proximity.

On average, field staff considered themselves closest to other field staff (1.87). They believed that they are the next closest to support staff (2.14), followed by middle management (2.35) and then senior management (3.06). This trend was consistently repeated for each of the five domains. With regard to external stakeholders, results were similar to other stakeholders, where the relationship was distinctly more distant compared to staff in the same country. Comparing all three stakeholders, the closest relationship was with the support office.

6.3.2.3.5 Relationships in WV PNG

This section summarizes the state of relationships in WV PNG.

In general, there was a trend for stakeholders to feel closest to individuals in the same stakeholder group as they were. Thereafter, they were closest to stakeholders in the same 'level', before their managers, or senior managers. It was clear that the hierarchy as depicted in parity, made a clear difference to how the relationship was perceived. Another key trend was the distant relationship that internal stakeholders reported regarding external stakeholders, particularly the Global Centre. This was evident for all categories of staff in the office. Finally, field staff who implemented projects reported the widest variation in the way they related with different stakeholders. This ranged from close relationships with other field staff (1.87) to significantly distant ones from the Global Centre (4.08).

6.4 Concluding the Collection Phase

The purpose of this chapter was to include measurement of World Vision's organizational culture. It documented the second part of the case study, which focused on perceptions of staff members in two different branch offices, WV Nepal and WV PNG. This shows the extent of the Christian identity in these two countries. The specific sub-questions that were answered include:

- What Christian values and assumptions are espoused by World Vision based on its core documents according to the organizational culture dimensions?
- Looking at two different offices of World Vision, what are the findings of actual values and assumptions held by members in each office connected to the dimensions as determined in the first question?
- Understanding an organization as an entity made up by a group of individuals, what is the state of relationships held by different internal stakeholders of the organization?

In answering these sub-questions, a clearer picture of the tacit Christian identity, as well as the social networks involved in the different branch offices is uncovered.
Summarizing the data collection in this chapter, it can first be concluded that World Vision deliberately includes Christian values explicitly in its core documents. The panel have found it possible to outline relevant Christian values for each of the organizational culture dimension. In reviewing the presence of these values in the two branch offices through the data obtained from the questionnaire, focus group discussions and interviews, it can be concluded that the impact of the Christian values on the organizational culture is not upfront. Other factors seem to influence

the overall organizational cultural dimension more than the Christian values.

In the study of the relationships, it was also clear that the field staff members, those implementing the projects feel closest to other field staff members. There seemed to be a wide distance of these staff members to the broader World Vision partnership in both offices. More analysis to the relationships are described in the following chapter.

This chapter concluded the collection phase of this dissertation. In the next chapter, we transition to the next phase, further analyzing the data that has been collected in this phase.

PART C: ANALYSIS PHASE

CHAPTER SEVEN

Analyzing the Field Research

Having just documented the results of the empirical research in the collection phase, we move to the analysis phase. In this analysis phase, two main tasks of the practical theological interpretation are taken up: interpretative and normative.

For the interpretative task, what is focused on is "wisely judgment." For this task, the identity formation model is used to explicate the identity in terms of the different 'selves' of World Vision as well as the resultant tacit identity of World Vision. This entails describing the findings of the case study in the different organizational 'selves': object, story and subject. Besides chronicling the different selves, the resultant tacit identity is also characterized using organizational culture. In addition, the state of relationships of the different staff members are also examined in their role as mediating the content and processes of the religious identity of the organization. In analyzing the collected data in this way, we understand the Christian identity of the organization further, as well as the areas that are lacking.

In the second task of this analysis phase, normative, the data is analyzed from a Christian perspective using the normative practice model. This moves beyond the interpretation of the organization as a socially constructed unit, providing an avenue for the data to be reflected from a clear Christian perspective. The normative practice model, rooted in Christian reality, evaluates the data from a Christian perspective. A Christian perspective on reality implies an intentional observation of the biblical narrative that underpins this reality. The normative practice model is appropriated in this normative task because of its clear understanding of reality as rooted in creation order, distinguishable by its modal aspects. At the same time, it is a model that seeks to analysis real life practices embedded in society. Before using this tool for the analysis of the data, the key concepts that root the normative practice model are first introduced to explicate its validity as a viable analytical tool. Secondly, the normative practice of development is outlined, integrating the existing research of development with the normative practice. Finally, the data collected are analyzed alongside the normative practice of development.

7.1 The Different Organization 'Selves' and the Mediated Self in Identity Formation of World Vision.

The identity formation model has been first introduced in chapter two as a means to grasp the religious identity of the organization. This model has also been used to determine the research methodology and in this chapter, will be used for further interpretation. As previously discussed, the organization is characterized as the self as object, story or subject in this model.[326] Through interaction of these different 'selves,' tacit religious identity is formed. Each of the different selves is discussed below in light of the data collected.

7.1.1 Self as Object

To focus on the organization as an object is to take seriously the content of the organization. In this dissertation, the religiosity of the organizational variables has been investigated to provide insight to the understanding of self as object. Based on the findings, it can be summarized that World Vision is clear and consistent in its Christian understanding as expressed in the different organizational variables as well as public documents.

As an overall partnership, World Vision has intentionally considered what it means for Christian faith to permeate through organizational variables. This commitment is held at the highest level of the organization where policies dealing with this Christian understanding are approved by the International Board of the entire World Vision partnership. The 'Witness to Jesus Christ' policy is an example of how World Vision has been intentional with its Christian understanding on different aspects of organizational variables. This include looking at elements with an impact on goal directness such as what witness looks like in its programs, or in activity systems related to different stakeholders, or dealing with environment by considering external partnerships.[327]

---

[326] Arne Carlsen, "On the Tacit Side of Organizational Identity: Narrative Unconscious and Figured Practice," *Culture and Organization* 22, no. 2 (2016): 107–135. See chapter 2.3.3.1 for further explanation.
[327] World Vision, "Witness to Jesus Christ Policy," Partnership Policy and Decision Manual (16 September 1995).

7.1.2 Self as Story

The next 'self' explores the organization as story. It focuses on the content of the organization as seen in its narrative through time. In this dissertation, the focus is on the influence of the Christian faith to the organization's narrative. Based on the findings, it is clear that World Vision has evolved since its early days. What began as an evangelical missionary organization "to meet critical needs of the Orient" has since evolved into an ecumenical organization with clear operating structures, working in sectors of relief, development and advocacy organization. It no longer exists primarily as an intermediary organization with the focus on churches and their involvement in the mission field, but rather is today aligned with known sectors in the wider development and humanitarian sectors in society, drawing funds from a wider base than the church.

In addition, people joining World Vision for work have also evolved. From predominantly evangelical Christians, people who work for World Vision currently include those from other denominations, as well as people of other faiths. At present, there is an intentional effort to communicate World Vision values to staff members through the mission statement, core values and the vision statement of the organization. These are included in orientation practices for new recruits. However, these efforts seem to be left wanting as staff members describe other priorities as more important than the organization's Christian values.

7.1.3 Self as Subject

The final 'self' focuses on the organization as subject. This focuses on the processes involved in the organization. Based on the findings, there has been a reported increase in the complexity of processes as the overall operations of World Vision have increased. From being an American organization, it has since expanded its operations in many different contexts with diverse cultures and religions. Much has been done to organize the work of World Vision as well as manage its decision making. Resources have been invested periodically to structure the organization in light of the change.

One of the earlier initiatives in structuring the different offices in World Vision was the covenant of partnership. This has since been further clarified, with World Vision structured as a federal model, accommodating diversity yet at the same time giving reserve powers to the Global Center. It can be concluded that this increase in complexity of processes resulted in rational bureaucratization. Policies and systems were drafted for smooth operation of the organization. At the same time, besides 'rational' policies drafted for the smooth operating of the organization, policy documents were also drafted to articulate how World Vision understands its Christian faith in different areas of its work. This include policies such as the Interfaith policy, Partnership with Churches, Children well-being etc.

Another obvious phenomenon with regard to the processes was the increasing diverse influence from the external environment with the increasing number of diverse stakeholders. As World Vision's spread across different cultures and in different sectors, there were more decision makers within the organization with different agendas. These different agendas pull the organization in different ways depending on the needs and particularities of World Vision in a given time and place. This has led the organization to evolve differently depending on its various contexts.

These findings show that rational bureaucratization as well as the increase diverse influence of stakeholders can indeed explain why the Christian identity is no longer core to the processes of the organization. The organization's Christian identity has been relegated to a supporting role that is not always prioritized.

7.1.4 Uncovering Tacit Christian Identity Through Study of Organizational Culture

So far, the three different organizational 'selves' have been discussed in relation to World Vision. These different selves described a part of the organization's content and process as depicted by the different 'selves' of the organization. What is left undiscussed is the interaction between these different 'selves' that results in the tacit religious identity. Organizational culture was measured to determine the tacit religious identity of the organization.

Organizational culture was measured to understand the assumptions held by staff members of the organization. In the collection phase, the different organizational cultural dimensions were first related to the stated Christian values of World Vision. Based on the findings, it was firstly evident that there were Christian values clearly articulated in World Vision's core documents. These values were however not forthcoming as resultant values of the staff members present in the two studied offices, Nepal and Papua New Guinea. Appendix 4 outlined a summary of reported values of both World Vision Nepal and World Vision PNG's values as comparted with World Vision's Christian values based on different organizational cultural dimensions. A summary analysis of the reasons why follows.

In Nepal, the non-Christian context was largely pointed out as the reason for difficulty in the transmission of Christian values. There was evidence of management activities (such as a deliberate internship program from churches, an appointed spiritual point person for each office location who was responsible for regular devotions, updates, etc.) which tried to foster Christian values. However, these activities did not seem to translate to deep Christian values embraced in World Vision Nepal.

In Papua New Guinea, the grant funded context was considered the primary reason for difficulty in the transmission of Christian values, this despite statistical indications that Papua New Guinea is a Christian country. The organization emphasized the need to focus on the project plan, its strict budget and timeline. Working in such a context, staff members emphasized the clear regulations that considered religious activities forbidden.

Based on the findings of the organizational culture in each country office, it could be concluded that despite the clear formal Christian identity of World Vision as described by the self as 'object', the overall tacit identity cannot be described as clearly Christian. This was possibly because of the evolving story of the organization as well as the processes the organization had embraced in light of its context. Christian values were not therefore not clearly dominant in the organizational culture as perceived by staff members of the organization. These results suggested congruence to the theories of isomorphism or bureaucracy previously described in earlier chapters.[328] In the final analysis of the tacit identity of the organization, relationships are discussed as this provide more insight to the interaction between process and content.

7.1.5 Relationships as key in mediating content and process

The dynamic tacit identity of an organization does not exist abstractly but through its expression by different members of the organization. Based on the identity formation model, people in the organization mediate the process through authoring and enabling through the relationships that they have with each other. As such, the state of relationships among different stakeholders have been studied as they shed light on the influence that different stakeholders have on the resultant tacit identity. The closer the relationship between stakeholders, the more influence these stakeholders can have due to an increased frequency of authoring and enabling. To un-

---

[328] The theory was discussed in more detail in chapter 1 in the section 3.3.

derstand the state of the relationship, a heuristic tool "relational proximity" was used.[329] This tool measured interaction between the different stakeholders based on five domains: directness, continuity, multiplexity, parity, and commonality. Based on this tool, the more stakeholders interacted on each of these five domains, the closer the relationship.

In both offices, field staff felt the most distance from senior management. This is noteworthy as senior management had the most links to other parts of the organization. This implied that senior management had ready access to different information such as partnership policies which detail the organization's Christian understanding. This access of partnership information to other staff members in a country office is often dependent on senior management. A reported distant relationship could result in limited access to partnership information, and therefore diminished influence of partnership information, including Christian understanding as being part of the daily operations of the office as implemented by field staff.

In addition, perceptions between different stakeholders had not necessarily been reciprocal. When one stakeholder deemed a relationship as close, the response of another stakeholder was not necessarily the same. This was particularly true for the senior management team. Senior management staff members reported a closer relationship to different staff members compared to what other staff members reported about their relationship with them. Differing perceptions on the relationship had an impact on actual "authoring" actions of the senior management team, since actions might not be "enabled" as often as desired.

It was also evident that most stakeholders had the closest relationship with other stakeholders who were in the same category. This could imply that field staff, who formed a majority of staff in each of the office locations, was significantly influential in the resulting organizational culture of World Vision in that a higher frequency of authoring and enabling takes place amongst them.

Finally, external stakeholders were held at a further distance compared to relationships in the local office. This can be problematic for the transmission of Christian values as these external stakeholders, the Global Centre or the Regional Office, are key offices responsible for the reserve powers of World Vision.[330] Included in the reserve powers is the need to

---

[329] For more information about this, refer to chapter 3 section 3.2.2.
[330] As described in chapter 4, reserve powers are decisions that are deemed as both high risk and broad in scope.

"promote the World Vision way" which is where the content and accountability of Christian identity lie. With a distant relationship to external stakeholders, it is no surprise that these stakeholders have little influence in the overall organizational culture in these locations.

In summary, the state of relationships analyzed are not conducive for promoting Christian values. Having described the way relationships impact the authoring and enabling of the identity formation model, we complete our first analysis of the case study interpreting the data using the identity formation model. While this model is useful to understand the dynamic existing in the organization, it does not address the reality that the organization is based on. This implies the need for a normative understanding. Reality is not neutral but is rather rooted in a particular worldview.[331] In completing this normative task, the assessment of an organization's Christian identity is analyzed alongside an understanding of the Christian reality or worldview. In the following section, further analysis is done from a decidedly Christian understanding of reality through the use of the normative practice model. This model is introduced next.

7.2 Introduction to the Normative Practice Model

The normative practice model is used to analyze the practice embodied in the organization. This model is used because of its clear Christian understanding of reality yet agility to practices in the broader society. This model was first developed as an alternative to mainstream applied ethics, to describe the complexities of different fields including medical care, nursing, education and development studies.[332] Instead of working of a

---

[331] Worldview is understood in this dissertation as a "framework or pattern that one follows like a guide to life. It has been defined as a commitment, a fundamental orientation of the heart, that can be expressed a story in a set of presuppositions (assumptions which may be true, partially true or entirely false) which we hold (consciously or subconsciously, consistently or inconsistently) about the basic constitution of reality, and that provides the foundation on which we live and move and have our being." See James W. Sire, *The Universe Next Door: A Basis Worldview Catalog* (Downers Grove: IVP Academic, 2004), 17.

[332] The understanding of normative practice as used in this dissertation is based on previous work by reformational philosophers. In applying the normative practice model, I have not sought to provide an exhaustive study on the underlying philosophy underpinning the model. Some articles that introduce this model include the following: Henk Jochemsen in articles such as "Normative Practices as an intermediate between theoretical ethics and morality," *Philosophia Reformata* 71 (2006): 96–112; "A Normative Practice for the Practice of Cooperation in Development as a Basis for International Social Justice," (paper presented during the ILE

general set of ethical principles and norms, the normative practice model focuses on a particular practice which is constituted by a constellation of norms typical for a specific practice. This model with the constellation of norms based on the particular practice can mitigate the tendency of following popular ethical trends within the social, scientific or economic domains blindly.

Before appropriating the normative practice model for the data collection at World Vision, key concepts that underpin the model are first described before focusing on how these concepts relate to the understanding of the organization. These key concepts include the outline of practices, norms and plurality.

7.2.1 Practices within Society Expressed in Institutions like Organizations

The first key concept that undergirds the normative practice model is the concept of practice. The understanding of practices refers to categories of human activity that exist in society. Formally, the definition of practice as given by MacIntyre is adopted in this understanding.[333]

> "By a 'practice' I am going to mean any coherent and complex form of socially established cooperative human activity through which goods internal to that form of activity are realized in the form of trying to achieve those standards of excellence which are appropriate to, and partially definitive of, that form of activity, with the results that human powers to achieve excellence, and human conceptions of the ends and goods involved, are systematically extended."[334]

Study Day in May 2012); Maarten Verkerk, "Spirituality, Organization and Leadership: Towards a Philosophical Foundation of Spirit at Work," in *Leadership, Innovation, and Spirituality*, ed. P. Nullens and J. Barentsen (Leuven: Peeters, 2014), 57–77 as well as Gerrit Glas, "Competence Development as Normative Practice – Educational Reform in Medicine as Heuristic Model to Relate Worldview and Education," *Koers – Bulletin for Christian Scholarship* 77, no. 1 (2012).

[333] The discussion of practice is described by MacIntyre as the context in which virtues are exercised. Concerned about the gradual disenchantment with virtue ethics in modern society, MacIntyre rejects the inevitability of relativism, as well as the limitations of generalization in social sciences. This discussion of practice is the first in his three stages in which the core conception of virtues can be understood.

[334] Alasdair MacIntyre, *After Virtue* (Notre Dame: University of Notre Dame Press, 1981), 187.

Examples of practices described by MacIntyre include chess, architecture, arts and politics.[335] This description of practices focuses on the internal goods present in the practice. Internal goods are goods that are specific and particular to the practice. They are identified and recognized by the experience of participating in the practice. Besides these internal goods, there can also be other goods, which Macintyre calls external goods, contingently attached to the practice due to social circumstances. These goods are not exclusive to the practice as they are not particular to the practice. Attainment of such goods are not specifically linked to the engagement of the practice as there are alternative ways of achieving these goods.[336]

To illustrate the difference between internal and external goods, MacIntyre uses the example of the practice of chess. In playing chess, what is necessary, the internal goods, are "certain highly particular kind of analytical skills, strategic imagination and competitive intensity, a new set of reason, reasons not just for winning on a particular occasion, but for trying to excel in whatever way the game of chess demands." This is differentiated from the external goods which are plausible reasons for playing and winning the chess game. These include prestige, power and money, as these can be found in other practices not related to chess.[337] This understanding of practice as expounded by MacIntyre is appropriated in the normative practice model. In using this definition, the normative practice model takes into consideration the understanding of internal and external goods, yet uses different terms to express these goods. These different goods are understood in the categories of the qualifying function, foundational and conditioning functions. These different functions are introduced in the next section in the outlining of Dooyeweerdian's social philosophy.

As a form of human activity, practices are complex and are not confined to any individual institution or organization. They manifest themselves in specific contexts, e.g. the practice of prosecutors in a variety of courts, alongside judges, lawyers and others. No one individual institution or organization can claim ownership of the entire practice. At the same time, this understanding of the practice, as well as its inherent internal goods can be useful to clarify organizational priorities. An organization is led by the practice it seeks to express in society, e.g. courts by administration of justice. For an organization to truly express a practice in society, it

---

[335] Alasdair MacIntyre, *After Virtue*, 187.
[336] Ibid., 188-189.
[337] Ibid., 188-189.

is important that the internal good, the purpose of the practice is prioritized in the organization. Care should be taken to prevent the corruption of practices, by giving more priority to external goods instead of internal goods.[338] The understanding of internal goods reemphasizes the importance of clarifying the purpose of the organization and ensuring that this purpose is prioritized in the goals of the organization as well as other characteristics of the organization such as the people and the systems.

Another way to think about the purpose of the organization is as the primary process of the organization as described in the variant of the normative practice model, the triple I model. In this model, the primary process, argued to be crucial refers to the "operational processes that constitute the core activities of an organization and that generate value for clients, citizens and society."[339] Describing the purpose of the organization in terms of a process clarifies the impact of this purpose on the activity systems of the organization as well as the people involved.

7.2.2 Norms rooted in the Christian View of Reality as described in Dooyeweerdian's social philosophy

The next key concept in the understanding of the normative practice model is the emphasis on the Christian view of reality. The understanding of reality is dependent on the "plausability structures" in society. Plausibility structures are constituted by the pattern of belief and practice in a society.[340] These basic patterns of beliefs are linked to the different worldviews that exist in society. Herman Dooyeweerd, reformational philosopher, affirmed the existence of different patterns of beliefs in society, arguing against neutrality presupposed in modernity. He described how all theoretical thought is based on a concept of "totality of meaning"

---

[338] Alasdair MacIntyre, *After Virtue*, 194.

[339] The triple I model, a variant of the normative practice model, is based on an organizational analysis of institutionalized professional practices. See Maarten Verkerk, "Spirituality, Organization and Leadership: Towards a Philosophical Foundation of Spirituality at Work," in *Leadership, Innovation, and Spirituality*, ed. Patrick Nullens and Jack Barentsen (Leuven: Peeters, 2014), 57-58.

[340] This understanding of plausibility structure was first coined by sociologist, Peter Berger as he studied the erosion of religion in secular societies because of the loss of the plausibility structure. This plausibility structure is the system of meaning within which these meanings make sense, or are made plausible within a particular sociocultural context. These systems of meanings are supported by, and embedded in, sociocultural institutions and processes. For more information, see Peter L. Berger, *The Sacred Canopy* (Garden City, NY: Doubleday, 1967).

rooted in religious presuppositions, otherwise described as the "Cosmonomic Idea." This is a "transcendental idea of subjectivity", that is diverse.[341] For him, there is no one united idea as different presuppositions ground different philosophical systems. "Each authentic system of philosophy is grounded in a Cosmonomic Idea of this or that type, even when the author does not account for it."[342]

Instead of simply adapting or accepting the patterns of beliefs prevalent in society, a Christian organization should critically analyze its alignment with the Christian view of reality. The choice of Dooyeweerdian philosophy is particularly useful because of his respect and intention to help one analyze everyday human experience. Instead of beginning with theoretical thought, his philosophy understands the theoretical through an analysis of the everyday life experience. Dooyeweerd believed that it is possible for everyday experience, meaning, to be directly and immediately engaged in his philosophical system alongside the biblical ground motive.[343] With due regard given to experiences, this philosophical system is appropriated in the practice model. An introduction to this system is described below.

7.2.2.1 Meaning in Multiplicity of Structures with Different Constellation of Norms

Dooyeweerd's Christian social philosophy is rooted in the biblical ground motive which he described as "creation, fall into sin, and redemption in Jesus Christ in the communion of the Holy Spirit."[344] Following in the tradition of Augustine, Calvin and Kuyper, Dooyeweerd believed that his understanding of the biblical ground motive captured the core of biblical Christianity.[345] For him, key to this understanding of the biblical ground motive is "God's holy sovereign creative will."[346] It is God's laws that set

---

[341] Yong-Joon Choi, *Antithesis and Thesis: A Philosohical Study on the Significance of Herman Dooyeweerd's Transcendental Critique* (Philadelphia, PA: Hermit Kingdom Press, 2006), 73–74.
[342] Herman Dooyeweerd, *A New Critique of Theoretical Thought*, trans. David H. Freeman and H. De Jongste, 3rd ed. (Ontario: Paideia Press, 1983), 1:94.
[343] For more information see, Understanding Everyday Experience and Lifeworld http://kgsvr.net/dooy/everyday.html
[344] Ibid., 1:507.
[345] Jonathan Chaplin, *Herman Dooyeweerd Christian Philosopher of State and Civil Society* (Notre Dame, Indiana: University of Notre Dame, 2011), 47.
[346] Dooyeweerd, *A New Critique of Theoretical Thought*, 1:507.

the boundaries between God and his creation.[347] Meaning on this earth is rooted in the understanding of the creator and his law. For him, the purpose of philosophy is to provide theoretical insight, uncover and discern meaning in the multiplicity of structures in created reality. This is done through his creative use of the modal aspects he distinguishes in reality. Modal aspects are unique and sovereign in its own sphere. They have been further explained using the metaphor of refracted light. "As the seven colours do not owe their origin to one another, so the temporal aspects of meaning in face of each other have sphere sovereignty or modal irreducibility."[348] Within Dooyeweerd's social philosophy system, there are fifteen different modal aspects. These include: Numerical, Spatial, Kinematic, Physical, Biotic, Psychic, Logical, Historical, Lingual, Social, Economic, Aesthetic, Juridical, Ethical and Faith.[349] These different aspects find their source in the creator and his laws.

To speak of sphere sovereignty of each modal aspect is to realize that each aspect contains a meaning kernel. It is this meaning kernel that gives the aspect its irreducible character. In Dooryeweerdian's philosophy, some of these modal aspects have meaning kernels that can be characterized by laws, while others are characterized by norms. Those characterized by law are thought to be "realized in the facts without human intervention" while those characterized by norms are thought to function like principles that require human agency.[350] Aspects with meaning kernel characterized by norms require "free, responsible, and rational human agents."[351] These included aspects like linguistic, social, economic, legal, aesthetical, ethical and pistical norms.[352] As humans work towards implementation of these norms, this has been described by Dooyeweerd as "positivization" of the norms. This also implies the free agency of people to deciding whether to follow through on these norms or not. Ultimately, the interpretation and actions of people, do not influence the validity of these norms.

---

[347] In describing the biblical ground motive, Dooyeweerd was not looking to pronounce the church, or the state as the all inclusive totality of social life. He believed that mankind in its spiritual root transcends the temporal order with its diversity of social structures. See Dooyeweerd, *A New Critique of Theoretical Thought*, 1:169.
[348] Dooyeweerd, *A New Critique of Theoretical Thought*, 1:102.
[349] Ibid., 1:55–59.
[350] Ibid., 237.
[351] Chaplin, *Herman Dooyeweerd*, 62.
[352] See Chaplin, *Herman Dooyeweerd*, 62 and Dooyeweerd, *A New Critique of Theoretical Thought*, 1:238.

For Dooyeweerd, different meaning structures exists as a complex order of all the irreducible modal aspects. While these structures always function in all the modal aspects, the way the aspects function in the structure differs for the different social structures. In describing social structures as composed of complex order of modal aspects, Dooyeweerd resisted against the reductionist tendencies present in understanding reality.

While the entire constellation of modal aspects is present in each structure, each structure is largely defined by two modal aspects in particular, the qualifying and founding aspects.[353] The qualifying aspect has been described as the function which exercises a leading role among various functions, directing the structure toward its specific destination. The founding aspect, on the other hand, provides key support to the structure, enabling the structure to reach its destination. These aspects take the lead for a particular structure.

Having provided a brief introduction to the understanding of meaning as expressed in modal aspects, the way that this meaning is expressed in organizations is introduced.

7.2.2.2 Constellation of Norms Expressed in organizations

In the discussion of practice, we have ascertained that an organization is led by the practice it seeks to express in society. This practice determines the overall purpose of the organization. The understanding of norms rooted in created reality is therefore useful to provide further understanding of the purpose of the organization.

A practice as a meaning structure is determined by the specific constellation of modal aspects whereby the qualifying aspect gives a practice its typical character. In other words, the internal goods, the telos of the practice is related to the qualifying aspect of the structure. Directly related to the overall purpose of the organization, this qualifying aspect influences the entire organization, the activity systems as well as the processes related to the interaction among members of the organization.

In addition, the norms can play a unifying function for organizations. As organized communities, organizations are social constructs and differ

---

[353] Chaplin, *Herman Dooyeweerd*, 66.

from natural communities such as families.[354] For Dooyeweerd, these organized communities are founded historically instead of biotically.[355] As they exist beyond the duration of any single member, the question of "continuous internal unity" beyond any one person becomes important. The question that needs to be answered for an organization is "How is it possible for the community to upkeep its "supra individual communal whole?"[356] To answer this question, experiences of the community are highlighted. For the community to sustain its identity, Dooyeweerd emphasizes the importance of this community being united along the qualifying aspect in interaction among different members.[357] With this move, he links the qualifying aspect to interaction of people in the organization. This qualifying aspect, linked to the practice that the organization seeks to express, unites the different people together. It is therefore important for the qualifying aspect to influence the different characteristics of the organization. This is echoed by organizational scientist who describe the importance of the purpose of the organization staying central to the other characteristics of the organization.[358] This implies the importance of the qualifying aspect influencing both the boundary maintenance and activity systems of the organization.

Having discussed the concept of practice as well as the norms rooted in the Christian reality, the last concept that needs to be elaborated is related to the plurality exemplified in an organization. This discussion of plurality focuses on the differences experienced by organizations who express the same practice. The work of Mouw and Griffoen is appropriated in this model as a framework to categorize the kinds of differences experienced.

7.2.3 Plurality in Practices and its Impact on Organizations

The last concept relates to the plurality in practices. While being involved in the same practice, it does not mean that organizations look or act the same. Evident from the data collected for World Vision, there were clear differences are reported in different locations. These differences happen for many different reasons: the cultural context, people who are part of the organization, or even the religious beliefs involved. These differences

---

[354] As socially constructed structures, organizations have the potential to be rooted in created reality.
[355] Chaplin, *Herman Dooyeweerd*, 102.
[356] Ibid.
[357] Ibid.,104.
[358] Stefan Kühl, *Organisationen: Eine sehr kurze Einführung* (Dordrecht: Verlag für Sozialwissenschaften, 2011), 18.

influence the organizations to different extents. As a means to distinguish the different kinds of plurality present in the organization, the normative practice model appropriates the understanding of plurality of Mouw and Griffioen. In their book *Pluralisms and Horizons*, three undeniable kinds of pluralisms important to public life are mentioned: directional, associational and contextual pluralism. These different kinds of pluralism exist in different social structures which include organizations. The following paragraphs further describe each kind of pluralism.

Directional pluralism is related to the different visions of good life as depicted by different religious beliefs. For the authors, the use of the term "directional pluralism" reflects their Christian worldview.[359] The term 'directional' presupposes a direction as understood in Christian anthropology that sees conflict in human life in the duality of obedience versus disobedience.[360] One's basic orientation in life can either be God honoring or God-dishonoring. The emphasis is on the response to the "divine call to obedience."[361] To be God honoring is to "orient (our) thinking toward the reality of God" and God dishonoring is when there is 'creature centered thought reductionist in character." In this instance, "people organize their understanding of reality around an absolutizing of some aspect creaturely."[362] Bearing this in mind, the directional pluralism of a social structure can be therefore be understood as the presuppositions that take priority and organize thought in the social structure. Do these presuppositions point towards the reality of God, or towards an alternative absolute ideal, forgoing the rest?

Associational pluralism is related to differences related to family as well as other associations such as voluntary groups or corporations. These differences are caused by the different setup or stakeholders involved. Contextual plurality refers to the cultural context. This can include different racial, ethic, geographic, gender and class experiences.[363] Contrary to directional plurality which looks at plurality as either moving towards obedience to God or disobedience, diversity in culture and associational plurality are understood as elements of creational diversity.[364] These pluralisms in themselves are not committed to a particular direction.

---

[359] As an example, see Albert M. Wolters, *Creation Regained: Biblical Basis for a Reformational Worldview* (Grand Rapids, MI: Eerdmans, 1985).
[360] Richard J. Mouw and Sander Griffioen, *Pluralisms and Horizons: An Essay in Christian Public Philosophy* (Grand Rapids, MI: W.B. Eerdmans, 1993), 89.
[361] Ibid.,88–89.
[362] Ibid.
[363] Ibid., 16–17.
[364] Richard J. Mouw and Sander Griffioen, *Pluralisms and Horizons*, 124.

These three different pluralities are not completely distinct but rather influence each other. Mouw and Griffioen write about the interwoven nature of associational and directional pluralisms, where "associational structures serve diverse directional orientations and our spiritual vision take on associational shapes."[365] In addition, they state that cultural pluralism is the result of "combine(d) directional visions and associational practices that must be taken seriously in their own right."[366]

Another key observation is the key role of directional pluralism evident in both associational and cultural pluralisms. At its core, these pluralisms reflect the direction that the social structure is taking.[367] For social structures that embrace the same Christian faith, these structures can work together to discern the will of God.[368] Sharing the same faith, this common biblical reference that should ground and guide the process of discernment for these different communities.[369]

At the same time, it is possible to work with other communities that do not hold the same Christian presuppositions, this through the focus on a common goal. While there might be disagreements on the ultimate religious presuppositions, it is nevertheless possible to work together with others on a common goal, gaining new insights from diverse points of view. For Mouw and Griffoen, it is because of "the eschatological vindication of the truth (at the end of time) that makes it possible to accept the pluralism in the here and now."[370]

The pluralities described by Mouw and Griffoen are also present in organizations. Mouw and Griffoen's understanding of plurality is a useful roadmap to understand the differences the organization is exposed to. It is a framework to analyze the differences that organizations face. Different organizations display different kinds of plurality. While contextual and associational pluralities that are present in organizations can be celebrated, more thought needs to be given to directional plurality. Directional plurality indicates the different direction that organizations are moving towards. Instead of moving towards the direction of the purpose, it is also possible for organizations to be moving away.

---

[365] Ibid., 88.
[366] Ibid., 153.
[367] Ibid., 153.
[368] Ibid., 103.
[369] Ibid., 104.
[370] Ibid., 107.

With this discussion of plurality we conclude the discussion of key concepts that underpin the normative practice model. What has been discussed include the explication of practices within society, the understanding of Christian norms with respect to Dooyeweerdian philosophy and finally, the discussion of plurality. In the next section, the key research pertinent to development studies is outlined as World Vision is understood to be part of the development practice. This outline of development studies is useful to construct the normative practice of development. The findings as collected in the empirical research is then analyzed alongside this development practice.

7.3 World Vision as Part of the Development Practice

In the mission statement of World Vision, World Vision clearly states that "World Vision sees itself as an international partnership of Christians whose mission is to follow our Lord and Savior Jesus Christ in working with the poor and oppressed to promote human transformation, seek justice and bear witness to the good news of the Kingdom of God."[371] This mission statement with its intention to work with the poor to promote transformation is understood in this dissertation to be primarily involved with the broader development practice. The work of advocacy and relief detailed as the other pillars of World Vision is done bearing in mind the mission of overall human transformation that World Vision works for. In this section, the current debate in development studies is broadly introduced as a prelude to the discussion of the normative practice of development. This development practice is understood as key to the practice that World Vision seeks to express in society.

The study of development is known for its breath and challenges in its multi-disciplinary approach.[372] As a concept, it is widely contested politically and theoretically, thought to be ambiguous and complex.[373] What

---

[371] World Vision, "Mission Statement," Partnership Core Documents (1992).
[372] The academic study of development began with British economists and other social scientists in the 1960s dissatisfied with existing traditional or classical economics that focused on the importance of quantitative paths to the study of societies and economies. See Robert B. Potter, "The Nature of Development Studies," in *The Companion to Development Studies*, ed. Vandana Desai and Robert B. Potter, 3rd ed. (Oxford: Routledge, 2014), 16–20.
[373] Andy Summer and Michael Tribe, *International Development Studies: Theories and Methods in Research and Practice* (Los Angeles: SAGE Publications, 2008), 8.

seems to be held commonly across different disciplines is the importance of change within society. Development has been described is as "encompassing continuous change in a variety of aspects of human society."[374] This notion of development focuses on societal change, often in societies that are considered "developing" or "third world." As a way to describe the diverse nature of change, the understanding of development has been classified into three different categories. The first is historical and long term influenced by existing metanarratives. The second is policy related and evaluative or indicator led, has short to medium term horizons 'development' such as the Millennium Development Goals or Sustainability Development Goals.[375] The third can be characterized as a post-modernistic understanding of the development concept, drawing attention to the ethnocentric and ideologically loaded Western conceptions of "development" and raising possibilities of alternative conceptions.[376] To gain a deeper understanding of the debate surrounding development, these categories are briefly introduced in the next section. This introduction does not pretend to be exhaustive, but rather illustrates the key trends involved in development studies.

7.3.1 Development as Long-term Process of Change

In the first category, development is considered a long-term process of change related to structural societal change. While changes are not directly 'prescribed', they are influenced by metanarratives.[377] This understanding of development as long-term change is recognizable from the start of the development discourse. President Truman first coined the word 'Development' in 1949 during his speech proposing the International Development Assistance. The perceived success in rebuilding Europe financially and technically after the war led Americans to consider the extension of "development" to other nations. In this speech, he highlighted two goals of this assistance: 1) creating markets for the United States by reducing poverty and increasing production in developing countries; 2) diminishing the threat of communism by helping countries prosper under capitalism.[378] President Truman's approach revealed a long-term approach

---

[374] Summer and Tribe, *International Development Studies*, 8.
[375] United Nations, "Sustainable Development Goals," accessed December 21, 2015, https://sustainabledevelopment.un.org/?menu=1300.
[376] Summer and Tribe, *International Development Studies*, 11.
[377] Summer and Tribe, *International Development Studies*, 12.
[378] United States Agency for International Development, "USAID History," accessed April 16, 2014, http://www.usaid.gov/who-we-are/usaid-history.

related to development which included structural societal change. His understanding was also built of metanarratives such as the emphasis on capitalism, as well as the possibility of progress implicit in modernization.[379] Development was understood to be the product of "intervention of the modern, scientific and democratic into the improvement of human existence."[380]

Gradually, there was a shift from the clear dependence on economic growth to the attention on local ownership and sufficient capacity. The understanding of development expanded to include sustainability, where future generations are taken into account in the changes proposed. More recently, the purpose of development was expanded to include promotion of a particular form of politics based on democratic representation, social justice, the rule of law, and adherence to international agreements on human rights.[381] One key proponent who highlighted the social objectives of development was Dennis Goulet, considered one of the forefathers of development ethics. He mentioned three components that he saw as important for understanding development, which was related to the opportunity for humans to lead full human lives. These three components included life sustenance, self-esteem and freedom. For him, self-sustenance is related to the provision of basic need, self-esteem, self-respect and independence and freedom, the ability for people to determine their own lives.[382]

This long-term perspective on development is often understood as the traditional view of development. The main critique of this view is the limited capacity of these metanarratives to guide the short term operational implementation of development. The first cracks in these metanarratives appeared in their promise to solve problems in society. For example, the 1980s recorded instances of failure in development, with indicators show-

---

[379] Jochemsen argues that development assistance was deeply rooted in modernization. See Henk Jochemsen, "A Normative Model for the Practice of Cooperation in Development as a Basis for Social Justice," in *Challenges of Moral Leadership*, ed. Patrick Nullens and Steven C. van den Heuvel (Leuven: Peeters, 2015), 129–150. This understanding of development as being part of the modern tradition was also repeated in the introduction of development by textbooks such as Richard Peet and Elaine Hartwick, *Theories of Development: Contentions, Arguments, Alternatives*, 2nd ed. (New York: Guilford Press, 2009).

[380] Peet and Hartwick, *Theories of Development*, 2–3.

[381] Alan Fowler, *Striking a Balance* (London: Earthscan Publications, 2002), 3–19.

[382] These ideas first appeared in the key work of Daniel Goulet, *The Cruel Choice: A New Concept in the Theory of Development* (New York: Athenaeum, 1971).

ing debt instead of growth in the South with problems of increased poverty, unemployment, landlessness reported despite development efforts.³⁸³ This led to the understanding of development to be defined in terms of specific indicators and policies.

7.3.2 Development as Progressive, Indicator-led change

Difficulties of operationalizing the metanarratives in development have led to a gradual shift of development to mean progressive change, centered around certain indicators. Often, this understanding of development is favored by development practitioners because of the clarity that these indicators bring. Poverty reduction objectives, Millennium Development Goals, and the newly minted Sustainability Development Goals are key for International Organizations such as the Organization for Economic Corporation Development (OECD) or United Nations Development Programme (UNDP).³⁸⁴ In addition, non-economic indicators thought to supplement the statistics on growth rate include the Human Development Indicator (HDI) or the Human Poverty Indicator (HPI) developed by the UNDP.³⁸⁵

One key issue of this understanding of development is its seemingly fragmented short-term modernist approach. With standard goals, it has been criticized for being "paternalistic," and not taking into consideration the local context where development takes place. This can lead to divided efforts of change within society as there is no integrated understanding of the change suitable for a particular society, where the views and understanding of local politics are represented.³⁸⁶ In fact, it is precisely because of a seemingly separate development agenda to the local context that civil society organizations advocated the inclusion of open, inclusive, accountable and effective governance in the setting up of sustainable development goals. This has resulted in the addition of goals to "build effective, accountable and inclusive institutions at all levels" within the sustainable development goals.³⁸⁷

---

[383] Potter, "The Nature of Development Studies," 22
[384] Ibid., 13.
[385] Ibid., 27.
[386] David Booth, "Missing Links in the Politics of Development: Learning from the PRSP Experiment," Overseas Development Institute (2005), accessed December 21, 2015, http://www.odi.org/sites/odi.org.uk/files/odi-assets/publications-opinion-files/2003.pdf.
[387] United Nations, "Sustainable Development Goals," accessed December 21, 2015, https://sustainabledevelopment.un.org/?menu=1300.

7.3.3 Development as Deconstructing Change

The third category of development arises from the postmodern critique regarding the imposition of the Western ethnocentric understanding of development on the rest of the world.[388] An increasing suspicion of modernization has led to the deconstruction of existing social relations as well as typical development buzzwords.[389] Often this perspective links the legacy of colonialism with the ideology of development, where the West determines the notion of "developed" and "developing" is based on its own experiences.[390] Sensitive to metanarratives, development from this perspective is more "down to earth," "de-mystifying the beliefs associated with development goals." Instead of clinging to lofty aspirations, a somber reflection of development has been defined as "the general transformation and destruction of the natural environment and of social relations in order to increase the production of commodities (goods and services) geared, by means of market exchange, to effective demand."[391]

One implication of the postmodern critique has been the heightened awareness of external influences in development. This has led to increased ownership of developing countries regarding the kind of development they think is necessary in their country. To this end, development aims at the "promotion or well-functioning of existing practices and institutions that are relevant within a certain setting."[392] Relevant practices and institutions are established and strengthened depending on the people in a particular context.

7.3.4 A Normative Understanding of Development?

In describing the three main perspectives to development, it is clear that existing development institutions embrace these different perspectives of development in varying degrees. Development institutions act depending on their understanding and opinions of the three perspectives.

---

[388] Potter, "The Nature of Development Studies," 14.
[389] Ibid., 22.
[390] Ibid., 8.
[391] Gilbert Rist, "Development as a Buzzword," in *Deconstructing Development Discourse: Buzzwords and Fuzzwords*, ed. Andrea Cornwall and Deborah Eade (Warwickshire: Practical Action Publishing, 2010), 23.
[392] Jochemsen, "A Normative Model for the Practice of Cooperation in Development as a Basis for Social Justice," 138.

As an alternative to choosing one of the three perspectives, a comprehensive approach to the practice of development is undertaken in the following section using the normative practice model. Such a view evaluates the validity of the different definitions from a normative lens, taking seriously the critique outlined in each perspective. In addition, this normative understanding is also rooted in Christian reality. As a unique social practice in society, the development practice is described in terms of norms that ought to be realized for the positive contribution to society. Elaborating on the normative practice of development contributes to development studies through outlining a normative understanding of development from a Christian perspective.

The term development is adopted instead of more specific terms such as "development corporation" or the traditional term "development aid" since "development" affirms the different branches involved in development studies that the normative practice of development draws upon.

7.4 Analysis of Field Research using the Normative Practice Model

For this normative task involved in the analysis phase, we have looked at the key concepts that underpin the normative practice model and its impact to an organization in section 7.2. This included the discussion of the practice, the understanding of reality as described by Dooyeweerd as well as the description of plurality. In addition, we have also introduced the debate surrounding development in section 7.3. In this section, the normative practice of development is outlined and used to interpret the data collected in the data collection phase.

There are three sides to this normative practice model: structural, directional and contextual. Figure 7.1 illustrates how the different sides come together in the normative practice model.[393]

---

[393] As mentioned earlier, the understanding of normative practices detailed in this section is based largely on the work of Henk Jochemsen, "Normative Practices as an Intermediate Between Theoretical Ethics and Morality," *Philosophia Reformata* 71 (2006): 96-112; as well as Gerrit Glas, "Competence Development as normative Practice: Educational Reform in Medicine as Heuristic Model to Relate Worldview and Education", *Koers: Bulletin for Christian Scholarship* 77, no. 1 (2012): Art. #411, 6 pages, http://dx.doi.org/10.4102/ koers.v77i1.411 (accessed February 20, 2015).

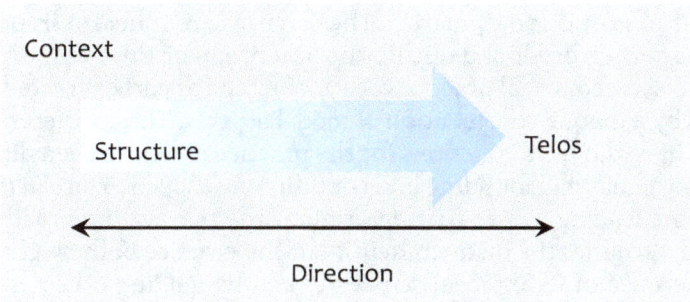

Figure 7.1: Sides of the Normative Practice Model

The following framework is used in this section to analyze the findings in the collection phase. This includes a) introducing each of the three sides and its expression in the organization, b) introducing the side in relation to development practice and finally, c) explicating World Vision field research findings based on the particular side. Through this analysis, the existing experience of World Vision is reflected against the normative ought of the development practice.

7.4.1 Introduction of the Structural Side

The structural side of the practice focuses on the nature of the practice. This nature of the practice can be further elaborated through explication of the telos, standard of excellences as well as qualifying rules, founding and conditioning rules.

The *telos* of a practice describes the reason, a certain finality or core value as to why the practice exists. This is similar to the description of internal goods as discussed by MacIntyre. Different activities that make up this practice should contribute to the realization of this telos.[394]

The *Standards of Excellence* are the rules of play as understood by the practice. They are the "know how" required to realize the telos of the practice. "These rules are embodied in professional conduct consisting in the ability to act according to a rule and to assess the correctness of this application even without making the rule explicit.[395] When these rules are well observed in different forms of the activity within the practice, the telos of the practice is being realized.

---

[394] Henk Jochemsen, "Normative Practices as an Intermediate Between Theoretical Ethics and Morality," *Philosophia Reformata* 71 (2006): 103.
[395] Ibid., 104.

The discussion of *telos* and standards of excellences affirm the importance of norms for a practice. These norms are inherent in practices, specify a certain order and qualify the practice in distinct ways.[396] As previously discussed, social practices are understood as part of created reality, defined by a unique constellation of modal aspects. These different modal aspects have different functions for the practice and have been differentiated into qualifying, founding and conditioning aspects. The *qualifying* aspect is the leading aspect that determines the telos of the practice. This aspect determines the distinct identity of the practice both by guaranteeing coherence of its internal structure, and by guiding other aspects as they each contribute in their own ways to proper functioning of the practice.[397] This aspect characterizes the primary processes of the practice.[398] The *founding* aspect furnishes indispensable support to the practice, making the practice possible. It prescribes activities that give the particular practice its characteristic content.[399] Finally, *conditioning* aspects are the rest of the modal aspects in which the practice functions. These aspects formulate conditions that should be observed in performing a practice but neither define the technicalities of the practice nor its finality. These aspects are observed to bring about proper integrity to the entire practice.

As a 'socially established cooperative human activity,' practices exist in society through institutions, of which organizations are an example. While it is not possible to confine the understanding of practice to any single organization, it is possible to recognize the practice in an organization. This is explored next.

One clear way that this understanding of the structure of the practice influences an organization is the emphasis on the overall telos that inspire the goal directedness or purpose of the organization. For the telos of the practice to truly influence the organization, there is a need to link this telos to the people in the organization. This link was first drawn in the discussion of institutions as molecular.[400] This overall telos should influence

---

[396] Gerrit Glas, "Competence Development as Normative Practice: Educational Reform in Medicine as Heuristic Model to Relate Worldview and Education," *Koers: Bulletin for Christian Scholarship* 77, no. 1 (2012): 4.
[397] Chaplin, *Herman Dooyeweerd*, 88.
[398] Maarten Verkerk, "Spirituality, Organization and Leadership: Towards a Philosophical Foundation of Spirituality at Work," in *Leadership, Innovation, and Spirituality*, ed. Patrick Nullens and Jack Barentsen (Leuven: Peeters, 2014), 67.
[399] Jochemsen, "Normative Practices," 104.
[400] See section 2.1.2.1 Institutions as Molecular

the purpose of the organization which would in turn influence staff membership as well as subsequent activity systems of the organization.[401] As a way to further understand this telos, the constellation of the modal aspects, particularly the qualifying aspect can be useful.

The qualifying function determines the distinct identity of the practice by guaranteeing the coherence of its internal structure. This qualifying aspect should unite the organization through the way it influences interaction among its people, as well as the people chosen. This means that this distinct identity caused by the qualifying function be reflected in the boundary maintenance as well as in the activity systems developed by the organization. For example, for a hospital who sees care as its qualifying function, this care should be reflected in the kind of people chosen to work in the hospital, as well as the activity systems that the hospital develops.[402]

In addition, this also implies that the overall *telos* should guide the general direction of the organization instead of other short-term goals. As short-term goals may or may not contribute to the overall telos of the practice, it is important that these goals stay secondary to the overall functioning of the organization. This implies that both the conditional or founding aspects cannot end up becoming central in the choice of people or activity systems developed in the organization. Using again the example of the hospital, the economic aspect, arguably a conditional aspect of the practice, which is interested in efficiency and the finances of the hospital, should not be prioritized over the qualifying aspect, care, in the decisions made.

Having introduced the structural side of the normative practice, the next section looks at the nature of development through detailing the structural side of the development practice. This is the next step in the actual analysis of World Vision's findings.

7.4.1.1 Structural Side of the Development Practice

The structural side has been discussed separately as the *telos*, standard of excellence consisting of the qualifying founding and conditioning rules. What each means for development practice is discussed below.

---

[401] Stefan Kühl, *Organisationen: Eine sehr kurze Einführung* (Dordrecht: Verlag für Sozialwissenschaften, 2011), 23.
[402] Jochemsen, "Normative Practices," 103.

7.4.1.1.1 Telos

The *telos* of a practice has been described as the reason why a practice exists. With development described as focusing on societal change, the telos of the development practice can be described as the "promotion of the well-functioning of the practices and institutions that are relevant in a certain setting."[403] This *telos* of development practice focuses on the intentional support of certain practices in society through promoting the well-functioning of the corresponding institutions involved in these practices such that positive change is evoked in society.

In the intentional support of the well-functioning of certain practices, development practitioners are required to critically evaluate the needs of the society based on the values they deem important. This is in contrast with prescribing practices and supporting relevant institutions based on current trends or existing external agendas. Such an understanding of development begins with an ethical basis where the values involved in the different decisions attached to social change are truly reflected prior to their implementation.

Once a decision has been made regarding the values and practices the development practice will support, it is important to note that this support should stay macro in nature. The development practice should not become in itself an institution in the practices that it is seeking to support. Instead, the development practice should be proactive and work with the existing institutions of the practice, supporting them to make positive change in society.

7.4.1.1.2 Standards of Excellence

The standards of excellence have been described as the rules of play as understood by the practice. They are the "know how" required to realize the telos of the practice. When these rules are well observed, the telos of the practice is being realized.

With the understanding of development as progressive, indicator led change, many different standards have been initiated. An example of a standard embraced by international NGOs is accountability, as described in the INGO Accountability Charter. "The INGO Accountability Charter is an initiative of international NGOs demonstrating their commitment to transparency, accountability and effectiveness. It provides the only global,

---

[403] Jochemsen, "A Normative Model for the Practice of Cooperation in Development as a Basis for Social Justice," 138.

cross-sectoral accountability framework for NGOs."[404] Members who adhere to this charter include international development organizations such as Care, ActionAid, Plan, World Vision, Oxfam etc. Members who belong to this charter are expected to hold to different accountability standards, including respect for human rights, participation, ethical fundraising etc. They are also expected to report their activities annually. Good practices of different NGOs are then shared with all members on the website.

Besides this charter, there are also other standards that are held by different countries. As an example, Germany has the *Spendenrat*, where organizations are committed to principles of transparency, efficiency and sustainability in dealing with the donations they receive.[405] Australia has an Australian Council for International Development (ACFID), where members adhere to the ACFID Code of Conduct, which defines minimum standards of governance, management and accountability of development for member non-government organizations.[406] Other known standards exist such as "Core humanitarian standard"[407] are a result of the merger of other standards like the HAP Standard in Accountability and Quality Management, or the People in Aid Code of good practice.

While these different standards are good to have, they are not in themselves sufficient to realize the *telos* of development. What is also important is the prioritizing of certain practices and their relevant institutions in determining the most important standards of excellence to adhere to. This includes a "critical and explicit reflection on the ends as well as the means of development, on the what as well as the how."[408] Key to this reflection is the ability to discern pressing priorities for the society, as well as skills and standards required to support the relevant institutions.

7.4.1.1.3 Qualifying, Founding and Constitutive Aspects of Development

Besides focusing on external standards, the constellation of the different modal aspects around which the practice is arranged is also important. As

---

[404] INGO Accountability Charter, "What is the Charter?" accessed January 15, 2016, http://www.ingoaccountabilitycharter.org/home/what-is-the-charter/.
[405] Deutscher Spendenrat, "Über uns," accessed January 15, 2016, http://www.spendenrat.de.
[406] Australian Council for International Development, "About us," accessed January 15, 2016, https://acfid.asn.au/about.
[407] Core Humanitarian Standard, "The Standard," accessed January 15, 2016, http://www.corehumanitarianstandard.org/the-standard.
[408] David A. Crocker, "Towards Development Ethics," *World Development* 19, no. 5 (1991): 467.

described, different aspects have different degrees of importance for different practices. They have been differentiated as qualifying, founding and conditioning aspects in the normative practice model. Having already described the role of each aspect earlier, this section looks directly at the different aspects in the development practice.

The qualifying aspect is the leading aspect that determines the telos of the practice, the intentional support of certain practices. For the development practice, the qualifying aspect should be involved with the intentional reflection of society. It is about discerning what practices to support in society. Taking this reflective intention seriously, it is proposed that the qualifying aspect of development is its historical aspect. In Reformational philosophy, this historical aspect has also been called the formative aspect as it focuses on the deliberate shaping of society. Dooyeweerd describes the modal meaning nucleus of the formative aspect as "the controlling manner of molding the social process."[409] This has also been described as the "irreducible modal manner of formation according to a free project."[410]

With the development practice involved in influencing society, this involves molding and forming which is key in the historical aspect. This molding and forming takes into account the past of the society as well as the future vision. This is in step with Dooyeweerd's understanding of the historical aspect, as he believes that "history unites the present, the past and the future. It is exactly in its historical aspect that time assumes this threefold articulation."[411]

Focusing on the historical or formative aspect as the qualifying aspect is to take into consideration the story of the society. It does not simply impose external standards but requires intentional reflection on the existing society to understand what is necessary. This involves the review of social practices in society and evaluating which practices to further develop in society. This implies that institutions that express the development practice are not just service providers. Instead, it is important for these institutions to critically evaluate what is necessary for society, support the growth of people through the intentional support of chosen practices in society that are presently lacking.

The next key aspect is the founding aspect of the practice. This aspect reveals the main aspects that make the practice possible. It outlines activities that give a particular practice its characteristic content. Looking at the history of the practice, the term "development" was first coined after

---

[409] Dooyeweerd, *A New Critique of Theoretical Thought*, 2:195.
[410] Ibid., 2:195.
[411] Ibid., 2:193.

the Second World War to support the rebuilding of Germany. In this rebuilding efforts, evaluation of needs in Germany resulted in the provision of technical and financial services. What was key was the role of evaluation and critical reflection in determining the needs required by Germany. In light of this importance of reflection, it is argued that the founding aspect for the development practice is also found in the formative aspect.

The formative aspect has been argued to be key to both the qualifying and founding aspects of the development practice. This implies that other modal aspects are part of the developing practice as constitutive aspects of the development practice. As constitutive aspects, these aspects formulate conditions that should be observed in the development practice. These aspects are not considered the most important aspects. They neither define the qualifying or founding aspects of the practice. It is therefore important that these aspects do not take primary focus in the practice.

So far, we have looked at the structural side of the normative practice, the implications of this structural side to the organization as well as the structural side of the development practice. In the next section, we analyze the data collected in the collective phase alongside this theory of the structural side of development.

7.4.1.2 Structural Reality as Explicated from the Field Research of World Vision

To uncover World Vision's understanding of the structure of the practice, data is derived mainly from the core documents of World Vision. These core documents reflect World Vision's intention for the work that it does. It is a good indicator of World Vision's official interpretation of the structure of the development practice.

7.4.1.2.1 Telos

The telos of World Vision can be traced from the main purpose that World Vision sets up for itself. As a starting point, World Vision describes itself as a "Christian relief, development and advocacy organization dedicated to working with children, families and communities to overcome poverty and injustice."[412] The three pillars, relief, development and advocacy make

---

[412] World Vision International, accessed March 23, 2016, http://www.wvi.org.

up the united mission "to follow our Lord and Savior Jesus Christ in working with the poor and oppressed to promote human transformation, seek justice and bear witness to the good news of the Kingdom of God."[413]

Despite the three pillars listed by World Vision, an organization is guided ultimately by one primary practice as the practice determines the overall purpose of the organization. With the mission focus of World Vision to "promote human transformation," this draws parallel to the telos of the development practice, particularly in its "support of certain practices... such that positive change is evoked." As these three pillars of the organization work together to support human transformation, it has been argued that World Vision is an organization that seeks to primarily express the development practice in society. This implies that instead of merely providing short term relief or advocacy for advocacy sake, the relief and advocacy done by World Vision has a wider purpose, that of human transformation. It is therefore important that each of the pillars clarify how they seek to promote human transformation individually. As a summary, it is clear from the documents of World Vision that the development pillar presents clear steps for how human transformation should be achieved. This however is not as clear for the other two pillars.

World Vision's strategy on development is clearly outlined in the "development program approach" in its development pillar. As described earlier, the main goal of this approach is "sustained well-being of children within families and communities, especially the most vulnerable."[414] There is a clear understanding that World Vision is child focused, developing projects based on joint decisions with the community, built on the basis of child well-being outcomes. Recognizing its role as transient within the society with the intention of transitioning out one day, World Vision works closely with the community, hiring local staff as well as working with external partners to achieve these well-being outcomes. The way that World Vision works with the community and external partners is clearly outlined in the "critical path," the process whereby this development approach

---

[413] World Vision, "Mission Statement," Partnership Core Documents (1992).
[414] In defining this goal, World Vision is not trying to replace the existing social practices in place. With the clearly chosen focus of children wellbeing, they work with the broader community to ensure that there are sufficient practices for children wellbeing in the community. This means that they are willing to introduce practices, work alongside others, doing so mindful that they will leave one day. World Vision, "The Handbook for Development Programs: The Essentials" (2011), 7, accessed June 15, 2015, http://www.wvi.org/sites/ default/files/Handbook_for_Development_Programmes.pdf.

turns into action in the community. Key to this critical path is the importance of developing partnerships and working closely with the community. With its clear choice for children well-being and its intentional support for the practices that support children well-being, it is clear that World Vision's development program approach aligns with the overall telos of the development practice.

The development program approach not only influences goals of the organization as described above, it also influences both boundary maintenance, and activity systems of the organization. As an example, key program staff are required to "live incarnational." This has been described to imply "humility and grace, recognition of the equality of all human beings, identification with the poor and vulnerable, and recognition of the right to life with dignity."[415] This need for staff to live incarnational implies the importance given to the community. It is the story of the community that should identify the staff and what they do.[416]

For activity systems, one obvious influence of the telos is the focus on learning and reflection in the process of development. From the resources provided, it is clear that this critical path should be a collaborative reflection led by World Vision together with the community.[417] Through this commitment to learning and reflection, this allows for more accurate understanding of the community, and clarification of which practices to support. In addition, World Vision is committed to working with other practices and institutions. This understanding of partnering is core in the identity of World Vision as partnership features in the core values of World Vision. With the intentional support of the community written into its development program approach permeating into the organization through the goals, boundary maintenance and activity systems, it is argued that World Vision's development program approach is in alignment with the telos of development practice.

What seems lacking is the clarity of how the advocacy and relief pillar adheres to the development practice. There is little in the documents of advocacy and relief that intentionally links with the development practice. If the organization truly wants to be led by development practice, more needs to be done by World Vision to intentionally link these pillars with overall development practice.

---

[415] World Vision, "Ministry Framework Revised – Summary" (November 2010), 5.
[416] In making this argument, it is noted that this is one of many reasons why World Vision wants their staff to live incarnationally. It is not the only reason.
[417] Example of resources available include http://www.wvi.org/development/guide/development-programming-guidance.

The next section introduces and analyzes the standards of excellence.

7.4.1.2.2 Standards of Excellence and the Presence of the Qualifying Aspect

World Vision's core documents show its adherence to a number of different standards of excellence such as the Red Cross code of conduct or the INGO accountability structure. These external standards provide indicators for development, but in themselves, do not bring the practice closer to the telos. It is the standards of excellence that bring the development practice closer to the telos. This refers to the ability of the organization to evaluate the particular societal context, with results of the evaluation leading to positive decisions on relevant practices and institutions that the organization should support. This evaluation involves a review of the different modal aspects in society and evaluating which aspects should be further developed for the society in question. It is dependent on the presence of the main qualifying aspect, the formative aspect, in the organization. Attention is now turned to the extent that World Vision reflects the qualifying aspect of the development practice in its existence. This is done through analyzing the emphasis given to the local context, the focus on learning and reflection in the work and finally, the goal of societal formation.

1. Emphasis Given to the Local Context

At World Vision, the story of the local society is valued in the development program approach as illustrated in their critical path. Integral to the critical path of the development program approach is the importance of collaboration between World Vision and its local partners. As part of its standard practice, this critical path shows a clear commitment of World Vision to work together with the community towards improving child well-being in families and communities. The local community has been described as partners of World Vision, not beneficiaries. As local partners, they work together with World Vision to decide which practices and institutions to support in their context. There is a strong tradition in World Vision to work at the grassroots level, leading to a clearer idea about the needs of a particular society. This is also evident in the empowerment principle, a key principle World Vision embraced when they adopted their federal model since the early 90s.

While clear commitment for local level partnership is noted, another contrasting trend is also evident at World Vision especially in the later years of World Vision: decision-making and power seem to be consolidated up the hierarchy. As described in the decision-making processes in the revival stage of the organization, a decision-making map was designed to clearly mark the relevant decision makers of the organization. Decision makers were assigned depending on the scope and risk of decisions.[418] In this map, staff members who are part of the field work are further distanced from the centers of excellences or the global center that decide riskier and broader decisions of the organization. This map risks neglecting the needs of local communities and becoming out of touch with the field. Decisions made in the centers of excellence or the global center of the organization about the direction of the organization do not include the feedback from staff members who work at the field level, individuals who are most in touch with the local community. This can result in a gap of understanding between the field operations and the broader partnership of World Vision.

2. Learning Necessary for the Formation of Society

To be able to reflect on the required formation necessary in society, it is necessary that staff members are able to discern how society should be formed. This implies that World Vision functions more than just a service provider but evaluates what practices are required in society. Based on the core documents, there is evidence that staff members are encouraged to continuously learn from their past experiences.

The importance of continuous learning is reflected in the core documents of World Vision. Example of its explicitness in the organization can be seen in various documents such as the development program approach, the strategic mandates of the organization, the core capabilities framework and the integrated competency framework. This continuous learning is described in the form of learning and reflection in the development program approach. This emphasis on learning is also reflected in the desire to "strengthen field capacity and ministry," one of five strategic mandates described in the "Our Future" initiative. World Vision states its desire to invest in people as they strengthen field capacity and ministry. In addition, this commitment to learning is also present in the core capabilities framework as well as the integrated competency framework that World Vision has developed for its staff.

This emphasis on continuous learning is clearly understood by staff members. In describing their perception, staff members believe that change

---

[418] See Chapter 4, section 4.3.4.4.

is desirable and therefore takes place frequently.[419] The main reason for change has been recorded to be "desire for continuous improvement and progress in office."[420] Instead of being expressed only in the core document, this reality of continuous learning is truly embraced by the staff members.

3. Goal of Societal Formation

Finally, it is imperative that all staff have a big picture understanding how societal formation should look like. Sources for this big picture understanding can be found in different partnership statements such as the Mission Statement, Vision Statement and Ministry Framework. In addition, other documents which pertain to specific pillars of the organization such as the development program approach also exist at World Vision. Suffice to say, there are ample sources available for staff members to be acquainted with World Vision's vision on societal formation.

From the field research, it is evident that the priority and overall value given to World Vision's understanding of societal formation differed in different offices. The big picture understanding of World Vision was not always pursued. For World Vision Nepal, the local context, followed by global and regional strategies, were considered to be the most important for decision making.[421] This affirms World Vision's vision, with the importance of the local context for World Vision Nepal as well as the strategy laid out by the central World Vision offices. This understanding was however not repeated in Papua New Guinea. In Papua New Guinea, donor expectations as well as the field financial guidelines were considered key in decision making.[422] This information can imply that World Vision's vision on societal formation took a back row. Donors and the importance to adhere to financial guidelines were perceived to be more important in the overall goal setting of the organization. Despite the documents available illustrating the World Vision way, it cannot be assumed that all offices will prioritize the same in the work they do.

Thus far, we have introduced the structural side, introduced the structural side for the development practice and analyzed the way World Vision expresses the structure of the development practice. In the next section, we turn our focus on the directional side of the practice.

---

[419] See Chapter 6, table 6.54
[420] See Chapter 6, table 6.56
[421] See Chapter 6, table 6.6.
[422] See Chapter 6, table 6.44.

7.4.2 Introduction of the Directional Side

As the normative practice model finds its basis from the creation order, the direction towards the telos of the practice is one where creation laws are positivized and applied to the specific situation.[423] To study the directional side is to look at the control beliefs, held by the practitioner, that influence the interpretation of the structural side of the practice.

This interpretation, done by the practitioners, depends on the worldview the practitioners embrace. In an organization context, the practitioners are the staff members involved. The staff members' worldview influences their motivations and beliefs about human life to motivations and conceptions of the value of the practice within one's society.[424] These beliefs and values are often so self-evident that they are assumed and not intentionally followed.[425]

One main reason that organizations that embody the same practice differ from each other is due to the differing interpretation of the practice structure by staff members. This interpretation becomes more complex for a faith-based organization with a clearly stated direction. The stated faith mission as determined in the documents can give an indication of the direction the organization is moving towards. However, instead of simply determining the direction of the organization through the stated faith mission in its core documents, the perceptions of the staff members are a better gauge of the interpretation of the practitioners. The perception of the staff members provide a better gauge to the overall interpretation of the practitioners.

Therefore, determining the directional side of the practice expressed within an organization moves beyond focusing only on the values of the founder of the organization, or on formal religious statements made by the organization in its core documents. It takes seriously the perceptions of individual staff members, and how these perceptions interact with the organization and the broader environment. One way that these perceptions can be studied, as done in this dissertation, is through uncovering assumptions held by individual members regarding the faith statements of the organization. In addition, the organizational life cycle is useful as it provides insight to the evolution of the organization, particularly in the way that

---

[423] This has been referred to as the Creational Mandate as stated in the Christian Worldview.
[424] Jochemsen, "A Normative Model for the Practice of Cooperation in Development as a Basis for Social Justice," 140.
[425] Verkerk, "Spirituality, Organization and Leadership," 68.

the organization has moved directionally since the start of the organization.

7.4.2.1 Introduction of the directional side of the development practice

To reflect on the direction of the development practice is to be aware and deliberate in positivizing creational structures within the development practice. The Lausanne Covenant describes one example of this reflection and intentionality of positivizing creation laws. For this broad evangelical network, development is understood as "Christians work(ing) towards poverty reduction through their concern for justice and reconciliation throughout human society. This includes liberation of men and women from every kind of oppression upholding the dignity of all mankind as they are created in the image of God."[426]

Besides moving towards the telos, it is also possible for the development practice to move away from the telos. This happens when development is pursued for other purposes in an extreme fashion. One common purpose done at an extreme is economic progress. A full focus on economic development can quickly distort the practice of development. This overemphasis on economic development can happen when economic indicators such as the Gross National Product[427] become one of the main indicators of development. When development is only viewed economically, this can result in the general transformation and destruction of the natural environment and of social relations in order to increase production of commodities (goods and services) geared, by means of market exchange, to effective demand.[428] To pursue economic development at all costs emphasizes the economic aspect at the expense of other modal aspects. This can quickly move the practice in the direction opposite from the telos.

---

[426] As an introduction, the Lausanne Covenant, a broad evangelical movement is used to describe the purpose of development. It is not meant to be exhaustive. See Lausanne Covenant 1974, point 5.

[427] OECD has been present since the start of development work and prides itself in providing evidence based statistics as well as promoting policies that will improve the economic and social well-being of people around the world. The Gross National Product, an indicator developed by the Organization for Economic Cooperation and Development (OECD) is one of the major indicators of poverty.

[428] Rist, "Development as a Buzzword," 23.

7.4.2.2 Directional Side as explicated from the Field Research of World Vision

Having introduced the directional side of the normative practice model as well as look at it specifically for the development practice, we can now turn our attention to the field research of World Vision. To understand the interpretation of the staff members with respect to the normative practice, the findings of the organizational culture as well as the organizational life cycle are focused on.

Based on the findings, World Vision has evolved from an American evangelical organization to an ecumenical organization working in sectors of relief, development and advocacy. Moving on from working primarily with the churches for mission purposes, World Vision has gradually aligned its work with known sectors in the wider development and humanitarian industry. In addition, World Vision has grown and spread across different cultures, sectors, with increased decision makers and different agendas. These changes have led to a diminished role in the Christian narrative of the organization.

From the core documents developed especially in the early phases of the organization, it is clear that World Vision actively seeks to pursue the Christian direction through its staff policy. An official preference is stated for staff to be followers of Christ if legally possible. "Staff should embody a vibrant Christian spirituality, subscribe to our core documents, and fulfill the individual indicators for Christ-centered life and work in the Core capabilities framework."[429] This preference for Christian spirituality is applicable for staff, particularly those in management positions, as well as in the choice of board members. While having an official preference for followers of Christ, there is also an understanding that it is not always viable to hire Christian staff. In such cases, the staff policies provide exceptions for hiring of non-Christian non-management staff, when these staff do not prevent the fulfillment of the mission of World Vision. This exception takes place more often at the field level, where the operational work of World Vision occurs especially in locations where it is not easy to find Christian staff.

Staff policies while important, are in itself not the only representative of the direction of the organization. The interpretation of staff members, particularly in the way the staff members make sense of the religious di-

---

[429] World Vision, "Witness to Jesus Christ Policy," Partnership Policy and Decision Manual (16 September 1995).

rection of the organization, is also important. In Papua New Guinea, a predominantly Christian country, 94% of the staff members described the organization's religious motivations and values as very important and important.[430] At first glance, this seems to be very important. However, a closer look illustrates a disconnect between the importance placed on the religious identity of World Vision and the impact it has on them. The values and mission of World Vision was ranked fourth out of seven choices in reasons why staff members would join the organization.[431] In addition, it was also evident that the mission and purpose of World Vision did not play a central role in motivating staff members. This mission and purpose was ranked third out of seven factors that motivated staff in their current role.[432] For World Vision Nepal, 87.3% of the staff members described the organization's religious motivations as important or very important.[433] Again, this seemed like a high percentage. However, when asked to compare the different reasons why staff members might choose to work for World Vision, this religious identity as well as the values and mission of World Vision take a lower position, ranked fourth out of seven, indicating the seeming low priority given by staff members.[434] In addition, the mission and purpose of the World Vision were also ranked third out of seven regarding the factors that motivated them in their current role.[435] Based on these results, it cannot be said that the Christian direction was primarily in the minds of the staff members, where they worked towards positivizing the development practice at World Vision.

In addition, based on the prior analysis of the tacit Christian identity of World Vision, it has also been concluded that the organization's Christian values were not prioritized in the organization's culture.

From the analysis on the directional side, it can be said that staff members do not fully share in the organization's Christian direction as depicted in their policies. This can result in gradual move away from the Christian direction. The next section looks at the final side, the contextual side.

7.4.3 Introduction of the Contextual Side

The contextual side focuses on the environment and the different stakeholders involved in the practice. As stakeholders from different contexts

---

[430] See Chapter 6, table 6.42.
[431] See Chapter 6, table 6.52.
[432] See Chapter 6, table 6.53.
[433] See Chapter 6, table 6.4.
[434] See Chapter 6, table 6.14.
[435] See Chapter 6, table 6.15.

become part of the practice, they bring along with them connections and links that might influence the final expression of the practice within a certain context.[436] In addition, stakeholders can also come from different cultural contexts and be different because of their particular racial, ethnic, geographic, gender and class experiences.[437]

Stakeholders bring along their own agenda and interests which can differ. Taking the example of health care organizations, key stakeholders include patients, insurance companies, medical associations and the government. These stakeholders influence the overall organization differently, depending on the context where the practice is located. There are contexts where insurance companies are more influential on health care organizations and others where patients are seen to be more influential.

A stakeholder analysis is a useful tool to characterize the influence different stakeholders have in the organization. This analysis evaluates different stakeholders based on their perceived influence and needs within the organization.[438] In performing this stakeholder analysis, it is important to note that different stakeholders are influenced by their own separate belief system. These different belief systems interact due to the different stakeholders and influence the overall direction that the practice takes.

7.4.3.1 Contextual Side of the Development Practice

The contextual side of the development practice is discussed in this section by describing the different stakeholders involved in the development practice as well as the influence of the cultural contexts where the practice is located.

Stakeholders involved in the development process are often involved in one way or other in the flow of foreign aid from one country to the

---

[436] Mouw and Sander, *Pluralisms and Horizons*, 16–17.
[437] Ibid.
[438] Stakeholder analysis is used in project management, business administration and even conflict resolution. It is useful to understand the different stakeholders that influence the organization. An example of the use of the stakeholder analysis can be seen in this journal article. Anne Fletcher, James Guthrie, and Peter Steane, "Mapping Stakeholder Perceptions for a Third Sector Organization," *Journal of Intellectual Capital* 4, no. 4 (2003): 505–27. There was a mapping of stakeholders' perception to understand what held most value and was considered performance for the different stakeholders in the work that the Australian Red Cross blood service did. This study was taken during an internal change process in the organization in the face of many external changes in the environment.

other. Often this foreign aid involves many intermediaries to deliver different physical, financial and knowledge resources. These can include UN bodies, international financial NGOs, government bodies giving and receiving aid, Red Cross, think tanks, universities as well as multilateral corporations. Other stakeholders might not be visible directly to the funders, yet are also extremely important in the process. These stakeholders can include local NGOs, local governments, community based organizations, small businesses as well as volunteers in the community that help people within their communities. Each stakeholder is unique with a starkly different professional background and personal background. Working with many stakeholders implies an increase in the complexity of relationships and dependencies, as well as frameworks used to deliver aid.[439] Figure 7.2 is an illustration of different stakeholders involved in the development aid industry.[440]

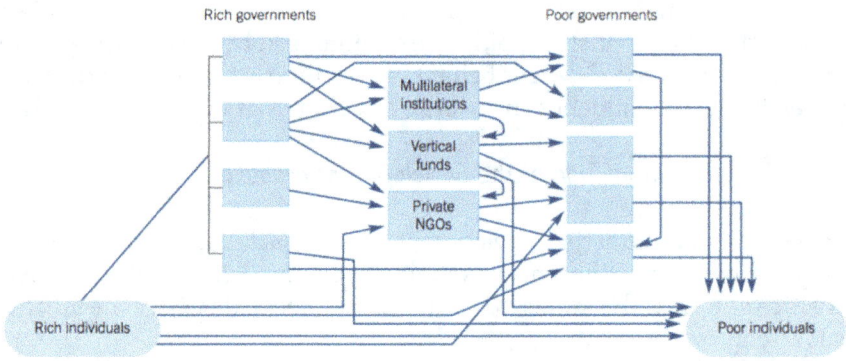

Figure 7.2 Reality of Aid Development

Source: Wolfgang Fengler and Homi Kharas, eds. *Delivering Aid Differently— Lessons from the Field* (Washington, DC: Brookings Institution, 2010).

---

[439] Ben Ramalingam, *Aid on the Edge of Chaos: Rethinking International Cooperation in a Complex World* (Oxford: Oxford University Press, 2013), 5.

[440] In using this figure to illustrate the different stakeholders involved, it is not my intention to assume that aid just moves in a singular direction, from rich to poor countries. The network of stakeholders is complicated usually involves different actors from the global North and South. What this figure seeks to illustrate is the multiple different stakeholders involved in the development process.

It is self-explanatory that different actors have different emphases and agendas in their development thinking and disciplines. For example, governments tend towards development thinking as economics, with their focus on economics, political science, public administration and demography whilst NGOs tend towards focusing on alternative development with their focus on disciplines such as sociology, anthropology, ecology, gender and cultural studies.[441] With different interests and agendas, the development process is a result of multi-level negotiations where different stakeholders struggle with different power relations. Relationships among different stakeholders are dynamic as they navigate the priorities and concerns of development (globalization, sustainability, gender, diversity, poverty alleviation). This can lead to new combinations of partnerships among different stakeholders.[442] To understand the context that World Vision is working in, the next section focuses on NGOs, the kind of stakeholder that World Vision belongs to.

7.4.3.1.1 Focus on NGOs

The term, "non-governmental organization" or NGO came to being in 1945 as a term used by the United Nations to categorize a unique kind of organizations with differing participation rights compared to those of intergovernmental agencies. As a unique category of organizations present in development, they are characterized by their independence from government control, non-profit making and non-criminal nature. They belong to the civil society as introduced earlier in this dissertation. As a wide category of different organizations, there are varying kinds of structures of NGOs. International NGOs have different member offices in different countries, while local NGOs work in only one country or transnationally.[443] World Vision belongs to the category of international NGOs.

NGOs have been considered one of the key implementers of development because of their strengths and distinctive competences as providers of "development alternatives" that offer more people-centered and grassroots-driven approaches to development.[444] Grassroots development was

---

[441] Jan Nederveen Pieterse, *Development Theory*, 2nd ed. (London: SAGE Publications, 2010), 10.
[442] Ibid., 11.
[443] Peter Willets, "What is a Non-Governmental Organization?" accessed December 15, 2016, http://www.staff.city.ac.uk/p.willetts/CS-NTWKS/NGO-ART.HTM.
[444] Anne G. Drabek, "Development alternatives: The challenge for NGOs – An overview of the issues," *World Development* 15, no. 1, supplement (1987): ix–xv.

understood as an alternative to development efforts by classical economics or Marxism. Disenchanted by the perceived failures of the top down approach, the grassroots approach was introduced as a means to alleviate the poverty of the poorest in developing countries. This was first promoted by introducing the concept of "basic needs" in society.[445] This led to greater attention on smaller scale activities and the poorer section in society.[446] NGOs, as grassroots oriented organizations, were viewed positively for their ability to connect with beneficiaries and became players in the development scene.[447]

While the endorsement of NGOs come from their grassroots links, the reality of NGOs being driven grassroots approaches for grassroots development might be more complicated. This is due to the reality of these NGOs being heavily reliant on donor funding or because of state control. Depending on the donor type, different requirements are set for the NGOs which influence the way that development is done by NGOs, particularly with the need to be operationally effective or to have its policies influenced by donor priorities and interests. At the same time, the work of NGOs can also be inhibited by state control in what they do.[448] NGOs are sometimes viewed negatively by governments in the countries that they work, hence limiting their breadth of action. One factor for this negative perception comes from the claim by some NGOs that they are the "voice of the people" and hence have "greater legitimacy."[449] This has led to different kinds of control imposed by governments. For example, in Ethiopia, regulations forbid NGOs that do any form of advocacy and human rights from receiving more than 10% of their income from overseas donors.[450]

As key institutions in development practice, NGOs can be influenced by different stakeholders in different ways depending on the context in

---

[445] The main basic needs approach was first highlighted by the International Labor Organization in 1976. The needs include basics of personal consumption, access to essential services, access to paid employment and qualitative needs (access to healthy and safe environment, ability to participate in decision-making) For more information, refer to Overseas Development Institute, Briefing Paper No.5 1978. http://www.odi.org/sites/odi.org.uk/files/odi-assets/publications-opinion-files/6616.pdf

[446] Katie Willis, *Theories and Practices of Development*, 2nd ed. (New York: Routledge, 2011).

[447] Nicola Banks, David Hulme, and Michael Edwards, "NGOs, States and Donors Revisited: Still Too Close for Comfort?" *World Development* 66 (2015): 708.

[448] Banks, Hulme, and Edwards, "NGOs, States and Donors Revisited," 709.

[449] Willetts, "What is a Non Governmental Organization."

[450] Banks, Hulme, and Edwards, "NGOs, States and Donors Revisited," 709.

which they are situated. The way that NGOs react to these different influences dependent on the mediated interpretation of staff members in the organization. This can lead to different organizations reacting differently in the same context depending on the staff members present.

7.4.3.1.2 *Country Culture and Religious Context*

Besides the stakeholders, another key contextual aspect that needs to be taken into consideration is the country culture and religious context.

Traditionally, culture has been described as a functional system where the functioning of society was the result of different processes working together as different parts of society interacted with each other.[451] Key proponents of a systemic understanding of culture include sociologists such as Bronislaw Malinowski and A.R. Radcliffe-Brown.[452] However, with the influence of postmodernism, this definition of culture as a system has slowly been replaced by the understanding of culture as a process. As a process, culture is seen as "fragmented rather than holistic, negotiated and constructed rather than a 'given' transmitted through unproblematic processes of socialisation and acculturation."[453]

Seeking to synthesize both the systemic and process view of culture, Clammer's understanding of culture is useful. He highlights three main characteristics of culture. Firstly, that culture is a process, secondly that talking about culture implies respecting indigenous knowledge as a rich knowledge system which is in itself valid and finally, if cultures are indeed relative, the understanding of the economy in different cultures is also a cultural construct, instead of being "objective."[454] Such an understanding of culture in the development practice emphasizes the importance of understanding the local context. It begins with discerning the starting point of the society in question. This is different from trying to fit and modify

---

[451] Eric Porth, Kimberley Neutzling, and Jessica Edwards, "Functionalism," accessed March 15, 2016, http://anthropology.ua.edu/cultures/cultures.php?culture=Functionalism.

[452] Walter Goldschmidt, "Functionalism," in *Encyclopedia of Cultural Anthropology*, vol. 2, ed. David Levinson and Melvin Ember (New York: Henry Holt and Company, 1996), 510.

[453] John Clammar, "Culture, Development, and Social Theory: On Cultural Studies and the Place of Culture in Development," *The Asia Pacific Journal of Anthropology* 6, no. 2 (2005): 103. For more information about culture as a process, see for example Jonathan Friedman, *Cultural Identity and Global Process* (London: SAGE Publications, 1996).

[454] Clammar, "Culture, Development, and Social Theory," 104.

development approaches that have been pre-designed from the outside. One way of looking at this is to place cultural concerns at the forefront of critical analysis in development. "Cultural concerns and notions of human fulfilment in a more holistic sense at their core."[455] In this instance, development is analyzed as discourse instead of ideology. The story of the society takes a central place in determining the actual development done.[456]

Another implication of discussing culture as process is a focus on the actual experiences of people living in a particular culture. This is contrasted with a view of an over-abstract and disembodied conception of culture that systems may provide.[457] Culture as understood in this dissertation is the constant creation of meaning, in particular to validate disordered experiences (illness, disasters, poverty).[458] It is a dynamic process that has a running narrative, with the possibility of changing the way things are done.

Often the cultural narrative is mediated by religious values held by the people in the particular cultural setting. These are real people involved in the development process, people with emotions and values, who suffer and seek meaning in their suffering, and who seek continually to expand their capacities and range of experience.[459] Such a view explicates the ambiguities and inconsistencies that are part of actual living culture. It also highlights the dangers of viewing culture as a closed system that doesn't change.

A focus of culture as process also increases the importance of a critical study of the existing state of culture and the role development plays in supporting its existing needs. The development practice has an active role in the meaning making of society.[460] Culture is not static but evolving. The actual beliefs and interpretation of the practitioners play an important role in the actual development undertaken by the organization. What they consider as important can influence the way the culture evolves over time.[461]

---

[455] Clammar, "Culture, Development, and Social Theory," 107.
[456] Pieterse, *Development Theory*, 14.
[457] Clammar, "Culture, Development, and Social Theory," 111.
[458] Ibid., 110.
[459] Ibid., 111.
[460] Ibid., 106.
[461] In this discussion, the discussion of culture has been kept at a generic level. Because of the vast indigenous context that should be considered, it is beyond this dissertation to describe how development functions in each individual culture.

7.4.3.2 Contextual side in World Vision

This analysis of the contextual side of World Vision focuses on stakeholders who are perceived to be influential for World Vision. To ascertain the influence of these different stakeholders in World Vision, staff members were asked to evaluate the role of different stakeholders in the organization. Responses revealed different perceptions regarding the influences of each stakeholder depending on the context of staff. What seems to be consistent in both offices is the perception of the strong influence of beneficiaries in the work of World Vision. This implies a clear sense of understanding that development work done by World Vision is ultimately for the beneficiaries, and should be therefore influenced by the needs of the beneficiaries. This also shows the understanding that attention should be given to the local context of the beneficiaries.

Apart from indicating the importance of direct beneficiaries, the responses in the field research varies in both offices. For World Vision Nepal, the local government was next in influential to the decision making of the office. This was followed by the regional office.[462] The influence of the local government and the regional office can influence the overall development done in the country, mediating the influence of the beneficiaries. With the local government having a large influence, the actual work that they do can be inhibited by state control.[463]

For World Vision Papua New Guinea, there was clear influence of the direct donors as well as support offices.[464] This importance of direct donors and support offices was also evident when staff was asked to evaluate the importance of different variables for decision making of the office.[465] The donors have a pronounced impact to the overall development done in World Vision Papua New Guinea. The priorities of the donor can have a long-term impact to the overall culture of the society.

7.4.4 Summary Analysis based on the Normative Development Practice Model

In this second analysis, the findings of the field research was analyzed using framework of the normative practice model, an established model

---

[462] See Chapter 6, table 6.33.
[463] Banks, Hulme, and Edwards, "NGOs, States and Donors Revisited," 715.
[464] As a reminder, support offices are offices that raise money for the work of World Vision in the field. See Chapter 6, table 6.71.
[465] See Chapter 6, table 6.44.

based on reformational philosophy. This model contains three sides: structural, directional and contextual. The practice of development was outlined before the actual analysis of the findings of World Vision.

In the analysis of the structural side, there was clear evidence that the core documents of World Vision were in alignment with the normative structure of the development practice. Operationally, it was also clear that World Vision's development program approach was in tune with the wider development practice. What remains unclear was how together the three pillars of World Vision—development, relief and advocacy—would work together to fulfill its mission of "human transformation," aligned to the telos of development practice. It is therefore important to have clarity as to how each pillar contributes towards the telos of human transformation.

For the directional side, it is clear that World Vision has evolved in its Christian understanding since its founding. Despite the official preference for Christian staff members at World Vision, staff members have expressed that the Christian values of the organization were not prioritized in the organizational culture and did not have much implication for the work that they do.

Finally, regarding the contextual side, World Vision had a clear understanding that beneficiaries influence the work that it does. Besides the beneficiaries, there were different influential stakeholders for both offices. For Papua New Guinea, donors were considered to be particularly influential whereas for Nepal, the local context seemed to be more influential with a focus on government relations as well as country statistics. These stakeholders can influence the overall development work done by World Vision in the different offices.

7.5 From Analysis to Recommendations

This chapter has gone to great lengths to analyze the findings of the field research, firstly through an analysis of the organization's tacit religious identity, and secondly, through an analysis of the findings using the normative practice model of development, which analyzes the findings of the case study from an intentional Christian perspective.

Having concluded the analytical phase, attention is turned to the last phase of the case study, the recommendations phase. In this recommendations phase, the tacit religious identity model is used as a framework to discuss specific recommendations for both the content and process of the organization. These recommendations build on the analyses of this chapter.

PART D: RECOMMENDATIONS PHASE

CHAPTER EIGHT

Appropriating The Trinity as Central for World Vision

Following the analysis of the case study, this chapter moves towards the recommendations phase of the case study. This recommendation phase coincides with the pragmatic task of theological interpretation. It focuses on forming and enacting strategies of action that influence events in ways that are desirable in light of the other tasks that have been taken up. This is done understanding that any change in an organization takes place in a process. It is important to know what has happened before moving forward.

With the research question in mind, recommendations are made to counter mission drift, by strengthening the Christian identity of World Vision. These recommendations take the form of content and process, key aspects of the tacit identity formation model that has been used throughout this dissertation. As described, identity is formed through the ongoing dialectic between the process and content of the organization.[466] In line with this model, two chapters are devoted to this recommendation phase, content and process recommendations.

In this chapter, the focus is on content recommendations. It takes into account the structure of the development practice that the organization is seeking to pursue. There are four main sections to this chapter. In the first section, the link between the analysis and the proposed recommendation is first made: the need to reemphasize the particularity of the Christian faith for an organization like World Vision. Secondly the argument for constructive theology is made for this discussion of the Christian faith. Thirdly, the trinity, as a core Christian doctrine is reflected in light of the development practice done by World Vision. This includes the discussion of each of the divine persons and how they contribute to the understanding of the development practice as well as practical ways that an organization like World Vision can respond to.

---

[466] For more information on the identity formation model, see chapter 2, section 2.3.3.

8.1 Content Analysis and the Proposed Recommendation

In the previous chapter, the analysis was done in two ways, first through looking at the organization's mediated identity as well as the use of the normative practice model. Based on this analysis, some main conclusions related to the analysis of content from the tacit identity model. From the understanding of the organization as an object, it is clear that there were clear and consistent Christian understanding in the different organizational variables as well as public documents. From the understanding of organization as self, it was also evident that World Vision significantly evolved since its founding. What began as a distinctly evangelical missionary organization has developed into a Christian organization focused on relief, development and advocacy. The focus on efficiency as well as expectations of others have indeed led to bureaucratization as well as isomorphism. It was also clear in the analysis that external stakeholders, ranging from government relations to donors, have affected the overall influence of faith values on the organization. The Christian influence on the overall ministry of the organization also diminished over time. More organizational attention has been placed on dealing with growth or efficiency. The newer ministry strategy plans of World Vision seem to highlight a quantitative goal. This overall goal of children's well-being that World Vision adopted was also discussed in different terms and approaches that World Vision employed.

In addition, reflecting on the content analysis using the normative practice model, it became clear that there was a lack of full understanding of the structure of the development practice throughout the organization. There were also signs that World Vision was moving in a wrong direction in terms of its organizational content. Staff members seemed to be more influenced by external stakeholders such as donors, government regulations, and beneficiaries.

8.1.1 Recognizing the Particularity of the Christian faith

In light of the analysis, it is recommended that the way the Christian faith uniquely influences the development practice that World Vision seeks to express, be explicated. As previously described, the telos of the development practice is the "promotion of the well-being of the practices and institutions that are relevant in a certain setting."[467] An intentional reflection of the Christian faith can shed light on which practices and institutions the development practice to support. It also describes the end goal of the practice, adding further information on the direction of the practice. This implies that the Christian faith should not only impact the organization historically, but also have continued value as it provides relevant information for the organization faced with contemporary challenges.

This recommendation affirms and validates the public role of faith. Considering that 80% of the world's population professes a religious faith, there is a rightful place for faith in development.[468] Long before the arrival of secular NGOs, faith-based institutions were already present in society, contributing in sectors which today are part of the development practice. There is a legitimate place of faith in society that should be reinforced. This affirmation and acceptance of religion in development is again gaining recognition in the development sector. As an example, DFID, the Department of International Development of the British government, has sought to develop faith partnership principles in a bid to work effectively with faith groups in fighting global poverty. In describing their current situation, they noted the avoidance of many development organizations to explicitly discuss how faith and religion influence development. As a way forward, DFID clearly puts religion back on the agenda of development. It is therefore important that "people working in development have sufficient understanding of the role played by faiths in the local, national and global contexts."[469] Faith-based organizations, like World Vision, can be confident and thoughtful about their faith identity, as they express this public role of faith in society.

To express this public role of faith in society, it is important that leadership prioritize Christian values and principles in the organization. This implies the understanding of faith being core to the organization, yet being sensitive to the different pressures at play in the organization. It is about being deliberate in making decisions to move the organization towards its *telos* of practice, described as the positivization of creation laws. As clarified in the analysis, this means more than having statements of its

---

[467] Jochemsen, "A Normative Model for the Practice of Cooperation in Development as a Basis for Social Justice," 138.

[468] Matthew Clarke, "Understanding the Nexus between Religion and Development," in *Handbook of Research on Development and Religion*, ed. Matthew Clarke (Cheltenham: Edward Elgar, 2013), 6.

[469] From their perspective, this reluctance stems from the Western influence of the 'sharp distinction between state and religion'.

Christian faith in its policy documents, but rather for staff members to be involved in robust engagement with the Christian content of the development practice. This engagement with the ability to influence the sense making of staff members have the potential to influence the overall assumptions held by the staff members. It can influence the overall direction of the organization towards the telos of the organization. For robust engagement to happen, it is first important to know what one is engaging with. This chapter attempts to provide content for this robust engagement.

8.1.2 Trinity as the Main Theological Motif

In order to prioritize the Christian faith in an organization, it is important that one is clear what this Christian faith entails. For an organization like World Vision, which operates in so many different faith contexts with staff from different faiths and Christian backgrounds, a standard understanding cannot be assumed. This chapter introduces the Trinity as the main theological motif in the Christian faith that should underpin the faith content of the organization. This understanding of the Trinity is unique to the Christian faith, different from other religious traditions.[470] At the same time, as a central doctrine of the Christian faith, the concept of the trinity is integral to orthodox Christian faith, unifying the different strands of the Christian faith.

The doctrine of the Trinity reveals God as one divine essence manifested in three divine persons.[471] This focus on the Trinity is prevalent in contemporary theology.[472] It has been claimed as "the rallying cry for modern dogmatics after Karl Barth."[473] Not only is it central to a basic understanding of who God is, it has also been central in the explication of different theological disciplines. As an example, in missions, Leslie Newbigin argued that it is "in terms of the Trinity that Christians were able to state

---

[470] Stanley J. Grenz, *Theology for the Community of God*, 7th ed. (Carlisle: Paternoster Press, 1994), 69.

[471] John S. Feinberg, ed., *No One Like Him: The Doctrine of God* (Wheaton, IL: Crossway Books, 2005), 487.

[472] Examples of systematic theologians that elevated the Trinity to the center of their systematic theology include Karl Barth, Jürgen Moltmann, Wolfhart Pannenberg, and Stanley Grenz. For an introduction to the development of the Trinity globally, see Veli-Matti Kärkkäinen, *The Trinity: Global Perspectives* (Louisville, KY: Westminster John Knox Press, 2007).

[473] Oliver D. Crisp and Fred Sanders, eds., *Advancing Trinitarian Theology Explorations in Constructive Dogmatics* (Grand Rapids, MI: Zondervan, 2014), 14.

both the unity and the distinctness of God's work in the forces of man's environment and God's work of regeneration within the soul of man."[474]

This centrality, uniqueness and recent renaissance of Trinitarian accounts renders the Trinity appropriate for the reflection of Christian content for organizations such as World Vision. It can be a starting point for reflection of the Christian content for the development practice done by the organization. At World Vision, review of its core documents shows many references to the Triune God briefly. While this is a good start, these references often presuppose a basic understanding of the Trinity which would not make much sense for non-Christian staff. One example of this claim can be seen in the *Witness to Jesus Christ* policy of World Vision, a key policy relating to the Christian Commitments at World Vision. The only explicit reference to the triune God in this policy states "As witnesses, we testify to God—Father, Son and Holy Spirit—who offers forgiveness and new life through faith in Jesus Christ."[475] This brief statement does not do justice to explicate the Trinity. For individuals who do not yet know the Christian faith, it does not mean much. In addition, while referencing the Father, Son and Holy Spirit, the way these persons relate to each other is not described. It also does not describe how the divine persons together are the Christian triune God. In addition, the text also does not clearly describe how this triune God relate to the world. A clearer articulation of the Trinity can be useful for providing content for engagement with the particularity of the Christian faith. It is particularly useful for explicating the structure of the development practice.

Taking into account the research findings as well as subsequent analyses, this discussion of the Trinity is done constructively. This means that the theological explication is sensitive to challenges brought about by the multi-cultural and religious operational contexts of World Vision. It is also mindful of the challenges of working with non-Christian staff, project partners with different agendas or beneficiaries who have very different worldviews. It also recognizes the broader pluralistic development sector that World Vision works alongside. This includes stakeholders such as donors who have different perceptions of what development constitutes. This theological reflection is therefore done in the spirit of allowing space for differing opinions to exist, yet at the same time clarifying what it means for the organization to pursue its Christian purposes.

---

[474] Leslie Newbigin, *Trinitarian Faith and Today's Mission* (Richmond, VA: John Knox Press, 1963), 32.
[475] World Vision, "Witness to Jesus Christ Policy," Partnership Policy and Decision Manual (16 September 1995).

Theologian Veli-Matti Kärkkäinen's constructive theological approach is appropriated in this theological reflection in light of the needs of the organization. This approach is adopted as Kärkkäinen's approach is unabashedly Christian, yet also sensitive to challenges of theology in the pluralistic "post" world. As a starting point, he describes his constructive theological approach as follows: "Constructive theology is an integrative discipline that continuously searches for a coherent, balanced understanding of Christian truth and faith in light of Christian tradition (biblical and historical) and in the context of the historical and contemporary thought, cultures and living faiths. It aims at a coherent, inclusive, dialogical and hospitable vision."[476] He further describes his approach in his systematic volume *A Constructive Christian theology for the Pluralistic World*.[477] In the following section, this constructive theological approach is introduced, clarifying its appropriateness for theological reflection of the trinity for organizations like World Vision.

8.2 Appropriating the Constructive Theological Approach for World Vision

The constructive theological approach as outlined by Kärkkäinen is used in the theological reflection of the trinity at World Vision. This theological approach engages in "continuous ecumenical and interdisciplinary dialogue."[478] It encompasses five aspects: integrative, coherent, inclusive, dialogical and hospitable. Before focusing on the Trinity as the subject for theological reflection at World Vision, each aspect of this approach is described below, highlighting its usefulness in an organization such as World Vision.

---

[476] Veli-Matti Kärkkäinen, *Christ and Reconciliation* (Grand Rapids, MI: Eerdmans, 2013), 13.

[477] The Constructive Christian Theology for the Pluralistic World is a five volume series that conceives the nature and task of Christian systematic/constructive theology in a new key. While robustly Christian in its convictions, building on the deep and wide tradition of biblical, historical, philosophical, and contemporary systematic traditions, it seeks to engage in present cultural and religious diversity. Veli-Matti Kärkkäinen, *Christ and Reconciliation* (Grand Rapids, MI: Eerdmans, 2013), xi.

[478] Ibid., 12.

8.2.1 Integrative

Theology that is integrative seeks to "utilize the results, insights, and materials of all theological disciplines. This includes fields such as religious studies, ethics and missiology."[479] It doesn't focus only on one discipline in theology, but rather sees links in different theological disciplines. Such an approach has also been echoed by missiologist David Bosch in his seminal work, *Transforming Mission*.[480] In describing missionary theology, David Bosch argues for the centrality of the missionary God in different theological disciplines as they exist to critically accompany this *Missio Dei*. He described the possibility to look for the missionary dimension in the Old and New Testament, in Church history, and even systematic theology.

This integrative aspect is particularly useful for an organization that focuses on the development practice, finding guidance from theology. This organization does not seek to specialize in a particular theological discipline, but rather seeks to find support within theology for a Christian understanding of development practice.

8.2.2 Coherent

One key aspect of the constructive theological approach is the realization that the study of theology should not ultimately be seen as a closed "system" of doctrine, but rather one that is "provisional historical and limited."[481] What is important then is to further advance this understanding of theology, appropriating both theological and non-theological resources through rational thinking. Adhering to coherence theory, Kärkkäinen uses the metaphor of a web to describe how different resources can relate. "Statements are related to other statements and ultimately to the whole."[482] Christian theology finds its "object in God and everything else stemming from the creative work of God." This coherence is found not only in traditional theological settings such as the church, but also evident in the widest possible notion of coherence, including various other resources (cultural, religious, socio-political).[483] What is important in this approach then is to provide a coherent and balanced response.

---

[479] Veli-Matti Kärkkäinen, *Christ and Reconciliation*, 13.
[480] David J. Bosch, *Transforming Mission: Paradigm Shifts in Theology of Mission* (Maryknoll, NY: Orbis Books, 2001), 494–495.
[481] Kärkkäinen, *Christ and Reconciliation*, 14.
[482] Ibid., 13.
[483] Ibid., 15.

Coherence is directly related to the overall theological interpretation that is used in this dissertation with the variety of disciplines used thus far.[484] While working through these different disciplines, the focus lies on how different disciplines shed light on the "creative work of God."[485] These disciplines are not viewed in closed systems, but rather are related to each other in search of answers. Bearing in mind the provisional nature of one's thinking, the theological reflection described in this chapter seeks to further contribute to the theological understanding of Christian organizations. It does not seek to be the final word, but rather an example of providing Christian resources for World Vision to respond to the challenges it faces.

8.2.3 Inclusive

The call for an inclusive vision "allows for diverse, at times even contradictory and opposing voices and testimonies to be part of the dialogue."[486] These voices should be multiperspectival, multidisciplinary and multicultural.[487] Multiperspectivalism has been described as "taking seriously the insights of all voices, especially those previously marginalized from the theological conversation." This inclusive vision recognizes the limitations of one's own position and the relativity because of one's particular environment.[488]

One implication of this inclusive approach is the serious consideration of the context in which theology is done. In calling for an inclusive vision, Kärkkäinen embraces ecumenism and seeks to be sensitive to the global nature of Christianity. This does not mean however that he devalues Christian tradition. For him, theological tradition is the whole heritage of the whole church and should continue to provide value for the growing living tradition. In being sensitive to the global nature of theology, he does not intend for a universal approach. Instead, he believes that this search for global theology is done "by employing theologies that are authentically local in the sense of being reflective of particular locations."[489] Ultimately, inclusive theology seeks to "present and argue for the truth of God in a coherent way that engages the whole catholic church of Christ, men and

---

[484] See Chapter 1 section 1.2 for initial discussion on coherence.
[485] Kärkkäinen, *Christ and Reconciliation*, 15.
[486] Amos Yong, *The Spirit Poured Out on All Flesh: Pentecostalism and the Possibility of Global Theology* (Grand Rapids: Baker Academic, 2005), 240.
[487] Yong, *The Spirit Poured Out on All Flesh*, 240.
[488] Kärkkäinen, *Christ and Reconciliation*, 17.
[489] Ibid., 21.

women, rich and poor, people from different ethnic and racial backgrounds."[490]

An inclusive approach in theology for an organization like World Vision which operates internationally is one that respects the local context. One way that this can happen is the intentional effort to embrace the different Christian traditions in the different contexts. Instead of insisting for a universally theological vision, it takes time to deliberate what it means in the specific context. What brings the different Christian traditions together is the development practice that the organization seeks to embrace. As an organization, World Vision has sought to be inclusive by embracing ecumenism since 1992 despite its founding as an evangelical organization.[491]

This call for an inclusive vision is also supported by sociological research that shows evidence of broader Christian ecumenism in Christian institutions. Religious sociologists have found that institutions which embody Christian thought in society can easily find themselves in a minority position. Against the backdrop of this broader pluralism, finer points of dogma in the different organizations seem to take a backseat.[492] As a means to strengthen their position in the broader society, these organizations work together. In addition to facilitating working together from a practical point of view, developing an inclusive Christian vision enables the theological understanding to be more relatable to the different contexts that the organization works in.

8.2.4 Dialogical

A dialogical vision highlights the importance of theology to engage with other faiths. It seeks to relate the Christian vision to the broader society. For Moltmann, to be capable of dialogue is to have "interest in the other religion, an open-minded awareness of its different life, and the will to live together."[493] This involves moving out of the Christian fraternity, where the "coherent argumentation of the truth of Christian doctrine must be

---

[490] Kärkkäinen, *Christ and Reconciliation*, 21.
[491] The Guiding Beliefs: The Church and World Vision document was developed in lieu of this organizational development. See World Vision, "Guiding Beliefs: The Church and World Vision," Partnership Policy Manual (19 September 2002).
[492] Barbara Hargrove, *The Sociology of Religion: Classical and Contemporary Approaches* (Arlington Heights, IL: Harlan Davidson, 1989), 151.
[493] Jürgen Moltmann, *Experiences in Theology: Ways and Forms of Christian Theology*, trans. Margaret Kohl (Minneapolis: Fortress Press, 2000), 18.

related to not only the internal but also the external spheres."[494] With a dialogical vision, religious studies, theology of religions and comparative theology become a part of the theological approach as they explicate other faiths. They are not "a materially different methodological choice, but should rather be seen as a necessary refinement and expansion of methodological orientation."[495]

In the same way, theological reflection done at World Vision, an international organization, should take seriously the different religious context in which it works. This implies the need to actively engage with other faiths, keeping an open mind to the possibility of learning from more about the development practice, yet at the same time, staying steadfast to one's faith claims.

8.2.5 Hospitable

The final aspect of this constructive theology is the importance of being hospitable. In order to be truly dialogical and inclusive, Kärkkäinen speaks about the need of a hospitable vision. This hospitable vision "honors the otherness of the other. It also makes space for an honest, genuine, authentic sharing of one's convictions."[496] At the same time, constructive theology also "seeks to persuade and convince with the power of dialogical, humble and respectful argumentation."[497] In describing hospitality, Kärkkäinen appropriated the understandings of Derrida and Levinas of 'the other', including the obligation of "unconditional hospitality" to those who are different.[498] For him, theology should be welcoming, not oppressing, particularly towards those who are different. Relationships with the other should be marked by grace, not violence.[499]

For World Vision to be truly hospitable in their theological reflection, it is important to have deep seated respect for the other while staying true to oneself. Drawing from its Christian roots, World Vision will have their own unique understanding of what good means. Instead of forcing others to insist on the same understanding of good, space should be created by inviting others for a discussion through "dialogical, humble and respectful argumentation."[500] This space for dialogue happens as World Vision's staff

---

[494] Jürgen Moltmann, *Experiences in Theology*, 18.
[495] Kärkkäinen, *Christ and Reconciliation*, 24.
[496] Ibid., 29.
[497] Ibid.
[498] Ibid., 31.
[499] Ibid., 32.
[500] Ibid., 29.

members work with others in the field. It is therefore critical that this theological reflection cascades down to the work activities of the organization instead of remaining at the policy level.

In this section, we have introduced the constructive theological approach that is appropriated for the theological reflection of World Vision. The way these different aspects can contribute to the theological reflection at World Vision have also been explicated. Having described this approach, we move on to the actual reflection on the Trinity.

8.3 The Trinity

The Trinity has been described as particular to the Christian faith. While a key doctrine in the Christian faith, it is not found in the Scriptures in any exact formula. It is instead a "logically warranted inference" from what Scripture says about God.[501] As a core tenet to the Christian faith, the Trinity is recommended as the main Christian content for the identity formation of the organization that staff members should engage in. This reflection of the trinity is done taking into consideration the constructive theological approach that has been introduced above.

In reflecting on the Trinity, this dissertation recognizes the rich tradition of theological reflection on the trinity. It is beyond the scope of this chapter to provide a systematic explication of the trinity. What is intended is the constructive appropriation of the Trinity as Christian content for organizations like World Vision to engage in as it seeks to strengthen their Christian identity. This is particular useful for developing a deeper understanding of the telos of the development practice, as well as the direction that one should take within the practice.

Four main sections are discussed in this reflection of the trinity in preparation for the engagement of this content by staff members. Firstly, the importance of the Trinity in Christian tradition is further underscored. Secondly, this conversation narrows the discussion on the Trinity as historical revelation. As God's character is revealed in his actions in the world, what happens in the world continues to be important to him. This characteristic of God leads to the understanding of the triune God as the *Missio Dei*, where World Vision participates in the mission particularly in the quest for justice in its expression of development practice. Finally, each divine person of the Trinity is studied separately for particular insights into the development practice.

---

[501] Feinberg, *No One Like Him*, 438.

8.3.1 Importance of the Trinity in Christian Tradition

The Trinity has been part of the Christian faith since its early years. This section gives a brief introduction to its inception. This introduction does not pretend to be historically comprehensive in nature, as it is impossible in the context of this dissertation. What it does seek to do is articulate how the Trinity has been central since the early years of the Christian faith. The Trinity bridges the Jewish roots and the revelation of Jesus. In fact, reformed theologian Herman Bavinck goes as far to say that "the entire Christian belief stands or falls with the confession of God's Trinity. It is the core of the Christian faith, the root of all its dogmas, the basic content of the new covenant."[502]

At the start of the Christian faith, early Christians struggled with the theological puzzle of how Jesus, who they believed, is related to the Jewish God. Stemming from its Jewish roots, the Christian faith was a continuation of what God initiated in the covenant with Abraham. In this covenant with Abraham, it was made clear that there was only one God and that this God alone was to be the object of worship. At the same time, early Christians, through their experiences, believed that God was revealed pre-eminently in the person of Jesus of Nazareth who had also given the ministry of the Holy Spirit, which enabled them to enjoy an intimate fellowship with the living God. This seeming contradiction finally came to a head in 318AD in the Arian controversy. Arius argued that while Jesus was a divine being, he was not God. He was instead a creature, truly human. Being human meant that he needed salvation, to be joined to God by grace and free will. It was this Arian controversy that sparked the call for the council of Nicea, whose first order of business was to clarify the nature of Jesus.[503] The council of Nicea in 325, further clarified the relationship of Jesus with God the Father. It was agreed that Jesus Christ, while the Son of God, was essentially the same substance as the Father. "... in one Lord Jesus Christ, the Son of God, the only begotten of his Father, of the substance of the Father, God of God, Light of Light, very God of very God, begotten, not made, being of one substance with the father..."[504] This creed took pains to clarify who Jesus was, an equal of the Father in being God.

---

[502] Herman Bavinck, *Reformed Dogmatics: God and Creation*, ed. John Volt, trans. John Vriend (Grand Rapids: Baker Academic, 2004), 260.

[503] For more information about Arius, see Roger E. Olson, *The Story of Christian Theology: Twenty Centuries of Tradition and Reform* (Downers Grove, IL: IVP Academic, 1999), 141–150.

[504] Henry Percival, *The Seven Ecumenical Councils, Vol 14, Library of Nicene and Post Nicene Fathers*, 2nd series (New York: Charles Scribners, 1990), *Vol XIV*, 3.

What was not fully clarified in AD325 was the relationship of the Holy Spirit to both God the Father and the Son. This was rectified at the Council of Constantinople in 381. At this council, there was further expansion of the creed to include the understanding of the Holy Spirit. Instead of the statement "And we believe in the Holy Ghost" of the Nicean council, the Council of Constantinople substituted "And we believe in the Holy Ghost, the Lord and Giver of Life, who proceeds from the Father, who with the Father and the Son together is worshipped and glorified, who has spoken through the prophets."[505] With this change, the Holy Spirit was understood in its full deity, worshipped together with the Father and the Son.

Together, these two creeds exhibited the commitment of the early Church to clarify the relationship between each of these divine persons. These creeds were constructed as a response to the grave theological problems faced in their times, of needing to reconcile the inherited commitment to the confession of one God with the Lordship of Jesus Christ, and with the experience of the Spirit that the first Christians had.

Since then, this understanding of the Trinity has been part of orthodox Christian faith tradition. As an organization that professes to be broadly Christian, the trinity is a rich theological doctrine that is worth engaging with. One key aspect for engagement is the understanding of the Trinity as revelation in the world.

8.3.2 The Trinity as Revelation in the World

Traditionally the study of the Trinity has evolved in two main ways. The first way focuses on relationships among the three divine persons, often described as the immanent (or ontological) understanding of the Trinity. The immanent Trinity refers to "God in himself, and concerns the internal relations members of the Godhead have with one another." The second way of studying the Trinity focuses on the way the triune God, as Father, Son and Holy Spirit, relates to the world, otherwise described as the economic Trinity. In discussing the Trinity for an organization like World Vision, the second approach is emphasized. This follows in the footsteps of Kärkkäinen who describes the Trinity as primarily historical revelation. This triune God reveals himself through time in this world. This understanding can be useful for organizations that are part of the world, seeking to do something good with the starting point in the Christian faith.

The events related to the Trinity, otherwise described as the triune event, is clearly linked to the history of the world. In fact, it can be argued

---

[505] Henry Percival, *The Seven Ecumenical Councils*, 3.

that any access to any knowledge of God moves up, so to speak, from the observation of "God's work in creation, providences, reconciliation, and consummation."[506] In the same way, this discussion about the Trinity can be traced back to how God relates to the world as described in the biblical narrative. "It is in the doctrine of the Trinity that we feel the heartbeat of God's entire revelation for the redemption of humanity."[507] Reflecting on the Trinity sheds light on how God relates to the world. Instead of being aloof, God is very much present and active in the world.

World Vision represents a small part of the universal history of the world. To reflect on the Trinity in the engagement of it's Christian vision is to be intentional about the presence of the triune God in the journey of World Vision. Such reflection takes the entire Christian narrative seriously, from creation to eschatology, intentionally considering how the Christian development organization fits into the narrative. It presupposes the Trinity and the biblical story as core to the development practice that the organization seeks to express. As an organization that embraces the identity of the Christian God, the organization should strive to "live in the biblical story as part of the community whose story it is, find in the story the clues to knowing God as his character becomes manifest in the story, and from within that indwelling try to understand and cope with the vents of our time and the world about us and so carry the story forward."[508] This speaks of the centrality of the biblical narrative in the understanding of development practice and the overall expression of this development practice in an organization context.

There are two main ways that World Vision can engage and reflect on the Trinity. This is discussed in detail below. In the first way, the triune God is further described as a sending God where World Vision participates in the mission of God. It is the triune God who forms the basis of understanding for the *Missio Dei*. Secondly, a deeper understanding of each of the divine persons individually can provide further insights into Christian perspectives in the development practice. This goes beyond a denominational divide. An intentionally ecumenical and inclusive discussion looks at how deeper understanding of the different divine persons tapped from different Christian traditions can further enrich the understanding of World Vision, an organization who seeks to move towards the direction of following God's law in the development practice.

---

[506] Kärkkäinen, *Trinity and Revelation*, 255.
[507] Bavinck, *Reformed Dogmatics: God and Creation*, 260.
[508] Leslie Newbigin, *The Gospel in a Pluralist Society* (London: SPCK, 1989), 99.

8.3.3 *Missio Dei* rooted in the Triune God

Thus far we have looked at the Triune God and its relation to this world. One way that this understanding of the Trinity was further developed was through focusing on the sending nature of God. The term, *Missio Dei*, the Mission of God, coined by German missiologist Karl Hartenstein, used the term to summarize the teaching of Karl Barth, who connected mission with the activity of God himself. The classic doctrine of the *Missio Dei* included the doctrine of the Trinity: God the Father sending the Son and God the Father and the Son sending the Spirit. This was then expanded to include sending the church into the world. This notion of *Missio Dei* reached a peak in missionary thinking at the Willingen Conference of the IMC in 1952.[509]

The understanding of the *Missio Dei* continues to be important for theologians today. Old Testament scholar Christopher Wright writes about the Bible as a product of and witness to the ultimate mission of God.[510] He described this as the missional hermeneutic of the Bible. From the Bible "the story of God's mission through God's people in their engagement with God's world for the sake of the whole of God's creation's is affirmed."[511] According to Wright the separate stories found within the Bible can be categorized into a wider metanarrative to think about God's mission. There are four main sections to this metanarrative: a) Creation: A God of purpose in creation, b) Fall: The conflict and problem generated by human rebellion against that purpose, c) Redemption: God's redemptive purposes being worked out on the stage of human history, and d) Future Hope: Horizon of its own history with the eschatological hope of a new history.[512] From Wright's perspective, the biblical narrative shows clearly how God's mission was always intertwined with his people. God is not absent or aloof. He is constantly interacting with his people, "is passionate, responsive and deeply relational."[513] As the triune God, God the Father sends his Son, and together, God the Father and Son send the Holy Spirit. The purpose of this sending was for the reconciliation of the world back to him. Instead of leaving his people alone, his mission was about his people and how he could redeem them back to himself. This understanding of the sending God

---

[509] Bosch, *Transforming Mission*, 390.
[510] Christopher J.H. Wright, *The Mission of God: Unlocking the Bible's Grand Narrative* (Downers Grove, IL: InterVarsity Academic, 2006), 48.
[511] Ibid., 58.
[512] Ibid., 64.
[513] Kärkkäinen, *Trinity and Revelation*, 287.

can be useful to understand World Vision's role as a Christian organization that is being sent.

8.3.3.1 Responding to the Missio Dei

In the doctrine of the *Missio Dei*, the church is sent by God to reconcile the world back to him. This reconciliation, described as "mission," is however not deemed positively in today's world. Instead, it often conjures up negative images.[514] The focus on the sending God can help in addressing the negative images related to mission. It affirms the emphasis on the character of God first before looking at the methods involved in mission. This has sometimes been described as the distinction between missions and Mission. Mission is understood as God reconciling his people to himself, and missions as the different ways that the church participates in this Mission. This is dependent on the specific times, places and needs. Such a distinction highlights missions as derivative, finding themselves in the source of the sending God.[515]

The sending God is a reconciler, bringing the world back to him. He seeks to foster his peace – shalom. Being a God of shalom, He is not inherently violent despite the alleged link between religion and violence.[516] Taking the cue from the nonviolent God, the church participating in his mission should also seek to participate in a nonviolent way. It is the agent of God's mission, the "instrument that God uses, representing God in and

---

[514] As examples of this negative image, mission has been perceived through its link to colonial expansion, occupation of land, conquests of other religion etc. In addition, the advancement of science and technology in society, as well as the ebbing influence of churches in the West, has led to the perception of increased secularization and guilt attached to the complication and crisis of mission. See David J. Bosch made this introductory point in his book transforming mission. He criticized the traditional understanding of the term before setting out his thesis of the Christian faith as a missionary faith. See Bosch, *Transforming Mission*, 1–4.

[515] Newbigin, *The Gospel in a Pluralist Society*, 135.

[516] Kärkkäinen, *Trinity and Revelation*, 324. Kärkkäinen makes four general statements to defend this claim. Firstly, he notes that violence was a mainstay in the ancient world. The Bible was not unusual in its passages about violence. Secondly, part of the understanding of the theology of revelation is the focus on progressive revelation. "God takes people at the level they are and patiently, over the ages, shapes them. To that progressive revelation also belong nuancing, balancing and finally forbidding the right to violence." Thirdly, through Jesus Christ, violence has been "superseded and replaced with unconditional love and embrace" and finally, violence is part of the fabric of the fallen world, it "will not come to an end until the righteous rule of God." See Ibid., 329, 330.

over against the world, pointing the world to God, holding up the God-child before the eyes of the world in a ceaseless celebration of the Feast of the epiphany." The church witnesses to the fullness of the promise of God's reign and participates in the ongoing struggle between that reign and the powers of darkness and evil.[517] As the agent of God's mission representing God, it is important to remember that what counts is more than the activities or priorities which the church undertakes. Instead, it is through the church's "total of a community enabled by the Spirit to live in Christ, sharing his passion and the power of his resurrection."[518] Together, the words and acts of the church reinforce each other, enabling the church to represent God

As the *Missio Dei* sends the church, the question that pertains to this dissertation is what about organizations like World Vision? What role do they play in participating in the sending process of God? Without getting into an in-depth ecclesiological discussion, this dissertation restates that because these organizations belong to the broader Christian pluralism within society, they are clearly part of the broader Christian family sent by God. This understanding is echoed by World Vision as its policy clearly states that World Vision "understands itself to be part of the one universal church with a particular calling and ministry to serve the poor in the name of Christ". It does not claim to be a "substitute, competitor or replacement for the Church." Instead, it seeks "to work with the diverse expressions of the church in the context of its work."[519] It is therefore clear from its policy statements that World Vision understands itself as participating in the mission of God. In the next section, the specific way that World Vision should participate in the mission of God is described.

8.3.3.2   World Vision as Primarily Participating in the Quest for Justice

To determine how World Vision participates in this mission of God, the understanding of the different elements that together constitute missions as described by Bosch is appropriated. These different elements, described collectively as the emerging ecumenical paradigm of missions was explicated for the postmodern paradigm of the world. For him, these elements are ecumenical and interlinked in nature. His list comprises of the following elements: mission as the church with others, *Missio Dei*, meditating sal-

---

[517] Bosch, *Transforming Mission*, 391.
[518] Newbigin, *The Gospel in a Pluralist Society*, 137.
[519] World Vision International, "Guiding Beliefs: The Church and World Vision."

vation, as quest for justice, as contextualization, as liberation, as inculturation, as common witness, as a ministry by whole of the people of God, as witness to people living of other faiths, as theology, and as action in hope.[520] In appropriating this list for World Vision, we recognize that this list is interrelated. These are not isolated and distinct components. It is argued that World Vision, in its expression of the development practice, primarily participates in the *Missio Dei* through her focus on the "quest for justice." This quest for justice takes seriously the social responsibility inherent in the Christian faith. As World Vision seeks to express the development practice, this is done in the context of working in society. At the same time, it is also clear that there can be other elements of missions involved in the work that World Vision does, these elements however take a more secondary role.

Social justice validates the important role of Christian faith in attending to social issues. This involves engaging the wider public, developing intentional coherence, working alongside other partners to uphold justice. True hospitality is also necessary in the quest for justice as it intentionally cares about the issues of others, accepting them for who they are.

As a faith-based organization, World Vision should participate in social justice by advocating an understanding of reality coherent with a Christian worldview in relation to broader society. This does not however mean that the organization expects everyone to embrace the Christian worldview. What is expected then is robust theological reflection for this Christian worldview in society and also the motivation to exhibit hospitality, where there is an intentional reaching out to the stranger, the other. Such a posture acknowledges religious differences that exist in society. However, this does not mean the mere toleration of differences. It goes a step further, accepting the other as different, welcoming the other for the glory of God. This implies "surrendering our biases: to make the interests, joys and sorrows of the stranger our own."[521]

8.3.3.2.1 Continued Importance of Evangelism?

While affirming participation through social justice, it is also clear from World Vision's documents that evangelism, described as witness, is important for World Vision as depicted in its core documents. In the *Witness to Jesus Christ* policy, "Witness to Jesus Christ" is seen as "an integrating principle in all that we do and one of the core ministries in World Vision

---

[520] David J. Bosch, *Transforming Mission*, 10.
[521] Kärkkäinen, *Trinity and Revelation*, 330–331.

Mission Statement."[522] World Vision testifies to "God—Father, Son and Holy Spirit—who offers forgiveness and new life through faith in Jesus Christ."[523] At the same time, this witness affirms "Christ's authority over the whole of creation—persons, communities, systems, structures and nature."[524] While clearly present in the core documents, it is also clear that this focus on witness has waned as the organization developed. As an illustration, the model of ministry framework outlined in 2010 did not mention the role of Christian witness at all. This document, created to bring together the different strategies and visions of World Vision, described the goal of World Vision as "sustained well-being of Children, within families and communities, especially the most vulnerable."[525] From this document, it can be clearly seen that the Christian role has diminished to be part of some ministry principles and approaches, instead of an overarching role.

While it has been argued that the quest for justice rather than evangelism is the primary element of missions that should be focused on, this does not mean that evangelism should be ignored in the organization. As elements of the missionary paradigm described by Bosch, evangelism and the quest for justice are not separate, but are clearly interlinked. There is a close link between this quest for justice and evangelism. This understanding was also echoed in the International Congress on World Evangelization in Lausanne in 1974, which stated that "evangelism and socio-political involvement are both part of our Christian duty. For both are necessary expressions of our doctrines of God and man, our love for our neighbor and our obedience to Jesus Christ."[526]

In light of the continued importance of witness, there is a need to critically reflect and engage on the importance of evangelism in the work that World Vision does. This means not avoiding the conversation but clarifying what it means, looking and aligning with external sources. As an example, Micah Network, a loose global alliance of evangelical Christian development NGOs, has sought to differentiate evangelism and proselytism in the following way: Evangelism has been described as "longing to see people coming to a personal faith in Jesus Christ," and proselytism "'unjustified manipulation or use of coercive techniques or force to achieve

---

[522] World Vision, "Witness to Jesus Christ Policy," Partnership Policy and Decision Manual (16 September 1995).
[523] Ibid.
[524] Ibid.
[525] See http://www.wvi.org/development/publication/ministry-framework-0 (accessed August 10, 2016).
[526] See point 5 of Lausanne Movement, "The Lausanne Covenant," 1974, accessed August 15, 2016, https://www.lausanne.org/content/covenant/lausanne-covenant.

conversion."[527] Evangelism refers to the deliberate efforts of articulating what God has already done in history and thereby inviting a response.[528] "The work of Christ has put the world on its way to full salvation and is realizing its destiny. Because of what Christ has done, people can be liberated from whatever power frustrates the flourishing of life."[529]

One way that evangelism can be engaged in the development practice is through continued focus on an individual's spirituality in the development process. This involves caring about the individual's faith journey, providing an opportunity to learn about the Christian God, the redeemer of all people. Individuals are presented a clear opportunity for evangelism, when they are told what God has done, is doing and will do. It is an invitation, aimed at a response.[530] Based on World Vision's model of ministry framework, one of the aspirations of the goal of child well-being was "Experience love of God and their neighbors." At first glance, the outcomes related to this aspiration does not explicate what this love of God is. It leaves one to wonder the extent to which the Christian God is described and communicated, and if World Vision truly has seized the opportunity for witness.[531] This can certainly be a starting point for further engagement.

At the same time, it is imperative that World Vision be particularly sensitive about not pressuring people but rather extending an invitation. This is important because of the inevitable imbalance of power present with a development organization.[532] One way that organizations like World Vision can witness to the Christian God is through the "possibility of living

---

[527] Micah Network, "Proselytism Policy Statement," 2007, accessed August 15, 2016, http://www.micahnetwork.org/sites/default/files/doc/library/proselytism_policy_statement.pdf.
[528] Bosch, *Transforming Mission*, 412–413.
[529] Henk Jochemsen, "A Normative Model for the Practice of Cooperation in Development as a Basis for Social Justice," in *Challenges of Moral Leadership*, ed. Patrick Nullens and Steven C. van den Heuvel (Leuven: Peeters, 2015), 143.
[530] Bosch, *Transforming Mission*, 412–413.
[531] Based on the ministry framework, outcomes related to "Experience love of God and their neighbors include "Children enjoy positive relationships with peers, family, and community members, Children grow in their awareness and experience of God's love in an environment that recognizes their freedom, Children value and care for others and their environment, Children have hope and vision for the future." These outcomes do not discuss what this love, hope and vision might look like from a Christian perspective.
[532] Steve Bradbury, "Mission, Missionaries and Development," in *Handbook of Research on Development and Religion*, ed. Matthew Clarke (Cheltenham: Edward Elgar, 2013), 425.

and doing development in a way that evokes questions to which the gospel is the answer."[533] This means that the way that World Vision completes its goal is important. It is important to critically consider how to live and do development in a way that evokes questions, namely, what kind of God is reflected in the work that is done?

8.3.3.2.2 Social Justice and Evangelism as Enabling Human Flourishing

The previous section described evangelism as intertwined in the quest for justice that World Vision does. Together, this quest for justice and evangelism at World Vision should lead to human flourishing. Operating in the public space, the term flourishing can be useful as this term is readily used in the public sphere. As a theme, it forms a good basis for encouraging dialogue with other religions. This has been the motivation of public theologian Miroslav Volf, in his book *Flourishing*.[534] Convinced of the importance of religion in society, he sought to show "how people with Christian convictions should relate to other religions and to globalization as well as how adherents of other world religions should relate to one another and globalization."[535] For him, speaking about flourishing is a good opportunity to dialogue with other faiths as it provides a broader framework to discuss overlapping visions of what the good life is.[536] Before having this dialogue, it is important for the organization to first establish an understanding of what this flourishing looks like from the Christian perspective. Three main points to flourishing are explicated here.

Firstly, flourishing can be understood in Christian faith as reconciliation to God as God actively relates to human creatures.[537] In one way, human beings "flourish" simply "in virtue of God's relating to it creatively." It is not through one's own efforts, but rather through being a creature of God. This "grounds the conviction that it (humans) has (have) a dignity that deserves unconditional respect no matter how diminished." One of the main implications this has for the quest for justice is the focus on people. "The human being and his or her well-being should be the end of all

---

[533] Myers, *Walking with the Poor*, 210.
[534] See Miroslav Volf, *Flourishing: Why We Need Religion in a Globalized World* (New Haven, CT: Yale University Press, 2015).
[535] Volf, *Flourishing*, 19.
[536] Ibid., 20.
[537] David H. Kelsey, "On Human Flourishing: A Theocentric Perspective," Yale Center for Faith and Culture Resources, accessed February 11, 2016, http://faith.yale.edu/sites/default/files/david_kelsey_-_gods_power_and_human_flourishing_0_0.pdf.

economic, social and political processes."[538] This focus on people is also the reason for continued evangelism, as seeking the flourishment of the other.

Another way that human beings "flourish" from a Christian perspective is when they "glorify God as they relate to God in response to God's relating to create them, including ways in which they relate to fellow human creatures and to their shared creaturely contexts so as to be loyal to their well-being." This understanding of flourishing focuses on relationships, first with God, second with other humans and even with the environment. The relationship with God is a response to the *Missio Dei* who has been pursuing his people. Besides being God the Father who creates, he is God the Son, Jesus who relates to created human beings, drawing them to himself,[539] as well as Holy Spirit, the "ever present life giving life supporting and energizing spirit of God."[540] To consider the relationship of an individual to this God is to consider flourishing as more than just material needs, but also one's spiritual needs.[541]

Finally, as a means to determine what a flourishing relationship can look like, the relationship among the different divine persons in the Trinity is referred to as a model. This focus on relationships within God as described by Kärkkäinen has been a focus of communion theology. Communion theology looks at God as a "dynamic living, engaging community of the three."[542] It is a fellowship of persons, categorized by "mutual relationality, radical equality and community in diversity."[543] This takes seriously the kind of relationships in the understanding of flourishing. The trinity can be a model of what relationships can aspire to.[544] As people are made in the image of God, the Trinity, as the "divine society" can provide a "pointer toward social life."[545]

An awareness of one's interpretation of flourishing relates to what one pursues as social justice. The section above has presented a Christian perspective of what flourishing constitutes, describing it as "reconciliation to

---

[538] Séverine Deneulin, "Christianity and International Development," in *Handbook of Research on Development and Religion,* ed. Matthew Clarke (Cheltenham: Edward Elgar, 2013), 57.
[539] Kelsey, "On Human Flourishing: A Theocentric Perspective," 3–4.
[540] Kärkkäinen, *Trinity and Revelation,* 338.
[541] Ibid., 58.
[542] Ibid., 320.
[543] Ibid., 321.
[544] In making this proposal, the danger and theological inaccuracy simply to relate the Trinity to a community's social program is noted. The divine community is not an equivalent to a worldly society but rather should inspire society.
[545] Kärkkäinen, *Trinity and Revelation,* 322–323.

God as God's actively relates to human creatures."⁵⁴⁶ This understanding of flourishing values people as created by God, as well as the relationship that people have with God, and subsequently to one another and to creation. It includes a clear relational focus characterized by love. Such an understanding should influence the overall interpretation of the development practice that World Vision is involved in. Having articulated a Christian vision of flourishing, we can now look at how flourishing as a concept can be a good basis for useful dialogical common ground within a pluralistic context.

8.3.3.2.3 Flourishing as Dialogical Common Ground

A Christian vision for flourishing presents itself as a starting point for dialogue with the other. Dialogue is not a neutral, disinterested exercise, but very much confessional in nature. It requires an open mind to the possibility of learning from others, yet at the same time, to be clear about one's faith claims.⁵⁴⁷ Dialogue needs to be executed in the spirit of hospitality, involving invitation, response and engagement.⁵⁴⁸ To speak about dialogue is to hope for authentic engagement between World Vision and the community. This means more than the prescription of development goals for the community. This dialogue entails the engagement with the existing

---

[546] In this brief discussion of human flourishing here on earth, it has not been my aim to equate human flourishing as the end goal of the Christian faith. The Christian faith is not a 'function of serving human needs.' Rather the concept of flourishing is part of an integrated broader holistic Christian vision that also include elements like salvation. It includes meaningful life on this earth, but also hope for the life to come. Kärkkäinen, *Trinity and Revelation*, 364.

[547] As an example of dialogue taking place academically, the understanding of flourishing as outlined in the capabilities approach, as well as Dietrich Bonhoeffer has been ventured. See Steven van den Heuvel, "The Flourishing of Human Life: Fostering a Dialogue between Theology and the Capabilities Approach Through Dietrich Bonhoeffer," *Theologica Wratislaviensia* 11 (2016): 55–66. In this paper, it is argued that despite their different starting points, there is a significant convergence regarding the vital theme of bodiliness. Instead of focusing on the differences, together, more can be achieved in the understanding of flourishing.

[548] Veli-Matti Kärkkäinen, *Trinity and Revelation: A Constructive Christian Theology for the Pluralistic World, Volume 2* (Eerdmans, 2014),364.

values of the community, responding to needs that are relevant and appropriate to the community.[549] This presents the organization with the opportunity to opt for moving towards the Christian direction. So important is the role of dialogue, and responding to needs in the community that a normative understanding of development cooperation has been described as "the promotion of the well-functioning of the practices and institutions that are relevant in a certain setting."[550] The context, and subsequent dialogue that takes place in the context where development is taking place is taken seriously.[551]

Finally, dialogue is also beneficial in explaining the work of the Christian organization within the community. The Christian organization should engage in dialogue that examines "the intention and nuance behind religious inspired definitions of mission and human development to reduce suspicion regarding the appropriate misuse of official development funds."[552] This entails an honest discussion to clarify what the organization actually prioritizes as important for the development practice.

Having discussed how World Vision participates in the *Missio Dei*, the following section narrows in on the individual persons of the Trinity, gleaning insights on how they individually can inform the development practice.

8.3.4 The Individual Contribution of the Divine Persons to the Understanding of the Development Practice

Earlier in this chapter, the Trinity has been described in its unity, focusing on how the three divine persons reveal God in this world. As Stanley Grenz puts it, "the Father functions as the ground of the world and of the divine program for creation. The Son functions as the revealer of God, the exemplar and herald of the Father's will for creation, and the redeemer of human kind. The Spirit functions as the divine power active in the world, the

---

[549] Matthew Clarke, "Understanding the Nexus between Religion and Development," in *Handbook of Research on Development and Religion*, ed. Matthew Clarke (Cheltenham: Edward Elgar, 2013), 8.
[550] See chapter 6, section 6.4.1.1
[551] Jochemsen, "A Normative Model for the Practice of Cooperation in Development as a Basis for Social Justice," 138.
[552] Steve Bradbury, "Mission, Missionaries and Development," in *Handbook of Research on Development and Religion*, ed. Matthew Clarke (Cheltenham: Edward Elgar, 2013), 426.

completer of the divine will and program."⁵⁵³ This Trinity illustrates a *Missio Dei*, where World Vision participates in its quest for justice. In this section, we shift our attention to each individual divine person and how they can individually provide further insight useful for understanding development practice. This understanding can provide further content for the development practice. Kärkkäinen, echoing Moltmann, describes the Trinity in constructive theology as beginning with "threeness, Father, Son and Holy Spirit."⁵⁵⁴

Each divine person of the Trinity is unique and worthy of study. Studying each individual divine person can provide a more inclusive Christian vision for World Vision. Different denominations have been observed to give different emphases to the different individuals of the Trinity. For Reformed Christians, particular attention is given to God the Father, Anabaptists as well as mainstream evangelicalism focus on the Son, and finally, in charismatic and Pentecostal circles the focus is on the Holy Spirit.⁵⁵⁵

In the following section, each divine person is focused on separately, detailing the unique contribution of each divine person to the challenge of social justice, particularly with regard to development practice.⁵⁵⁶ A suggested response is given thereafter. Following in the constructive theological approach, it is reiterated that the purpose of the following section is not meant to be systematically comprehensive, but rather, to provide integrative and coherent content for further engagement and reflection.

8.3.4.1 God the Father

Reformed tradition emphasizes God the Father as the one who revealed the law in creation. Creation, grounded in God's goodness is created for the glory of God.⁵⁵⁷ One implication of this is the strong focus on God himself, particularly his sovereignty, and the need for unconditional human obedience.⁵⁵⁸ God the Father is sovereign in all things, over creation, providence,

---

⁵⁵³ Grenz, *Theology for the Community of God*, 86.
⁵⁵⁴ Kärkkäinen, *Trinity and Revelation*, 264.
⁵⁵⁵ Richard J. Mouw, *The God Who Commands* (Notre Dame, IN: University of Notre Dame Press, 1990), 151–152.
⁵⁵⁶ This approach follows in the example of focusing on each divine person in its contribution to moral theology.
⁵⁵⁷ Bavinck, *Reformed Dogmatics: God and Creation*, 432.
⁵⁵⁸ Henk Jochemsen, "Calvinist Spirituality and its Meaning for Ethics," in *Seeing the Seeker: Explorations in the Discipline of Spirituality*, ed. H. Blommestein et al. (Leuven: Peeters, 2008), 465.

salvation and restoration.[559] This sovereignty applies to "the whole of life and all of life." God should not be limited only to the spiritual side of one's life, or in isolating oneself from the rest of society. Instead, God's sovereignty extends to the whole of society. In response to his sovereignty, God's moral commandment is understood as good for the whole of society.[560] This has led Reformed Christians to develop a "faith-inspired understanding" and approach to issues in society at large.[561] This understanding of the sovereign creator is relevant to the social justice efforts involved in the development practice. In the following section, the relationship between creation and God is further described. An understanding of this relationship is vital as the basis for responding to the sovereign God.

8.3.4.1.1 Relationship between Creation and God

To speak about creation is to recognize that the world is created by God the Father. The Father takes the initiative for creation, thinks the idea of the world.[562] "Creation is the handiwork of God the Father, in fact, studying creation "gives an expression of His own character."[563] Reflecting the character of God, creation is normatively structured.[564] It reflects the beauty of God, and because of this link, one can have a basic positive attitude to created reality, to bodily life and to human activity in this world.[565] This implies "a correlation of the sovereign activity of the creator and the beauties of creation—the created order."[566]

Whilst reflecting the handiwork of God the Father, creation unfortunately did not stay in a state of paradise. The fall took place when Adam and Eve disobeyed God, resulting in pervasion of the entire creation.[567] Adam and Eve chose to decide apart from God's commands on what good

---

[559] Ibid.
[560] Mouw, *The God Who Commands*, 151.
[561] Jochemsen, "Calvinist Spirituality," 470.
[562] Bavinck, *Reformed Dogmatics: God and Creation*, 425.
[563] Ibid., 463.
[564] This understanding of creation as revelation to who God is reminiscent to the understanding of natural theology, where God is revealed through his creation. Proponents of such thinking include David van Drunen, *Divine Covenants and Moral Order: A Biblical Theology of Natural Law* (Grand Rapids, MI: Eerdmans, 2014). However, such thinking has also been rejected by key theologians in the 20th century like Karl Barth who believed that God only revealed himself through special revelation.
[565] Jochemsen, "Calvinist Spirituality," 466.
[566] Wolters, *Creation Regained*, 13.
[567] Ibid., 144.

and evil is. In doing so, they destroyed their relationship with God, with each other and with nature.[568] Sin has perverted creation as well as men's understanding of it. This corruption cannot be repaired by mankind alone.[569] At the same time, while sin has led to irreparable corruption, sin has not replaced creation but rather distorted creation.[570] Today's sinful fallen nature continues to possess recognizable characteristics of creation that will shine through despite its brokenness and distortion.[571] Bavinck describes this in the following way: "Sin spoiled and destroyed everything, but because it is not a substance, it could not alter the essence or substance of the creation."[572]

In Reformed thinking, the difference between creation and the effects of sin has been described as the distinction between structure and direction.[573] Structure ultimately roots creation as it attempts to elucidate the constant creational structures in reality. Despite sin and the fall, these structures remain in place. They do not depend on decisions taken by humankind. The decisions humankind takes are described in terms of direction. In his disobedience and guilt humankind can choose to move away from God towards the order of sin resulting in further distortion or perversion of creation or it can, through submission and discernment, move towards God, to the order of redemption.[574] In reality, it is not always obvious what constitutes structure and direction as underlying created structures and their corruption are inextricably mixed. This requires discernment and careful ethical deliberation.

While the story of creation and fall is described primarily in the first three chapters in Genesis, the rest of Scriptures outlines God's redemptive purpose for his people Israel and finally for the whole world. Through the sacrifice of Jesus Christ, the Son of God, there is redemption.[575] The gospel calls people to Jesus and to follow his example of proclaiming his kingdom and doing good. It is in this phase of redemption that we are living. Proclaiming the kingdom of God and doing good includes the possibility of restoring one's fellowship back to God, and the privilege of participating in the restoration and glorification of the creation order.

---

[568] Jochemsen, "Calvinist Spirituality," 466.
[569] This has been described as total depravity.
[570] Wolters, *Creation Regained*, 45.
[571] Ibid., 47-48
[572] Bavinck, *Reformed Dogmatics: God and Creation*, 573,574.
[573] The discussion of direction was first discussed in its role in the normative practice model. See 6.2.2.3 Plurality in Practices Expressed in Organizations
[574] Wolters, *Creation Regained*, 49-52.
[575] Ibid., 57.

At the promised consummation for the people of God, God will come again with his promise of a new heaven and earth. In this new reality, sin will be no more and the world will be filled with God's glory and holiness. This promise of God's coming brings hope. It provides Christians with perspective on their current work. Consummation is not dependent on human efforts.[576] It is God who guides history to its fulfilment in his kingdom in which He will be all in all. While people participate in the redemption of the earth, it is also clear that peoples' efforts in themselves will never result in the new heaven and earth. It remains the work of God to provide the final solution to the earth.

8.3.4.1.2 Responding to the Creator

To respond to God the Father, one needs to first have a strong understanding of God's goodness expressed in creation. This involves one's role in the creation mandate. This creation mandate has been described as the "responsibility of mankind, as co-workers with God to positivize creation laws and apply them to the specific situations in their lives."[577] This entails working towards restoration in all spheres of the original creation while waiting for final regeneration in the second coming.[578] With such an understanding, nothing is neutral but rather a fight between God's kingdom and the world.[579]

This understanding of the sovereignty of God the creator as well as the creation mandate can be applied to the development practice. In fact, the normative practice model that was used to analyze the findings of the field research, appropriates the sphere sovereignty, a key innovation of Neo-Calvinism. It was Abraham Kuyper who developed the idea of "sphere sovereignty" to describe the claims of sovereign Christ to different spheres in life.[580] Based in the biblical narrative, reality as experienced today can be mapped to the redemptive phase of the biblical narrative. As a way to make sense of reality, Kuyper described reality as being made up of different spheres and Christians as performing their different roles in society "to restore, transform and redeem the natural spiritual, cultural and social realms of God's creation; to bear upon society, to influence and to change it, redeeming and claiming it for Christ to whom the whole created order

---

[576] Jochemsen, "Calvinist Spirituality," 467.
[577] Wolters, *Creation Regained*, 15.
[578] Ibid., 58.
[579] Ibid., 60.
[580] Abraham Kuyper, "Sphere Sovereignty," in *Abraham Kuyper: A Centennial Reader* (Grand Rapids: Eerdmans, 1998), 488.

belongs."[581] Since then, this understanding of sphere sovereignty has been worked out by Reformed philosophers, with key proponents such as Herman Dooyeweerd (1889-1977) and D.H. Th. Vollenhoven (1892-1978).

This understanding of sphere sovereignty is a core concept for the normative practice model and has been used to analyze practice. Following in the tradition of Kuyper, it appropriates Dooyeweerd's understanding of created reality as a multiplicity of modal aspects. These modal aspects, each with its ontologically grounded, irreducible dimensions, prevent the possibility of theoretical reductionism. This takes seriously the created order in the ethical analysis done. It is to accept the dependency of creation on the creator.

Specific to the development practice as outlined in the analysis chapter, the historical aspect, more recently also called the formative aspect, has been described as both the qualifying and founding aspect. This aspect gives the development practice its discrete and distinct identity. For the historical/formative aspect, the nucleus is in "the controlling manner of moulding the social process."[582] This refers to the molding and forming of society, taking into consideration the story of the society. One way that the development organization can take into account the story of the society is to take a serious interest in the society. This involves building trusting relationships in such a way that an honest dialogue on fundamental beliefs and convictions in the society is possible.[583]

At the same time, it remains important that certain norms are observed in the molding and forming of society. Henk Jochemsen, the director of Prisma, a Dutch Christian network that brings together twenty-one Christian Development corporations describes the role of the creation motive for Christian organizations with regard to the development practice:

> This emphasizes the unique value and equality of all people as created in the image of God. God the Creator is also the God of the people who holds their leaders accountable (cf. Psalm 82). God has created the world in an ordered way (for example, the plants and animals according to their nature). This requires respect and care for human beings and creatures in their individuality; core value here is stewardship. This motif represents a commitment to doing justice to creatures and creation as a whole and it opposes any exploitation and destruction of God's creation and any absolutization of created reality. So no worshipping of wealth, health or even of nature itself. But

---

[581] Ibid.
[582] Dooyeweerd, *A New Critique of Theoretical Thought*, 1:195.
[583] Jochemsen, "A Normative Model for the Practice of Cooperation in Development as a Basis for Social Justice," 142.

neither of spiritual powers in the world, which originally are also part of the created order but that when they are worshipped, always lead to a form of slavery.[584]

This quote reinstates the implications of God as creator for the development practice. Created equally, people act within a certain structure and are required to be good stewards of creation. Humans have been given the natural environment as God's gift to provide for their needs, but it is a gift they have to cherish and protect. They are stewards, not owners of creation. Material goods are not the property of humans, but ultimately belong to God and serve God's glory."[585] In addition, the understanding of the creation motive takes seriously the danger of reductionism that can take place in the understanding of development, especially if any part of created reality eclipses all other parts of created reality. It is important for creation to be considered in its totality, recognizing that it is God who created it. Factors such as economic growth, total control of life or happiness cannot be used as the only indicator of development.[586] Discussing the creator also implies the role of individuals who are involved in the development process. There is an understanding that "for those who profess that God is the creator of all that exists, not respecting creation implies not respecting God. Humankind are not in control of the pace or the result of what they do. As they work alongside God, they do not ultimately dictate the pace, or the result of what they do. This calls for the importance of perseverance in what they do."[587]

Having looked closely at God the father and the specific implications for the development practice, we turn our attention now to God the son.

8.3.4.2 God the Son

The focus on God the Son, Jesus Christ, has been traditionally emphasized by evangelical Christians, the group that World Vision originated from. To focus on God the Son is to emphasize Jesus Christ, the divine person who shared our human condition. It is to emphasize the gospel as the climax of

---

[584] Prisma, "Development Cooperation and Religion: A Prisma contribution to reflection and policy" (December 2014), 18, http://www.prismaweb.org/media/203248/religion%20and%20development%20cooperation%20prisma%20contribution.pdf.
[585] Deneulin, "Christianity and International Development," 53.
[586] Jochemsen, "A Normative Model for the Practice of Cooperation in Development as a Basis for Social Justice," 142.
[587] Jochemsen, "Calvinist Spirituality," 470.

the biblical narrative: Jesus as the Son of God, his incarnation, ministry, death, resurrection and ascension. In this section, the discussion of Jesus is done in the context of Jesus as the revealer of the kingdom of God. The understanding of the kingdom of God is a powerful impetus as it reveals the goal of the biblical story. It is also directly related to the development practice and has been used broadly in the evangelical circle. For an organization such as World Vision, the kingdom of God can be useful in developing their understanding of social justice.[588] In this section, a brief introduction to how the kingdom of God ended up as an imagery for social justice is first described. This is followed by describing the specific ways in which the kingdom of God can provide further direction to the solving of social problems.

8.3.4.2.1 The Kingdom of God as an Imagery for Social Justice

The kingdom of God was used as an imagery for Social Justice in the movement known as Neo-Evangelicalism. Neo-Evangelicalism, largely taking place in North America was one key historical trend that led to the founding of World Vision. Neo-Evangelicalism, the revival of evangelism, can be traced to the ministry of Billy Graham. As a renowned evangelist, he became central to the National Association of Evangelicals (NAE). As a corporate expression of evangelical churches, the NAE was founded by a group of diverse conservatives who were looking for a less divisive and more constructive association compared to the exclusivist American Council of Churches. Moving away from the anti-intellectual and antiscientific spirit that according to them had discredited original evangelism, this movement proactively published *Christianity Today*, a fortnight publication, as well as produced critical and apologetic literature in different areas, including social issues. This interest in social issues by the NAE included acting upon them. One issue of that time was the cold war. During this period of time, "the patriotism of this nation with the soul of a church was aroused." Speaking about religion favorably and being a church member were understood as part of the American way of life.[589] While the NAE did

---

[588] The Kingdom of God already features in the policy documents of World Vision. such as the Mission Statement or the Witness to Jesus Christ policy. What is however necessary is a longer explication of this Kingdom of God and its relation to social justice.

[589] Sydney E. Ahlstrom, *A Religious History of the American People* (New Haven, CT: Yale University Press, 1974), 951.

not agree with the approaches taken by liberal churches, they were challenged to demonstrate an active concern for these issues.[590]

It is in this context of neo-evangelicalism and the issue of the cold war World Vision was founded. In 1960, World Vision was founded in support of missions in Korea to meeting the needs of the Orient. At that point, World Vision's mission was understood to be about supporting religious people who found themselves in an atheistic community context.[591] However, instead of focusing only on the conversion of the soul, Bob Pierce, the founder of World Vision, was also acutely aware of the impact of spiritual conversion on an individual's social needs. Having witnessed the abandonment by the local community of someone converted to the Christian faith, he became clear that "it was not God's purpose to save her soul, so she can starve to death. God cares, Jesus lived, taught, loved and so the ingredients of wholeness began to come back into the understanding of what is the gospel and what is our ministry."[592] This double concern of both spiritual conversion as well as meeting social needs has been present since the founding of World Vision.

This concern of social needs was present in the Neo-evangelicalism movement as evident in the work of Carl Henry, one of the key theologians in Neo-evangelism and editor of *Christianity Today*. He used the imagery of the kingdom of God in one of the earliest evangelical works on social needs. *The Uneasy Conscience of Modern Fundamentalism* was written "to urge evangelicals the necessity for a deliberate restudy of the whole kingdom question, that the great evangelical agreements may be set effectively over against the modern mind, with the least dissipation of energy on secondary issues."[593] Instead of being stuck in the dichotomy of the social gospel at the left and the fundamentalists at the right, both of which he considered to be wrong, Henry described a kingdom theology that should engage socio-politically yet be rooted in the gospel.[594] This understanding of the

---

[590] Ibid., 959.
[591] Roberta Hestenes, "1996 World Vision International Board Founder's Chair Address," World Vision Partnership Historical Information (1996).
[592] Ibid.
[593] Carl F.H. Henry, *The Uneasy Conscience of Modern Fundamentalism* (Grand Rapids, MI: Eerdmans, 1947), 51.
[594] The social gospel was a North American movement that began late 19th century early 20th century that "concentrates religious interest on the great ethical problems of social life." In this theology of the social gospel, "thy Kingdom come, thy will be done" meant that attention was given to social problems like poverty, economic inequality etc. with social issues prioritized over individual piety. It was

kingdom of God informs the "redemptive priorities of Christianity."[595] Also a lecturer-at-large for World Vision between 1974-1987, Carl Henry had a direct impact on the theological development of World Vision. The kingdom of God was described in policy documents such as the "Ministry Policy Witness to Jesus Christ."[596]

Since Carl Henry, other theologians have followed in his footsteps, imagining the kingdom of God from what is revealed in the gospel. One example of the broad reach of the use of the Kingdom of God is in the International Congress on World Evangelization at Lausanne. This covenant started with clarifying that God was "sending his people back into the world to be his servants and his witnesses, for the extension of his kingdom." As people are "born again into his kingdom" … they "must seek not only to exhibit but also to spread its righteousness in the midst of an unrighteous world."[597] It is this understanding of the kingdom of God that informs the Christian social responsibility.

As a valuable imagery that has taken root in the work of World Vision and the broader evangelical world, the imagination of the kingdom of God is further expounded on. As a theological motif, the kingdom of God has been widely discussed by theologians. In this section, it is impossible to incorporate the broad scholarship done with this topic. What is intended is to broadly increase the understanding of the Kingdom of God through incorporating voices from other different Christian traditions.[598] This inclusivity is useful to incorporate different perspectives in the discussion of the practice of development. We begin by first looking at the relationship

---

charged by evangelical Christians as being liberal, having "lost a genuinely theological perspective, substituting it with a political program." See Carl F.H. Henry, *Aspects of Christian Social Ethics* (Grand Rapids, MI: Eerdmans, 1964), 116.

[595] Carl F.H. Henry, *Aspects of Christian Social Ethics*, 116.

[596] In the Witness to Jesus Christ policy, the Kingdom of God is explicated as "Through the work of Christ and the presence of the Holy Spirit, God's reign is experienced in the present. We believe that God suffers with the poor and oppressed, and the grace and mercy we have received from Jesus Christ compel us to share in the suffering in the world. Evidences of God's reign are seen wherever people show compassion to those who suffer, relationships are reconciled and people live with dignity, justice, peace and hope. We anticipate a future when all creation is restored and suffering and evil are defeated."

[597] Lausanne Movement, "The Lausanne Covenant," 1974, accessed August 15, 2016, https://www.lausanne.org/content/covenant/lausanne-covenant.

[598] This includes theologians like Dietrich Bonhoeffer, Ronald J. Sider., Leslie Newbigin and NT Wright. These theologians represent diverse denominations within the Christian tradition and their relevant theologies will be explicated in the following section.

of the life of Jesus and the kingdom of God. This information is then appropriated for the development practice.[599]

8.3.4.2.2 Jesus and the Kingdom of God

Through the act of coming into the world historically, the reality of God encountered the reality of the world.[600] Jesus came to this earth as the promised messiah of the Jewish people scattered all over the land. As the messiah, his kingdom was described as having no end. As one of the prophecies read, "he will reign on David's throne and over his kingdom, establishing and upholding it with justice and righteousness from that time on and forever."[601] It is therefore no surprise that this kingdom of God was central to his message. In this section, we focus on two aspects of Jesus and the kingdom of God. Firstly, we look at how Jesus reveals the kingdom of God. Secondly, on how his life and ministry exemplifies the characteristics of the kingdom of God.

Jesus reveals the kingdom of God by coming to this earth. In his ministry, Jesus preached that the kingdom of God was at hand.[602] One way that this kingdom of God can be explicated is in understanding proximity as spatial instead of temporal. This reign of God is not a time period but a person, the man Jesus.[603] It is Jesus who represented the reign of God on earth. "The kingdom of God is before all else a person with the face and name of Jesus of Nazareth the image of the invisible God."[604] Jesus Christ as

---

[599] In bringing up the imagery of the Kingdom of God, it is not my intention to negate the importance of the creation order as discussed earlier in the discussion of God the father. Both the discussion on the creation order as well as the kingdom of God can be held together. Oliver O'Donovan points to the resurrection of Christ as the bridge between the Kingdom of God and creation. For him, the resurrection of Christ points towards God's original intention for Adam to live, which in turn, reaffirms the creation order of things in which humanity has a place. At the same time, this same resurrected Christ also reveals the new Kingdom that Christians can look forward to in the eschatological participation in the kingdom of God. To focus solely on the kingdom of God and reject the understanding of creation is likened to a 'denial of its beginnings.' See Oliver O'Donovan, *Resurrection and Moral Order: An Outline for Evangelical Ethics* (Leicester: Inter-Varsity Press, 1986), 15.

[600] Dietrich Bonhoeffer, *Ethics*, vol. 6 of *Dietrich Bonhoeffer Works* (Minneapolis: Fortress Press, 2005), 159.

[601] Isaiah 9:7.

[602] Newbigin, *The Gospel in a Pluralist Society*, 104.

[603] Ibid., 105.

[604] Ronald J. Sider, *One Sided Christianity* (Grand Rapids, MI: Zondervan House, 1993), 263.

the self-revelation of God reveals God's kingdom to humankind. He is the reality of the kingdom in human form.[605] Through the story of Jesus, the world receives its boundaries, its legitimacy and limitation.[606]

There are two implications to Jesus revealing the Kingdom of God. Firstly, this reveals the deeply relational characteristic of this kingdom.[607] Jesus, the Son of God, was sent by God the Father to reveal this kingdom.[608] Secondly, with the kingdom of God founded in Jesus Christ, God's reign has arrived on this earth. This reign on earth is not divided into two realms, the sacred or religious versus the profane or worldly. Only one reality is revealed in Christ. The whole reality of the world has already been drawn into and is held together in Christ."[609] This reality of God and the reality of the world are united. Through Christ, the world is reconciled to God.[610] These two implications are well summarized by John Stott who noted: "The kingdom of God is God's dynamic rule, breaking into human history through Jesus, confronting, combating and overcoming evil, spreading the wholeness of personal and communal well-being, taking possession of his people in total blessing and total demand."[611]

Besides representing the reign of the kingdom, the second aspect that is revealed is the characteristics of the kingdom of God through his life and ministry. "The son of God did not stay in the safe immunity of his heaven. He emptied himself of his glory and humbled himself to serve."[612] From this point of view, Jesus' earthly ministry could be categorized by his suffering. He did not explicitly use his power with the religious authorities but went about in a humble, powerless way which led to his crucifixion. At the same time, his ministry was also filled with mighty works. He did perform great signs and wonders, and also resurrected.[613] Instead of being an odd event, or another new religious possibility, "the resurrection of Jesus offers itself . . . as the utterly characteristic, prototypical, and foundational

---

[605] Another way that this has been described is the kingship of Jesus.
[606] Ronald J. Sider, *One Sided Christianity*, 263.
[607] Jayakumar Christian, *God of the Empty-Handed Poverty: Power and the Kingdom of God* (Victoria: Acorn Press, 2011), 180.
[608] Ibid.
[609] See Bonhoeffer, *Ethics*, 42, 44.
[610] Ibid., 48.
[611] John Stott, Issues Facing Christians Today (Grand Rapids: Zondervan, 2006), 56.
[612] Ibid.,54.
[613] Newbigin, *The Gospel in a Pluralist Society*, 107–108.

event within the world."⁶¹⁴ Through his death and resurrection, Jesus presented a way forward against powers and principalities. This "consists in abiding in him, sharing his passion so that we may share his victory over death."⁶¹⁵ It is only through the service and giving of His life is the kingdom of God accessible. The kingdom of God is a gift, it cannot be earned.⁶¹⁶ As described by Bonhoeffer: "In the body of Jesus Christ, God is united with humankind, all humanity is accepted by God, and the world is reconciled to God. In the body of Jesus Christ, God took on the sin of all the world and bore it."⁶¹⁷

The story of Jesus does not end with the death and resurrection of Christ. Jesus has ascended to heaven and is at the Father's right hand today. Jesus has started something here on earth. His work marks a new beginning in the plan of redemption. However, it is not yet finished. The kingdom of God has "already been inaugurated, yet awaits a future consummation."⁶¹⁸ Jesus in heaven will not stay hidden forever and will someday come back to this world. In his arrival, he will appear as "God's right hand and he will reign in manifest glory."⁶¹⁹ Instead of a delay, this hidden period is an opportunity for all to respond to the life of Jesus. It is an opportunity 'to repent, to be converted and to believe and recognize the presence of the reign of God in the crucified Jesus."⁶²⁰ As a gift to all, this kingdom of God invites a response from those to whom it is presented.⁶²¹

8.3.4.2.3 Responding to Jesus who Reveals the Kingdom of God

The story of Jesus entering into this world reveals the kingdom of God. It is historical, yet at the same time, transcends history. In responding to this Jesus, what is required is not detachment or ambivalence, but rather a "whole person engagement and involvement", otherwise described as love."⁶²² "Love is the deepest mode of knowing because it is love that, while completely engaging with reality other than itself, affirms and celebrates

---

⁶¹⁴ Nicholas T. Wright, *Surprised by Hope: Rethinking Heaven, the Resurrection, and the Mission of the Church* (New York: Harper Collins Publishers, 2008), 67.
⁶¹⁵ Ibid., 114.
⁶¹⁶ Wright, *Surprised by Hope*, 56.
⁶¹⁷ Bonhoeffer, *Ethics*, 54.
⁶¹⁸ Wright, *Surprised by Hope*, 385.
⁶¹⁹ Ibid.
⁶²⁰ Newbigin, *The Gospel in a Pluralist Society*, 106.
⁶²¹ Christian, *God of the Empty-Handed Poverty*, 183.
⁶²² Wright, *Surprised by Hope*, 71.

that other than self-reality."[623] To respond to Jesus is to respond in love in him. It is intentionally subscribing to the underlying plausibility structures of the different knowledge and truths that one loves. "Every exercise of reason depends on a social and linguistic rendition which is, therefore, something which has the contingent, accidental character of all historical happenings."[624]

Responding in love for him requires the desire to "inhabit an alternative plausibility structure that is found in the biblical story."[625] This involves more than articulating a body of ideas but rather, to be part of an actual community. This implies that as an organization, World Vision should aspire to be the faithful community that lives the biblical narrative. It is to be a "faithful witness of Christ" as the revealer of the kingdom during the period of his ascension and his coming again.[626] He, the crucified, risen and regnant Christ is the one in whom the whole purpose of God for cosmic history has been revealed and effected.[627]

To be the faithful community, this includes modeling one's understanding of one's mission on Christ's mission.[628] As Jesus entered the brokenness of this world, his mission was marked with the costly identification with people in their actual situations.[629] At World Vision, this incarnational nature of mission has been taken seriously as noted in the ministry framework.[630] For World Vision to remain this faithful community, this should be actively noted for the organization.

In addition, there are also societal ramifications to the incarnation of Christ. The purpose of God for cosmic history is for all of this world and not for the select few. The resurrection of Christ that happened in this world have implications for and effects on this world.[631] What is done on earth will last into God's future. People are not just saved for the afterlife, but also for life before death. Salvation is not only about "going to heaven," there are also effects on earth. People who have been saved live a life in God's new heaven and new earth, and become a "part of the means by which God makes this happen."[632] In response, these people are to be a sign

---

[623] Ibid.
[624] Ibid., 57.
[625] Ibid., 99.
[626] Newbigin, *The Gospel in a Pluralist Society*, 125.
[627] Ibid.
[628] John Stott, Issues Facing Christians Today, 55.
[629] Ibid., 55.
[630] This was first mentioned in chapter 7, section 7.4.1.2.1.
[631] Wright, *Surprised by Hope*, 191.
[632] Ibid., 198.

and foretaste of what God wants to do for the entire cosmos.⁶³³ This includes proclaiming precisely to this world its reconciliation with God to disclose the reality of the love of God, against which the world so blindly rages.⁶³⁴

Bonhoeffer makes a distinction between ultimate and penultimate things in the life of a Christian in advocating for the work of social reconciliation. The ultimate thing, he described as "the event of justification of a sinner" takes place at the end of time while the penultimate thing consists of events that take place before the end of time.⁶³⁵ The penultimate on the other hand involves "some action, suffering, movement, intention, defeat, recovery, pleading, hoping," taking place during the "time of God's permission, waiting and preparation."⁶³⁶ This penultimate exists in the here and now. It is important to care for this penultimate so as to not hinder the way of the ultimate. Because Jesus entered the world, this penultimate is neither "self-sufficient" or "destroyed."⁶³⁷ Instead, it now exists with the reality of Jesus. By Jesus coming down to earth, taking on humanity and affirming it, the world is reconciled to God and not destroyed. At the same time, this penultimate reality is not self-sufficient. It remains fallen. Not because the "world was worthy that God came down, but precisely because it had fallen did God take up the suffering and 'curse' of the divine No."⁶³⁸ To care for the penultimate is to take the perspective and example of Christ in the world. It "allows the world to be world and reckons with the world as world, while at the same time never forgetting that the world is loved, judged, and reconciled in Jesus Christ by God."⁶³⁹ It acknowledges the real powers of darkness that are present that cannot be eliminated by human projects. As succinctly put, "no human project however splendid is free from the corrupting power of sin."⁶⁴⁰ Evil continues to permeate this world.

Embracing the development practice, an organization like World Vision works towards caring about the penultimate. This implies bringing signs and symbols of God's renewed creation to birth on earth as it is in heaven. It is to respond to the needs of others. "The hungry person needs bread, the homeless person needs shelter, the one deprived of rights need

---

[633] Wright, *Surprised by Hope*, 198.
[634] Bonhoeffer, *Ethics*, 54.
[635] Ibid., 140.
[636] Ibid., 141–142.
[637] Ibid., 150.
[638] Ibid., 262.
[639] Ibid., 264.
[640] Ibid., 138.

justice, the lonely person needs community, the undisciplined one needs order and the slave needs freedom."[641] This involves following Jesus' example who acted and suffered for all men.[642] It is to be the vicarious representation for one's concrete neighbor, considering their concrete reality instead of reducing them to a mere idea or value. Another way that this has been described is in bringing the essence of Christ's personhood: being-there-for-man (*Daseinfürandere*) out in the world.[643] This is done in the spirit of confidence and certainty of Christ, yet also accepting suffering and struggle with "patience and endurance" as Jesus did in his earthly ministry.[644]

8.3.4.2.4 The Development Practice as Caring for the Penultimate

The question that we seek to answer now is how then should World Vision, an organization that seeks to express the development practice care about the penultimate? Two main answers are pursued in this section. Firstly, it is important to note the uniqueness of the context of this development practice and secondly, it is critical to elucidate the goal of the development practice based on the understanding of the kingdom of God.

One unique characteristic found in the context of the development practice is the intentional work with poverty and oppressive structures in society. Liberation theologian Gustavo Gutierrez writes that "Sin is evident in oppressive structures, in the exploitation of humans by humans, in the domination and slavery of peoples, races and social classes. Sin appears, therefore, as the fundamental alienation, the root of situations of injustice and exploitation." Collective sinful actions of individuals create a structure of sin, which in turn influences the behavior of individuals. These sin structures are difficult to change, can create a sense of blindness as it is taken for granted in society, and can often lead to exasperation for the experience of an impossible choice.[645] It is in the particular context of poverty with its existing sin structures that the development practice takes place in.

In the face of this injustice, there is the need to accept that this broken situation is part of the fallen world, bringing about a certain amount of

---

[641] Bonhoeffer, *Ethics*, 156.
[642] Ibid., 258.
[643] Nullens, "Dietrich Bonhoeffer, a Third Way of Christian Social Engagement," 60–69.
[644] Bonhoeffer, *Ethics*, 109.
[645] Gutierrez Gustavo, *A Theology of Liberation* (London: SCM Press, 2000), 62.

realism that "prevents utopian fanaticism."[646] John Stott describes this as one of the six essential "marks" of a Christian mind – the awareness of evil.[647] At the same time, this should not lead to despair, as it is possible to keep one's faith with Jesus. Jesus has defeated the power of evil. Knowing that he has begun his reign on earth and will return someday gives hope. The work that is done today, however incomplete, is done "as an offering to the Lord who is able to take it and keep it for the perfect kingdom which is promised."[648] It is building for the Kingdom that will one day find its way into the new creation that God will make.[649]

In addition, this understanding of the kingdom of God can inform the ultimate goal of development. In describing the future envisaged for communities, Myers described the "unshakable kingdom" as the best future, and the "unchanging person" as the best means.[650] He used the term *shalom* to describe what he meant: "just, peaceful, harmonious, and enjoyable relationships with each other, ourselves, our environment and God."[651] This definition covers more than one kind of brokenness. It is all-encompassing, looking at the physical, social, mental and spiritual manifestations of poverty. In practice, this means that development can include "Immunizing children, improving food security, and providing portable water, . . . reconciliation, peace building and values formation toward the end of including everyone and enabling everyone to make their contribution, . . . working to make social systems, and those who manage and shape them, accountable to work for the well-being, stress counselling, critical incidence debriefing and simply listening and being with those whose poverty begins in the inner heart or broken spirit."[652] In summary, the goal of development practice is life and life in abundance.

Having completed the section of Jesus Christ, the kingdom of God and the plausible response by World Vision, we turn our attention to the Holy Spirit.

8.3.4.3   *God the Holy Spirit*

God the Holy Spirit has been emphasized in the Pentecostal movement as well as the Eastern Orthodox Church, rich in pneumatological and spiritual

---

[646] Gutierrez Gustavo, *A Theology of Liberation* (London: SCM Press, 2000), 62.
[647] John Stott, Issues Facing Christians Today, 61.
[648] Newbigin, *The Gospel in a Pluralist Society*, 115.
[649] Wright, *Surprised by Hope*, 208.
[650] Myers, *Walking with the Poor*, 113.
[651] Ibid.
[652] Ibid.

tradition. Within contemporary theology, the discussion of the Holy Spirit has received renewed attention due to the engagement with the Pentecostal movement as well as the Eastern Orthodox Church in official ecumenical organizations. Has led to a renewed interest in the Holy Spirit.[653]

A deeper appreciation of the Holy Spirit emphasizes experience. As defined by Moltmann, "Christian faith is the experience of the quickening Spirit – experience of the beginning of the new creation of the world."[654] Moltmann referred to experiences as consisting of two references: outward – perception of the thing happening, and inward, the perception of the change in self.[655] He argues that while it can be argued from a modern philosophical perspective the impossibility to describe an outward reference of the objective experience of God, it is still possible to understand the experience of God through an inward reference of the self.[656]

Moltmann includes the experience of God within the inward reference of self. This inward reference of the self is not limited to the individual's experience of his or her own self. It can also include experiences of God. As God is in all things, and if all things are in God, the experience of the Holy Spirit is everywhere. This experience of God "found in human experience of the self has its inalienable and indestructible character."[657] To include the experience of God as one's inward reference is to take seriously the presence of God in one's life.[658] In the following discussion of the Holy Spirit, what is focused on is the understanding of the experience of God, particularly as the completer of the divine program and also the understanding of the Spirit of life, equipping the individual.

8.3.4.3.1 The Spirit as the Completer of the Divine Program

The Spirit is present from the start of time to today. It is possible to trace the presence of the spirit in the biblical narrative throughout history. The Spirit was understood as *ruach*, the life-giving force to his people in the Old Testament. He was "God's creative action and the one by whom God sustains the world."[659] From several incidents in the Old Testament, it can be

---

[653] Veli-Matti Karkkainen, *Pneumatology: The Holy Spirit in Ecumenical, International, and Contextual Perspective* (Grand Rapids, MI: Baker Academic, 2002), 12.
[654] Jürgen Moltmann, *The Spirit of Life*, trans. Margaret Kohl (London: SCM Press, 1992), 68.
[655] Ibid., 23.
[656] Jürgen Moltmann, *The Spirit of Life*, 28-31.
[657] Ibid., 34.
[658] Ibid., 35.
[659] Grenz, *Theology for the Community of God*, 472–473.

said that the Spirit's presence "provided the recipient with the resources necessary to complete a divinely-ordained task."[660] This Spirit continues to be present in the gospel, beginning with the conception of Jesus. In fact, integral "both chronologically and theologically, the operation of the divine spirit becomes the precondition or premise for the history of Jesus of Nazareth."[661] It was the dove present at Jesus' baptism, as well as proclaimed by Jesus to be upon him during the inauguration of his ministry (Luke 4:18-19). Throughout his ministry, there were instances where the Spirit was clearly present with Jesus. During his farewell message to his followers, Jesus promised the Spirit. This Spirit would be a helper, mediating the presence of the Lord with his people.[662] The Holy Spirit was also involved in the resurrection of Jesus. During the event of Pentecost, Jesus' promise to his followers was fulfilled as the book of Acts recorded an outpouring of God's Spirit on his people.[663] It is through the Spirit that mankind can be brought back into fellowship back with God the Father and God the Son.[664]

The Spirit continues to be present in the world today. This Spirit that created the world at the start of time, continues in his role as the Spirit of Life in the world.[665] God's presence reaches into the depths of human existence.[666] As the Spirit, he is "the power of God at work in the world bringing to completion the divine program."[667] This experience of the spirit results in the "category of the new in the biblical history of promise and the glance into the future of the world in that light of Christ's resurrection."[668] The Holy Spirit present from creation onto the sending of Christ, is the same spirit that ultimately effects the new creation of humankind at the end of time. In the meantime, this Spirit is also operating *enroute*, before the final completion of this divine program. Working both in individual lives as well as the wider world, the spirit is bringing the new creation into

---

[660] Grenz, *Theology for the Community of God*, 472–473.
[661] This point was made by Jürgen Moltmann, *The Spirit of Life*, trans. Margaret Kohl (London: SCM Press,1992), 60 who was referencing James D.G. Dunn, *Jesus and the Spirit. A study of the Religious and Charismatic Experience of Jesus and the First Christians as reflected in the New Testament* (London: SCM Press,1975).
[662] As described by Jesus, this Spirit will be a helper, mediating the presence of the Lord with his people. See John 16:12.
[663] Grenz, *Theology for the Community of God*, 479.
[664] Ibid., 489.
[665] Kärkkäinen, *Trinity and Revelation*, 264.
[666] Jürgen Moltmann, *The Spirit of Life*, 42.
[667] Grenz, *Theology for the Community of God*, 472–473.
[668] Jürgen Moltmann, *Ethics of Hope*, trans. Margaret Kohl (Minneapolis: Fortress Press, 2012), 36.

the world. This Spirit is the "pledge of the new creation," the "dynamic by whom God brings creation into existence."[669]

8.3.4.3.2 Holy Spirit Experienced as the Spirit of Life

Besides being the completer of the divine program, the Spirit also acts as the Spirit of life in the world. This implies that through the Spirit, creation is drawn into God's fellowship into true community. "He mediates human participation in the eternal relationship between the Father and the Son."[670] The Spirit is revealed through human experiences, particularly through the transcendent inward side as earlier described. As God is in all things, it is possible to experience God in, with and beneath each everyday experience of the world.[671] This Spirit is not confined to the church, but rather is present in the wider world. He is found in "the wholeness of the community of creation, which is shared by human beings, the earth and all other created beings and things."[672] As the eternal Spirit, he is the "divine well spring of life – the source of life created, life preserved and life daily renewed, and finally the source of the eternal life of all created being."[673] It is through the Spirit that we come to God.

8.4.4.3.3 Responding to the Spirit in the Development Practice

Having described the Holy Spirit as present in one's life experiences and is the completer of the divine program, we can now consider the implication of the Spirit on the understanding of the development practice. In general, the Holy Spirit provides us with the assurance of God's great future for the world. This Spirit is "the active connection between the promised future and the experienced coming of the new creation of all things."[674] There are two main implications to responding to the spirit. Firstly, the need to discern the Spirit that is already at work and secondly, to remember that God's spirit empowers.

As the life-giving Spirit of the world, God is already present in the world. Organizations like World Vision that seek to express development practice participate in the story of the community where God's Spirit is

---

[669] Grenz, *Theology for the Community of God*, 491.
[670] Ibid., 493.
[671] Ibid.
[672] Jürgen Moltmann, *The Spirit of Life*, 37.
[673] Ibid., 82.
[674] Jürgen Moltmann, *Ethics of Hope*, 36.

already present. They are not there alone and should therefore intentionally consider what it means to be part of God's story of redemptive work in the world.[675] It is not the organization's responsibility to set a new agenda for the community, but rather to actively discern the presence of God that is there. This means to "expect, look for, and welcome all the signs of the grace of God at work in the lives of those who do not know Jesus as Lord."[676] The Spirit is already at work where the organization is at. What is important is the discernment of what the spirit is already doing. Moltmann describes this as the "anticipation-ethics of his (Jesus) future."[677] It is about opening one's eyes "to perceive the subsequent outpouring of the Spirit, and the experiences of the vital powers of the divine Spirit, as being 'powers of the world to come' (Heb. 6.5)."[678] This suggests the need for the organization to look for these signs of grace and the experiences of the spirit, instead of blindly following other external agenda, such as donor requirements, or government regulations.

Secondly, the Spirit empowers the people of God. Jesus calls his followers to live in him and by the power of his Spirit, to be new-creation people here and now, bringing signs and symbols of the kingdom to birth on earth as in heaven.[679] This extends to people working at World Vision. People at work in these organizations can have hope because of the active presence of the Spirit.[680] The Holy Spirit is the "universal advocate, chief defender of all". He works against victimizing ideologies, provides incontrovertible proof that, in the long run, there is no life outside of God's norms for life.[681] The work that is done is not in vain. God's people can continue in the work and even be hastening or anticipating.

This entails "go(ing) swiftly in space from one place to another."[682] This means to do what one can to "cross the frontiers of present reality into the spheres of what is possible in the future." It is to move towards the new creation while anticipating the "righteousness and justice out of which, on the Day of the Lord, a new and enduring earth is to come into being."[683]

---

[675] Jürgen Moltmann, *The Spirit of Life*, 114.
[676] Newbigin, *The Gospel in a Pluralist Society*, 180.
[677] Jürgen Moltmann, *Ethics of Hope*, 38.
[678] Ibid.
[679] Wright, *Surprised by Hope*, 209.
[680] Bob Goudzwaard, Mark Vander Vennen, David van Heemst, Hope in Troubled Times: A New Vision for Confronting Global Crises (Grand Rapids: Baker Academix, 2007), 172.
[681] Goudzwaard, Vennen and van Heemst, Hope in Troubled Times, 174.
[682] Jürgen Moltmann, *Ethics of Hope*, 8.
[683] Ibid.

This hastening compels people to pursue justice through the development practice. The development practice is not a passive process, but one that seeks to move towards the new creation. It is done anticipating justice and righteousness, the new creation of the Lord to come. Choosing to follow God is an act of faith. As the Spirit is living, choosing the Spirit can lead to the "experience of the quickening Spirit—experience of the beginning of the new creation of the world."[684]

To choose for the Spirit is to recognize the waiting time between Jesus' resurrection and his return. The goal of work is not completion of the new creation, but rather, to bring signs and symbols. This has been described as the "patient revolutionaries who know that the whole creation, with all its given structures, is groaning in the travail of a new birth, and that we share this groaning and travail, this struggling and wrestling, but do so in hope because we have already received, in the Spirit, the first fruit of the new world (Romans 8:19-25)"[685] This waiting includes an active expectation, hope that "carries the promised future of righteousness into one's own life. God's coming unfolds a transforming power in the present."[686] In addition, waiting also implies "not conforming to the conditions of this world of injustice and violence." People can wait because "they know that a better world is possible and that changes in the present are necessary."[687] Finally, waiting also involves staying steadfast in faith. It entails perseverance in the face of difficulty.[688] The notion of waiting can be useful when thinking about success for the development practice. Besides the completion of specific performance indicators related to project goals, success can also be classified in terms of faithfulness. This means including success to mean resistance from disbelief and persevering in having faith in God's future and in doing good.

8.3.4.4 Ecumenical Understanding from Each Divine Person

Thus far, we noted the particular contribution that each divine person makes to the understanding of the development practice. This information is particularly useful for World Vision as an ecumenical organization. This discussion seeks to be inclusive of different Christian traditions in its interaction with the development practice. Drawing from the understanding

---

[684] Moltmann, *The Spirit of Life*, 68.
[685] Leslie Newbigin, *The Gospel in a Pluralist Society*, 209.
[686] Jürgen Moltmann, *Ethics of Hope*, 7.
[687] Ibid.
[688] Ibid.

of God the Father, God the Son, and God the Holy Spirit can further supplement its existing understanding of the development practice particular in the understanding of the structure as well as the Christian direction.

In making this recommendation for World Vision, it is noted that this information is not exclusive for World Vision. Instead, it can be useful for other Christian organizations wanting to strengthen their understanding of the development practice. This information further strengthens the understanding of the structure of the practice, providing a wealth of knowledge for a Christian directional understanding of the development practice.

8.4 From Content Recommendations to Process Recommendations

This chapter presents the first recommendation in this dissertation, focusing on the Christian content of the identity formation model. An intentional clarification of the Christian faith outlines the particularity of the Christian faith for the development practice. This provides a clearer understanding of the structure as well as the Christian direction that the organization should move towards. Instead of having only a historical role in the organization, there is continued value in engaging with the Christian content to provide relevant information for the organization. This is particular important for an organization that operates in different settings that may or may not have an understanding of the Christian faith.

In recommending how the Christian faith can impact the development practice, the context that the organization is in was taken seriously. As an organization, World Vision works in multi-cultural and religious contexts, employs non-Christian staff, project partners with different agendas or beneficiaries who have very different worldviews surfaced. This context influenced the theological approach used in explicating the Christian content. The constructive theological approach of Kärkkäinen was appropriated in this theological reflection. This constructive theological reflection seeks to be integrated, coherent, dialogical, inclusive and hospitable.

The Trinity, as historical revelation in the world, was introduced as the main theological motif that the organization should engage with. This meant a reemphasis on the significance of the world for God. It is because of the "Father's love that he sent his Son, offering a word of hope not only to men and women but also to the whole of creation."[689] Validating the

---

[689] Jürgen Moltmann, *Ethics of Hope*, 22.

importance of the world, the Trinity was further outlined in two main areas. The first area considered the Trinity as the basis of the *Missio Dei* and World Vision, as an expression of the development practice participating in this mission, particularly in its quest for justice. The second focused on each of the individual divine persons in the Trinity and how they could provide further insight to the development practice. A clearer understanding of the structure of the development practice as well as the Christian direction emerges in this theological reflection.

While it is useful to have thorough theological reflection, this does not automatically imply a stronger Christian identity in the organization. Care needs to be taken to internalize this Christian content within the organization. As discussed in chapter 3, section 3.3.2.5, this is not an automatic process but is dependent on the significance of this Christian meaning for the organization. One way that this Christian meaning can be further internalized is in the focus on the processes involved. We turn our attention to the next recommendation which concerns the processes of the organization.

CHAPTER NINE

Strengthening Leadership in the Organization

This chapter is a continuation of the recommendation phase which focuses on the content and processes of identity formation. In the previous chapter, the recommendation focused on the content aspect of identity formation, clarifying the particularity of the Christian faith in the development practice as content valuable for further engagement. In this chapter, the focus is on the processes in the organization. To focus on the processes is to focus on the authoring and enabling that takes place in the organization. This involves the organizational practices that are put in place in the organization as well as staff members involved.

In the first section of this chapter, the issues and subsequent analysis related to the existing processes are outlined. In addition, the relation between organizational processes and the leadership process is made. Linking organizational processes to the leadership process, the recommendations in this chapter are centered on the leadership of the organization. Leadership in this chapter is defined as a process whereby an individual influences a group of individuals to achieve a common goal.[690] It is not centered only on the individual leader, but is understood as a process whereby the context, purpose and followers of the organization are constitutive.[691]

To do justice to this leadership moment, the second section of this chapter focuses on the theology of work. This is used as a framework to evaluate the existing leadership of the organization as it focuses on the work experience of staff members, based on the ontological instrumental and relational aspect of work. Recommendations are made for World Vision with regard to each aspect.

The third section analyses the individual leader as the main driver of the leadership process. The implementation of these recommendations is dependent on the leader of this leadership process. This leader is not passive, but rather an active agent in the leadership process. What he decides

---

[690] Peter G. Northouse, *Leadership: Theory and Practice* (London: SAGE Publications, 2007), 3.
[691] Donna Ladkin, *Rethinking Leadership: A New Look at Old Leadership Questions* (Cheltenham: Edward Elgar, 2010), 25.

as priority is dependent on his being. Authentic leadership is introduced as a leadership theory that focuses on who the individual leader is and how that impacts the way the leader executes his or her leadership role. In describing the theory, recommendations for leader development are also made.

9.1 Identifying Issues in Processes at World Vision and their Link to Leadership

The processes of identity formation include "processes of participation in and performance of embodied, value-producing activity" within the organization.[692] The emphasis is on the stream of acts of authoring and enabling that results in a broader pattern of self-enacting in formative practice.[693] One general finding gleaned from the field research is the gradual rational bureaucratization of World Vision. More policies and systems were drafted for the smooth operation of the organization. This emphasis on functional efficiency has at times resulted in the diminished role of religious values within the organization.

Focusing on the structural side of the normative practice model, it can first be said that the *telos* of the development practice does not influence the humanitarian and advocacy work that World Vision does. In addition, World Vision seems to be conflicted regarding the qualifying aspect of the development practice which has been described earlier as the formative aspect. To take the formative aspect as the qualifying aspect of the development practice, it is important to take seriously the story wherein development practice is taking place. Based on the analysis as reported in this dissertation, we have seen that the actions of World Vision seem contradictory. On the one hand, there is a strong tradition and commitment at World Vision to work with grassroots communities, where the story of the community seems to be taken seriously. On the other hand, there is also the trend where decision-making and power is consolidated up the hierarchy. Strategic decisions of World Vision that impact the overall development process are taken apart from local communities.

With regard to the directional side, it is evident that World Vision is moving away from the Christian direction. As described in the analysis, staff members do not actively consider what makes their work Christian in the work that they do. Finally, with reference to the contextual side,

---

[692] Arne Carlsen, "On the Tacit Side of Organizational Identity: Narrative Unconscious and Figured Practice," *Culture and Organization* 22, no. 2 (2016): 107–135.
[693] Ibid.

there is an understanding that the most important stakeholders were the local beneficiaries of the development work. The next key stakeholder was determined by the particular context of the organization. In Papua New Guinea, the funding organizations were considered to be the most important because of the grant-funding nature of the office; in Nepal, the government was considered more important. These stakeholders played a significant role in the overall actions of the organization.

The issues raised for each of the three sides are the result of the existing authoring and enabling of the people in the organization. These authoring and enabling can be the result of intentional management control with decisions made by leaders regarding the choice of streams of authoring that are put in place in the organization. However, just like the organizational culture, management control does not have full control over all the authoring and enabling in the organization. Individual staff members and their perceptions are also at play in this process.

The leadership process in an organization involves more than the leader and management control. It involves setting the tone of the organization by establishing the direction, aligning people to this direction and being motivating and inspiring to the people.[694] Besides the individual leader, the interpretation of the followers, the goal of the organization and the context of the organization are other factors that can influence the overall leadership process. This leadership process constitutes different factors which imply the limitation of the individual leader, as well as the importance of the interpretation of staff members in the organization.

Taking seriously the different factors in leadership, the understanding of leadership in this chapter references the understanding of leadership scholar Donna Ladkin, whereby leadership is as a moment, constitutive on the "things of which they are part."[695] These different things or pieces are: the leader, context, purpose and follower. As a moment, the reality of leadership is dependent on these different pieces and cannot be separated from them.[696] "Leaders relate to followers and together they interact within a particular context and move towards an explicit or implicit purpose."[697] Figure 9.1 shows the central role that the leadership moment has on the processes involved in the organization, which is the result of authoring and enabling within the organization.

---

[694] John P. Kotter, *A Force for Change: How Leadership Differs from Management* (New York: Free Press, 1990).
[695] Ladkin, *Rethinking Leadership: A New Look at Old Leadership Questions*, 25.
[696] Ibid., 26.
[697] Ibid., 27.

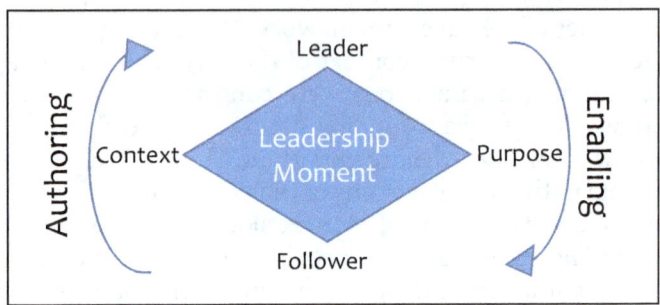

Figure 9.1 Leadership Moment in Organizational Processes

In addition, understanding leadership as a moment acknowledges that this leadership moment is made concrete in the work experiences of staff members in a specific context working for an organization with a specific purpose. This emphasizes the "mobilization of the different pieces" instead of the singular understanding of each individual piece.[698] The different pieces are interconnected such that changing one piece can result in the overall change in the experience. Depending on the purpose of study, different leadership theories gives attention to different pieces to improve the overall leadership moment.

Taking the work experience seriously, it is recommended that theology of work be appropriated as the hermeneutical lens used to review the existing leadership moment at World Vision. It emphasizes the Christian presuppositions with respect to work. These Christian presuppositions influence not only the desired outcome of the work, but also the understanding of work itself. We begin our discussion on the theology of work below.

9.2 Appropriating the Theology of Work as the Hermeneutical Lens for Leadership

Reflecting on a distinct Christian perspective to the work experience at World Vision is a good way of safeguarding Christian values in the leadership experience. In this section, the theology of work is appropriated to illuminate the gaps and opportunities faced by World Vision from a distinctly Christian perspective. Working through these gaps provides an opportunity for the organization to change the processes introduced by management control, as well as influence the interpretation made by staff

---

[698] Ladkin, *Rethinking Leadership: A New Look at Old Leadership Questions*, 28.

members. This can influence the processes involved in the organization, thereby strengthening the organization, countering the mission drift experienced.

The theology of work represents an important shift in the theological discussion of work. It is a theological perspective that encompasses a broader theological framework, as well as takes seriously the existing work realities faced in modern times.[699] This term, "theology of work" was first used by French Catholic theologians as they sought to come up with theologies of social realities.[700] It was formally mentioned by Catholic theologian M-D Chenu in his book, *The Theology of Work: An Exploration.*[701]

In appropriating the theology of work in this chapter, we follow in the tradition of theologians like Miroslav Volf and Darrell Cosden to whom the purpose of reflecting on the theology of work is transformative and not merely descriptive. Within this tradition, the new creation roots the broad theological framework of work. "Work is done under the inspiration of the spirit and in light of the coming new creation."[702] Moved by the Spirit and striving towards the new creation, this implies a clear Christian perspective, with norms that work should strive for.[703] It envisages the possibility

---

[699] Traditionally, work has been discussed in the context of the doctrine of sanctification. It considered how the new life in Christ should influence daily's work. Other doctrines or scriptures were also consulted as it provided the impetus to work. Other examples of theologians that have engaged in the subject of work include Karl Barth in his Christological anthropology, or a Trinitarian framework to discuss work as expounded by Richard Higginson, *Called to Account: Adding Value in God's World* (Guildford: Eagle, 1993), and Gorden Preece, *Changing Work Values: A Christian Response* (Melbourne: Acorn, 1995). Pope John Paul's II's encyclical *Laborem Exercens* sees work as indirectly referred to in Scriptures, with God's command to "Be fruitful and multiply, and fill the earth and subdue it" (Gen. 1:27). In carrying out this mandate, "human beings reflect the very action of the Creator of the universe." (John Paul II, *Laborem Exercens*, 4).

[700] Cosden, *A Theology of Work*, 4.

[701] Marie-Dominique Chenu, *The Theology of Work: An Exploration* (Dublin: M. H. Gill & Son, 1963). It is not the intention of this dissertation to evaluate the different positions found in the theology of work. This is beyond the scope of this chapter. Instead, this section focuses mainly on the understanding of the theology of work as described by Miroslav Volf and Darrell Cosden. As a key leading theologian in the theology of work, Cosden followed in Volf's tradition and forwarded his arguments.

[702] Miroslav Volf, *Work in the Spirit: Toward a Theology of Work* (New York: Oxford University Press, 1991), 79.

[703] In describing the implication of the new creation to the normative ethical claims, Volf makes a distinction between the ethical maximum and minimum and its implications to his theology of work. The ethical minimum are principles that cannot

of evaluating one's work reality according to a theology of work, "facilitating the transformation of work toward ever greater correspondence with the new creation."[704] This transformational view of work is appropriate for this chapter of strengthening leadership as it takes seriously the dynamic nature of identity formation in the organization.

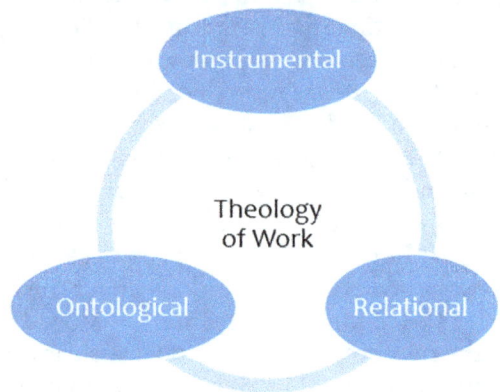

Figure 9.2 The Three Dimensions of Work Theology

Work is a transformative activity essentially consisting of dynamically interrelated instrumental, relational and ontological dimensions, whereby along with work being an end in itself, the workers' and others' needs are providentially met, believers sanctification is occasioned, and workers express, explore and develop their humanness while building up their natural social and cultural environments thereby contributing protectively and productively to the order of this world and the world to come.[705]

---

be set aside if justice is to prevail based on the concept of the new creation. These ethical minimum forms the criterion for structuring the world of work. At the same time, the new creation implies principles that point beyond justice to the way of love, this he termed the ethical maximum. Bearing the ethical minimum and maximum in mind, all Christian behavior need to at least satisfy the ethical minimum. However, inspired by the sacrificial love of Christ demonstrated on the cross and guided by the vision of the new creation, this should not be enough. Rather, they should be motivated to move toward the ethical maximum. This ethical maximum functions like a necessary regulative ideal. It is not forced on as a criterion at work because this can lead to unhelpful distortions. At the same time, without love, it is impossible to talk about a humane society. See Volf, *Work in the Spirit*, 81–83.

[704] Ibid, 85.
[705] Cosden, *A Theology of Work*, 179.

This definition of work by Cosden validates the multi-faceted perspectives of work. As illustrated in figure 9.2, the three different dimensions of work: instrumental, relational and ontological, are equally important in the understanding of work.[706] In addition, this definition also prevents the long-term monopoly of having any one dimension of work dominate the understanding of work. These three dimensions are distinct, yet at the same time interrelated in the totality of work. The change of one dimension inevitably influences the other dimensions. Together, these three distinct but interrelated dimensions enable a more holistic ethical framework of work.[707]

In the following section, the different dimensions of work theology are briefly introduced. Taking into mind the transformative intention of the theology of work, the case of World Vision is evaluated and specific recommendations are given. The intention of these recommendations is to inspire leadership development in World Vision. In general, leadership development has been defined as the expansion of an organization's capacity to enact basic leadership tasks needed to accomplish shared, collective work.[708] This involves the intentional influence of organizational processes, the overall authoring and enactment within the organization. We begin our focus now with the ontological dimension.

9.2.1   The Ontological Dimension of Work

The ontology of work refers to the intrinsic value of work, the understanding that work is important for human existence.[709] This value is more than what it achieves as well as the relationships developed through it.[710] An inherent value to work is accorded when a *Transformatio Mundi* opinion of the eschatological future of the world. According to this view, the world is not destroyed. There is continuity between the present age and the age to come.[711] Work is then understood as a positive cultural involvement in the

---

[706] Cosden, *A Theology of Work*, 178.
[707] Ibid.
[708] Ellen Van Velsor and Cynthia D. McCauley and Marian N. Ruderman, "Our View of Leadership Development," in *The Center for Creative Leadership Handbook of Leadership Development* (San Francisco: Jossey-Bass, 2010), 3.
[709] It is not the intention of this section to provide a complete argument of the ontological dimension of work. The arguments presented in this section follows in the tradition of Cosden, Volf and Moltmann.
[710] Cosden, *A Theology of Work*, 184.
[711] This perspective is in contrast to an understanding of the world ending in apocalyptic destruction where work will not have any ultimate significance. Such an understanding of the work implies that work only possesses earthly significance,

present age that has eternal consequences. "The results of cumulative work of human beings have intrinsic value and gain ultimate significance, for they are related to the eschatological new creation, not only indirectly through the faith and service they enable or sanctification they further, but also directly."[712] Through work, "human beings contribute in their modest and broken way to God's new creation."[713] What is done on earth will last into God's future. The work that is done is done in hopes that it "will one day find its way into the new creation that God will make."[714]

Understanding work as having inherent ontological value, we focus on two main points in the evaluation of work at World Vision providing recommendations for improvement. These two points: the kind of work that constitutes positive cultural involvement, and the value of work for the individual.

9.2.1.1 Positive Cultural Involvement of Work done by World Vision

Taking the inherent value of work seriously, work should "come into line and promote the values theologically associated with the new creation."[715] As evident from the overall findings of the case study, work is however not primarily understood in terms of its Christian values. Without a clear understanding of the Christian values by its staff members, this will make it difficult for staff members to be motivated by the positive cultural involvement of World Vision.

As a way to clarify the work by its Christian values, the previous chapter reflects on the Trinity, focusing on its implications to the structural and directional understanding of the development practice. It begins first with understanding the Trinity as historical revelation. From the biblical narrative, God intricately involves himself with the world till the end of time. The work that World Vision does is a small contribution to the overall participation of the body of Christ in the mission of God, with the focus on their quest for social justice. Within social justice, the particular kind of social justice that World Vision engages in is further detailed as the de-

---

namely for the well-being of the worker, the worker's community, and posterity. Volf, *Work in the Spirit*, 89.
[712] Ibid., 91.
[713] Ibid., 92.
[714] Gustavo Gutiérrez, *A Theology of Liberation* (London: SCM Press, 2000), 62.
[715] Ibid. 185.

velopment practice. In addition, an inclusive understanding of the development practice was also outlined from studying the individual divine persons: Father, Son and Holy Spirit.

What is important to note is the inherent value involved in the quest of social justice by World Vision. This work is not done in vain. It "is an offering to the Lord who is able to take it and keep it for the perfect kingdom which is promised."[716] To be able to effectively work for social justice, this theological understanding of the work done by World Vision should not be neglected in the overall leadership of the organization. Rather, it should be taken into consideration as integral to the normative practice of development. As World Vision seeks to express the development practice, this theological reflection illuminates the direction that the organization should move towards, as well as clarify the Christian underpinnings involved in the structure of the practice.

As a recommendation, the normative practice of development, together with its theological underpinnings, should stay central in the hermeneutical process within the organization.[717] Describing leadership as a moment, the purpose of the organization should be emphasized in all that the organization does. This implies that the structure, particularly the *telos*, often expressed as the purpose of the organization, stays key in determining the other characteristics of the organization, such as the staff members of the organization, as well as the subsequent activity systems.[718] One example of how the purpose of the organization can be central to the organization is found in the discussion of people management in development organizations. The purpose, encapsulated in the structure of the practice, was used as a framework for people management in the organization.[719]

This focus on the practice of development provides a "common ground for moral reflection and debate in a pluralist society and also create op-

---

[716] Dietrich Bonhoeffer, *Ethics*, vol.6 of *Dietrich Bonhoeffer Works* (Minneapolis: Fortress Press, 2005), 258.
[717] Donna Ladkin, *Rethinking Leadership: A New Look at Old Leadership Questions* (Cheltenham: Edward Elgar, 2010), 124.
[718] See Stefan Kühl, *Organisationen: Eine sehr kurze Einführung* (Dordrecht: Verlag für Sozialwissenschaften, 2011).
[719] See Peirong Lin, "An Ethical Consideration of People Management in Development Organizations," in *Challenges of Moral Leadership*, ed. Patrick Nullens and Steven C. van den Heuvel (Leuven: Peeters, 2016), 183–98.

portunities to show the relevance of the Christian faith to realizing the finality of social practices in our fragmented society."[720] It takes seriously the Christian reality, yet at the same time provides space for plurality in its contexts and association. Finally, describing development as a normative practice can be useful in considering where the common ground is, inviting dialogue with other worldviews in the practice of development in pursuit of the common good.[721] This entails critically considering the structure of the development practice and the extent to which they can authentically support different themes within the broader civil society.

9.2.1.2 Fulfilling Work for Individual Staff Members

If work has inherent value, it is important then that work itself is treated as a transformative act with the possibility of flourishing. For one to flourish, there should be the potential for staff members to experience fulfilling work. Moltmann echoes this by describing work as more than "purpose and usefulness," instead, it should also include "freedom for self-presentation and thus playfulness."[722] To work well, work needs to "provides latitude for individual formation and thereby allows possibilities for self-expression."[723] In addition, the process of work is also important. "Human beings are called to achieve something efficiently as well as gifted to enjoy the process of achieving it."[724] In the same way, work at World Vision should strive to be fulfilling, where staff members enjoy the process, with sufficient latitude for individual formation and self-expression.

Based on the case study of World Vision, the job description was a main reason why staff members joined World Vision. This motivation is kept up by learning and development activities as well as career advancement opportunities. In addition, when asked why their colleagues would join World Vision, responses such as the industry World Vision is in (NGOs, In-

---

[720] Johan Hegemann, Margaret Edgell, and Henk Jochemsen, *Practice and Profile: Christian Formation for Vocation* (Eugene, OR: Wipf and Stock, 2011), 86.
[721] In chapter 8, section 8.3.3.2.3, flourishing has been described as useful for dialogical common ground. This is useful for determining the extent of working together towards common good.
[722] Jürgen Moltmann, *On Human Dignity*, trans. M. Douglas Meek (Minneapolis: Fortress, 2007), 41.
[723] Ibid., 54.
[724] Cosden, *A Theology of Work*, 198.

ternational Organizations) or the compensation and benefits that they receive took center stage.[725] From these results, there was some evidence of space for individual formation and self-expression at World Vision. However, this self-expression was not central to the reasons for working at World Vision. The industry that World Vision was in or the actual compensation and benefits were deemed more important. It is clear that more can be done by World Vision to support the process of finding enjoyment and individual formation at work.

As a recommendation, this chapter focuses on the individual through a detailed discussion on the authentic leader described later in this chapter. As the leader leads authentically, there is space for self-expression and for one to potentially flourish.

9.2.2 The Instrumental Dimension of Work

The instrumental dimension of work gives attention to the other purposes why people work. It looks at work as a means to an end. The two aspects related to the instrumental dimension of work are an individual's sustenance as well as the concern for a person's spiritual growth through work. To be concerned about sustenance is to focus on work as "providing the necessary resources for human survival and flourishing."[726] At the same time, providing resources, while important, is not sufficient. It needs to be balanced with the concern of spiritual growth of a person through work. This means looking at work as an occasion for grace. In the following section, the experience of World Vision is looked at.

9.2.2.1 World Vision's Ability to Provide for Individual's Sustenance and Spiritual Growth

Based on the findings of the case study, changes in work conditions (Salary and Benefits),[727] was perceived to be the largest demotivating factor for both WV Nepal and WV PNG. One plausible reason for this dissatisfaction is because World Vision is generally compared with other international organizations. Staff members reported that the sector (INGOs, NPOs) that

---

[725] See chapter 6, table 5.14 and 5.15 for WV Nepal and table 5.52 and 5.53 for WV PNG.
[726] Cosden, *A Theology of Work*, 181
[727] See chapter 5, table 5.15 and 5.53.

World Vision was in was one key reason for joining World Vision.[728] Because of this comparison, there is an apparent expectation of salary and benefits at World Vision to be comparable to other international organizations.

An example of a compensation system widely adopted by international organizations is the established compensation system, pay for performance, as developed by the Society of Human Resources Management (SHRM).[729] SHRM is an advocate for a pay for performance system which rewards individual employee performance.[730] This system is designed to 1) motivate people to join the organization, 2) motivate employees to stay at the top of their skill set and 3) motivate employees to stay.[731] This is dependent on the external factors that the organization is in.[732] Depending on the different factors, the organization will choose between different "pay positions" in the market, which can include the position of lagging the market, meeting the market or leading the market. The final step involves determining the actual position of different employees based on their performance.[733]

As World Vision determines their own compensation system in the face of other organizations, it is insufficient to compare only with the external

---

[728] See chapter 5, table 5.14 and 5.52.
[729] This claim is made as international organizations adopt prevalent business practices, where pay for performance is known as a benchmark compensation system. See for example Human Resources (HR) Support Package, resource of CHS alliance, a network of international organizations. In section 3.1, merit increases are described as integral for performance management. "Human Resource Support Package," accessed 20th June 2016, http://www.chsalliance. org/files/files/Resources/Tools-and-guidance/HRSupportPackage-December% 202016.pdf.
[730] For more information about the SHRM's work, see Sharon K. Koss, *Solving the Compensation Puzzle: Putting Together a Complete Pay and Performance System* (Alexandria, VA: Society for Human Resource Management, 2008).
[731] Koss, *Solving the Compensation Puzzle*, 29.
[732] In describing the system, the pay philosophy of the employer should first be detailed depending on the prevailing constraints of the organization. This philosophy should incorporate factors such as the company's financial position, the size of the organization, the industry, business objectives, salary survey information, and the level of difficulty in finding qualified talent based on the economy, as well as the unique circumstances of the business. At the same time, it is reviewed regularly to compare its effectiveness with the times that it is facing. The compensation philosophy of the organization is typically developed by the human resources department in collaboration with the senior leadership team. See "Compensation Philosophy," accessed 20th June 2016, https://www.shrm. org/Templates-Tools/hrqa/Pages/Compensationphilosophy.aspx.
[733] Koss, *Solving the Compensation Puzzle*, 32.

market. The values that World Vision wants to foster in society need to also be critically considered. This pay for performance system sees money as the main motivation for staff to join the organization, be productive and stay at the organization. Taken to the extreme, this pay for performance system seems to promote certain values that may not be in alignment with the values espoused by World Vision, or the broader development practice. This pay for performance system with money as the main motivator seems to promote the importance of money over other practices and institutions in society. It can also suggest that the relationship between the individual staff member and the organization is merely transactional. While it may be possible that this pay for performance is an expectation from its staff members, seen as necessary for recruiting good staff, it is also important to critically evaluate and appropriate this system and to be clear about the communication to its staff members.

In addition, underlying this pay for performance system is the assumption that money is a good motivation. The importance of money as a motivator seems to be indeed true as staff members reported dissatisfaction about the work conditions at World Vision in the questionnaire.[734] One reason for this dissatisfaction in work conditions could be due to the dynamic nature of felt product needs. As described by Volf, felt product needs are not static, but rather dynamic as these product needs were previously yesterday's desires.[735] These felt product needs are not satisfied but continue to expand. In this sense, the solution might not be to pay staff members more money. It is recommended that World Vision intentionally support its staff members on developing other fundamental needs that are non-product related.[736]

These other fundamental needs provide a balance to the product need felt by staff members. It complements the understanding of sustenance needed by staff members for flourishing. In addition, they include the key element of spiritual growth that has been described as another key element in the instrumental dimension of work. As World Vision critically appropriates the pay for performance system, a knowledge of the other fundamental needs can be useful to further balance and orientate the compensation system towards the purpose of World Vision. These fundamental needs are described below.

---

[734] Based on questionnaire, work conditions imply salary and benefits. See Appendix 1, section 3.1.2.3 Motivation, questions 23, 26 and 27. The findings regarding motivation are found in table 6.15 and 6.53.
[735] Volf, *Work in the Spirit*, 15
[736] Ibid, 152.

9.2.2.2 *Fundamental Needs as Complementing Sustenance*

This understanding of fundamental needs adopts a Christian anthropology as they are rooted in the normative human nature. As described by Volf, fundamental non-products are "objectively rooted in the nature of human beings as creatures made in the image of God, but are subjectively awakened and satisfied by the activity of the Spirit of God. The same spirit that empowers people to work in order to satisfy their product-needs also motivates them to satisfy their fundamental needs that might limit these product needs."[737] Besides product needs, there are also fundamental needs that are necessary for the flourishing of the individual. An organization employing individuals should focus not only on providing for sustenance that affords for product needs, but also on fundamental needs.

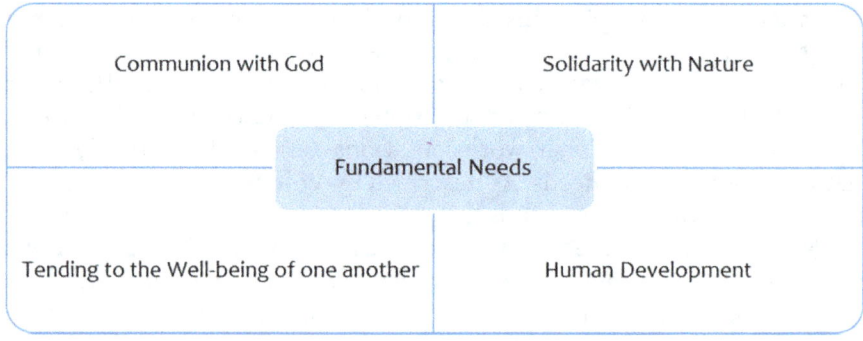

Figure 9.3 Illustration of Fundamental Needs

Source: Volf, *Work in the Spirit*, 152

Volf described four fundamental needs that are anthropologically grounded as illustrated in figure 9.3. These needs are: 1) the need for communion with God, where God's presence guards people from "an insatiable desire for material wealth" 2) solidarity with nature, where people are conscious of their destiny that belongs with nature in the one eschatological new creation 3) tending to the well-being of one another, where from the spirit of fellowship, a person is liberated from an individualistic search for satisfaction of product needs to focus on the needs of the community 4) human development, which consists of both moral capacities and of

---

[737] Volf, *Work in the Spirit*, 152.

practical and intellectual skills.[738] Further development of these fundamental needs serves as a counter weight to the expansion of product needs as they have the potential of limiting the desire of product needs.

Taking into account that the instrumental dimension of work focuses on work as a means to an end, which include both spiritual growth as well as sustenance, the fundamental need-communion with God-is further outlined in the following section. This however does not mean that the other fundamental needs will be ignored, but instead, they are discussed in the other dimensions.[739]

9.2.2.3 Spiritual Growth at Work as Contributing to the Fundamental Need of Communion with God

Volf describes the need for communion with God as the most fundamental of all human needs. This implies that it is in the experience of the fullness of life in God's presence that health is brought to the soul.[740] One place in which this communion with God can be experienced is in the work place, through spiritual growth. Spiritual growth focuses on "work's contribution to sanctification."[741] From this point of view, work is described as an occasion for grace, where "through working, a person grows spiritually through humble obedience to and dependence upon God, demonstrating to himself or herself and others the nature of their relationship to God, being kept from idleness and sin, having resources to share with others and so forth."[742]

While highlighting the opportunity of work for spiritual growth, it is also important to note that work is not be the primary center where the fundamental need – communion with God should be focused on. In other words, work's qualifying aspect is not pistic. Therefore, while taking the spiritual growth of staff members seriously, it is equally important to note that work will never be able to entirely fulfill all the needs of the individual with regard to his or her communion with God. In supporting spiritual growth, the organization should not harbor unrealistic expectations of be-

---

[738] Volf, *Work in the Spirit*, 152.
[739] The need "solidarity with nature" as well as "human development" are referred to in the ontological work aspect while the tending to the well-being of one another is discussed in the relational aspect.
[740] Ibid.
[741] Ibid.
[742] Ibid., 182.

ing the center of the communion of God. It should rather seek to contribute to the spiritual growth of the individual, intentionally setting up conditions to support the individual's spiritual growth.[743] As an example of how an organization like World Vision can support spiritual growth, workplace spirituality should be focused on. This is looked at in the next section.

9.2.2.3.1 Workplace Spirituality as an Avenue for Communion with God

Workplace spirituality has been defined as "a framework of organizational values in a culture that promotes employee experience of transcendence though the work that provides feelings of compassion and joy."[744] The individual worker is explored as more than *Homo laborans*, but rather one who also has body, mind, heart and spirit.[745] This concept has been lauded as a possible solution to the challenges in the business world as it provides an alternative lens to respond to challenges that were seen to exceed the rational. Workplace spirituality programs have reportedly benefited both the organization as well as the individual worker. For the organization, these programs increased commitment, improved productivity, and reduced absenteeism and turnover.[746] In the following section, two main variables transcendence and connectedness are first briefly introduced. This is followed by outlining implications of this for the discussion of spiritual growth of staff members at World Vision.

Transcendence is derived from a sense of purpose in the work that one does, a sense of being called (vocationally). Because of the sense of calling, the individual believes in his or her ability to perform the job, to be able to journey into new and untraveled territories with confidence and vigor.[747]

---

[743] It should be restated that this is done bearing in mind the hospitable and dialogical aspects of constructive approach. Instead of forcing the other to this Christian God, speaking about the Christian God at a work context should be done in a hospitable and engaging way. It should seek to meaningfully relate with other faiths, honor the otherness of the other, and make space for true exchange of different perspectives.

[744] Robert A. Giacalone and Carole L. Jurkiewicz, "Toward a Science of Workplace Spirituality," in *Handbook of Workplace Spirituality and Organizational Performance*, ed. Robert A. Giacalone and Carole L. Jurkiewicz (New York: M.E. Sharpe, 2003), 3–28.

[745] See R.S. Moxley, *Leadership and Spirit* (San Francisco, CA: Jossey-Bass, 2000).

[746] Chris Start and Peirong Lin, "The Search for Spirituality in the Business World" in *Leadership, Innovation and Spirituality*, ed. Patrick Nullens and Jack Barentsen (Leuven: Peeters 2014), 34.

[747] Louis Fry, "Toward a Theory of Spiritual Leadership," *The Leadership Quarterly* 14,

Transcendence comes from an intimate appreciation of the purpose of one's work. This motivates the individual to rise up to challenges that happen at work. Because of the weight given to the work one does, organizational scientists recommend the deliberate creation of a vision that allows organizational members to experience meaning in the building of transcendence. This vision, future oriented, should include some implicit or explicit commentary on why people should strive to create that future.[748] In the same way, staff members should foster feelings of transcendence at World Vision. This happens when individual staff members see the link of their work with the larger purpose that World Vision exists for. This includes clearly articulating the telos of the development practice, as well as clearly laying out how each individual worker can contribute to reaching this telos. Besides setting formal statements, institutional practices are also useful to reinforce the feelings of transcendence. Based on the findings in the collection phase, existing practices that have been useful included devotions as well as yearly events such as the day of prayer.

Connectedness or membership is the second variable in workplace spirituality. This refers to the need of individuals for social connection.[749] This social connection can be derived from the different cultural and social structures that the individual is embedded in. Through these structures, the individual finds an understanding and appreciation of who he or she is.[750] Besides being influenced by external social connection, this connectedness is influenced by the individual. Human agency determines the extent of connectedness.[751] The connectedness to different social structures is dependent on one's connectedness within oneself, "where there is sustained comfort with oneself irrespective of the circumstances involved." This connected person, when engaging with society, will then seek to do good, thinking positively about society, nature and universe.[752]

There are two main implications for World Vision with regard to connectedness. Firstly, it is important to be aware of the possible social con-

---

no. 693 (2003): 727.
[748] For more information, see John.P. Kotter, *Leading Change* (Boston, MA: Harvard Business School Press, 1996).
[749] Louis Fry, "Toward a Theory of Spiritual Leadership," *The Leadership Quarterly* 14, no. 693 (2003): 727.
[750] Ibid., 704.
[751] Start and Lin, "The Search for Spirituality in the Business World," 34.
[752] N.T. Sree Raj, "Spirituality in Business and Other Synonyms: A Fresh Look at Different Perspectives for its Application," *Journal from the School of Management Science* 4, no. 2 (2011): 71–85.

nections that the individual staff members are part of, as these connections impact organizational practices. This implies the importance of relationships, as well as the context that the organization is in. In addition, besides the importance of external connections, another key implication is the way an individual makes sense of his or her work at World Vision. The sense of calling in the work that one does influences the extent to which the individual makes sense of his or her work.

In light of the understanding of workplace spirituality, the spiritual guidance model is recommended for World Vision to further support the spirituality of staff members. This model intentionally reflects on the individual's social connections as well as the purpose of one's job from a spiritual perspective. Spiritual guidance has been defined as a form of interaction that assists in "directing and organizing his/her personal course of life through orientation on the mystery we call God."[753] In recommending this model for World Vision, it invites the individual to notice the Christian God in their experiences at work. It also takes into account the social connections at the workplace.

9.2.2.4 Recommendation of Spiritual Guidance Model with a Clear Christian Perspective

The spiritual guidance model developed by Dutch priest and professor of pastoral theology, Tjeu van Knippenberg is recommended in this section as a tool for workplace spirituality at World Vision. This model focuses on supporting the individual staff member in making sense of his or her work experience based on the Christian perspective form whence World Vision is working. In recommending this model to World Vision, it is suggested that this model be used as a framework to strengthen the spirituality of their staff members.

While this model was developed by a Dutch priest for the Dutch context, this dissertation describes the potential of using this in the context of World Vision because of the emphasis given to the path of life of the individual. The teachings and tradition of the Christian faith is then connected to the experiences of the individual through the reflection of the spiritual perspective of these experiences. This model takes seriously the presence of God in all dimensions of life – including work. It seeks to develop "a new awareness of oneself, God and the world."[754] It doesn't stay at

---

[753] Tjeu Van Knippenberg, *Towards Religious Identity: An Exercise in Spiritual Guidance* (Leiden: Brill, 2002), 48.
[754] Van Knippenberg, *Towards Religious Identity*, 64.

a fixed point in time, but is interested in the guidance of the human being through one's course in life.[755]

In making this recommendation, this dissertation does not assume that all staff members have pre-knowledge or belief in the Christian faith. It does however deliberately provide an opportunity for individual staff members to develop an awareness of themselves and the invitation to connect this awareness with the Christian faith.[756] For this to be possible, it is assumed that the administrators of this spiritual guidance model have knowledge and belief in the Christian faith and are willing to support others on this journey. Before introducing the model, the understanding of perspectives is further unpacked.

A perspective has been described as "a network of affects, intentions and concepts whereby reality is perceived in a particular way."[757] It is possible to draw different perspectives depending on what one observes. Different perspectives provide different lenses to understand reality. Four different perspectives were listed by van Knippenberg: somatic, psychosocial, existential and spiritual. Each of these perspectives provides a different layer of understanding the nuance and layered reality that the individual is experiencing.[758] These different layers are not separate but are intricately related. At the deepest level, the spiritual perspective involves every other dimension.

To concentrate on the spiritual perspective is to surface "the deepest, that which is most individual about oneself, allowing the self to rise up through everything else that covers it and shields it from itself."[759] It is to uncover that which gives the individual ultimate meaning. Focusing on the spiritual reality implies being intentional about surfacing the spiritual meaning at work. It makes space to question this reality, instead of sticking only to the surface lens of the somatic or psychosocial. As this deepest layer is the most individual of who a person is, at the same time, it is often also the most difficult to discuss because of the lack of common under-

---

[755] Van Knippenberg, *Towards Religious Identity*, 48.
[756] This takes seriously the importance of evangelism as described in Chapter 8 section 8.3.3.2.1 Continued Importance of Evangelism. Recognizing that staff members are practitioners in the field and are paramount to the overall development practice that is implemented, this model invites staff members to see what God has done, is doing and will do in their lives. It is an invitation, aimed at a response.
[757] Van Knippenberg, *Towards Religious Identity*, 53.
[758] Ibid.
[759] Ibid, 58.

standing of the presence and effect of the spirit in the events that are experienced.[760] It is easier to articulate an issue in a perspective shared by many. This has resulted in research from organizational science focusing on the somatic or psychosocial. Recognizing the importance of the spiritual, the spiritual guidance model is introduced below as a way to intentionally make space to discuss the spiritual from a Christian perspective.

9.2.2.4.1 Introduction of Spiritual Guidance Model

The spiritual guidance model is designed to support the meaning making of people, focusing on how the experienced reality can be connected with God.[761] To use this at World Vision is to connect the work experiences of an individual with the Christian God. This supports staff members to make spiritual sense of their work experience. Figure 9.4 provides the basic structure of this model. In the following, the basic structure of the model is first introduced. Recognizing that meaning is dependent on a larger narrative, the language used to further explicate the Christian tradition is explored thereafter. In the third section, the way that this spiritual guidance model can be used in workplace spirituality is described. Finally, the implications of this model to World Vision is described.

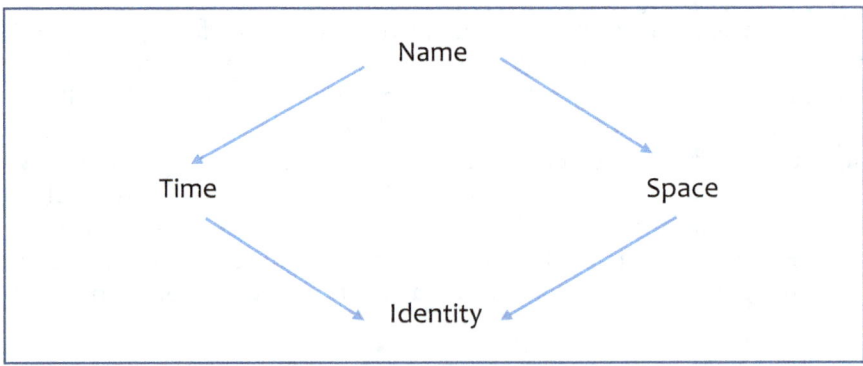

Figure 9.4 Basic Structure of Spiritual Guidance Model

Source: Van Knippenberg, *Towards Religious Identity*, 152

Taking seriously the individual's story, the model begins with the name, the uniqueness of who the individual is. "This particular name belongs to

---

[760] Van Knippenberg, *Towards Religious Identity*, 62.
[761] Ibid., 70.

the only person who was born at that time and in that place."⁷⁶² This takes seriously who the individual is. An individual's journey or existence exists in the conditions of space and time. To speak about time is to recognize that individuals understand themselves as existing in a time continuum, with a past, a present and a future. The experiences that one faces are reflected against time continuum. Space refers to the spheres that one lives in. This indicates one that has a front, back, side, above, below etc.⁷⁶³ This focuses on the spatial character of one's journey. To appropriate this spiritual guidance model in the work context is to take seriously the condition of time and space at work, acknowledging work as an integral part of life in the meaning making of life.

The understanding of identity in this model is the unique Christian vantage point. It is a context for framing experiences of existence, providing a certain content and concretizes them.⁷⁶⁴ In stating the Christian vantage point as the frame for work experiences, this is done recognizing the plural society and public space that World Vision is part of. The Christian vantage point is therefore used with hospitality and dialogue in mind. It is an invitation to view work from a Christian perspective. This approach "honors the otherness of the other," and at the same time, "seeks to persuade and convince with the power of dialogical humble and respectful argumentation."⁷⁶⁵ In the following, the language used to articulate this Christian vantage point is explicated.

9.2.2.4.2 Introduction of Language Used to Articulate Christian Vantage Point

From a Christian faith tradition, the spiritual perspective is understood as "putting oneself in God's presence." Meaning is generated as one understands oneself as part of creation that is on a journey. This implies an active awareness of one's shared nature and therefore the need of the other.⁷⁶⁶ This journey, experienced in space and time, is done while having ultimate reality, the creator in mind.⁷⁶⁷ As created reality, "normal things

---

[762] Van Knippenberg, *Towards Religious Identity* 152.
[763] Ibid., 53.
[764] Ibid, 106.
[765] Veli-Matti Kärkkäinen, *Christ and Reconciliation* (Grand Rapids, MI: Eerdmans, 2013), 31.
[766] Van Knippenberg, *Towards Religious Identity*, 108.
[767] Ibid., 106.

have parable character, indications of kingdom of God."[768] As part of created reality, it is possible to seek out spiritual meaning in work experiences. This meaning directly relates to transcendence, the higher purpose that an individual seeks out in workplace spirituality. A Christian perspective clearly anchors this transcendence in the Christian tradition.

In addition, meaning is not individualistic. It is "never restricted to the person or to the personal experience of this person." Instead, meaning should have an "active awareness that I am an element and that I need others."[769] This is in alignment with the understanding of workplace spirituality that emphasizes the importance of connections. Van Knippenberg used three main descriptors: co-heirs, guest and travel companion as useful for initiating the perception of a collective context of meaning as it explicitly focuses on the conditions of space and time.[770] Using these points enables one to "not fall victim to a staccato perception and not be the slave of further and more."[771] It is one way to reflect on work experiences from a Christian perspective, where experiences are clearly described in terms of the journey of life, felt within space and time. These terms are useful for World Vision as they clearly show the connection to transcendence and connectedness, key variables in workplace spirituality, as well as provide vocabulary to articulate the reflection of spiritual meaning at the workplace at World Vision. We turn to the separate images and discuss their applicability to World Vision.

Coheir

Coheir denotes the identity people have on this earth – created as children of God.[772] This implies that identity is not individualistic, but rather collective. As children of God, people are coheirs. They "inherited life as individual and a collective."[773] The life that individual lives exists in a particular space and time.[774] At the same time, this individual does not exist alone, but rather alongside other things that have been created. This requires the individual to provide hospitality as a guest, as well be a travelling companion to the other. Both roles of guest and travelling companion are undertaken by people at the workplace and will be further expounded later.

---

[768] Van Knippenberg, *Towards Religious Identity*, 55.
[769] Ibid., 108.
[770] Ibid., 109.
[771] Ibid., 115.
[772] Ibid., 109.
[773] Ibid.
[774] Ibid, 110.

Coheirs make meaning in their specific time and space alongside other parts of creation. They are guardians of part of creation,[775] intentionally being part of a journey whose destination is determined by creation.[776] A clear understanding of being a coheir impacts how one participates in creation. An understanding of being a coheir can result in a deep sense of calling in the work one does, where the creating God remains the long-term source and critical body for the consciousness. This understanding of the coheir roots the understanding of transcendence in workplace spirituality. The calling at work is an expression of what one does within the wider creation.

In addition, to understand oneself as co-heir is to recognize that one is created by God. The relationship that one has with the creator God qualifies all other relationships that one can have.[777] This has important implications to the understanding of connectedness, as we are all connected through our connection to our creator. Rooted in the identity as coheirs, people perform their roles of guest and travelling companion at their work. This is further described and imagined in an organization like World Vision below.

Guest

The notion of guest describes the way individual deals with space as he or she recognizes that this world is not a permanent home. In using the term guest, what is emphasized is the importance of hospitality, as "a sign of quality in the contact with space."[778] Hospitality has been described as a "model of communicative acting with meaning, on the conditions that people are able to discover what the stranger means." It "makes room for the new, the unexpected, providing an opportunity to lose images."[779]

As World Vision works with different cultures and in different countries, this understanding of guest and hospitality should influence the way individuals connect and work with each other. The place of work, actual

---

[775] Van Knippenberg, *Towards Religious Identity*, 110.
[776] This understanding of coheirs presupposes a specific understanding of creation. Creation is "an order that has existed since the beginning of time, that one can take as a starting point and on which one can rely for the future." It is not a "closed system of creation" where everything has already been created, rather, creation is understood as "a continual event." It continues to take place in the concrete conditions of time and space. See Van Knippenberg, *Towards Religious Identity*, 124.
[777] Van Knippenberg, *Towards Religious Identity*, 122.
[778] Ibid., 112.
[779] Van Knippenberg, *Towards Religious Identity*, 113.

tasks and how it links to the development practice are work experiences that links with space. World Vision should intentionally consider how work experiences reflect quality contact with space.

Travelling Companion

The notion of travelling companion is described in the context of one's interaction with time. Time is not understood to be static or having arrived, but rather "constructed as becoming." There is a desire in people for continuity – "connecting what is and what not yet be."[780] One way that this understanding of time as a continuity is concretized is in being each other's travelling companion. This means being deliberate about travelling meaningfully *enroute* with others towards an "ultimate destination."[781] As travelling companions, individuals are not in competition with one another. Together, they move from what is to what will be. To reflect on oneself as a travelling companion is to be reflective of the time one is in. In addition, it is intentional with the people around. It focuses on people at work and considers how the work can be done together with a sense of corporation.

This understanding of travelling companion is useful at World Vision as it clarifies the importance of people. The work that is done is done alongside others. Goals at World Vision should be perceived as a collective goal, shared with other staff members and the broader society. In the same way, World Vision should intentionally consider work experiences that involve others and how it truly reflects walking enroute to an ultimate destination.

Together, co-heir, guest and travelling companions are terms that World Vision can use in articulating workplace spirituality from a Christian vantage point. In the next section, this language is incorporated in the structure of the spiritual guidance model and is described as a framework that can be used at World Vision for workplace spirituality.

9.2.2.4.3 Appropriating the Spiritual Guidance Model at World Vision

In appropriating the spiritual guidance model, two main aspects are focused on. Firstly, the model can be understood as a hermeneutic framework used to interpret one's experiences, making what's unarticulated

---

[780] Van Knippenberg, *Towards Religious Identity*, 113.
[781] Ibid, 114.

Strengthening Leadership in the Organization

conscious.[782] Secondly, this hermeneutical framework is also linked to the agogic framework for further support to staff members. The agogic framework describes communicative key steps that can be useful for the administrator of the spiritual guidance model to provide direction to the individual at each circuit of the hermeneutical framework. This administrator is the guide that supports the individual through this spiritual guidance process. Knowing these different steps helps the administrator support the individual in his or her reflection. Figure 9.5 shows the basic structure of the spiritual guidance model alongside the different circuits in the hermeneutic framework as well as the agogic steps relevant for each circuit. Both of these frameworks are discussed together below illustrating how they can be used by World Vision.

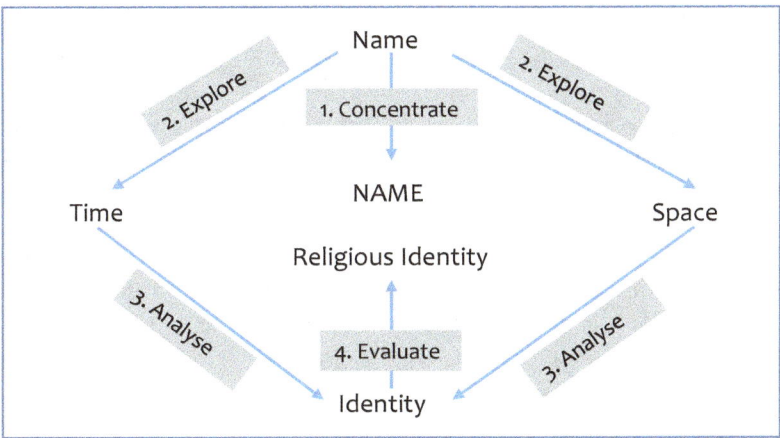

Figure 9.5: Spiritual Guidance Model with the Hermeneutical and Agogic Framework

Source: Van Knippenberg, *Towards Religious Identity*, 156 and 159

As a hermeneutical framework, Van Knippenberg describes this framework as made up of four circuits:

1. The first circuit focuses on the name of the individual. As a unique individual, it is not by chance where the person is at. It is through divine time and space, with the presence of the Holy Spirit that an individual finds himself or herself in.[783] Taking seriously the time and space where the individual is at, the agogic step that the administrator should focus on

---

[782] Van Knippenberg, *Towards Religious Identity*, 162.
[783] Ibid., 157.

is to support the individual to concentrate. This implies creating conditions for the individual to draw attention to the here and now.[784] This involves developing a greater self-awareness as well as an understanding of the context the individual is in.

2. The second circuit is related to the narrative of the individual. It is an understanding of the individual's story in terms of the space and time. This story is in the middle of a past and a future and is formed in a particular location. In this circuit, what is important is the authenticity of the story. It is also important to be "attentive to the relation between the psychological constellation of the person and his incidental occurrence."[785] This relationship provide more understanding to the story of the individual as a whole. Taking seriously the story of the individual, the agogic step that the administrator should focus on is explore. This refers to the active listening and enquiring of the individual experiences, feelings and actions to understand the personal meaning of these in the individual's path of life.[786]

3. The third circuit focuses on the interaction between the individual and the administrators of this guide. These administrators, coming with their own story as well as representing World Vision, can influence the individual in their interpretation.[787] Recognizing the direct interaction and the possible influence of the administrator to the individual, the agogic step that the administrator should focus on is analyze.[788] It means actively looking for patterns, offering alternative perspective. The purpose of this is to widen the individual's understanding of his or own story, dealing with a certain amount of "narrative competence."[789]

4. Finally, the last circuit looks at how the administrator interprets his or her own story. This looks at the way the administrator's faith tradition can influence his or her own interaction with the individual. As representatives of World Vision, the resultant faith tradition of the individual can be mediated by the theological references of World Vision. What is key in this circuit is the importance of finding an administrator who has the "competence in making a connection between the actual world of experience and the inheritance of the Christian faith."[790] The corresponding agogic step is evaluate. This evaluation is a continuation to the exploration

---

[784] Van Knippenberg, *Towards Religious Identity*, 160.
[785] Ibid., 157.
[786] Ibid., 161.
[787] Ibid., 158.
[788] Ibid., 162.
[789] Ibid., 162.
[790] Ibid., 159.

and the analysis step. The purpose of evaluation is to connect viewpoints derived from the process of spiritual guidance derived from the earlier circuits to the Christian tradition.[791]

As the individual goes through this hermeneutic framework with the support of the administrator implementing agogic steps, it is possible to bring awareness to the religious perspective of his or her experiences. This religious perspective, focusing on the deepest layer of meaning goes beyond the boundary of the other perspectives: biological, spatio-temporal. This framework takes into serious consideration the conditions of existence, space and time that this spiritual perspective is developed.[792] Through this process of spiritual guidance with the focus on time and space at each step, autobiographic competence as well as relational competence of the individual are further developed. These competences strengthen one's awareness of who one is. It also provides a way of connecting the experiences of the individual to the Christian language introduced earlier in section 9.2.2.4.2. Both these competences are described next.

Autobiographic competence is related to the ability to describe one own's story meaningfully across time. This means more than the separate events that take place in one's life through time. It includes meaning that has been put into the events in an autobiographic way. Through developing this competency, one should also critically consider what does it mean to be a "travelling companion whilst enroute."[793] This implies an awareness of being alongside others as one makes meaning through the different events in life. The others at work can include the different stakeholders that one comes into contact with.

Relational competence concerns itself with the space condition of human existence. This understanding of space concerns itself with the physical locality, or the social standing one has. The ability to change space, adopt a new social position is part of one's existence and is necessary for identity formation. An individual's understanding of space is dependent on one's socialization and one's mental condition. In strengthening this competency, there is the increased ability to be a guest as well as offer hospitality should the opportunity arise.[794] The actual work tasks, locality of work that one experiences can be linked to the understanding of guest and hospitality.

---

[791] Van Knippenberg, *Towards Religious Identity*, 162.
[792] Ibid., 163.
[793] Ibid., 164
[794] Ibid., 166.

9.2.2.4.4 Appropriation of Spiritual Guidance Model by World Vision

So far, we have introduced the spiritual guidance model as a useful framework to strengthen workplace spirituality at World Vision, contributing to the fundamental need of communion with God. It is a holistic model that takes seriously the story of the individual, seeking to provide Christian perspective to their experiences. It validates that events at the workplace impact the overall journey and meaning making of an individual. In using this model, it develops the individual's competence for self-awareness and invites individuals to consider their work experiences from a Christian perspective. In this final section of the spiritual guidance model, we explore the implications of this model to World Vision.

Firstly, it is important that ample resources are given to the implementation to this model. In describing its appropriation, an administrator of the model has been described as key to the appropriation of this model. This administrator works to ensure that the different hermeneutical circuits takes place as well as deliberately include agogic steps for each circuit. A good administrator is also necessary for making this a meaningful exercise. This administrator requires certain competencies[795] as well as inhabiting the Christian tradition. One key competence is the ability to make a "connection between the actual world of experience and the inheritance of the Christian faith."[796]

Secondly, there are existing spiritual practices at World Vision like devotions or day of prayer that can be understood within this model. What is not present is a comprehensive framework to look at the spirituality at the workplace. Practices like devotions or day of prayer generally operate within the third circuit, the point of interaction between the individual and the administrator. Looking at the spiritual guidance model, it should be clear from this model that this in itself is insufficient. While important practices, the individual staff members might not have gone through all the other circuits that are relevant for the building of autobiographic and relational competencies. It is therefore important that other practices that can influence the other circuits and support the concentrating and exploring agogic steps are also introduced at World Vision.

In this chapter, the common language of travelling companion and guest have been described as useful for understanding one's role on this

---

[795] See discussion on page 172–177 on discussion of competence necessary for the guide.
[796] Van Knippenberg, *Towards Religious Identity*, 159.

earth. The way that they relate to the autobiographic and relational competency was also made. In making this suggestion, it is important to note that having mere terms that are not used is insufficient. The validity of the terms proposed is dependent on the confidence conversation partners have, where this language is understood as adequate in the situation in which they find themselves.[797] This implies the importance of having sufficient understanding of these terms among staff members. It is important that the language is introduced frequently and repeated throughout the organization in its different activity systems and by different staff members. Further linkage of these terms with the experience of expressing its purpose of development practice needs to be established. In addition, the usage of this spiritual guidance model needs to be prioritized by management control for use by staff members. As management control is determined by the leaders of the organization, this implies the validity of this model is very much dependent on the individual leaders.

What is asked is for individual leaders to believe and prioritize this model in the workplace, recognizing this model as an invitation for all staff to consider their work experiences alongside the Christian perspective. Only with this belief will the leader provide sufficient resources for the implementation of this model. Sufficient resources would be needed for the administration of this model, completing the different hermeneutical circuits as well as the different agogic steps.

9.2.3 The Relational Dimension of Work

The final dimension, the relational nature of work, focuses on the broader social ethical significance related to work. It is this dimension that is focused on when work is understood to "first and foremost unite people." In this consists its social power: the power to build a community."[798] Through this unity of its people, there is the potential to create community.[799]

Cosden describes two main aspects with regard to this dimension. Firstly, he recognizes that at the basis for social development "man has a tendency to self-realization," and work must "serve his humanity, to fulfill the calling to be a person that is his by reason of his own humanity."[800] A relational dimension of work needs to therefore take into account the in-

---

[797] Van Knippenberg, *Towards Religious Identity*, 62–63.
[798] John Paul II, *Laborem Exercens*, 20.
[799] Cosden, *A Theology of Work*, 212.
[800] John Paul II, *Laborem Exercens*, 6.

dividual working, focusing on the "existential development or self-fulfillment of the person through work."[801] Secondly, society is developed through the exchange of values. This exchange is made concrete during the work experience of the individuals and has impact to the broader society and its development.[802]

The existential development of the individual at work validates the importance of work. In the discussion on the ontology of work, this existential development of the individual has been discussed through highlighting the importance to create space for individual formation and enjoyment. "Work, one of the primary ways that humans apply themselves to the task of living life, will thus be a central contributor to the evolution of the self both individually and socially."[803] In the previous sections, extensive reflection on how work should develop the individual has been described. This includes the discussion of fundamental needs, particularly workplace spirituality as well as the importance of fulfilling work. These discussions make clear the importance of the individual at the workplace. Having already extensively discussed the individual at the workplace, the second aspect of this dimension is focused on at this juncture.

The next aspect in the relational aspect of work focuses on the impact of work on the broader society. It recognizes the values exchange in the different personal and non-personal relationships that take place at work. Through the relationships at work, values for the society are formed. It is therefore important to reflect on the kind of values that matter in society, and to consider the relevant organizational structures and patterns that should produce and sustain these values.[804] This focus on values is especially important for a development organization that sees its purpose as supporting the formation of society. It is also related to the context side of the normative practice model. Before making specific suggestions to the relational dimension, the existing state of relationships of stakeholders in the organization are looked at with a special focus on the values exchanged.

9.2.3.1 Relationships among Stakeholders and Values exchanged

In a work setting, the parties involved in relationships have been described as stakeholders because of the stake they have in the organization. This

---

[801] Cosden, *A Theology of Work*, 183.
[802] Ibid.
[803] Ibid.
[804] Ibid.

relationship and influence of the different stakeholders with the organization is a two-way street. It influences the organization through its influence on each other.[805] In this section, both internal and external stakeholders of World Vision, as well as their subsequent values are considered.

Based on the findings of the field research, staff members believed that the beneficiaries were the most important external stakeholders in both offices.[806] What was considered as the next most important stakeholder(s) were the government officials in Nepal as well as the direct donors in PNG. Held in such high esteem by the staff members, the values embraced by the beneficiaries, the government officials as well as the direct donors are the most influential to the organization. This is noteworthy as these stakeholders may or may not share the same Christian values espoused by the organization.

With regard to the stakeholders in the office, the findings reported distant relationships the senior management team had with all other internal stakeholders in the office.[807] This can be problematic because the senior management team interacts most with the broader World Vision Partnership. It is in this broader partnership, particularly the Global Centre that values related to the "World Vision way" are transmitted. With a perceived distant relationship to the rest of the staff, it is possible that values as described in the "World Vision way" do not enter into the discussion of the office, therefore having little influence on the actual values discussed and exchanged at the office.

One obvious way that the office can influence the value exchange is to narrow the gap for this relationship between the senior management team and everyone else. This involves making recommendations on ways to narrow the gaps on each of the different dimensions such as directness, continuity, multiplexity, parity and commonality. In making the suggestion to narrow the gap, it is also understood that the actual decision on how the gaps should be narrowed is dependent on the cultural context of the organization. For example, the different preferences for power distance can influence relational proximity in dimensions such as parity and multiplexity. Therefore, instead of insisting only on one way of how this gap can be narrowed, the final analysis should be made and decided at the branch office level.

---

[805] O. C. Ferrell, John Fraedrich, and Linda Ferrell, *Business Ethics: Ethical Decision Making and Cases* (Stamford, CT: Cengage Learning, 2015), 31.
[806] See chapter 5, table 5.33 and 5.71.
[807] See chapter 5, table 5.36 – 5.39 for WV Nepal and table 5.74 – 5.77 for WV PNG.

What is suggested here as a recommendation is the importance of developing relationships that are rooted in justice, a form of love. When love and justice become the basis of the relationship, the relationship becomes consistent with the value of social justice that World Vision seeks to further. This can further impact the authoring and enabling that takes place within the organization. This understanding of the relationship is described below.

9.2.3.2 Love Characterizing relationships

To speak about relationships as characterized by love is to reassert the inherent value of relationships and people. This inherent value of relationships seemed to be amiss in the branch offices. When asked about the purpose of relationships in the field research, members reported the main role of relationships with external stakeholders as "to provide new networks that might be useful in work context." For internal stakeholders, the main role of relationships was "to lead to trust which is effective for accomplishing work." The understanding of relationships seemed to be a means for a different end. In addition, respondents did not believe that relationships were a priority in the office. Policies and structures, as well as pre-agreed tasks took priority in the office.[808]

The inherent value of people and relationships have long been part of the Christian tradition and should be emphasized in this relational dimension of work. Described in chapter eight, the Christian concept of flourishing is rooted in people, particularly in their reconciliation to God. Flourishing has a clear relational focus that is characterized by love. To impart value of flourishing, characterized by love, the relationships at work should also be marked by love. This implies an understanding of the inherent value of the other person more than the benefits the relationship might have. The question that follows then is, what love should look like in relationships in an organizational setting. In this chapter, it is recommended that this love be expressed through the focus on justice and care of the other. This understanding of love and justice should inform the people management activity systems of the organization. This implies the importance of having it actively lived out in the organization.

---

[808] See chapter 5, table 5.23 and 5.61.

Justice in love is love that "seeks to enhance a person's wellbeing or flourishing and love that seeks to secure that a person's rights are honored, that she be treated with due respect for her worth."[809] Such an understanding of love values the individual inherently, looking out for the rights of the other. This is more than a sentiment, but rather a concrete action towards the wellbeing of the other. This love seeks to promote what one believes to be that person's good or right.[810] It is a love that aims for wholeness in relationships and is motivated by the care of the individual. This love it is not dependent on the actual success of the concrete action.

To apply this understanding of love in the relationships at work is to take into consideration the well-being of the other in the completion of work tasks. It is to recognize the importance of care to the other as a valid priority. This care is an obligation owed to that individual, treating the individual as one's "moral counterpart." This implies the just treatment of the individual as a way of loving him.[811] It is about caring for the "standard of wellbeing for all parties in a given community."[812]

This priority of love for the other reinforces the understanding of flourishing that World Vision embraces. The needs of the others should be intentionally deliberated in the activity systems for it to not be left out. It is the basis of the relationship between the different stakeholders external and internal of the organization.

With the recommendation on love in relationships, we have now reviewed the experience of work from all the three dimensions of work theology. This was done in a transformative way, with recommendations given for each dimension of work. These recommendations are given in light of the leadership moment. In the next section, the attention shifts to the individual leader as the main driver in the leadership process. It recognizes that recommendations made can only be implemented if individual leaders believed and acted on them. A better understanding of the individual leader and its impact to the leadership process is therefore necessary and forms the final recommendation given in this chapter.

---

[809] Nicholas Wolterstorff, *Justice in Love* (Grand Rapids, MI: W.B. Eerdmans, 2011), 101.
[810] Ibid, 103.
[811] Wolterstorff, *Justice in Love*, 83.
[812] Bruce C. Birch, Rebekah Miles and Allen Verhey, "Justice" in: Joel B. Green et al., *Dictionary of Scripture and Ethics* (Grand Rapids, MI: Baker Academic, 2011).

9.3 Leadership and the Individual Leader

Specific recommendations have been made in the previous section with the appropriation of work theology. Firstly, there is the need to focus on the purpose of the organization as the basis of decision making. This purpose of the organization should also be central to the decisions made regarding other organizational characteristics such as the activity systems and boundary maintenance. Secondly, a turn to focus on the spiritual growth of the staff members as a form of workplace spirituality and finally, intentional focus on the care of staff members such that relationships can be characterized by justice in love.

In making these recommendations, it is clear that the implementation of these recommendations is dependent on the leader of this leadership process. In this section, the central role of the leader to the overall leadership process is highlighted. The leader is not passive, but rather an active agent in the leadership process. He or she carries out his role depending on who he or she is. This involves more than the task at hand. The very being of who this individual is can impact the leadership process that the leader is involved in.

What the leader discerns as important for the leadership process is dependent on his or her being. The leader navigates and mediates the information through his own understanding of what's right or wrong. The traits of leaders alone are not sufficient to determine the success of the leadership process. They are too simplistic and do not account for the other factors involved in the leadership process. Research has shown that what is preferred differs depending on factors such as the norms of the group,[813] as well as the cultural context of the followers.[814]

Moving beyond the individual traits, one leadership theory that focuses on the being of the leader is authentic leadership. Authentic leadership focuses on who the leader is and how that impacts the way the individual executes his or her leadership role. This leadership theory can be traced to the roots of humanistic and positive psychology. Humanistic psychologists such as Carl Rogers and Abraham Maslow are particularly influential with their research on fully functioning self-actualized persons. For them, fully actualized humans are individuals who are in alignment with

---

[813] Daan Van Knippenberg, "Embodying Who We Are: Leader Group Prototypicality and Leadership Effectiveness," *Leadership Quarterly* 22, no. 6 (2011): 1078–1091.

[814] Anne S. Tsui, Sushil S. Nifadkar, and Amy Yi Ou, "Cross-National, Cross-Cultural Organizational Behavior Research: Advances, Gaps, and Recommendations," *Journal of Management* 33, no. 3 (June 1, 2007): 426–78.

their basic nature, are unfazed by others' expectations for them, and therefore, are able to make better personal choices.[815] This individual is often seen as autonomous, with sufficient inner essence that is the basis of authentic action as a leader.[816] In the discussion of the individual leader, the authentic leadership theory is appropriated. This focus on the being of the individual is consistent with the way people have been discussed throughout this dissertation. People are valuable, their interpretation have real impact to the organization and therefore are deserving of the effort to further understand them.

The authentic leadership theory is appropriated in this section as a way of understanding a good authentic leader. Since the inception of the authentic leadership theory, different scholars have focused on different aspects of the theory.[817] In explicating the theory of authentic leadership in this section, we keep our focus on the discussion of the individual leader.[818] We begin by outlining an understanding of the leader self that is rooted in self-awareness, developed within a particular context as well as embedded

---

[815] Bruce J. Avoilo and William L. Gardner, "Authentic Leadership Development: Getting to the Root of Positive Forms of Leadership," *Leadership Quarterly* 16 (2005): 319.

[816] William George, *Authentic Leadership: Rediscovering the Secrets to Creating Lasting Value* (San Francisco: Jossey-Bass, 2003).

[817] Some have described the features of authentic leadership to include the need for self-awareness, the enduring nature of the true self, self-regulation and consistency as well as the link between authenticity and moral leadership. See Raymond Sparrowe, "Authentic Leadership and the Narrative Self," *Leadership Quarterly* 16 (2005): 420. Others have sought to group the existing literature on authentic leadership in key aspects such as being true to oneself, being self-aware of this true self as well as this true self being morally good. See Donna Ladkin and Steven S. Taylor, "Enacting the 'True self'": Towards a Theory of Embodied and Authentic Leadership," *Leadership Quarterly* 21, no. 1 (2010): 64–74. Another way that authentic leadership has been studied is the relationship of this self to the function of leadership. Themes that were described included, knowing one's true self in terms of preferences, beliefs, strengths and so on (Self-awareness), representing oneself in relation to others according to how one perceives one true self (relational transparency), gathering and employing objective information that may challenge self-awareness (balanced processing) and exhibiting a moral perspective referring to self-regulation and self-determination. Arran Caza and Brad Jackson, "Authentic Leadership," in *The Sage Handbook of Leadership*, ed. A. Bryman et al. (London: SAGE Publications, 2011), 352–64.

[818] In this section, we have not defined who the leader is specifically. Keeping the definition broad, a leader is understood in the section as an individual who has influence over followers and is able to cause change in a particular context.

within a narrative discourse. The morality of this narrative self is also described. After developing this understanding of self, we focus on how the individual enacts his or her leadership role, particularly in his or her communication with followers. Recommendations on different leader development opportunities for the organization are also made.

9.3.1 Understanding of Self

At the core of authentic leadership is an assumption of high levels of self-awareness.[819] This awareness focuses on one's values, thinking behind identity, emotions, and purposes.[820] Often, this definition is described as an internal process where one continually comes to understand his or her "unique talents, strengths, sense of purpose, core values, beliefs and desires. It can include having a basic and fundamental awareness of one's knowledge, experience and capabilities."[821]

Besides being self-aware, the theory of authentic leadership has often included the acceptance of who one is. This acceptance has been described in theory as optimal self-esteem. Self-esteem "involves favorable feelings of self-worth that arise naturally from successfully dealing with life challenges; the operation of one's core, true, authentic self as a source of input to behavioral choices; and relationships in which one is valued for who one is and not for what one achieves." Because of this individual positive acceptance, there is "relative absence of defensiveness, that is, being willing to divulge negative behaviors or self-aspects in the absence of excessively strong desires to be liked by others."[822] In theory, an understanding and acceptance of who one is enables one to lead more authentically, instead of simply fulfilling the expectations of others.

9.3.1.1 *Influenced by the Environment and Others*

In making this claim about self-awareness, this does not imply an individualistic, independent understanding of the self. In fact, an individual self is situated, influenced by the context that he or she comes from. This self is not separate from the wider context, something that can be managed

---

[819] Avoilo and Gardner, "Authentic Leadership Development," 324.
[820] William L. Gardner et al., "Can You See the Real Me? A Self-Based Model of Authentic Leader and Follower Development," *The Leadership Quarterly* 16, no. 3 (2005): 343–72.
[821] Avoilo and Gardner, "Authentic Leadership Development," 324.
[822] Michael H. Kernis, "Toward a Conceptualization of Optimal Self-Esteem," *Psychological Inquiry* 14 (2003): 13.

like a "project", with this project outputs being the possibility of self-realization.[823] The individual self has sometimes been understood as an individual that is contained and entangled in relational and contextual holds, needing to be freed from society.[824] Society is painted negatively, with the mindset that there is "something fundamentally false or dishonest about social life, and for that reason, it is crucially important to be who you are and be the person you are in all you do."[825]

In reality, it is not possible to make clear distinctions between the self and the wider society. An individual self belongs to a certain tradition by virtue of his or her environmental context, which influences the individual's thrownness, immersion and formation. This context can include political, religious and historical concerns.[826] This tradition has a big influence on how one interprets and understands situations.[827] This is particularly interesting for World Vision as it works with individual leaders from different tradition and contexts. Even if leaders come from the Christian tradition, there continues to be much diversity within this Christian tradition.

In addition, one's "true self is not discovered absent of others, but rather is constituted in relation to others."[828] However, this does not mean that the individual self is fully passive, adopting all the opinions of the other. Instead, this individual continues to retain an element of control that he or she can exert in deciding the extent that he or she would be influenced by the social environment. Meaning making of an individual is developed by a sense of self, experienced by action.[829] Focusing only on the internal self can result in 'shutting out' the context that this self is in, as well as the different meaningful relationships that this self has. By shut-

---

[823] Nicholson and Carroll, "So You Want to Be Authentic in Your Leadership," 290.
[824] Helen Nicholson and Brigid Carroll, "So You Want to Be Authentic in Your Leadership: To Whom and for What End?" in *Authentic Leadership Clashes, Convergences and Coalescences*, ed. Donna Ladkin and Chellie Spiller (Cheltenham: Edward Elgar, 2013), 289.
[825] Charles Guignon, *On Being Authentic* (New York: Routledge, 2004), 146.
[826] Guignon, *On Being Authentic*, 140.
[827] For more information, see Hans-Georg Gadamer, *Truth and Method*, trans. Joel Weinsheimer and Donald G. Marshall (New York: Crossroad, 2004).
[828] Sparrowe, "Authentic Leadership and the Narrative Self," 422.
[829] For more information, see E. Goffman, *Stigma: Notes on the Management of a Spoiled Identity* (Englewood Cliffs, NJ: Prentice-Hall, 1963).

ting out the context and relationships, this is akin to blocking out the influences and demands of history, society, nature and solidarity, eliminating "all the candidates for what matters."[830]

The self then is situated in a particular context, mediated by people as well as the environment that he or she is in. This self is situated in a particular context, yet at the same time dynamic, open to change. There is opportunity for the individual self to be changed through their work experience. A dynamic self can at first glance seem contrary to the description of self that is described in authentic leadership. This self in authentic leadership has often been described as fixed, static and constant. Self-constancy is thought to be necessary to anchor self-regulatory processes such that the individual's actions are in alignment to their true selves. This understanding of self- constancy can however represent a truncated view of the self. People do change, and are not always consistent. One way that this tension between constancy and change can be addressed is through the appropriation of narrative thought by Ricoeur, particularly the relationship between an individual's character and self-consistency.[831] This focus of the narrative is consistent with the recommendation of the spiritual guidance model. The narrative approach of the self is further explored below.

9.3.1.2 Narrative Approach to the Self Rooted in a Social Horizon

A narrative approach of the self assumes an individual who reflects on his or her life experiences and makes meaning in the context of his or her own story. This includes the recognition of the cultural context one comes from. This indicates an individual who has high autobiographic and relational competency. This self plays an active role reflecting and making meaning. He or she does not merely allow others to completely override or subvert who he or she is. This process of making meaning in the context of one's narrative has been described as an authentic living story web, when an individual integrates his or her past experiences, his or her future expectations and his or her potentiality for being a whole-self while deconstructing their inauthentic selves.[832] Similar to the spiritual guidance

---

[830] Charles Taylor, *The Ethics of Authenticity* (Cambridge, MS: Harvard University Press, 2003), 41.
[831] Sparrowe, "Authentic Leadership and the Narrative Self," 422.
[832] David M. Boje, Catherine A. Helmut, and Rohny Saylors, "Cameo: Spinning Authentic Leadership Living Stories of the Self," in *Authentic Leadership Clashes, Convergences and Coalescences*, ed. Donna Ladkin and Chellie Spiller (Cheltenham: Edward Elgar, 2013), 271–273.

model, this understanding of the living story web takes seriously the conditions of space and time. In the following paragraph, this living story web is further described as the process that the individual self goes through as they seek to develop an authentic self. As the spiritual guidance model recommended earlier supports the development of an individual's self-awareness, similarities to the spiritual guidance model are pointed out.

More than a shallow or short term thinking of oneself, a self that seeks to create an authentic living story requires emergent awareness, defined as the "ability to distinguish between reaching a potentiality for an authentic whole self or the inauthentic they-self through ontological inquiry."[833] Ontological inquiry takes reflection of the self seriously, drawing on the individual's past experiences and future expectations. This implies reflection being future focused or 'ahead of itself' which influences the present and re-historicizes the past.[834] This reflection is useful in the understanding of one's story, especially according to a clear chronological order. It seeks to critically consider the theme, the generalized plot structure and character traits of the individual.[835] Through a series of steps, it makes it possible to re-historicize the individual's experiences such that the individual stays in control over his or her living story. The individual becomes an active agent, conscious about which experiences to focus on and which to ignore, as well as the themes that are implicit in the experiences. Through this ontological inquiry, the individual can create a more authentic living story web, and in return, a more authentic self.[836] The spiritual guidance model as described earlier is an example of an ontological inquiry model. In this model, a guide is included to supports the self in weaving this narrative.

To gain further insight into this reflection process, the process of emplotment as described by Ricoeur can provide further insight. Emplotment "draws a meaningful story from a diversity of events or incidents."[837]

---

[833] David M. Boje, Catherine A. Helmut, and Rohny Saylors, "Cameo: Spinning Authentic Leadership Living Stories of the Self," in *Authentic Leadership Clashes, Convergences and Coalescences*, ed. Donna Ladkin and Chellie Spiller (Cheltenham: Edward Elgar, 2013), 271–273.

[834] Martin Heidegger, *Being and Time*, trans. John Macquarrie and Edward Robinson (New York: Harper and Row, 1962), 202, 246.

[835] David M. Boje and Grace A. Rosile, "Restorying the Authentic and Inauthentic Self," Seminar at Benedictine University, St. Louis, MO (2011).

[836] Boje, Helmut, and Saylors, "Cameo: Spinning Authentic Leadership Living Stories of the Self," 274–276.

[837] Paul Ricoeur, *Time and Narrative*, trans. K. McLaughlin and D. Pellauer (Chicago: University of Chicago Press, 1984), 65.

Events that may not seem related are drawn together so that their temporal and logical interdependencies can be understood.[838] The outcome of emplotment is to "'integrate into a larger narrative, the discordant nature of events into the unity of a life considered a temporal totality which is itself singular and distinguished from all others."[839] This understanding of emplotment is also similar to the discussion of autobiographic and relational competence as described earlier in the spiritual guidance model. What is key is the ability to make sense of the individual events in one's life into a larger plot.

For Ricoeur, the unity in the different events or incidents points to one's character – or what is enduring about the self. During the emplotment process, the character intertwines with the plot thereby lending self-constancy to an individual's identity. This provides consistency to the individual. As this process of emplotment repeats itself, the brief plots are retrospectively weaved together into a larger narrative with an implied actual beginning, middle and ending. This larger narrative is the framework that people use to narrate their lives as originating at some point.[840] This involves "creation and construction as well as discovery, originality and frequently, opposition to the rules of society and even potentially to what we recognize as morality. At the same time, it also requires openness to horizons of significance and a self-definition in dialogue."[841] With the dynamic understanding of self, what stays constant is this character that the individual refers to.

This theme or character that an individual uses as a reference point has also been described as the processing "against a background of intelligibility" which Charles Taylor describes as a horizon. Bigger than any individual, Taylor describes these horizons as given. An individual makes decisions about what takes up significance against the backdrop of pre-existing horizons of significance. These horizons of significance are not neutral, but rather have different values attached to them as prescribed by the different horizons of significance. The Christian perspective, that of being a co-heir, described in the spiritual guidance model is an example of one kind of horizon that the individual self can choose to frame the events of work and even the broader life around in making a narrative. As an in-

---

[838] Sparrowe, "Authentic Leadership and the Narrative Self," 425.
[839] Paul Ricoeur and Kathleen Blamey, *Oneself as Another* (Chicago: University of Chicago Press, 1994), 147.
[840] Sparrowe, "Authentic Leadership and the Narrative Self," 428.
[841] Paul Ricoeur, *Time and Narrative*, 66.

vitation, it is clear that not all individuals would use this horizon of significance. The individual self, as part of the environment that they are in and constituted by the relationships that they have, may be predisposed to choose some horizons over others. What the individual self, as leader in an organization chooses as the horizon of significance can cascade through the whole organization.

Having described the process of achieving self-consistency in the narrative self through ontological enquiry, the next section focuses on the morality of this individual leader.

9.3.1.3 Morality of One Self

In theory, the authentic leader has often been assumed to be ethical.[842] This stems from positive psychology that assumes that the authentic fully actualized person has strong ethical convictions.[843] The individual leader's ethics is central in the practice and scholarship of authentic leadership.[844] Being true to one self and others is thought to lead to high moral and ethical standards.[845] This authentic leader goes beyond his or her own concerns and management effectiveness to issues involving society that can be greater than each individual self.[846]

One reason for this link is the understanding that as one clarifies who one is, authenticity results in one being involved with something bigger, a connection to a wider whole.[847] It is living responsibly from an individual's standpoint, resulting in a richer mode of existence.[848] This was described in Guignon's understanding of a social embodiment of authenticity where authenticity requires people to consider their commitment to wider social

---

[842] See authors like Arran Caza and Brad Jackson, "Authentic Leadership," 352–64, Donna Ladkin and Steven S. Taylor, "Enacting the 'True self': Towards a Theory of Embodied and Authentic Leadership," 64–74 and Owain S. Jones and Keith Grint, "Authentic Leadership and History," 21–38.
[843] Abraham Maslow, *The Farther Reaches of Human Nature* (New York: Harper, 1971), 346.
[844] Suze Wilson, "Viewpoint: The Authentic Leader Reconsidered: Integrating the Marvelous, Mundane and Mendacious," in *Authentic Leadership Clashes, Convergences and Coalescences*, ed. Donna Ladkin and Chellie Spiller (Cheltenham: Edward Elgar, 2013), 61.
[845] Bernard M. Bass and Paul Steidlmeier, "Ethics, Character and Authentic Transformational Leadership Behavior," *Leadership Quarterly* 10, no. 2 (1999): 184.
[846] Nicholson and Carroll, "So You Want to Be Authentic in Your Leadership," 298.
[847] Charles Taylor, *The Ethics of Authenticity* (Cambridge, MS: Harvard University Press, 2003), 91.
[848] Ibid, 74.

community and to engage from a place of authenticity.[849] "The authentic person becomes more clear-sighted and reflective about the issues, engaging in political action aimed at preserving and reinforcing a way that allows for such worthy personal life projects as that of authenticity."[850] This possibility of being authentically engaged in social issues perpetuates the belief that the authentic leader will be moral.

While it is certainly possible that the social embodiment of authenticity can lead to positive action, it is also not necessary that the authentic self will decide on positive values and principles. It might very well be possible that when one is seeking to be true to oneself, one can end up choosing to be narcissistic instead of well-intentioned.[851] Not all authentic people share the same idea of morality. One's morality depends again on the reflection based on one's chosen character, theme and horizon of significance. The ethical interpretation of an individual has been described as the "unending work of interpretation applied to action and to oneself that we pursue the search for adequation between what seems to us to be best with regard to our life as a whole and the preferential choices that govern our practices."[852] The individual is constantly interpreting depending on the narrative that he or she is weaving.

9.3.1.4 Implications of the Individual Self to Leader Development

So far, we have outlined the theory involved in outlining the individual self in authentic leadership. We began first by describing the self as one with high levels of self-awareness and self-esteem. The self is not a free agent but rather is situated, influenced by the environment as well as the relationships he or she has. He or she is not static but rather grows, weaving a narrative around the experience he or she lived through based on his or her chosen theme. He or she makes meaning and ethical interpretation based on this chosen theme, character and horizon. In outlining this theory, what is clear is the importance for the individual leader to be able to reflect. Through reflection, he or she becomes aware about who he or she is, the character, theme or horizon he or she would like to weave into his or her narrative.

Reflection is a process that clarifies for an individual who he or she is. Until one knows who one is, it is difficult to know what is truly important

---

[849] Guignon, *On Being Authentic*, 163.
[850] Ibid., 161-163.
[851] Sparrowe, "Authentic Leadership and the Narrative Self," 424.
[852] Paul Ricoeur, *Time and Narrative*, 65.

to oneself. This ability to reflect and discern is particularly important for leaders leading an organization in the development practice. With the telos of the practice described as the "promotion of the well-functioning of the practices and institutions that are relevant in a certain setting,"[853] it is important for leaders to be able to reflect and discern which practices and institutions to promote. The choice of practices and institutions to promote is best done by the authentic leader who is more discerning during decision making because of the ability to reflect. This reduces the tendency for the individual leader to follow existing trends, or to do that which seems convenient.

At the same time, it is not assumed that all authentic individuals will share the moral inclination of the organization, or the development practice. An authentic individual can also be authentically incompatible to the values of the organization and genuinely choose practices and institutions that clash with what is understood as relevant from a Christian perspective. However, with the emphasis on reflection, it is assumed that an authentic individual would at an early stage be clear about who he or she is and will decide whether there can be a potential fit between the organization and the individual self.

In the next section, the increase space for reflection within an organization is outlined. This increased space for reflection nudges the individual to become more aware of who he or she is at the work place, leading to reflected action and discerning decision making.

9.3.1.5 Opening Space for Reflection at Work

Reflection involves the process of knowing oneself better as reflective thinking focuses on one's spiritual and moral sources. Through the process of deep reflection, one begins to know oneself deeper, as the core of one's being is being approached.[854] This importance of deep reflection is not only reserved for the leaders, but is also relevant for all staff. Reflection is a big part of the spiritual guidance model, the recommendation given to strengthen communion with God. What is argued here is the added importance of reflection for leaders. As influential people, who they are and the decisions they make have a profound impact on the organization. It is therefore important that these leaders are reflecting and have clarity

---

[853] Jochemsen, "A Normative Model for the Practice of Cooperation in Development as a Basis for Social Justice," 138.
[854] Ibid., 135.

about their employment process. The process of deep reflection is described below.

Deep reflection has been described to be the interpretation or reinterpretation of experience, knowledge and beliefs. It enables one to think actively and consciously about one's experiences, actions, behaviors, choices and views.[855] This is similar to the ontological inquiry described earlier, or the hermeneutical framework described in the spiritual guidance framework. This reflection exists within the conditions of time and space, takes into consideration the self as embedded in society with others. The following paragraphs outline the possibility of reflecting deeply at work at two levels, as well as critically considering the social relationships involved at work.

The first level of reflection asks the question "Do I do it properly?"[856] Properly in this instance is understood as the extent that the proficiency of the role is met. This focuses on one's performance according to existing standards.[857] While a start, this is insufficient as it does not consider the broader purpose of the role that the individual does, neither does it engage the individual at the level of his or her spiritual and moral source.

A second level is necessary for the individual to relate his role to his or her spiritual and moral sources. This involves reflecting on the question "Do I engage the proper values with which to perform properly?" At this level of reflective thinking, the individual looks at the experience of the work role from a more personal level. There is the willingness to engage in a deeper understanding of the purpose of the role that one fulfils, as well as the purpose of the organization within society.[858] This goes beyond completing the role well. Instead, it is about relating the role with who the individual is. At its deepest level, this involves discerning one's suitability to the role, "accepting a task that is in harmony with the movement people sense in their inner self."[859] It is about questioning the compatibility be-

---

[855] Johan Hegemann, Margaret Edgell, and Henk Jochemsen, *Practice and Profile: Christian Formation for Vocation* (Eugene, OR: Wipf and Stock, 2011), 9.
[856] Ibid., 10.
[857] Jochemsen, "A Normative Model for the Practice of Cooperation in Development as a Basis for Social Justice," 136.
[858] Ibid., 136.
[859] Johan Verstraeten, "Spirituality as Source of Inspired, Authentic and Innovative Leadership," in *Leadership, Innovation and Spirituality*, ed. Patrick Nullens and Jack Barentsen (Leuven: Peeters, 2014), 92.

Strengthening Leadership in the Organization 353

tween the role that one holds with who one is such that there is inner freedom to act. This involves being introspective about one's own individual's spirituality in this contemplation.[860]

With the spiritual guidance model discussed earlier, one's work experiences is reflected based on the understanding of being a co-heir to the kingdom of God, where the connection of one's work experience to being a travelling companion *enroute* one's journey of life as well as guest and hospitality in the space that one is has been outlined. This second level reflection described here relates this understanding of traveling companion and guest/hospitality to the specific purposes of the organization and the context where the organization is in. In chapter eight, the theological reflection of the development practice can be a useful starting point for leaders to use as they question their compatibility of who they are and the needs of the organization.

For the organization encouraging deep reflection, this involves creating intentional space for dialogue and critical reflexivity in tandem with the development practice as well as the other key categories of meaning that the individual make at the workplace. Individuals are invited to consider how they can contribute to this common ground from a place of authenticity. Instead of remaining distinct from the organization, it is possible for a fusion of horizons to take place between the individual and the organization. Besides having guides as per the spiritual guidance model, another way that this fusion of horizon can happen is through the process of translation, where the organization deliberately develops processes and content that can act as translators, articulating the significance of the development practice in a way "that can be comprehended in the perceptual and linguistic worlds of others."[861] It is possible for the content in chapter eight to be used for the process of translation. In addition, as the self has been understood as an agent "engaged in a variety of conversations, identifications, points of view and dialogues," the organization can support the dialogue through reframing possibilities, engaging in "a different self-talk, calling on the different selves that already exist."[862]

The development practice as embodied by the organization provides "a starting point for aligning meaning among organizational members as a basis for coherent action." The leader engages intentionally with this practice, recognizing their own prejudices and viewpoints yet are willing

---

[860] Ibid, 90.
[861] Ladkin, *Rethinking Leadership*, 120.
[862] Nicholson and Carroll, "So You Want to Be Authentic in Your Leadership," 295–296.

to be open to the vision of the organization.[863] In this way, the work that the individual leader does at World Vision becomes a legitimate way for him or her to engage with the community and the larger society. What this also implies is the autonomy given to the leader for him or her to have some control over the priorities of the work goals based on the normative practice. This is in contrast to directing the organization in a different direction because of external pressures.

Besides the development practice, another key aspect in this reflection is the understanding of the self as embedded in social relationships. In thinking of oneself as a travelling companion or guest, this implies the importance of involving the reflection of others in the understanding of one self. As detailed by Ricoeur, who one is becomes an object of reflection. Through the reflection of the self as the other, the other becomes valuable. Statements such as "I cannot myself have self-esteem unless I esteem others as myself,"[864] or the "esteem of the other as oneself and the esteem of oneself as an other"[865] indicates the equitable value of the other as oneself. A critical evaluation of who one is from the view of the other takes the opinion of the other seriously. It focuses on how one is viewed as a companion. One way that this can be done is to solicit feedback from others on individual's strengths.[866] At the same time, it is also clear that for feedback to be honest, the staff members should be able to trust these leaders. The relationship between the authentic self and the followers are looked at, particularly how the authentic leader communicates his or her leadership role.

9.3.2 Communication between Authentic Leaders and Followers

The way the authentic self enacts his or her leadership role involves the way he or she communicates with his or her followers, particularly through the discussion of self-regulation. As an introduction, self-regulation is described as a key characteristic in authentic leadership. Often, this concept is linked to the transparency and consistency of the leader. It has been defined as the process "through which the behavior of authentic

---

[863] Ladkin, *Rethinking Leadership*, 124.
[864] Paul Ricoeur, *Oneself as Another*, 193.
[865] Ibid, 194.
[866] Sparrowe, "Authentic Leadership and the Narrative Self," 432.

leaders become transparent (consonant) with their self-awareness."[867] Self-regulation is made apparent when leaders align who they are in terms of their values, purposes and goals with their actions, making it known to the followers. The leader's observed behavior is assessed depending on the consistency with identifiable qualities. This process has been categorized as the model of prototype matching.[868] In this discussion of self-regulation, the context involved in the narrative discourse that the self is embedded in as well as other processes, can alter this process of self-regulation. This is described below.

9.3.2.1 *Narrative Discourse in Self-Regulation*

Understanding the self as embedded in the narrative discourse can make it challenging to determine the transparency and consistency of the individual leader through prototype matching, where "observed behavior is assessed in terms of its consistency with identifiable qualities." This narrative self is less straightforward with less obvious identifiable qualities. As a solution, Sparrowe suggests that instead of prototype matching, this self should be understood with the concept of "re-conceptualization."[869]

Re-conceptualization implies more responsibility on the reflective leader to be transparent and consistent. To be transparent is to be intentionally explicit about one's true intentions, and to be consistent is to maintain the same character through different events in one's narrative discourse.[870] In seeking to be transparent and consistent, there are other processes such as balanced processing and relational transparency that the leader is confronted with. Both these processes are described particularly in the way it impacts communication between the leader and the followers.

Balanced processing refers to the ability of leaders to consider multiple different perspectives as they evaluate information in a relatively balanced way. It refers to the "unbiased processing of self-relevant information which involves objectivity and acceptance of one's positive and

---

[867] Fred Luthans and Avoilo, Bruce J., "Authentic Leadership: A Positive Development Approach," in *Positive Organizational Scholarship: Foundations of a New Discipline*, ed. K.S. Cameron, J.E. Dutton, and R.E Quinn (San Francisco: Barett-Koehler, 2003), 241–58.

[868] Sparrowe, "Authentic Leadership and the Narrative Self," 432.

[869] Ibid., 432.

[870] Ibid.

negative aspects, attributes, and qualities."[871] A reflective self is aware of the different perspectives present and seeks to evaluate the information in a balanced way. This impacts the ultimate action of the leader. Relational transparency refers to the relationship between the leader and the follower. It considers the value given to openness and truthfulness in the relationships with the other. In the theory of authentic leadership, there is an expectation that the ideal relationship between the leader and the followers should be characterized by transparency, openness and trust.[872] This leader as self should choose to relate to the other through a process of self-disclosure and the development of mutual intimacy and trust.[873] While this has been described as an expectation in theory, this relationship between the leader and his or her followers should not be assumed.

The inescapability of power within the relationship might make the relationship between the leader and the followers less than ideal. In addition, "the inevitability of human imperfection, the local and broader social context, including the existence of prejudice, poverty and inequality, plus a greater sense of the multifaceted and often contradictory aspects of our 'selves' would also be taken seriously."[874] This implies that transparency cannot be assumed but rather needs to be actively worked on.

The narrative discourse can cause the self to be too complex for understanding. Alternatively, it can "portray what is a contingent choice today in the form of a consequence one must live with tomorrow."[875] There is a pattern of behavior that can be uncovered. An organization should support the individual self in self-regulation. In the relational dimension as described, the importance of a relationship characterized by love in the form of justice has been emphasized. This love should also characterize the relationship between the leader and follower. In addition, in the discussion of deep reflection, the reflection of social relations was added as a key aspect that should not be forgotten. The self should reflect on himself as a subject. To complement these existing recommendations, the following section describes the importance of moral intelligence to strengthen balanced processing of the leaders.

---

[871] Michael H. Kernis, "Toward a Conceptualization of Optimal Self-Esteem," *Psychological Inquiry* 14 (2003): 14.

[872] William L. Gardner et al., "Can You See the Real Me? A Self-Based Model of Authentic Leader and Follower Development," *The Leadership Quarterly* 16, no. 3 (2005): 345.

[873] Ibid.

[874] Wilson, "Viewpoint."

[875] Sparrowe, "Authentic Leadership and the Narrative Self," 432.

9.3.2.2 Building Moral Intelligence in the Organization

Balanced processing requires the leader to be able to contemplate different perspectives while considering who one is. One way in which the organization can support this. Is to actively build the moral intelligence of the leaders. In leadership studies, the discussion of ethics seems to be scathing to say the least.[876] To speak about moral intelligence is to once again reinforce the role of ethics in the actions of the individual leaders. As these authentic leaders work to influence the overall moral climate, it is important for them to be equipped with moral intelligence.

Moral intelligence considers the capacity for the individual to "have the mental capacity to determine how universal human principles should be applied to our values, goals and actions."[877] To be morally intelligent is to recognize one's particular starting point, including cultural situatedness, yet at the same time, be sympathetic to the complex reality the individual is in. This requires the ability for the individual to interpret reality in a non-simplistic way.[878] In this discussion of moral intelligence, we focus on two main aspects. Firstly, a model is introduced as a framework for moral reasoning. Secondly, moral intelligence through the cultivation of virtues are described.

One who has moral intelligence has high moral reasoning abilities. He or she is able to "draw on more sophisticated conceptualization of interpersonal situations, to think about problems in different ways, and are cognizant of a larger number of behavioral options."[879] As a tool to guide moral reasoning, a framework that incorporates different dimensions of reality according to different ethical theories has been created.[880] This

---

[876] In describing the role of ethics in leadership studies, Joanne Ciulla argues that "the discussion of ethics in leadership literature is fragmented; there is little reference to other works on the subject, and one gets the sense that most authors write as if they were starting from scratch." Joanne B. Ciulla, *Ethics: The Heart of Leadership* (Westport, CT: Praeger Publishers, 2004),4.

[877] Doug Lennick and Fred Kiel, *Moral Intelligence 2.0: Enhancing Business Performance and Leadership Success in Turbulent Times* (Upper Saddle River: Prentice-Hall, 2011), xxxi.

[878] This means more than studying ethical issues through looking at the interest of different stakeholders' analysis, a key method considered in business ethics.

[879] Nick Turner et al., "Transformational Leadership and Moral Reasoning," *Journal of Applied Psychology* 87 (2002): 305.

[880] In his framework, these dimensions include the practice that the organization seeks to express, the individual self, the micro-context – people that the self is in contact with, macro-context, the society that one is in, and finally, the transcendental reality. Each of these dimensions can input the influence the ethical matrix

model is an alternative to reductionist ethical tendencies, focusing only on one category of ethical theories, for example, consequential ethics. It is recommended in this dissertation as it affirms the importance of different ethical categories to providing different ethical perspectives. These different categories have been categorized to include principle, consequential, virtue and value ethics.[881] This framework is useful for leaders in their balanced processing and moral reasoning in the interpretation of reality.

Finally, leaders should be encouraged to follow through with their moral reasoning. Generally speaking, individuals with high ability to morally reason are thought to act morally too, in order to achieve consistency, reducing uncomfortable cognitive dissonance. This however should not be assumed. Moral utilization describes the extent to which individuals actually utilize their capacity for principled thinking in ethical decision making. Should the individual leader utilize their moral reasoning, this can result in a strengthened relationship between the leader and the overall moral climate in the organization.[882] One way that this can be further supported is through the deliberate embedding of organizational mechanisms that support the selection and management of the leader in the organization. Embedding mechanisms have been described as "tools" that support the vision of the organization.[883] These mechanisms range from primary embedding mechanisms to secondary articulation and reinforcement mechanisms. These mechanisms have been described in chapter 3, figure 3.5.

9.3.2.3 Developing Appropriate Virtues Depending on the Practice

Besides the framework for moral reasoning, the emphasis on virtue ethics is also made. With the focus on the being of the leader in authentic leader-

---

that should be used in moral reasoning. See Patrick Nullens, "Slim omgaan met ethische dilemma's: Een hermeneutisch model," *Tijdschrift voor Management en Organisatie* 68, no. 5–6 (2014): 91–107.

[881] For a philosophical and theological description of these different models, see Patrick Nullens and Ronald T. Michener, *The Matrix of Christian Ethics: Integrating Philosophy and Moral Theology in a Postmodern Context* (Colorado Springs: IVP Books, 2010).

[882] Michael E. Brown and Linda K. Treviño, "Ethical Leadership: A Review and Future Directions," *The Leadership Quarterly* 17 (2006): 605.

[883] See Chapter 2, section 2.4.4.2.

ship, the inclusion of the discussion of virtue ethics is appropriate as it approaches ethics from the perspective of the leader's character.[884] In addition, as a theological dissertation, there is something unique that the Christian tradition can certainly contribute to the content of virtues required in leadership. As human nature has "remained fairly constant," there is much that humanities such as theology can offer to the understanding of the moral expectation of leaders.[885]

In this section, two virtues are described as necessary for leaders at World Vision. A full reflection of each of these virtues is beyond the scope of this section. What is aimed at is the reasoning and introduction of why these virtues are vital for World Vision. Knowing the virtues necessary for individual leaders should inform the leader management processes involved. This can impact for example, the selection criteria of the leader as well as processes that intentionally cultivate these virtues.

The choice of the virtues mentioned are related to the role of the leader within the overall leadership moment at World Vision as illustrated in this case study.[886] In making recommendations for particular virtues, this list is by no means exhaustive. These virtues support the leader in solving moral issues that they are currently facing. It recognizes the leader as key in the leadership moment. Through the actions of the leader, other pieces of the leadership moment are influenced. Two moral issues and the suggested virtues are described in the following.

The first category of moral issues is related to the purpose of the organization. In chapter seven, the purpose of World Vision has been described to be related to the development practice. In dealing with the purpose of the organization, virtues are understood as "the embodiment of normative principles in the profession."[887] This implies that the leader should embody normative principles that are directly related to the ultimate purpose of the organization. In chapter seven, we have established that for the development practice, the related normative principle is the historical or formative principle.[888] This involves evaluating the needs of

---

[884] Peter G. Northouse, *Leadership: Theory and Practice*, (London: SAGE Publications, 2007), 345.
[885] For example, see Joanne B. Ciulla, "The Moral Dangers of Leadership," in *Challenges of Moral Leadership*, ed. Patrick Nullens and Steven C. van den Heuvel (Leuven: Peeters, 2016), 26.
[886] The understanding of leadership as a moment was introduced earlier in section 9.1 Issues in processes and their link to leadership.
[887] Hegemann, Edgell, and Jochemsen, *Practice and Profile: Christian Formation for Vocation*, 83.
[888] See chapter 7, section 7.1.4.2 Standards of Excellence.

society taking into consideration its context. The virtue of discernment embodies this principle of evaluating the needs of the society.

Discernment is described as "an awareness of that which is deemed ultimately important." It entails listening, "opening oneself up to the context and to God's involvement in the context."[889] This understanding of discernment emphasizes the importance of reflection, listening to the experience, to God, the word, one another and the context.[890] Discernment can then be described as "a chain of reasoning whose first premises concern the human good, whose intermediate steps specify what virtues require, if the human good is to be achieved, and whose conclusion is the action that is good and best for us to perform here and now."[891] This discernment recognizes God's presence, his action towards and through human beings. Human good or flourishing is understood as the reconciliation to God as God actively relates to human creatures.[892]

The second category of moral issues related to the leader is the required virtues to deal with followers. Justice is discussed as an integral virtue, particularly because of the unequal power relations between the leader and the follower. Leaders play a "high stakes game because their moral behavior can harm or benefit followers, groups, organizations, institutions, countries and possibly the world." By nature of the role they play, the "cost and benefits of complying or not complying are greater."[893] In the leader-follower relationship, there is a clear imbalance of power that can lead to abuse. Echoing the importance of love in relationships that was mentioned as the standard for relationship, the virtue justice in love becomes a vital virtue. For justice to be experienced, this understanding of virtue must first be embodied by the leaders. It becomes a key virtue for

---

[889] Cornelius J.P. Niemandt, "Discerning Spirituality for Missional Leaders" (paper presented at the conference on Leadership, Spirituality and Discernment, Leuven, Belgium, 6 May 2017).

[890] Gert S. Cordier and Cornelius J.P. Niemandt, "Core capacities for the minister as missional leader in the formation of a missional congregational culture. Part 2: Capacities and conclusions," *Journal for Missional Practise* 6(Autumn 2015), accessed August 20, 2017, http://journalofmissionalpractice.com/core-capacities-for-the-minister-as-missional-leader-in-the-formation-of-a-missional-congregational-culture-part-2-capacities-and-conclusions.

[891] Alasdair MacIntyre, Dependent Rational Animals: Why Human Beings Need the Virtues (Chicago, IL: Open Court Press, 1999), 158-159.

[892] See 8.3.3.2.2 Social Justice and Evangelism as Enabling Human Flourishing.

[893] Joanne B. Ciulla, "The Moral Dangers of Leadership," in *Challenges of Moral Leadership*, ed. Patrick Nullens and Steven C. van den Heuvel (Leuven: Peeters, 2016), 14.

leaders to develop. In linking leading to justice, ethics takes a center stage in the decisions making of the leaders.[894]

From a Judeo-Christian perspective, justice is rooted in the inherent rights of human beings simply because of "the worth of beings of their sort."[895] It is God who confers the value of worth to human beings because His love seeks to enhance and preserve their wellbeing.[896] In this sense, justice as rights is understood as "bestowing of wellbeing on other people's lives and history."[897] For justice to be a virtue that influences one's leading, this requires one to remember God's example. As God the savior kept his covenant to his people faithfully, justice entails following God's example of faithfulness. This entails treating human beings as loved by God and seeking their wellbeing. It is "an act in imitating God as savior and maker of a covenant with his people."[898]

9.4. Concluding the Recommendations on Processes

This chapter has focused on the second and final recommendation of the case study, strengthening the processes involved in the organization. To focus on the processes is to focus on the authoring and enabling that takes place in the organization, the organizational practices that are put in place in the organization as well as the human agency involved. As processes are influenced by leadership, the recommendations in this chapter centered on the process of leadership, the individual leader as well as specific leadership development recommendations.

In the first broad section of this chapter, the theology of work was appropriated as the hermeneutical lens for the investigation of leadership. Work theology takes seriously people's work experience and focuses on the ethical evaluation of work on three aspects, instrumental, relational and ontological. As a theological model that is transformative, recommendations were made for World Vision in light of the evaluation.

The extent that these recommendations take place is very much dependent on the priorities of the leader. Recognizing the key role the leader

---

[894] Patrick Nullens, ""Let Justice Roll Down Like Waters": Ethical Leadership as Generating Justice in an Evil World," in *Challenges of Moral Leadership*, ed. Patrick Nullens and Steven C. van den Heuvel (Leuven: Peeters, 2016), 77.
[895] Nicholas Wolterstorff, Justice: Rights and Wrongs (Princeton: Princeton University Press, 2008), 10–11.
[896] Ibid., 189-190.
[897] Ibid.
[898] Patrick Nullens, "Let Justice Roll Down Like Waters", 93.

plays, the second section studied the leader, a key piece in the overall leadership process. The leader is not a passive agent, but influences the followers based on the purpose and context of the organization. As this leader influences based on his or her individual being, the theory of authentic leadership is outlined as a means to understand this leader, as well as the way he communicates with his follower. Specific recommendations for leader development include increasing space for reflection, building moral intelligence and developing virtues have been discussed.

CHAPTER TEN

Conclusion

This dissertation focused on the case study of World Vision to understand the phenomenon of mission drift. As a case study, much space has been given for rigorous investigation of the real-life context experienced by World Vision.

The specific research question posed in this dissertation is "how can the four different tasks involved in practical theological interpretation, as well as the appropriation of different academic disciplines and theological sub-disciplines, be used to strengthen the Christian identity of the organization thereby countering mission drift?" This practical theological interpretation consists of four different tasks that interact and mutually influence each other. Recognizing the complexity found in the realities of this case study, different academic disciplines are appropriated to support the different practical tasks for this theological interpretation.

In this dissertation, a case study strategy has been employed for this theological interpretation. This allows sufficient space to be given to each task and phase. It also takes seriously the process of arriving at the final recommendations. It seeks to be an example of the interaction between theory and practice. In the next section, key findings from each phase are detailed. Concluding thoughts are then discussed in light of these findings. Finally, future research ideas that are related to this dissertation are outlined.

10.1 Case Study Strategy to Answer Research Question

The four phases of the case study have been used as a framework for this dissertation. They include the phases: design, collection, analyzing and recommendation. The different ways the different phases contribute to the overall answer of the research question is described.

10.1.1 Design Phase

Chapter two and three form the design phase of this dissertation. This design phase outlines the necessary theoretical basis for the case study as well as the descriptive task of the practical theological interpretation.

The second chapter begins to set out the necessary background information. First of all, the context where faith-based organizations is situated in, civil society, is described. The civil society is described as the context where common good in society is pursued via institutions. This is a space where different kinds of institutions exist in. Faith-based organizations, a form of institution with established and prevalent social rules, contribute to the Christian pluralism in civil society. It contributes uniquely to the civil society from a Christian perspective. As the organization is the particular institution focused on in this dissertation, an in-depth understanding of the organization is included. This includes describing the different characteristics of the organization, as well as the different approaches that are available for studying the organization. In addition, we looked at how different organizational approaches can be appropriated to achieve a comprehensive understanding. The socio-interpretative approach, in particular, is described to be important to supplement the modern organizational approach that has already been employed by World Vision during their change management process. This refers to the importance given to the interpretation of staff members for the overall performance of the organization. In the final section of this chapter, different sociological models related to the influence of religion in society as well as within the organizations is described. This chapter concludes with explicating the tacit identity formation model which describes the identity formation in an organization to be a dialectic, consisting of process and content. This understanding of identity formation has been used throughout the dissertation in the discussion of the Christian identity of World Vision.

The third chapter investigates the different possible ways that World Vision's Christian understanding can be described. The first way focuses on established methods of utilizing typologies, the second on studying the different organizational characteristics determining their influence by religious ideas. The third method emphasizes the organizational culture in each office. These different ways complement each other as they correspond to different organizational approaches. The typologies correspond to a classical organizational approach, the organizational variables to a modern approach and the organizational culture to a socio-interpretative approach. This socio-interpretative approach measures the extent to which staff members embraced World Vision's Christian values. Together, both chapter two and three provide the theoretical basis of this case study.

10.1.2 Collection Phase

The collection phase documents the actual findings of the empirical research of World Vision. This is found in chapters four to six. This continues the descriptive task of the practical theological interpretation. The extent that the Christian identity permeates World Vision is studied. This empirical research has been described in two levels, one at the level of the entire partnership, and the other at the level of its branch offices. Specific research has also been done in these two branch offices with similar sized operation, one in Nepal and one in Papua New Guinea. Conducting the case study in two locations shed further light on the impact of the environmental context to the overall Christian identity of World Vision offices.

Chapter four describes specific research methods employed in the actual empirical research. This include the description of specific data collection sources, discussion of the limitation of the field research as well as responding to issues of validity and reliability. These different methods relate to the different organizational selves in the tacit identity formation model.

Chapter five outlines information of World Vision as a partnership. This chapter focuses on the first level of the case study and answers the following question: How is World Vision's Christian understanding expressed in its organizational variables and how has this Christian understanding evolved in the development of the organization? Official statements of World Vision based on their policies have been studied. To further understand the dynamic nature of the organization, the chapter details how the organization has evolved with relation to its Christian identity. Based on the findings in chapter five, it is evident that there is a rich inclusion of religiosity in the organizational variables. At the same time, it can also be said that the organization has evolved significantly through time. A diminished Christian influence to the overall ministry of the organization can be deduced.

Chapter six focuses on the collection of the Christian identity at the second level, uncovering the organizational culture in two separate locations, Nepal and Papua New Guinea. Research questions posed in this chapter include:

1) Using the framework of Organizational Culture dimensions, what are the Christian values and assumptions espoused by World Vision based on its core documents?
2) Looking at two different offices of World Vision, what are the actual values and assumptions held by members in each office based on values and assumptions identified in the second question?
3) Understanding an organization as an entity made up by a group of individuals, what is the state of relationships held by different internal stakeholders of the organization?

Based on the findings as outlined in chapter six, it can generally be said that the Christian values as stated in the core documents were not central to the overall organizational culture in either location. With regard to the state of relationships in general, relationships within the office in each location are stronger than relationships with other World Vision offices in other locations. In addition, all the different internal stakeholders perceived the relationship with senior management as the most distant in the office. Through the findings recorded in this collection phase, it is clear that Christian identity has generally diminished in the organizational culture.

10.1.3 Analytical Phase

Chapter seven analyzes of the case study in two ways. First through describing the different organizational 'selves' that interacted to make up the resultant tacit identity in the organization. This includes the self as object, content and subject. In addition, the analysis includes the discussion of organizational culture which explicates the resultant tacit identity. This analysis focuses on the interpretative task of practical theological interpretation.

Based on this first analysis, it can be concluded that despite the clear inclusion of religiosity in the organizational characteristics, the tacit identity of the organization is not clearly Christian. Reasons for this include the diminishing role of the Christian identity in the organization, as well as the processes that the organization has embraced.

In the second analysis, the normative practice model is used. Centered on norms, this analysis corresponds to the normative task of the practical theological interpretation. This normative practice model is an ethical model that focuses on a particular practice, understanding the practice as constituted by a constellation of norms. These norms are based on the understanding of sphere sovereignty as described by Reformational philosopher Herman Dooyeweerd. There are three sides to this model: structural, directional and contextual. In the analysis of the structural side, there is clear evidence that the core documents of World Vision are generally in alignment with the normative structure of the development practice. What is lacking is the clarification of how advocacy and relief, the two other pillars of World Vision would work together to fulfill the telos found in the development practice.

From the analysis of the directional side, World Vision as an organization has evolved and gradually moved away from its Christian direction. Despite the official preference for Christian staff members at World Vision, staff members have expressed that the Christian values of the organization were not prioritized in the organizational culture. These Christian values do not seem to have much implications to the work that is done.

Finally, with regard to the contextual side, World Vision had a clear understanding that the beneficiaries influenced the work that they do. Both case studies reflected different influential stakeholders. For Papua New Guinea, donors are considered to be particularly influential whereas for Nepal, the local context seemed to be more influential with the focus on government relations as well as country statistics.

10.1.4 Recommendation Phase

The final phase offers recommendations that can be made in light of the findings and subsequent analysis. This corresponds to the pragmatic task of theological interpretation. To frame the recommendations, the identity formation model, mediated by process and content, is used. Chapter eight focuses on the content recommendations while chapter nine focuses on the process recommendations.

In chapter eight, the related content of the Christian faith for the development practice is outlined. This provides a timely reminder of the particularity of the Christian faith and its implications to the development practice, particularly in its structure and direction. It is recommended that the Christian faith of the organization should have more than a historical role. It needs to be reconsidered in light of its situation today. The theological reflection in this chapter appropriates the Trinity, a core theological motif of the Christian faith since its early stages. It is recommended that this understanding of the trinity be rigorously engaged with at the organization.

The Trinity is chosen as it explicitly describes the Christian God, and the relationship this God has with the world. As World Vision works in a multi-cultural and religious context, this theological reflection is done in consideration of the context World Vision exist in. The constructive theological approach of Kärkkäinen is appropriated in light of this context. This discussion of the Trinity emphasizes the significance of the world to God. Validating the importance of the world, the Trinity is further outlined in two main areas. The first area looks at the Trinity as the basis of the *Missio Dei* and World Vision as participating in this mission, particularly in its quest for justice. The second focuses on each of the individual divine persons in the Trinity and how they can provide further insight to the development practice. For God the father, the attention is on the Creator God, for God the Son, the focus is on Jesus revealing the Kingdom of God and for God the Holy Spirit, the emphasis is on the completer of the divine program. Specific recommendations on how the organization can respond to each of these divine persons are also discussed.

In chapter nine, recommendations focus on the processes involved in the organization. This complements the content recommendations made in the previous chapter. To focus on the processes is to focus on the authoring and enabling that takes place in the organization. This includes the organizational practices that are put in place as well as the human agency involved. As processes are influenced by leadership, the recommendations in this chapter centers on leadership.

In the first section of this chapter, the work experience of staff members is evaluated using work theology. Specific recommendations are given in light of this evaluation. Work theology takes people's work experience seriously and focuses on the ethical evaluation of work on three dimensions, instrumental, relational and ontological. Particular insights include the need to focus on the purpose of the organization as the basis of decision-making in the organization. This include decisions on other organizational characteristics such as the activity systems and boundary maintenance. Secondly, the possibility of focusing on the spiritual growth of staff members as a form of workplace spirituality and finally, the petitioning of relationships within the organization to be characterized as justice in love. In the second section of this chapter, the leader, a key piece in the overall leadership process, is focused on. The leader is not a passive agent, but influences the followers based on the purpose and context of the organization. As this leader influences based on his or her individual being, authentic leadership is studied to further understand what a good authentic leader is. Specific recommendations on leader development for World Vision are given in light of this study.

10.1.5 Implications of Research

In this dissertation, an interdisciplinary approach is taken to answer a research question situated in the real world. These different academic disciplines are appropriated and brought into dialogue with theology in addressing the issue of Mission Drift in the organization. Several implications of this research are listed here.

The first implication of this is the limitation of the positive modernist approach to reducing mission drift. Management control in itself is insufficient for changing the perceptions of its staff members. From the empirical research, it is clear that staff perceptions regarding the value of World Vision's Christian mission persisted despite the management practices introduced. The perceptions of staff members are important and should be taken seriously. These perceptions are further influenced by social processes and networks involved, as well as the external environment.

Despite the limited control, leadership should continue to focus on the purpose of the organization. While people are key to meaning transmission, meaning should be first and foremost be determined by the purpose of the organization. This purpose is in return decided by the practice it seeks in society. The normative practice model is a useful tool to root the practice in the Christian perspective. The structure of the practice impacting the purpose of the organization should be consistent throughout the organization. In this dissertation, we discussed World Vision as an organization seeking to express the development practice. This means that the structure of the practice, particularly the *Telos* should influence the overall purpose of the organization as well as the activity systems and the people of the organization. Specific ways have been discussed in this dissertation. Focusing on the telos can keep the structure of the practice intact for the organization.

Another useful implication is the regular deliberate engagement of the Christian content related to the purpose of the organization. Existing in a pluralistic context, engaging with this Christian content can remind the staff members of the intended direction of World Vision, ensuring that this Christian context remains relevant. In recommending this, it is the constructive approach that should be taken seriously. In this dissertation, the Trinity has been used as a theological concept for further engagement and reflection. This content provides clear Christian insight that shows the particularity of the Christian faith. It also provides concrete examples of the relevance of faith in the work that they do.

With people and their perceptions key to meaning transfer, the overall work experience of staff members becomes key too. The work experience influences the overall perception of the staff members. The theology of work has been appropriated as a way to evaluate work experiences from a distinct Christian perspective. Specific recommendations to this work experience have been drawn based on this evaluation.

Finally, it is the leader, with his or her control beliefs who has a large impact to the leadership process and the overall direction that the organization moves towards. This implies the importance of choosing and developing the leader of the organization. This choice and development needs to be purpose of the organization taken into consideration. Who the leader is and the virtues the leader embodies are important and cannot be neglected.

10.2 Future Research Opportunities

Having summarized the dissertation and listed the implications of this research, it is noted that there are some outstanding issues that would make good future research opportunities moving forward. Three of these future research opportunities are discussed briefly here.

10.2.1 Implement Recommendations Listed in the Dissertation

This dissertation has been a case study that has ended with recommendations. These recommendations, while a result of a rigorous process as outlined in this dissertation, have not been tested. It remains a contribution on the clarification of the organizational phenomenon taking place as well as a list of hermeneutical models in Reformational philosophy and theology. It is recommended that as a practical step forward, the recommendations mentioned in this case study be implemented and further evaluated for its validity and for further refining.

10.2.2 Expansion in scope: More Organizations, More Offices

This dissertation has clearly focused on World Vision as a case study at two levels. Firstly in its entirety as a partnership and secondly, in its operations in two different locations. While sufficient for a dissertation as it provided ample space to develop an in-depth understanding of the organization, this is in itself a very narrow scope. Recommendations that were suggested were also not tested. As a future research idea, the transferability of recommendations to other Christian development organizations, as well as the studying of other offices is suggested.

10.2.3 National Cultural Implications

In this dissertation, the national culture found in Nepal and Papua New Guinea were not focused on in the way this culture interacts with the recommendations suggested in the dissertation. With culture described as a process that can be transmitted, what was not further explored, was how the existing collective culture systems interacted with the recommendations posed in this dissertation.

As a follow up research, it would be interesting to consider the existing cultural norms in Papua New Guinea or Nepal, and to consider the implications of these norms on the specific recommendations mentioned in this dissertation. This could include searching for common ground for dialogue, uncovering existing horizons of significance with the Christian perspective. This can be useful for further uptake of the recommendations.

10.2.4 Virtues Required in Leaders of World Vision

In the discussion about leaders, the two virtues required by leaders have been briefly mentioned. The discussion has been brief, written as an example of how virtues can be included in the discussion. A longer list of virtues required by leaders in development organizations is potentially an important future research opportunity. In addition, a deeper understanding of the different virtues can also be helpful for the organization. This list of virtues can potentially provide a basis for the recruitment of staff in countries where it can be difficult to find Christian staff. These virtues with a broader understanding can be applied to the pluralistic world.

APPENDICES

Appendix 1: Organizational Culture Questionnaire

1. Introduction

The introduction of the questionnaire raises initial consciousness about World Vision's Christian Identity to an individual. It lists two core documents of World Vision that provides key ideas about World Vision's Christian Identity. This include the Mission Statement as well as the core value – We are Christian. The way that individuals respond to the questions indicate the overall importance that they individually give to the religious identity of the organization. The table below lists the questions related to the introduction.

---

1. How important is the Organization's religious motivation and values in choosing a job?

☐ Very important
☐ Important
☐ Not Important
☐ Unrelated

Mission Statement

World Vision is an international partnership of Christian whose mission is to follow our Lord and Savior Jesus Christ in working with the poor and oppressed to promote human transformation, seek justice, and bear witness to the good news of the Kingdom of God.

Preamble of World Vision Mission Statement

2. When did you learn about the Mission Statement of World Vision?

☐ Before applying for my role, it influenced by decision to work with World Vision

☐ During the recruitment process, the recruiters shared the Mission Statement during the interview

☐ During orientation, this was shared as part of my induction documents

☐ During the course of my work

☐ Others – please specify _____

3. Does the Mission Statement influence your work?

☐ Yes
☐ No

If yes, please provide some examples, if no, please provide some reasons why?

_____

_____

4. Does the Mission Statement influence your office?

☐ Yes
☐ No

If yes, please provide some examples, if no, please provide some reasons why?

_____

_____

5. What more do you suggest the office do to fulfill the mission of World Vision?

___

___

We Are Christian

We acknowledge one God; Father, Son and Holy Spirit. In Jesus Christ the love, mercy and grace of God are made known to us and all people. From this overflowing abundance of God's love we find our call to ministry.

We proclaim together, "Jesus lived, died, and rose again. Jesus is Lord." We desire him to be central in our individual and corporate life.

We seek to follow him -- in his identification with the poor, the powerless, the afflicted, the oppressed, the marginalized; in his special concern for children; in his respect for the dignity bestowed by God on women equally with men; in his challenge to unjust attitudes and systems; in his call to share resources with each other; in his love for all people without discrimination or conditions; in his offer of new life through faith in him. From him we derive our holistic understanding of the gospel of the Kingdom of God, which forms the basis of our response to human need.

We hear his call to servanthood and see the example of his life. We commit ourselves to a servant spirit permeating the organization. We know this means facing honestly our own pride, sin and failure.

We bear witness to the redemption offered only through faith in Jesus Christ. The staff we engage are equipped by belief and practice to bear this witness. We will maintain our identity as Christian, while being sensitive to the diverse contexts in which we express that identity.

Core Values – we are Christian

6. Does the Core Value – we are Christian, affect your work?

☐ Yes
☐ No

If yes, please provide some examples, if no, please provide some reasons why?

7. Does the Core Value – we are Christian affect your office?

☐ Yes
☐ No

If yes, please provide some examples, if no, please provide some reasons why?

_____
_____

8. What more do you suggest the office does to fulfill the Core Value – We are Christian?

_____
_____

2. Organizational Cultural Dimensions

In this questionnaire, all eight Organizational Culture dimensions are asked. In this section, the Christian value in each organizational culture dimension is outlined, as well as the corresponding practices. The questions that are asked of each dimension is outlined thereafter.

2.1 Basis of Truth and Rationality in the Organization

For the dimension "Basis of truth and rationality," World Vision would make decisions by taking into account the Bible as it provides us with an increased understanding of Christ in his identification with the poor and the oppressed. In discussing this value with the panel, organizational practices that express this value include the following:

Appendix I: Organizational Culture Questionnaire

- Staff members understand Christ's identification with the poor and oppressed as described in the Bible.
- Decision-making processes in the organization incorporate the biblical understanding in its processes

The table below provides the actual questions asked in the questionnaire regarding this dimension.

---

9. Please rank the following information according to the most important to the least important in their use in decision making in your office? (1 being most important)

- [ ] Global & Regional Strategies
- [ ] Donor Expectations
- [ ] Country Statistics (e.g. Poverty Index etc.)
- [ ] Relationship with the government and other stakeholders in the community
- [ ] Field Financial guidelines
- [ ] Human Resources policies
- [ ] Biblical perspectives on the decision that is being made
- [ ] Local cultural practices – please provide an example: _____
- [ ] Others – please specify _____

10. Are scriptures consulted as part of the decision making process of your office?

- [ ] Yes
- [ ] No

11. How are Scriptures considered in the decision making process?

☐ Scriptures are referred to collectively by the decision makers during the decision making process

☐ Scriptures are referred to individually by the decision makers and should influence the actions of the different decision makers

Please provide concrete examples of how Scriptures are considered.

_____
_____

12. What are some obstacles in using Scriptures in the decision making process?

☐ One needs to be sensitive to the Non Christian country context that we are operating in

☐ Scriptures are not relevant in the decision making process

☐ Use of Scriptures is personal and should not be used in work related decisions

☐ One needs to be sensitive to other staff in the office that are not Christian

☐ Others – please specify
   _____

2.2 Nature of Time and Time Horizon

For the Organizational cultural dimension "nature of time and time horizon," it was established that for World Vision, this meant that as an organization, it seeks to be responsive to God's direction in diverse context, as it seeks to bring God's reign in the present. In discussing the expressed organizational practices with the panel, this dimension should be practiced in the organization in the following way:

Appendix I: Organizational Culture Questionnaire

- Earnestly seeking God's direction in decision-making
- Decisions are made at a timely manner, responding to current issues while making room for emergencies

The table below provides the actual questions asked in the questionnaire regarding this dimension. Goals are discussed as a way of understanding the decision-making process.

18. Rank each of the following in its role for setting goals in your office according to the most important to the least important with 1 being most important.
☐ Compliance to pre discussed strategy and objectives for the office
☐ Consideration of operational challenges as they arise at the current moment
☐ Planning for future objectives and direction of the office
☐ Consideration of emergencies in the country context and the response of the office to the emergency
☐ The following of God's direction in the completion of the goal
☐ Others- please specify _____

19. To what extent are goals set by your office time bound with timelines observed?
☐ Goals are not time bound, timelines are not observed at all
☐ Goals are seldom time bound, timelines are not observed most of time
☐ Goals are somewhat time bound, timelines are observed as far as possible
☐ Goals are extremely time bound, timelines are observed strictly

20. Do you see your office seek God's guidance in setting of goals in the organization?

- [ ] Yes
- [ ] No

21 How is God's direction sought in the setting of goals in the organization?

- [ ] Setting aside time for prayer during office hours
- [ ] Reading the bible
- [ ] Regular devotions
- [ ] Personal reflection
- [ ] Setting aside time for decision makers to reflect on the work issues
- [ ] Using Christian principles for work practices
- [ ] others- please specify _____

22. What are some obstacles in seeking God's direction in the setting of goals?

- [ ] To be sensitive of the Non Christian country context that we are operating in
- [ ] God's direction is not related to the setting of goals of the organization
- [ ] To be sensitive to staff who are not Christian
- [ ] I do not know what God's guidance is
- [ ] Others – please specify
  _____

Appendix 1: Organizational Culture Questionnaire

2.3 Motivation

In the dimension "Motivation," World Vision is intrinsically motivated to do a good work as the love of God compels them. The organizational practices that express that include

- Religious orientation of World Vision is a key factor in the quality of work that World Vision produces
- Staff choose to work for World Vision because of the religious orientation of World Vision

The table below provides the actual questions asked in the questionnaire regarding this dimension.

---

23. Rank the following in terms of the most important to the least important reasons for you joining World Vision with 1 being most important.

- [ ] Job Description
- [ ] Industry (INGO, NPO etc.) that World Vision is a part of
- [ ] Existing Staff in the Office
- [ ] Religious Identity of World Vision
- [ ] Espoused values and mission of World Vision
- [ ] Conditions offered by World Vision (salary & benefits)
- [ ] Others – please specify _____

24a. What do you like best about working with World Vision?
_____
_____

24b. What do you like least about working with World Vision?
_____
_____

25. Rank the following in terms of the most important to the least important reasons why staff choose to work with World Vision with 1 being most important

- [ ] Job Content
- [ ] Industry (INGO, NPO etc.) that World Vision is a part of
- [ ] Existing Staff in the Office
- [ ] Religious Identity of World Vision
- [ ] Espoused values and mission of World Vision
- [ ] Conditions offered by World Vision (salary & benefits)
- [ ] Others – please specify _____

26. What are top three factors that motivate you in your current role?

- [ ] Management Style of Senior Leadership Team
- [ ] Work Place Environment
- [ ] Job Scope
- [ ] Career Advancement Opportunities
- [ ] Learning and Development Activities
- [ ] Changes in work conditions (Salary & Benefits)
- [ ] Mission and Purpose of World Vision
- [ ] Others – please specify _____

27. What are the top three factors that demotivate you in your current responsibility?

- [ ] Management Style of Senior Leadership Team
- [ ] Work Place Environment
- [ ] Job Scope
- [ ] Career Advancement Opportunities

Appendix I: Organizational Culture Questionnaire   385

☐ Learning and Development Activities
☐ Changes in work conditions (Salary & Benefits)
☐ Mission and Purpose of World Vision
☐ Others – please specify _____

2.4 Stability vs Change/ Innovation/ Personal Growth

In the dimension "stability vs change/innovation and personal growth," the value that World Vision embraces is to be open to change and innovation, it understands the importance of intentionally discerning the Holy Spirit's guidance as it understands it limitations and its dependence on God.

The practices that should be expressed include:

- World Vision is open and positive to changes
- Organizational Systems are put in place for reliance on the Holy Spirit during change and innovation. E.g. through prayer, discernment material in strategy process

The table provides the actual questions that are asked regarding dimension.

28 How often do changes in your office take place?
☐ Very Often
☐ Often
☐ Sometimes
☐ Seldom
29. How does your office consider change?
☐ Change is extremely undesirable
☐ Change is somewhat undesirable
☐ Change is somewhat desirable
☐ Change is extremely desirable

30. Rank the following types of changes that take place most often in your office from the most often to the least often with 1 being most often

- [ ] Organizational Processes
- [ ] Field Financial Manual
- [ ] Human Resources Policies
- [ ] Organizational Structure
- [ ] Long Term Organizational Strategy and Objectives
- [ ] Project Logframes
- [ ] Staff Turnover
- [ ] Available Funding
- [ ] Others – please specify _____

31. What is the main reason for changes in your office?

- [ ] Sudden Change in Environmental conditions in country context
- [ ] Management style of Senior Leadership within the office
- [ ] Change in Partnership Direction
- [ ] Desire for continuous improvement and progress in office
- [ ] Others – please specify _____

32 Do you see your office seek God's guidance in the changes made in the office?

- [ ] Yes
- [ ] No

33 When is God's guidance considered in the change process? Please tick all that is appropriate.

- [ ] In the evaluation of need for change
- [ ] Planning Process for change
- [ ] During change process
- [ ] After change process, as means of reflection

34 How is God's guidance considered in the changes experienced by the Organization? Please provide examples if possible

- [ ] Setting aside time for prayer during office hours
- [ ] Reading the bible
- [ ] Regular devotions
- [ ] Personal reflection
- [ ] Setting aside time for decision makers to reflect on the work issues
- [ ] Using Christian principles to understand change
- [ ] Others - please specify _____

35 What are some obstacles in seeking God's guidance in changes that take place in the Organization?

- [ ] To be sensitive of the Non Christian country context that we are operating in
- [ ] The Holy Spirit speaks to individuals and not corporately to the organization
- [ ] To be sensitive to staff who are not Christian
- [ ] God's guidance is not required to assist in changes in the Organization.
- [ ] I do not know what God's guidance is.
- [ ] Others – please specify _____

2.5 Orientation to Work/Task/Coworkers

With the dimension "Orientation to work/task/coworkers," World Vision sees people as priority before money, structure, systems and other institutional machinery. This can be expressed in practices like the following:

- People and Culture (Human Resources) practices consider the value of staff above other constraints
- Time is provided for staff fellowship as well as other staff spiritual nurture activities.

The table below provides the questions of the questionnaire regarding this dimension.

36. Please rank the following in terms of its priority for your office from the most important to the least important with 1 being most important.
☐ Completion of pre-agreed tasks as determined by formal documents of World Vision
☐ Observation of organizational structures and the relevant levels of authority
☐ Observation of field financial manual
☐ Observation of people & culture policies
☐ Relationships between individuals within and outside of the organization.
☐ Others – please specify _____

2.6 Isolation vs Collaboration/Cooperation

With the dimension "isolation vs collaboration/cooperation," World Vision considers relationships key to the success of its work. It is through relationships that World Vision would be are able to succeed in its goals. In the organization, this is understood to take place through the following practices.

- There is an understanding that relationships with internal stakeholders are key for the organization's success

Appendix I: Organizational Culture Questionnaire   389

- The working environment should be supportive for the building of work relationships

The table below indicates the questions posted on the questionnaire that is related to this dimension.

---

37. How is work normally accomplished in the office?

☐ Work is done individually with individuals responsible for work outputs

☐ Work is done collectively with team collectively responsible for work outputs

☐ Others – please specify _____

38. What are your views on relationships of internal stakeholders? (Internal stakeholders are considered as colleagues within current office context)

☐ Relationships are very important and are considered to be key to success to the office.

☐ Relationships are important and are considered to be a useful component in the office.

☐ Relationships are somewhat important and are considered good to have in the office.

☐ Relationships are not important to the success of the office

39. What is the role of relationships for internal stakeholders? You may choose more than one.

2.7 Control/Coordination/Responsibility

With this dimension "Control/coordination/responsibility," World Vision actively makes decisions together with the different members of the organization as the organization corporately seeks to rely on the Holy Spirit for inspiration and guidance. This is seen in organization practices such as:

- Staff seek for the Holy Spirit's inspiration and guidance collectively
- Staff's point of views are represented in the decision making process

The table below provides the actual questions that were asked in the questionnaire.

---

13. How are decisions generally made in the office?

- [ ] Decisions are made mainly by the National Director with little or no consultation with others
- [ ] Decisions are made mainly by the Senior Leadership Team with little or no consultation with others
- [ ] Decisions are made by the Senior Leadership Team in consultation with some managers
- [ ] Decisions are made collectively by the Senior Leadership in consultation with different levels of staff

14. How are decisions communicated to different members of the office?

- [ ] through email
- [ ] 1-to-1 meetings with direct managers
- [ ] corporate staff meetings
- [ ] others- please specify _____

15. Do you think that God's guidance is sought in the decision making of your office?

- [ ] Yes
- [ ] No

16. If yes, how do you think God's guidance is sought in the decision making process in the office?

☐	Setting aside time for prayer during office hours
☐	Reading the bible
☐	Regular devotions
☐	Personal reflection
☐	Setting aside time for decision makers to reflect on the work issues
☐	Using Christian principles for work practices
☐	others- please specify _____

2.8 Orientation and Focus

In the final dimension, "Orientation and Focus," World Vision actively engages in external partnerships as it seeks to respond to honor God and his direction in diverse contexts. This is expressed in the following organizational practices:

- External partners of World Vision are clearly mapped keeping in mind mutual participation in ministry
- Clear strategy and work plan on how World Vision intends to work with external partnerships

The questions related to this dimension that were used in this questionnaire are found in the table below:

41. What is the role of relationships in the office with external stakeholders? You may choose more than one.

☐	Relationships do not have a role. Work tasks should be completed independent of relationships
☐	Relationships are able to provide new networks that might be useful in work context
☐	Relationships are important in current cultural contexts as basis for working in said context.

	Relationships lead to trust, which is effective for accomplishing work
	Relationships provide opportunities to witness to God's love
	Relationships enable diversity of people to work together
	Others – please specify _____

42. What are your views on relationships with external stakeholders in the office?

	Relationships are very important and are considered to be key to success to the office.
	Relationships are important and are considered to be a useful component in the office.
	Relationships are somewhat important and are considered good to have in the office.
	Relationships are not important to the success of the office

3. Stakeholders Relationships

The final section of the questionnaire asks questions to ascertain state of relationship held by different stakeholders of the organization. As a prelude, the main section of the questionnaire posed a question to understand which the importance of the different stakeholders in their ability to influence the strategy and direction of the office.

40. Rank each of the following stakeholders In the way it influences the strategy and direction of the office according to the most important to the least important with 1 being most important.

	Beneficiaries of the work of World Vision
	Other NGOs working in the same country context
	Global Centre
	Relevant Support Office
	Regional Office

Appendix 1: Organizational Culture Questionnaire 393

☐	Local churches within area of work of World Vision in country context
☐	Government officials in country context
☐	Direct Donors
☐	Others – please specify _____

The stakeholders that are studied in detail were categorized in this questionnaire in the following way:

☐	Field Staff (Works directly with beneficiaries in the field)
☐	Support Staff (Works primarily to support staff in the field, does not work directly with the beneficiaries in the field)
☐	Middle Management (Manages a team and reports to a member of the Senior Management Team
☐	Senior Management (Part of the Senior leadership team. This includes the National Director as well as staff reporting to the National Director)
☐	External Partner (Global Centre)
☐	External Partner (Regional Office)
☐	External Partner (Donor Office)

To have a general idea about the relationships in the office, general questions that are asked of the different stakeholders include the following.

a. How would you consider your relationship with	Very Close	Somewhat close	Somewhat distant	Very distant
Field Staff (Works directly with beneficiaries in the field)				
Support Staff (Works primarily to support staff in the field, does not work directly with the beneficiaries in the field)				

Middle Management (Manages a team and reports to member of Senior Leadership Team				
Senior Management (Reports directly to National Director)				
External Partner (Global Centre)				
External Partner (Regional Office)				
External Partner (Donor Office)				

b. How influential is the following stakeholder in your work?	Extremely influential to my work	Very influential to my work	Somewhat influential to my work	There is little or no influence
Field Staff (Works directly with beneficiaries in the field)				
Support Staff (Works primarily to support staff in the field, does not work directly with the beneficiaries in the field)				
Middle Management (Manages a team and reports to member of Senior Leadership Team)				
Senior Management (Reports directly to National Director)				
External Partner (Global Centre)				
External Partner (Regional Office)				
External Partner (Donor Office)				

As mentioned in chapter 3, the relational proximity of the different stakeholders. As previously mentioned, this framework looks at the relationship through five different domains. These five domains include directness, continuity, multiplexity, parity and commonality. In general, directness is

Appendix 1: Organizational Culture Questionnaire

focused on the proximity in contact, continuity focuses on the proximity through time, multiplexity focuses on the proximity in multiple spheres, parity is the proximity in levels of power and commonality is the proximity of purpose.

The questions are divided into each of the five domains, where each section seeks to understand the individual relationships of different stakeholders according to the different domains. The first part of the questions seeks to grasp the relationship of the different stakeholders depending on the domain. The next part of the questions seeks to understand if the relationships between the different stakeholders experienced the positive outcomes that are expected of each domain. This framework follows the structure of the relational proximity that has been discussed in its literature.[899]

D1. Directness	Strongly Agree	Agree	Neutral	Disagree	Strongly Disagree
a. I have direct access to Stakeholder					
Field Staff					
Support Staff					
Middle Management					
Senior Management					
External Partner (Global Centre)					
External Partner (Regional Office)					
External Partner (Donor Office)					
b. I meet Stakeholder regularly					
Field Staff					
Support Staff					
Middle Management					

---

[899] For more information read: Michael Schulter and David Lee, *The R Factor* (London: Hodden and Stoughton Ltd,1993).

Senior Management					
External Partner (Global Centre)					
External Partner (Regional Office)					
External Partner (Donor Office)					
c. I feel connected to Stakeholder					
Field Staff					
Support Staff					
Middle Management					
Senior Management					
External Partner (Global Centre)					
External Partner (Regional Office)					
External Partner (Donor Office)					
d. Stakeholder and I are able to communicate freely					
Field Staff					
Support Staff					
Middle Management					
Senior Management					
External Partner (Global Centre)					
External Partner (Regional Office)					
External Partner (Donor Office)					

What other comments do you have of this section?

_____

_____

Appendix 1: Organizational Culture Questionnaire

D2. Continuity	Strongly Agree	Agree	Neutral	Disagree	Strongly Disagree
a. I meet Stakeholder on a regular basis					
Field Staff					
Support Staff					
Middle Management					
Senior Management					
External Partner (Global Centre)					
External Partner (Regional Office)					
External Partner (Donor Office)					
b. The regular meeting between Stakeholder helps me to understand SH/SH representative better					
Field Staff					
Support Staff					
Middle Management					
Senior Management					
External Partner (Global Centre)					
External Partner (Regional Office)					
External Partner (Donor Office)					
c. I understand where I stand in my relationship with Stakeholder through regular meetings					
Field Staff					
Support Staff					

Middle Management					
Senior Management					
External Partner (Global Centre)					
External Partner (Regional Office)					
External Partner (Donor Office)					

d. Stakeholder and I are able to progress in our relationship

Field Staff					
Support Staff					
Middle Management					
Senior Management					
External Partner (Global Centre)					
External Partner (Regional Office)					
External Partner (Donor Office)					

What other comments do you have of this section?

_____

_____

Appendix 1: Organizational Culture Questionnaire 399

D3. Multiplexity	Strongly Agree	Agree	Neutral	Disagree	Strongly Disagree
a. I meet Stakeholder at different contexts (e.g. personal, work etc.)					
Field Staff					
Support Staff					
Middle Management					
Senior Management					
External Partner (Global Centre)					
External Partner (Regional Office)					
External Partner (Donor Office)					
b. I have a deeper knowledge of Stakeholder esentative					
Field Staff					
Support Staff					
Middle Management					
Senior Management					
External Partner (Global Centre)					
External Partner (Regional Office)					
External Partner (Donor Office)					
c. I understand Stakeholder because of the knowledge I have.					
Field Staff					
Support Staff					
Middle Management					
Senior Management					

External Partner (Global Centre)					
External Partner (Regional Office)					
External Partner (Donor Office)					
d. The understanding of Stakeholder leads to further transparency in our relationship.					
Field Staff					
Support Staff					
Middle Management					
Senior Management					
External Partner (Global Centre)					
External Partner (Regional Office)					
External Partner (Donor Office)					

What other comments do you have of this section?

D4. Parity	Strongly Agree	Agree	Neutral	Disagree	Strongly Disagree
a. Stakeholder and I are on the same level in the Organizational Structure					
Field Staff					
Support Staff					
Middle Management					
Senior Management					

Appendix I: Organizational Culture Questionnaire

External Partner (Global Centre)					
External Partner (Regional Office)					
External Partner (Donor Office)					
b. I know that Stakeholder is treating me fairly					
Field Staff					
Support Staff					
Middle Management					
Senior Management					
External Partner (Global Centre)					
External Partner (Regional Office)					
External Partner (Donor Office)					
c. I have respect for Stakeholder					
Field Staff					
Support Staff					
Middle Management					
Senior Management					
External Partner (Global Centre)					
External Partner (Regional Office)					
External Partner (Donor Office)					
d. The respect I have for Stakeholder leads to increased participation					
Field Staff					
Support Staff					
Middle Management					

	Strongly Agree	Agree	Neutral	Disagree	Strongly Disagree
Senior Management					
External Partner (Global Centre)					
External Partner (Regional Office)					
External Partner (Donor Office)					

What other comments do you have of this section?

D5. Commonality	Strongly Agree	Agree	Neutral	Disagree	Strongly Disagree
a. I have a lot in common with Stakeholder					
Field Staff					
Support Staff					
Middle Management					
Senior Management					
External Partner (Global Centre)					
External Partner (Regional Office)					
External Partner (Donor Office)					
b. Our commonality leads to alignment in work tasks					
Field Staff					
Support Staff					
Middle Management					
Senior Management					

Appendix 1: Organizational Culture Questionnaire

External Partner (Global Centre)					
External Partner (Regional Office)					
External Partner (Donor Office)					
c. I feel a shared identity with Stakeholder					
Field Staff					
Support Staff					
Middle Management					
Senior Management					
External Partner (Global Centre)					
External Partner (Regional Office)					
External Partner (Donor Office)					
d. There is synergy in the work that Stakeholder and I do					
Field Staff					
Support Staff					
Middle Management					
Senior Management					
External Partner (Global Centre)					
External Partner (Regional Office)					
External Partner (Donor Office)					

What other comments do you have of this section?

Appendix 2: Questions for Focus Group Discussions and Interviews

What is positive and negative about working with World Vision?

What are the differences between World Vision as a Christian Organization as well as other organizations that are not religious? How does this influence the work that is done organizationally as well as in your area of work.

Where do you learn Christian Values? Please provide some examples of values that you have found important.

How are Christian values applied in your work? Please provide some specific examples.

What are some challenges to applying these Christian values at your work place? Can you please provide concrete examples?

How are core documents referred to in the office? This includes Mission Statement, Vision Statement, Core Values etc.

Relationships Mapping – Who are the key people that your team works with? How are Christian values considered in these relationships?

Appendix 3: Relational Proximities as answered by respondents in WV Nepal and WV PNG

WV Nepal

Table 36. Average Perception regarding Relational Proximity for Senior Management (1= Strongly Agree, 2= Agree, 3= Neutral, 4=Disagree, 5=Strongly Disagree)							
	Field Staff	Support Staff	Middle Management	Senior Management	External (GC)	External (RO)	External (SO)
Directness							
I have direct access to Stakeholder	1.80	1.80	1.60	1.80	3.40	2.60	2.40
I meet stakeholder regularly	3.00	2.60	2.20	2.20	4.00	3.00	3.20
I feel connected to Stakeholder	2.60	2.20	2.00	1.80	3.80	2.60	3.20
Stakeholder and I are able to communicate freely	2.60	2.00	2.20	1.80	3.40	2.80	2.80
Average on Directness	2.50	2.15	2.00	1.90	3.65	2.75	2.90
Continuity							
I meet stakeholder on a regular basis	3.00	2.75	2.00	1.75	3.25	2.50	3.50
The regular meeting between Stakeholder and I helps me to understand Stakeholder better	1.60	1.80	1.80	1.60	2.80	2.40	3.00

I understand where I stand in my relationship with Stakeholder through regular meetings	2.20	2.20	2.40	2.00	3.00	2.60	3.20
Stakeholder and I are able to progress in our relationship	2.00	2.00	1.80	1.80	2.75	2.25	3.00
Average on Continuity	2.20	2.19	2.00	1.79	2.95	2.44	3.18
Multiplexity							
I meet stakeholder at different contexts (e.g. Personal, work etc.)	2.20	2.20	2.20	2.40	3.60	3.00	3.80
I have a deeper knowledge of Stakeholder	1.25	1.50	1.50	1.25	2.33	2.00	2.00
I understand Stakeholder because of the knowledge I have	1.33	1.67	1.33	1.33	2.50	2.00	2.00
The understanding of stakeholder leads to further transparency in our relationship	2.00	2.00	2.00	1.75	2.33	2.25	2.00
Average on Multiplexity	1.70	1.84	1.76	1.68	2.69	2.31	2.45
Parity							
Stakeholder and I are on the same level in the Organizational Structure	2.75	2.50	2.50	1.75	2.67	2.67	2.67
I know that Stakeholder is treating me fairly	2.40	2.40	2.20	2.20	3.00	3.00	2.40
I have respect for stakeholder	1.60	1.80	2.00	1.60	2.20	2.00	2.20
The respect I have for stakeholder leads to increased participation	2.00	2.00	2.00	1.50	2.33	2.00	2.00
Average on Parity	2.19	2.18	2.18	1.76	2.55	2.42	2.32
Commonality							
I have a lot in common with stakeholder	2.80	2.60	2.60	2.00	3.00	2.40	2.60

Appendix 3

Our commonality leads to alignment in work tasks	2.00	1.75	2.00	1.50	2.75	2.25	2.50
I feel a shared identity with stakeholder	1.75	1.75	1.75	1.25	2.75	2.25	2.25
There is synergy in the work that stakeholder and I do	2.00	2.00	2.25	2.00	3.00	2.50	2.50
Average on Commonality	2.14	2.03	2.15	1.69	2.88	2.35	2.46
Overall Average scores for Senior Management	2.14	2.08	2.02	1.76	2.94	2.45	2.66

Table 37. Perception regarding Relational Proximity for Middle Management
(1= Strongly Agree, 2= Agree, 3= Neutral, 4=Disagree, 5=Strongly Disagree)

	Field Staff	Support Staff	Middle Management	Senior Management	External (GC)	External (RO)	External (SO)
Directness							
I have direct access to Stakeholder	2.00	1.82	2.00	2.32	3.55	3.18	3.45
I meet stakeholder regularly	2.18	2.18	2.09	2.27	4.00	3.73	4.09
I feel connected to stakeholder	1.45	1.64	1.73	2.27	3.55	3.45	3.82
Stakeholder and I are able to communicate freely	1.55	1.45	1.64	2.36	3.73	3.64	3.82
Average on Directness	1.80	1.77	1.86	2.31	3.70	3.50	3.80
Continuity							
I meet stakeholder on a regular basis	2.33	1.78	1.89	2.44	4.22	4.11	4.11

The regular meeting between stakeholder and I helps me to understand Stakeholder better	1.11	1.11	1.67	2.22	3.44	3.44	3.44
I understand where I stand in my relationship with Stakeholder through regular meetings	1.89	2.00	1.89	2.56	4.22	4.11	4.11
Stakeholder and I are able to progress in our relationship	1.44	1.44	2.00	2.22	3.89	3.67	3.89
Average on Continuity	1.69	1.58	1.86	2.36	3.94	3.83	3.89
Multiplexity							
I meet stakeholder at different contexts (e.g. Personal, work etc.)	1.80	1.70	1.90	2.70	3.90	3.80	3.80
I have a deeper knowledge of Stakeholder	2.10	2.10	2.22	3.00	3.70	3.70	3.70
D3c I understand stakeholder because of the knowledge I have	1.78	2.00	2.11	3.78	4.00	3.89	3.89
The understanding of stakeholder leads to further transparency in our relationship	1.56	1.56	1.67	2.11	2.89	2.89	2.89
Average on Multiplexity	1.81	1.84	1.98	2.90	3.62	3.57	3.57
Parity							
Stakeholder and I are on the same level in the Organizational Structure	3.22	3.10	1.90	3.89	4.22	4.22	4.22
I know that Stakeholder is treating me fairly	1.56	1.80	1.75	2.00	2.89	2.75	3.00
I have respect for stakeholder	1.22	1.33	1.60	1.78	1.89	1.67	1.89
The respect I have for stakeholder leads to increased participation	1.50	1.60	1.60	1.89	2.44	2.33	2.56
Average on Parity	1.88	1.96	1.71	2.39	2.86	2.74	2.92

Appendix 3

Commonality							
I have a lot in common with stakeholder	2.22	2.33	2.30	2.89	3.56	3.56	3.67
Our commonality leads to alignment in work tasks	1.78	2.00	1.80	2.56	3.00	2.89	3.11
I feel a shared identity with stakeholder	1.56	1.67	1.70	2.22	3.00	2.89	3.11
There is synergy in the work that stakeholder and I do	1.44	1.50	1.78	2.40	2.89	2.89	3.00
Average on Commonality	1.75	1.88	1.89	2.52	3.11	3.06	3.22
Overall Average scores for Middle Management	1.78	1.81	1.86	2.49	3.45	3.34	3.48

Table 38. Perception regarding Relational Proximity for Support Staff (1= Strongly Agree, 2= Agree, 3= Neutral, 4=Disagree, 5=Strongly Disagree)

	Field Staff	Support Staff	Middle Management	Senior Management	External (GC)	External (RO)	External (SO)
Directness							
I have direct access to Stakeholder	1.64	1.73	2.09	3.55	4.00	3.73	3.60
I meet Stakeholder regularly	2.36	1.73	2.18	3.55	4.55	4.45	4.30
I feel connected to Stakeholder	1.91	1.82	2.45	3.00	4.27	4.18	3.73
Stakeholder and I are able to communicate freely	1.73	1.91	2.18	3.00	4.18	4.09	3.64
Average on Directness	1.91	1.80	2.23	3.27	4.25	4.11	3.82
Continuity							

I meet stakeholder on a regular basis	1.91	1.82	2.73	3.18	4.73	4.55	4.27
The regular meeting between Stakeholder and I helps me to understand Stakeholder better	1.91	1.82	2.27	3.00	4.18	4.18	4.09
I understand where I stand in my relationship with Stakeholder through regular meetings	1.73	1.73	2.18	2.45	4.09	4.27	4.09
Stakeholder and I are able to progress in our relationship	2.00	1.73	2.55	2.73	3.82	3.73	3.27
Average on Continuity	1.89	1.77	2.43	2.84	4.20	4.18	3.93
Multiplexity							
I meet stakeholder at different contexts (e.g. Personal, work etc.)	2.64	2.27	2.91	3.27	4.36	4.27	4.45
I have a deeper knowledge of Stakeholder	1.90	2.00	2.30	2.90	4.05	4.00	4.30
I understand Stakeholder because of the knowledge I have	2.00	2.09	2.36	2.55	3.91	4.00	3.91
The understanding of Stakeholder leads to further transparency in our relationship	1.82	1.91	2.18	2.36	3.45	3.55	3.64
Average on Multiplexity	2.09	2.07	2.44	2.77	3.94	3.95	4.08
Parity							
Stakeholder and I are on the same level in the Organizational Structure	3.25	3.00	3.50	4.27	4.27	4.18	4.27
I know that Stakeholder is treating me fairly	2.25	2.45	2.50	3.18	3.82	3.82	3.82
I have respect for Stakeholder	1.75	1.82	1.83	1.86	2.00	2.00	2.00
The respect I have for Stakeholder leads to increased participation	1.92	1.92	2.00	2.27	2.91	3.00	2.91

Appendix 3

Average on Parity	2.29	2.30	2.46	2.90	3.25	3.25	3.25
Commonality							
I have a lot in common with stakeholder	2.67	2.50	3.25	3.67	4.00	4.00	4.08
Our commonality leads to alignment in work tasks	2.50	2.08	2.58	2.83	3.42	3.42	3.50
I feel a shared identity with stakeholder	2.33	2.33	2.50	3.17	3.50	3.50	3.58
There is synergy in the work that stakeholder and I do	2.00	2.08	2.17	2.67	3.08	3.17	3.25
Average on Commonality	2.38	2.25	2.63	3.08	3.50	3.52	3.60
Overall Average for Support Staff	2.11	2.04	2.44	2.97	3.83	3.80	3.74

Table 39. Perception regarding Relational Proximity for Field Staff
(1= Strongly Agree, 2= Agree, 3= Neutral, 4=Disagree, 5=Strongly Disagree)

	Field Staff	Support Staff	Middle Management	Senior Management	External (GC)	External (RO)	External (SO)
Directness							
I have direct access to Stakeholder	1.15	1.78	2.25	3.30	4.40	4.40	4.26
I meet Stakeholder regularly	1.20	1.84	2.30	3.15	4.35	4.25	4.25
I feel connected to Stakeholder	1.10	1.75	2.35	3.37	4.18	4.20	3.95
Stakeholder and I are able to communicate freely	1.10	1.78	2.13	3.15	4.15	4.25	4.10
Average on Directness	1.14	1.79	2.26	3.24	4.27	4.28	4.14
Continuity							

I meet Stakeholder on a regular basis	1.20	1.95	2.35	3.37	4.30	4.25	4.20
The regular meeting between Stakeholder and I helps me to understand Stakeholder better	1.25	1.95	2.25	2.95	3.95	4.05	4.00
I understand where I stand in my relationship with Stakeholder through regular meetings	1.35	1.90	2.21	2.95	4.10	4.10	4.00
Stakeholder and I are able to progress in our relationship	1.40	1.85	2.25	3.05	4.00	4.05	3.95
Average on Continuity	1.30	1.91	2.27	3.08	4.09	4.11	4.04
Multiplexity							
I meet stakeholder at different contexts (e.g. Personal, work etc.)	1.75	2.25	2.60	3.65	4.30	4.30	4.35
I have a deeper knowledge of Stakeholder	1.63	2.16	2.42	3.32	4.05	4.16	4.05
I understand stakeholder because of the knowledge I have	1.70	2.10	2.58	3.47	4.00	4.16	4.11
The understanding of Stakeholder leads to further transparency in our relationship	1.53	2.00	2.28	3.39	3.83	3.89	3.89
Average on Multiplexity	1.65	2.13	2.47	3.46	4.05	4.13	4.10
Parity							
Stakeholder and I are on the same level in the Organizational Structure	2.20	2.70	3.25	3.95	4.35	4.45	4.35
I know that Stakeholder is treating me fairly	1.70	2.10	2.65	3.26	3.80	3.85	3.85
I have respect for Stakeholder	1.55	1.60	2.00	2.35	2.85	2.85	2.80
The respect I have for Stakeholder leads to increased participation	1.45	1.70	2.26	2.65	3.15	3.15	3.05

Appendix 3

Average on Parity	1.73	2.03	2.54	3.05	3.54	3.58	3.51
Commonality							
I have a lot in common with Stakeholder	1.85	2.35	2.90	3.45	4.05	4.10	4.00
Our commonality leads to alignment in work tasks	1.60	1.90	2.26	2.80	3.25	3.25	3.15
I feel a shared identity with Stakeholder	1.90	2.10	2.75	3.30	3.70	3.70	3.65
There is synergy in the work that stakeholder and I do	1.33	1.56	2.11	3.11	3.56	3.56	3.67
Average on Commonality	1.67	1.98	2.51	3.17	3.64	3.65	3.62
Overall Average for Field Staff	1.50	1.97	2.41	3.20	3.92	3.95	3.88

WV Papua New Guinea

Table 74. Average Perception regarding Relational Proximity for Senior Management (1= Strongly Agree, 2= Agree, 3= Neutral, 4=Disagree, 5=Strongly Disagree)							
	Field Staff	Support Staff	Middle Management	Senior Management	External (GC)	External (RO)	External (SO)
Directness							
I have direct access to Stakeholder	2	1.75	1.5	1	2.75	2.25	3
I meet stakeholder regularly	2.25	2.00	1.75	1.00	3.75	3.25	3.00
I feel connected to Stakeholder	2.25	1.75	1.25	1.00	3.25	2.50	2.25
Stakeholder and I are able to communicate freely	2.25	1.50	1.50	1.25	3.75	2.50	3.25
Average on Directness	2.19	1.75	1.50	1.06	3.38	2.63	2.88

Continuity							
I meet stakeholder on a regular basis	3.25	2.25	1.50	1.25	4.00	3.75	3.00
The regular meeting between Stakeholder and I helps me to understand Stakeholder better	2.50	2.25	2.00	2.00	3.33	3.33	2.75
I understand where I stand in my relationship with Stakeholder through regular meetings	2.25	1.75	1.75	1.50	3.00	3.00	2.50
Stakeholder and I are able to progress in our relationship	2.75	1.75	2.00	1.75	3.00	3.00	2.50
Average on Continuity	2.69	2.00	1.81	1.63	3.33	3.27	2.69
Multiplexity							
I meet stakeholder at different contexts (e.g. Personal, work etc.)	3.00	3.33	3.00	2.00	3.50	2.00	3.00
I have a deeper knowledge of Stakeholder	2.50	2.00	1.75	1.50	3.00	3.00	2.75
I understand Stakeholder because of the knowledge I have	2.25	2.00	2.00	2.00	3.00	3.00	2.75
The understanding of stakeholder leads to further transparency in our relationship	2.00	2.25	2.00	2.00	3.00	3.00	2.50
Average on Multiplexity	2.44	2.40	2.19	1.88	3.13	2.75	2.75
Parity							
Stakeholder and I are on the same level in the Organizational Structure	4.00	3.75	3.00	2.50	4.00	4.00	4.00
I know that Stakeholder is treating me fairly	2.25	2.25	2.25	2.00	2.50	2.50	2.50
I have respect for stakeholder	1.25	1.25	1.25	1.25	1.50	1.50	1.75

Appendix 3

The respect I have for stakeholder leads to increased participation	1.75	1.75	1.75	1.75	2.00	2.67	2.50
Average on Parity	2.19	2.18	2.18	1.76	2.55	2.42	2.32
Commonality							
I have a lot in common with stakeholder	3.00	2.75	2.25	2.00	3.75	2.50	3.50
Our commonality leads to alignment in work tasks	2.50	2.50	2.50	2.50	3.00	3.00	3.00
I feel a shared identity with stakeholder	1.75	2.50	1.75	2.25	3.00	2.75	3.50
There is synergy in the work that stakeholder and I do	2.25	2.25	2.00	1.75	2.75	2.75	3.00
Average on Commonality	2.14	2.03	2.15	1.69	2.88	2.35	2.46
Overall Average scores for Senior Management	2.33	2.07	1.97	1.60	3.05	2.68	2.62

Table 75. Perception regarding Relational Proximity for Middle Management
(1= Strongly Agree, 2= Agree, 3= Neutral, 4=Disagree, 5=Strongly Disagree)

	Field Staff	Support Staff	Middle Management	Senior Management	External (GC)	External (RO)	External (SO)
Directness							
I have direct access to Stakeholder	1.62	1.62	1.62	2.38	4.23	4.00	3.54
I meet stakeholder regularly	1.67	1.62	1.77	2.54	4.38	4.23	3.69
I feel connected to stakeholder	1.69	1.69	1.54	2.23	4.08	3.83	3.42

Stakeholder and I are able to communicate freely	1.54	1.62	1.31	2.08	4.42	4.17	3.75
Average on Directness	1.63	1.63	1.56	2.31	4.28	4.06	3.60
Continuity							
I meet stakeholder on a regular basis	1.77	1.69	1.54	2.46	4.25	4.25	3.67
The regular meeting between stakeholder and I helps me to understand Stakeholder better	1.69	1.69	1.62	2.25	3.91	4.00	3.55
I understand where I stand in my relationship with Stakeholder through regular meetings	1.54	1.62	1.54	2.23	4.00	4.17	3.75
Stakeholder and I are able to progress in our relationship	1.62	1.69	1.50	2.17	4.00	3.82	3.36
Average on Continuity	1.65	1.67	1.55	2.28	4.04	4.06	3.58
Multiplexity							
I meet stakeholder at different contexts (e.g. Personal, work etc.)	1.62	1.54	1.62	2.46	4.17	3.92	3.50
I have a deeper knowledge of Stakeholder	1.77	1.77	1.85	2.77	4.08	3.92	3.67
D3c I understand stakeholder because of the knowledge I have	1.62	1.62	1.77	2.31	3.25	3.42	2.83
The understanding of stakeholder leads to further transparency in our relationship	1.33	1.42	1.50	1.83	3.00	2.92	2.58
Average on Multiplexity	1.58	1.58	1.68	2.34	3.63	3.54	3.15
Parity							
Stakeholder and I are on the same level in the Organizational Structure	2.73	2.45	2.08	3.36	4.30	4.40	4.30

Appendix 3

I know that Stakeholder is treating me fairly	2.09	2.18	2.09	2.64	3.60	3.70	3.50
I have respect for stakeholder	1.08	1.17	1.17	1.25	1.64	1.64	1.55
The respect I have for stakeholder leads to increased participation	1.50	1.50	1.50	1.92	2.27	2.27	2.09
Average on Parity	**1.85**	**1.83**	**1.71**	**2.29**	**2.95**	**3.00**	**2.86**
Commonality							
I have a lot in common with stakeholder	1.75	1.92	1.83	2.50	3.91	3.82	3.55
Our commonality leads to alignment in work tasks	1.50	1.50	1.42	2.42	3.27	3.09	2.82
I feel a shared identity with stakeholder	1.50	1.67	1.58	2.25	3.27	3.18	3.09
There is synergy in the work that stakeholder and I do	1.50	1.58	1.50	2.25	3.00	2.91	3.09
Average on Commonality	1.56	1.67	1.58	2.35	3.36	3.25	3.14
Overall Average scores for Middle Management	**1.66**	**1.68**	**1.62**	**2.31**	**3.65**	**3.58**	**3.26**

Table 76. Perception regarding Relational Proximity for Support Staff (1= Strongly Agree, 2= Agree, 3= Neutral, 4=Disagree, 5=Strongly Disagree)

	Field Staff	Support Staff	Middle Management	Senior Management	External (GC)	External (RO)	External (SO)
Directness							
I have direct access to Stakeholder	2.14	1.86	2.05	2.62	3.85	3.95	3.75
I meet Stakeholder regularly	2.05	1.91	2.18	2.95	4.45	4.50	4.20

I feel connected to Stakeholder	2.18	2.18	2.05	3.00	4.24	4.29	4.05
Stakeholder and I are able to communicate freely	1.82	1.64	2.00	2.77	4.33	4.38	4.10
Average on Directness	2.05	1.90	2.07	2.84	4.22	4.28	4.02
Continuity							
I meet stakeholder on a regular basis	2.14	2.14	2.24	2.76	4.40	4.35	4.20
The regular meeting between Stakeholder and I helps me to understand Stakeholder better	1.90	2.00	2.35	2.80	4.16	4.21	4.00
I understand where I stand in my relationship with Stakeholder through regular meetings	1.86	1.86	2.05	2.57	4.05	4.05	3.80
Stakeholder and I are able to progress in our relationship	1.81	1.95	2.10	2.57	4.00	4.00	3.75
Average on Continuity	1.93	1.99	2.18	2.68	4.15	4.15	3.94
Multiplexity							
I meet stakeholder at different contexts (e.g. Personal, work etc.)	2.20	2.20	2.60	2.95	4.26	4.26	4.16
I have a deeper knowledge of Stakeholder	2.30	2.30	2.65	3.00	3.74	3.68	3.67
I understand Stakeholder because of the knowledge I have	1.90	1.90	2.29	2.57	3.60	3.55	3.55
The understanding of Stakeholder leads to further transparency in our relationship	1.71	1.81	1.95	2.29	3.53	3.47	3.35
Average on Multiplexity	2.03	2.05	2.37	2.70	3.78	3.74	3.68
Parity							
Stakeholder and I are on the same level in the Organizational Structure	3.05	2.74	3.16	3.47	4.06	4.11	3.94

I know that Stakeholder is treating me fairly	2.25	2.30	2.55	2.90	3.17	3.22	3.00
I have respect for Stakeholder	1.70	1.65	1.70	1.80	2.11	2.11	1.95
The respect I have for Stakeholder leads to increased participation	1.80	1.75	1.84	2.00	2.56	2.50	2.22
Average on Parity	2.20	2.11	2.31	2.54	2.97	2.98	2.78
Commonality							
I have a lot in common with stakeholder	2.53	2.26	2.74	3.21	3.94	4.00	3.89
Our commonality leads to alignment in work tasks	2.32	2.37	2.32	2.74	3.33	3.28	3.22
I feel a shared identity with stakeholder	2.26	2.37	2.37	2.68	3.17	3.17	3.00
There is synergy in the work that stakeholder and I do	2.32	2.42	2.32	2.78	3.12	3.06	3.00
Average on Commonality	2.36	2.36	2.43	2.85	3.39	3.38	3.28
Overall Average for Support Staff	2.11	2.08	2.27	2.72	3.70	3.71	3.54

Table 77. Perception regarding Relational Proximity for Field Staff (1= Strongly Agree, 2= Agree, 3= Neutral, 4=Disagree, 5=Strongly Disagree)

	Field Staff	Support Staff	Middle Management	Senior Management	External (GC)	External (RO)	External (SO)
Directness							
I have direct access to Stakeholder	1.50	1.65	2.00	2.81	4.19	4.19	4.13
I meet Stakeholder regularly	1.50	2.00	2.00	2.87	4.20	4.13	3.93

I feel connected to Stakeholder	1.50	2.00	2.07	2.73	3.93	3.87	3.73
Stakeholder and I are able to communicate freely	1.56	2.00	2.20	3.00	4.27	4.20	4.13
Average on Directness	1.51	1.91	2.07	2.85	4.15	4.10	3.98
Continuity							
I meet Stakeholder on a regular basis	1.72	1.93	2.20	3.20	4.53	4.47	4.33
The regular meeting between Stakeholder and I helps me to understand Stakeholder better	1.78	1.93	2.13	3.13	4.27	4.20	4.13
I understand where I stand in my relationship with Stakeholder through regular meetings	1.89	2.13	2.40	3.40	4.60	4.53	4.47
Stakeholder and I are able to progress in our relationship	1.72	2.00	2.33	3.13	4.40	4.27	4.27
Average on Continuity	1.78	2.00	2.27	3.22	4.45	4.37	4.30
Multiplexity							
I meet stakeholder at different contexts (e.g. Personal, work etc.)	1.83	2.07	2.40	3.07	4.13	4.13	4.27
I have a deeper knowledge of Stakeholder	2.06	2.27	2.53	3.27	4.47	4.47	4.36
I understand stakeholder because of the knowledge I have	1.94	2.00	2.47	3.13	4.00	4.00	4.00
The understanding of Stakeholder leads to further transparency in our relationship	1.72	2.00	2.27	2.86	3.80	3.80	3.73
Average on Multiplexity	1.89	2.08	2.42	3.08	4.10	4.10	4.09
Parity							
Stakeholder and I are on the same level in the Organizational Structure	3.17	3.60	3.60	3.80	4.64	4.64	4.64

I know that Stakeholder is treating me fairly	2.39	2.36	2.71	3.23	4.00	4.00	3.93
I have respect for Stakeholder	1.33	1.60	1.67	2.07	2.67	2.67	2.60
The respect I have for Stakeholder leads to increased participation	1.56	1.73	2.00	2.60	3.47	3.47	3.47
Average on Parity	2.11	2.32	2.50	2.92	3.69	3.69	3.66
Commonality							
I have a lot in common with Stakeholder	2.11	2.47	2.60	3.40	4.13	4.07	4.07
Our commonality leads to alignment in work tasks	1.94	2.36	2.36	2.92	4.00	3.92	3.85
I feel a shared identity with Stakeholder	2.11	2.40	2.53	3.27	3.93	3.93	3.87
There is synergy in the work that stakeholder and I do	2.06	2.40	2.60	3.33	4.07	4.00	3.93
Average on Commonality	2.05	2.41	2.52	3.23	4.03	3.98	3.93
Overall Average for Field Staff	1.87	2.14	2.35	3.06	4.08	4.05	3.99

Appendix 4: Summary of Organizational Cultural Dimensions in Nepal and Papua New Guinea

Organizational Cultural Dimensions	World Vision Values
1. Basis of truth and rationality in the organization	World Vision takes the Bible seriously as it provides the organization an increased understanding of Christ in his identification with the poor and the oppressed.
World Vision Nepal	Whilst there is an understanding that scriptures are key to the organization, members have questioned the explicit applicability of scriptures for their day to day work. In addition, staff have an assumption that the scriptures and the Christian worldview are being worked out at the global and regional levels, and as such, not necessary to be thought through at the country level.
World Vision Papua New Guinea	There is no clarity that scriptures are key to decision making in the organization. Instead, the use of Scriptures is left to the discretion of individual leaders.
2. Nature of time and time horizon	World Vision seeks to be responsive to God's direction in diverse context, as it seeks to bring God's reign in the present.
World Vision Nepal	While it was clear that goals are time bound, it is not clear that emergencies are planned for and that God's direction was actively sought in the decision making of WV Nepal.
World Vision Papua New Guinea	It is not unanimous that God's direction was intentionally sought in decision making of WV PNG. As goals set by the organization were linked to project plans pre-agreed, they are not pre-planned for emergencies.

3. Motivation	World Vision is intrinsically motivated to do good work as the Love of God compels it.
World Vision Nepal	The religious orientation of the organization is not seen to be the primary motivation for staff working in the organization or for them to continue in their jobs.
World Vision Papua New Guinea	The religious orientation of the organization is not the primary motivation for staff to work for World Vision. Other factors like needs in the community and employment terms were more influential at motivating/demotivating staff to do a good job.
4. Stability vs change/innovation/personal growth	World Vision is open to change and innovation, understands the importance of intentionally discerning the Holy Spirit' guidance as it understands it limitations and its dependence on God.
World Vision Nepal	Change is embraced in World Vision Nepal. However, its relationship to God's dependence is not clearly expressed and embraced by members of the office.
World Vision Papua New Guinea	In general, respondents embraced change, with planning for changes discussed and prayed for during devotions. However, the extent to which God's guidance influences these changes is dependent on individual leaders.
5. Orientation to work/task/coworkers	World Vision sees people as priority before money, structure, systems and other institutional machinery
World Vision Nepal	It is not clear for the respondents that World Vision values people as priority before money, structure, systems and other institutional machinery.
World Vision Papua New Guinea	Staff members do not believe that people were valued above other constraints in the People and Culture policies. They do, however, experience intentional time spent on organizational fellowship events
6. Isolation vs collaboration/cooperation	World Vision considers relationships key to the success of its work. It is through relationships formed

	that World Vision will be able to succeed in their goals.
World Vision Nepal	World Vision encourages a positive working environment, where relationships are considered important for the success of the office.
World Vision Papua New Guinea	The leadership of World Vision encourages a positive working environment. However, it is not clear that the current state of relationships was strong enough or meant for witness.
7. Control/Coordination/Responsibility	**World Vision makes decisions the different members of the organization as the organization corporately seeks to rely on the Holy Spirit for inspiration and guidance.**
World Vision Nepal	In general, respondents believed that decisions were made in consultation with at least some staff members. However, it seems that the final decision made does not represent the views of all staff members as support to decisions were less forthcoming.
World Vision Papua New Guinea	In general, decisions were made in consultation with staff members. These decisions were made in response to external realities or pressures that the office felt instead of representing staff members' point of view.
8. Orientation and Focus	**World Vision actively engages in external partnerships as it seeks to honor God and respond to God's direction in diverse contexts**
World Vision Nepal	There is a clear strategy and openness to work with external partners, where partners are involved with the intention of sustainability and collaboration in their work. What is not as clear is how relationships with external partners honor God.
World Vision Papua New Guinea	External stakeholders are taken seriously in WV PNG with the main role for these relationships meant for networking purposes. It is not clear that these relationships were considered in light of World Vision's 'ministry'.

Consolidated Bibliography

Primary Sources

World Vision. *Statement of Faith.* 1950.

------. *Covenant of Partnership.* Partnership Core Documents. 1978.

------. *A Declaration of Internationalization.* 1978

------. *Core Values.* Partnership Core Documents. March 1990.

------. *Mission Statement.* Partnership Core Documents. 1992.

------. *Partnership with Churches.* Partnership Policy and Decision Manual. 1995, revised 2003.

------. *Witness to Jesus Christ Policy.* Partnership Policy and Decision Manual. 1995.

------. *Understanding Child Sponsorship: A Historical Perspective.* 1996.

------. *WV History Briefs.* 1996.

------. *Guiding Beliefs: The Church and World Vision.* Partnership Policy Manual. 2002.

------. *Vision Statement.* Partnership Core Documents. 2004.

------. *Children's Well-Being.* 2005.

------. *Partnership Principles in Action, World Vision's Governance, Decision Making and Accountability Principles.* 2007.

------. *From Genesis to Exodus: Our Future Legacy.* 2008.

------. *How is World Vision Governed?* World Vision Partnership Orientation. 2010.

------. *Ministry Framework Revised – Summary.* 2010.

———. *Partnership Affirmation of Christian Witness.* 2011.

———. *Principles to Guide Formation of National Policies on Spiritual Nurture of Children.* World Vision Partnership Policy and Decision Manual. 2010.

———. *World Vision in the 1960s.* Accessed March 10, 2015. https://www.youtube.com/watch?v=g_lSI-QAMAo&index=2&list=PL48EDE1AEFD3A43F3.

World Vision International. Accessed March 23, 2016. http://www.wvi.org.

———. "Accountability." Accessed June 29, 2015. http://www.wvi.org/accountability.

———. "Annual Review 2012." Accessed March 3, 2015. http://www.wvi.org/international/publication/world-vision-international-annual-review-2012.

———. "Annual Review 2015." Accessed March 23, 2016. http://www.wvi.org/sites/default/files/20161030_WVIAnnualReview.pdf

———. "Board of Directors." Accessed April 2015. http://www.wvi.org/board-directors.

———. "Board Policy on Boards and Advisory Councils of World Vision National Offices." Amended November 2014.

———. "Good Partners and Best Practice." Accessed July 20, 2015. http://www.wvi.org/accountability/structure-and-funding.

———. "The Ministry Framework." Accessed May 15, 2015. http://www.wvi.org/development/publication/ministry-framework-0.

———. "The Handbook for Development Programs, The Essentials." 2011. Accessed June 15, 2015. http://www.wvi.org/sites/default/files/Handbook_for_Development_Programmes.pdf.

———. "Principles to Guide Formation of National Policies on Spiritual Nurture of Children." Partnership Ministry Policy. 2010. Accessed

May 15, 2015. http://www.wvi.org/development/publication/brief-overview-development-programmes-approach.

---. "Our Work for Children." Accessed March 23, 2016. http://wvi.org/our-work-children.

Secondary Sources

Ahlstrom, Sydney E. *A Religious History of the American People.* New Haven, CT: Yale University Press, 1974.

Aldrich Howard E., and Martin Ruef. *Organizations Evolving.* London: SAGE Publications, 2003.

Anheier, Helmut K. *Nonprofit Organizations: Theory, Management, Policy.* Cornwall: Routledge, 2005.

Australian Council for International Development. "About us." Accessed January 15, 2016. https://acfid.asn.au/about.

Avoilo, Bruce J., and William L. Gardner. "Authentic Leadership Development: Getting to the Root of Positive Forms of Leadership." *The Leadership Quarterly* 16, no. 3 (2005): 315–338.

Banks, Nicola., David Hulme, and Michael Edwards. "NGOs, States and Donors Revisited: Still Too Close for Comfort?" *World Development* 66 (2015): 707–18.

Bass, Bernard M., and Paul Steidlmeier. "Ethics, Character and Authentic Transformational Leadership Behavior." *Leadership Quarterly* 10, no. 2 (1999): 181–217.

Barth, Karl. *Church Dogmatics.* Edited by Geoffrey W. Bromiley and Thomas F. Torrance. Translated by Geoffrey W. Bromiley. 14 vols. Edinburgh: T. & T. Clark, 1956.

Bauckham, Richard. "Jesus the Revelation of God." In *Divine Revelation*, edited by Paul Avis, 174–200. Eugene, OR: Wipf and Stock, 2004.

Bavinck, Herman. *Reformed Dogmatics: God and Creation*, Vol 2, Edited by John Volt. Translated by John Vriend. Grand Rapids: Baker Academic, 2004.

Berger, Julia. "Religious Nongovernmental Organizations: An Exploratory Analysis." *Voluntas: International Journal of Voluntary and Nonprofit Organizations* 14 no. 1 (2003): 15–39.

Berger, Peter L. *The Sacred Canopy.* Garden City, NY: Doubleday, 1967.

Bielefeld, Wolfgang, and William S. Cleveland. "Defining Faith-Based Organizations and Understanding Them through Research." *Nonprofit and Voluntary Sector Quarterly* 42, no. 3 (2013): 442–67.

Birch, Bruce C., Rebekah Miles, and Allen Verhey. "Justice." In *Dictionary of Scripture and Ethics*, edited by Joel B. Green. Grand Rapids, MI: Baker Academic, 2011.

Boje, David M., Catherine A. Helmut, and Rohny Saylors. "Cameo: Spinning Authentic Leadership Living Stories of the Self." In *Authentic Leadership Clashes, Convergences and Coalescences*, edited by Donna Ladkin and Chellie Spiller, 271–278. Cheltenham: Edward Elgar, 2013.

Boje, David M., and Grace A. Rosile. "Restorying the Authentic and Inauthentic Self." A Seminar Held at the Benedictine University in St Louis, MO. 2011.

Bonhoeffer, Dietrich. *Ethics.* Vol. 6 of *Dietrich Bonhoeffer Works.* Translated by Reinhard Krauss, Charles C. West, and Douglas W. Stott. Edited by Clifford J, Green. Minneapolis: Fortress Press, 2005.

Booth, David. "Missing Links in the Politics of Development: Learning from the PRSP Experiment." Accessed December 21, 2015. http://www.odi.org/sites/odi.org.uk/files/odi-assets/publications-opinion-files/2003.pdf.

Bosch, David J. *Transforming Mission: Paradigm Shifts in Theology of Mission.* Maryknoll, NY: Orbis Books, 2001.

Bradbury, Steve. "Mission, Missionaries and Development." In *Handbook of Research on Development and Religion*, edited by Matthew Clarke, 413–429. Cheltenham: Edward Elgar, 2013.

Bratt, James D. *Abraham Kuyper: A Centennial Reader.* Grand Rapids, MI: Eerdmans, 1998.

Brown, Michael E., and Linda K. Treviño. "Ethical Leadership: A Review and Future Directions." *The Leadership Quarterly* 17, no. 6 (2006): 595–616.

Bryman, Alan. *Social Research Methods*, 3rd ed. New York: Oxford University Press, 2008.

Buchanan David A., and Andrzej Huczynski. *Organizational Behaviour*. New York: Prentice Hall, 2007.

Caputo, Richard K. "Religious Capital and Intergenerational Transmission of Volunteering as Correlates of Civic Engagement." *Nonprofit and Voluntary Sector Quarterly* 38, no. 6 (2009): 983–1002.

Carlsen, Anne. "On the Tacit Side of Organizational Identity: Narrative Unconscious and Figured Practice." *Culture and Organization* 22, no. 2 (2016): 107–135.

Caza, Arran, and Brad Jackson. "Authentic Leadership." In *The Sage Handbook of Leadership*, edited by A. Bryman et al, 352–64. London: SAGE Publications, 2011.

Central Bureau of Statistics. "National Population and Housing Census 2011." Last modified December 11, 2015. Accessed October 6, 2016. http://cbs.gov.np/nada/index.php/catalog/54.

Chang, Patricia M.Y. "Escaping the Procrustean Bed: A Critical Analysis of the Study of Religious Organizations, 1930 – 2001." In *Handbook of the Sociology of Religion*, edited by Michele Dillon, 123–135. New York: Cambridge University Press, 2003.

Chaplin, Jonathan. *Herman Dooyeweerd: Christian Philosopher of State and Civil Society*. Notre Dame, IN: University of Notre Dame, 2011.

Chenu, Marie-Dominique. *The Theology of Work: An Exploration*. Dublin: M. H. Gill & Son, 1963.

Choi, Yong- Joon. *Antithesis and Thesis: A Philosophical Study on the Significance of Herman Dooyeweerd's Transcendental Critique*. Philadelphia, PA: Hermit Kingdom Press, 2006.

Ciulla, Joanne B. *Ethics, the Heart of Leadership*. Westport, CT: Praeger, 2004.

------, "The Moral Dangers of Leadership." in *Challenges of Moral Leadership*, edited by Patrick Nullens and Steven C. van den Heuvel, 13-27. Leuven: Peeters, 2016.

------, Clancy Martin, and Robert C. Solomon. *Honest Work: A Business Ethics Reader*, 3rd ed. New York: Oxford University Press, 2013.

Clammar, John. "Culture, Development, and Social Theory: On Cultural Studies and the Place of Culture in Development." *The Asia Pacific Journal of Anthropology* 6, no. 2 (2005): 100–119.

Clarke, Matthew. "Understanding the Nexus between Religion and Development." in *Handbook of Research on Development and Religion*, edited by Matthew Clarke, 2–13. Cheltenham: Edward Elgar, 2013.

Clarke, Gerard, and Michael Jennings. *Development, Civil Society and Faith Based Organizations: Bridging the Sacred and the Secular*. Basingstoke: Palgrave Macmillan, 2008.

Cosden, Darrell. *A Theology of Work: Work and the New Creation*. Carlisle: Paternoster Press, 2004.

Crocker, David A. "Towards Development Ethics." *World Development* 19, no. 5 (1991): 457–483.

Core Humanitarian Standard. "The Standard." Accessed January 15, 2016. http://www.corehumanitarianstandard.org/the-standard.

Corley, Kevin G., Celia V. Harquail, Michael G. Pratt, Mary Ann Glynn, C. Marlene Fiol, and Mary Jo Hatch. "Guiding Organizational Identity Through Aged Adolescence." *Journal of Management Inquiry* 15, no. 2 (2006): 85–99.

Crisp, Oliver D., and Fred Sanders. *Advancing Trinitarian Theology: Explorations in Constructive Dogmatics*. Grand Rapids, MI: Zondervan, 2014.

Critchley, Simon, and Robert Bernasconi. *The Cambridge Companion to Levinas*. Cambridge: Cambridge University Press, 2002.

Davie, Grace. *The Sociology of Religion*. London: SAGE Publications, 2007.

Deneulin, Séverine. "Christianity and International Development." In *Handbook of Research on Development and Religion*, edited by Matthew Clarke, 51–65. Cheltenham: Edward Elgar, 2013.

Detert, James R., Roger G. Schroeder and John J. Mauriel. "A Framework for Linking Culture and Improvement Initiatives in Organizations." *Academy of Management Review* 25 (2000): 850–862.

Deutscher Spendenrat. "Über uns." Accessed January 15, 2016. http://www.spendenrat.de.

Dickson, Marcus, Renee S. Beshears, and Vipin Gupta. "The Impact of Societal Culture and Industry on Organizational Culture." In *Culture Leadership and Organizations: The Globe Study of 62 Societies*, edited by Robert J. House, Mansour Javidan, Vipin Gupta, Peter W. Dorfman, and Paul J. Hanges, 74–90. Los Angeles: SAGE Publications, 2004.

DiMaggio, Paul J. "Interest and Agency in Institutional Theory." In *Institutional Patterns and Organizations*, edited by Lynne G. Zucker, 3–22. Cambridge, MA: Ballinger, 1988.

------ and Walter W. Powell. "The Iron Cage Revisited: Institutional Isomorphism and Collective Rationality in Organizational Fields." *American Sociological Review* 48, no. 2 (1983): 147–60.

Dobbelaere, Karel. *Secularization: An Analysis at Three Levels.* Brussels: Peter Lang, 2002.

Dooyeweerd, Herman. *A New Critique of Theoretical Thought.* Translated by David H. Freeman and H. De Jongste. 3rd ed. 4 vols. Ontario: Paideia Press, 1983.

Drabek, Anne G. "Development Alternatives: The Challenge for NGOs – An Overview of the Issues." *World Development* 15, no. 1, supplement (1987): ix–xv.

Dunker, Marilee P. *Man of Vision.* Waynesboro, GA: Authentic Media, 2010.

Durkheim, Emile. *The Elementary Forms of the Religious Life: The Totemic System in Australia.* New York: Free Press, 1912.

Dutton, Jane E., Laura M. Roberts, and Jeffrey Bednar. "Pathways for Positive Identity Construction at Work: Four Types of Identity and the Building of Social Resources." *Academy of Management Review* 35, no. 2 (2010): 265–93.

Epitropaki, Olga, and Robin Martin. "Implicit Leadership Theories in Applied Settings: Factor Structure, Generalizability, and Stability over Time." *Journal of Applied Psychology* 89 (2004): 293–310.

Fayol, Henri. *General and Industrial Management*. Translated by Constance Storrs. London: Pitman and Sons, 1916.

Feinberg, John S. *No One Like Him: The Doctrine of God*. Wheaton, IL: Crossway, 2005.

Fenn, Richard. *Key Thinkers in the Sociology of Religion*. London: Continuum, 2009.

Ferrari, Silvio. "Religion and the Development of Civil Society." *International Journal for Religious Freedom* 4, no. 2 (2011): 29–36.

Ferrell, O. C., John Fraedrich, and Linda Ferrell. *Business Ethics: Ethical Decision Making and Cases*. 10th ed. Stamford, CT: Cengage Learning, 2015.

Fletcher, Anne, James Guthrie, and Peter Steane. "Mapping Stakeholder Perceptions for a Third Sector Organization." *Journal of Intellectual Capital* 4, no. 4 (2003): 505–27.

Ford, David F. *Theology: A Very Short Introduction*. 2nd ed. Oxford: Oxford University Press, 2014.

Fowler, Alan. *Striking a Balance.* London: Earthscan, 2002.

Franke, John R. *The Character of Theology: An Introduction to Its Nature, Task, and Purpose*. Grand Rapids: Baker Academic, 2005.

Freeman, R. Edward. *Strategic Management: A Stakeholder Approach*. Boston: Pitman, 1984.

Friedman, Jonathan. *Cultural Identity and Global Process*. London: SAGE Publications, 1996.

Fry, Louis. "Toward a Theory of Spiritual Leadership." *The Leadership Quarterly* 14, no. 6 (2003): 693–727.

Furseth, Inger, and Pål Repstad. *An Introduction to the Sociology of Religion: Classical and Contemporary Perspectives.* Aldershot: Ashgate Publishing, 2006.

Gadamer, Hans-Georg. *Truth and Method.* Translated by Joel Weinsheimer and Donald G. Marshall. 2nd ed. New York: Crossroad, 2004.

Gardner, William L., Bruce J. Avolio, Fred Luthans, Douglas R. May, and Fred Walumbwa. "Can You See the Real Me? A Self-Based Model of Authentic Leader and Follower Development." *The Leadership Quarterly* 16, no. 3 (2005): 343–72.

George, William. *Authentic Leadership: Rediscovering the Secrets to Creating Lasting Value.* San Francisco: Joosey-Bass, 2003.

Giddens, Anthony. *The Constitution of Society: Outline of the Theory of Structuration.* Cambridge: Polity Press, 1984.

Gill, John, and Phil Johnson. *Research Methods for Managers.* 4th ed. Los Angeles: SAGE Publications, 2010.

Glas, Gerrit. "Competence Development as Normative Practice- Educational Reform in Medicine as Heuristic Model to Relate Worldview and Education." *Koers - Bulletin for Christian Scholarship* 77, no. 1 (2012): 1–6.

Giacalone, Robert A., and C.L. Jurkiewicz. "Toward a Science of Workplace Spirituality." In *Handbook of Workplace Spirituality and Organizational Performance*, edited by Robert A. Giacalone and Carole L. Jurkiewicz, 3–28. New York: M.E. Sharpe, 2003.

Globe Project. Accessed February 1, 2015. http://www.tlu.ee/~sirvir/IKM/Leadership%20Dimensions/globe_project.html.

Goulet, Daniel. *The Cruel Choice: A New Concept in the Theory of Development.* New York: Athenaeum, 1971.

Goffman, Erving. *Stigma: Notes on the Management of a Spoiled Identity.* Englewood Cliffs, NJ: Prentice-Hall, 1963.

Goldschmidt, Walter. "Functionalism." In *Encyclopedia of Cultural Anthropology*, vol. 2, edited by David Levinson and Melvin Ember, 510. New York: Henry Holt and Company, 1996.

Goudzwaard, Bob, Mark Vander Vennen, and David Van Heemst. Hope in Troubled Times: A New Vision for Confronting Global Crises. Grand Rapids: Baker Academic, 2007.

Graeme, Irvine. "A New Partnership." Chapel Address. 1989.

Gray, Barbara, Michel G. Bougon, and Anne Donnellon. "Organizations as Constructions and Destructions of Meaning." *Journal of Management* 11, no. 2 (1985): 83–98.

Gray, David E. *Doing Research in the Real World*. London: SAGE Publications, 2004.

Greer, Peter, and Chris Horst. *Mission Drift*. Bloomington, MN: Bethany House Publishers, 2014.

Grenz, Stanley J. *Theology for the Community of God*. 7th ed. Carlisle: Paternoster Press, 1994.

Grint, Keith. *The Sociology of Work: Introduction*. Cambridge: Polity Press, 2005.

Guignon, Charles. *On Being Authentic*. New York: Routledge, 2004.

Gustavo, Gutierrez. *A Theology of Liberation*. London: SCM Press, 2000.

Hargrove, Barbara. *The Sociology of Religion: Classical and Contemporary Approaches*. 2nd ed. Arlington Heights, IL: Harlan Davidson, 1989.

Harrison, P.M. *Authority and Power in the Free Church Tradition*. Princeton: Princeton University Press, 1959.

Hatch, Mary J. *Organization Theory: Modern, Symbolic, and Postmodern Perspectives*. 3rd ed. Oxford: Oxford University Press, 2013.

------, and Majken Schultz. "The Dynamics of Organizational Identity." *Human Relations* 55, no. 8 (2002): 989–1018.

Hegemann, Johan, Margaret Edgell, and Henk Jochemsen. *Practice and Profile Christian Formation for Vocation.* Eugene, OR: Wipf and Stock, 2011.

Heidegger, Martin. *Being and Time.* Translated by John Macquarrie and Edward Robinson. New York: Harper & Row, 1962.

Hestenes, Roberta. "1996 World Vision International Board Founder's Chair Address." World Vision Partnership Historical Information. 1996.

Henry, Carl F.H. *The Uneasy Conscience of Modern Fundamentalism.* Grand Rapids, MI: Eerdmans, 1947.

――――. *Aspects of Christian Social Ethics.* Grand Rapids, MI: Eerdmans, 1964.

Higginson, Richard. *Called to Account: Adding Value in God's World.* Guildford: Eagle, 1993.

Hill, Charles W. L., Gareth R. Jones and Melissa A. Schilling. *Strategic Management Theory: An Integrated Approach.* 11th ed. Stamford, CT: Cengage Learning, 2014.

Hodgson, Geoffrey M. "What are Institutions?" *Journal of Economic Issues* 40, no. 1 (March 2006): 1–25.

Hofstede, Geert, Gert Jan Hofstede, and Michael Minkow. *Cultures and Organizations Software of the Mind.* New York: Mc Graw Hill, 2011.

Houston, Tom. "Address to WVI Council 1986; Partnership in Transition." Prepared for World Vision International Council September 16, 1986.

Hirsch, Dean. "The Last Three Years in Perspective." September 1998.

INGO Accountability Charter. "What is the Charter?" Accessed January 15, 2016. http://www.ingoaccountabilitycharter.org/home/what-is-the-charter/.

Irvine, Graeme. "Our Pilgrimage: An Historical Perspective WV Field Directors' Conference." Address to the World Vision Field Directors' Conference, Melbourne, October 18, 1982.

------. "The Core Values Process." Address to the WV Field Directors' Conference, October 1988.

------. "The Internationalization Journey." Prepared at the request of the chair of the Partnership Task Force. Date unknown.

James, Rick. "Creating Space for Grace. God's Grace in Organizational Change." Swedish Mission Council, 2004. http://www.missioncouncil.se/wp/wp content/uploads/2011/05/04_02_space_for_grace.pdf

------. "What is distinctive about FBOS." INTRAC 22 (February 2009). Accessed April 1, 2014. http://www.intrac.org/data/files/resources/482/Praxis-Paper-22-What-is-Distinctive-About-FBOs.pdf.

James, William. "A World of Pure Experience." In *Writings of William James: A Comprehensive Edition*, edited by John J. McDermott, 194–214. Chicago: University of Chicago Press, 1977.

Jayakumar, Christian. *God of the Empty-Handed Poverty, Power and the Kingdom of God.* Victoria: Acorn Press, 2011.

Jeavons, Thomas H. "Identifying Characteristics of 'Religious' Organizations." In *Sacred Companies Organizational Aspects of Religion and Religious Aspects of Organizations*, edited by N.J. Demerath III, Peter Dobkin Hall, Terry Schmitt, and Rhys H. Williams, 79–95. New York: Oxford University Press, 1998.

Jennings, Michael. "'Do Not Turn Away a Poor Man': Faith-Based Organizations and Development." In *Handbook of Research on Development and Religion*, edited by Matthew Clarke, 359–375. Cheltenham: Edward Elgar, 2013.

Jochemsen, Henk. "Normative Practices as an Intermediate between Theoretical Ethics and Morality." *Philosophia Reformata* 71 (2006): 96–112.

------. "Calvinist Spirituality and its Meaning for Ethics." In *Seeing the Seeker: Explorations in the Discipline of Spirituality*, edited by H. Blommestein et al., 463–474. Leuven: Peeters, 2008.

------. "A Normative Model for the Practice of Cooperation in Development as a Basis for Social Justice." In *Challenges of Moral Leadership*, edited by Patrick Nullens and Steven van den Heuvel, 129–150. Leuven: Peeters, 2015.

Kalberg, Stephen. "Max Weber's Types of Rationality: Cornerstones for the Analysis of Rationalization Process in History." *American Journal of Sociology* 85, no. 5 (1980): 1145–79.

Kärkkäinen, Veli-Matti. *Pneumatology: The Holy Spirit in Ecumenical, International, and Contextual Perspective.* Grand Rapids, MI: Baker Academic, 2002.

------. *The Trinity: Global Perspectives.* Louisville, KY: Westminster John Knox Press, 2007.

------. *Christ and Reconciliation.* Grand Rapids, MI: Eerdmans, 2013.

------. *Trinity and Revelation.* Grand Rapids, MI: Eerdmans, 2014.

Kelsey, David H. "On Human Flourishing: A Theocentric Perspective." Yale Center for Faith and Culture Resources. Accessed February 11, 2016. http://faith.yale.edu/sites/default/files/david_kelsey_gods_power_and_human_flourishing_0_0.pdf.

Kernis, Michael H. "Toward a Conceptualization of Optimal Self-Esteem." *Psychological Inquiry* 14 no. 1 (2003): 1–26.

Kilduff, Martin and David Krackhardt. *Interpersonal Networks in Organizations: Cognitive, Personality, Dynamics, and Culture.* New York: Cambridge University Press, 2008.

Koss, Sharon K. *Solving the Compensation Puzzle: Putting Together a Complete Pay and Performance System.* Alexandria, VA: Society for Human Resource Management, 2008.

Kotter, John P. *A Force for Change: How Leadership Differs from Management.* New York: Free Press, 1990.

------. *Leading Change.* Boston, MA: Harvard Business School Press, 1996.

Kühl, Stefan. *Organisationen: Eine sehr kurze Einführung.* Dordrecht: Verlag für Sozialwissenschaften, 2011.

Ladkin, Donna. *Rethinking Leadership: A New Look at Old Leadership Questions.* Cheltenham: Edward Elgar, 2010.

------. "What Is So Important about the 'Vision-Thing'?" In *Rethinking Leadership A New Look at Old Leadership Questions*, edited by Donna Ladkin, 101–126. Cheltenham: Edward Elgar, 2010.

------, and Steven S. Taylor. "Enacting the 'True self': Towards a Theory of Embodied and Authentic Leadership." *Leadership Quarterly* 21, no. 1 (2010): 64–74.

Lausanne Movement. "The Lausanne Covenant 1974." Accessed August 15, 2016. https://www.lausanne.org/content/covenant/lausanne-covenant.

Lennick, Doug, and Fred Kiel. *Moral Intelligence 2.0: Enhancing Business Performance and Leadership Success in Turbulent Times.* Upper Saddle River: Prentice-Hall, 2011.

Lester, Donald L., John A. Parnell, and Shawn Carraher. "Organizational Life Cycle: A Five Stage Empirical Scale." *The International Journal of Organizational Analysis* 11, no. 4 (2003): 339–354.

Lin, Peirong. "Appropriating the Normative Practice Model in People Management of Development Organizations" In *Challenges of Moral Leadership*, edited by Patrick Nullens and Steven van den Heuvel, 183–198. Leuven: Peeters 2016.

------. "An Ethical Consideration of People Management in Development Organizations." In *Challenges of Moral Leadership*, edited by Jack Barentsen and Steven van den Heuvel, 173–188. Leuven: Peeters, 2016.

Linstead, Stephen, and Robert Grafton-Small. "On Reading Organizational Culture." *Organizational Studies* 13, no. 3 (1992): 331–355.

Lord, Robert G., Christy L. De Vader, and George M. Alliger. "A Meta-Analysis of the Relation between Personality Traits and Leadership Perceptions: An Application of Validity Generalization Procedures." *Journal of Applied Psychology* 71 (1986): 402–410.

Luthans, Fred, and Bruce J. Avoilo. "Authentic Leadership: A Positive Development Approach." In *Positive Organizational Scholarship: Foundations of a New Discipline*, edited by K.S. Cameron, J.E. Dutton, and R.E Quinn, 241–258. San Francisco: Barett-Koehler, 2003.

MacIntyre, Alasdair. *After Virtue*. Notre Dame, IN: University of Notre Dame Press, 1981.

------. *Dependent Rational Animals: Why Human Beings Need the Virtues*. Chicago, IL: Open Court Press, 1999.

Maslow, Abraham. *The Farther Reaches of Human Nature*. New York: Harper, 1971.

Mason, Chris. "Isomorphism, Social Enterprise and the Pressure to Maximize Social Benefits." *Journal of Social Entrepreneurship* 3, no. 1 (2012): 74–95.

McKenna, Christopher D. *The World's Newest Profession: Management Consulting in the Twentieth Century*. New York: Cambridge University Press, 2006.

Meyer, M., R. Buber, and A. Aghamanoukjan, "In Search of Legitimacy: Managerialism and Legitimation in Civil Society Organizations." *Voluntas*, 24 (2013): 167–93.

Micah Network, "Proselytism Policy Statement." 2007. Accessed August 15, 2016. http://www.micahnetwork.org/sites/default/files/doc/library/proselytism_policy_statement.pdf.

Michener, Ron. "Face to Face with Levinas: (Ev)angelical Hospitality and De(constructive) Ethics?" *European Journal of Theology* 19, no. 2 (2010): 153–62.

Miller, Danny, and Peter H. Friesen. "A Longtitudinal Study of the Corporate Life Cycle." *Management Science* 30, no. 10 (1984): 1161–1183.

Miller, Seumas. "Social Institutions." *The Stanford Encyclopedia of Philosophy* (Winter 2014 Edition), edited by Edward N. Zalta. Accessed August 7, 2015. http://plato.stanford.edu/archives/win2014/entries/social-institutions/.

Moltmann, Jürgen. *The Spirit of Life*. Translated by Margaret Kohl. Minneapolis: Fortress Press, 1992.

------. *God for a Secular Society: The Public Relevance of Theology*. Translated by Margaret Kohl. London: SCM Press, 1997.

------. *Experiences in Theology: Ways and Forms of Christian Theology*. Translated by Margaret Kohl. Minneapolis: Fortress Press, 2000.

------. *On Human Dignity*. Translated by Margaret Kohl. Minneapolis: Fortress Press, 2007.

------. *Ethics of Hope*. Translated by Margaret Kohl. Minneapolis: Fortress Press, 2012.

Monsma, Stephen V. *When Sacred and Secular Mix: Religious Non-Profit Organizations and Public Money*. Lanham, MD: Rowman and Littlefield, 1996.

Mouw, Richard J. *The God Who Commands*. Notre Dame, IN: University of Notre Dame Press, 1990.

------ and Sander Griffioen. *Pluralisms and Horizons: An Essay in Christian Public Philosophy*. Grand Rapids, MI: W.B. Eerdmans, 1993.

Moxley, Russ S. *Leadership and Spirit*. San Francisco: Jossey-Bass, 2000.

Myers, Bryant L. *Walking with the Poor: Principles and Practices of Transformational Development*. Maryknoll, NY: Orbis Books, 2008.

National Statistical Office. "Papua New Guinea 2011 National Report." Accessed May 15, 2015. http://sdd.spc.int/en/resources/document-library?view=preview&format=raw&fileId=218.

Newbigin, Leslie. *Trinitarian Faith and Today's Mission*. Richmond: John Know Press, 1963.

------. *The Open Secret: An Introduction to the Theology of Mission*. Grand Rapids, MI: Eerdmans, 1978.

------. *The Gospel in a Pluralist Society*. London: SPCK, 1989.

Nicholson, Helen, and Brigid Carroll. "So You Want to Be Authentic in Your Leadership: To Whom and for What End?" In *Authentic Leadership*

Clashes, Convergences and Coalescences, edited by Donna Ladkin and Chellie Spiller, 286–302. Cheltenham: Edward Elgar, 2013.

Nick Turner et al. "Transformational Leadership and Moral Reasoning." *Journal of Applied Psychology* 87 (2002): 304–311.

Niebuhr, Richard H. *The Social Sources of Denominationalism.* New York: H. Holt and Company, 1929.

Niemandt, Nelus. "Discerning Spirituality for Missional Leaders" (paper presented at the conference on Leadership, Spirituality and Discernment, Leuven, Belgium, 6 May 2017.

------, and Gert S. Cordier. "Core capacities for the minister as missional leader in the formation of a missional congregational culture. Part 2: Capacities and conclusions." *Journal for Missional Practise* 6 (Autumn 2015), accessed August 20, 2017, http://journalofmissionalpractice.com/core-capacities-for-the-minister-as-missional-leader-in-the-formation-of-a-missional-congregational-culture-part-2-capacities-and-conclusions

Northouse, Peter G. *Leadership: Theory and Practice.* 6th ed. Los Angeles: SAGE Publications, 2013.

Nullens, Patrick. "Dietrich Bonhoeffer: A Third Way of Christian Social Engagement." *European Journal of Theology* 20, no. 1 (April 2011): 60–69.

------. "Slim omgaan met ethische dilemma's: Een hermeneutisch model." *Tijdschrift voor Management en Organisatie* 68, no. 5–6 (2014): 91–107.

------. "Let Justice Roll Down Like Waters": Ethical Leadership as Generating Justice in an Evil World." In *Challenges of Moral Leadership*, edited by Patrick Nullens and Steven C. van den Heuvel, 75–109. Leuven: Peeters, 2016.

------, and Ronald T. Michener. *The Matrix of Christian Ethics: Integrating Philosophy and Moral Theology in a Postmodern Context.* Colorado Springs, CO: IVP Books, 2010.

O'Donovan, Oliver. *Resurrection and Moral Order: An Outline for Evangelical Ethics.* Leicester: Inter-Varsity Press, 1986.

Offermann, Lynn R., John. K. Kennedy Jr., and Philip W. Wirtz, "Implicit Leadership Theories: Content, Structure and Generalizability." *The Leadership Quarterly* 5, no. 1 (1994): 43–58.

Olson, Roger E. *The Story of Christian Theology: Twenty Centuries of Tradition & Reform.* Downers Grove, IL: IVP Academic, 1999.

Overseas Development Institute, Briefing Paper No. 5, 1978. Accessed January 15, 2016. http://www.odi.org/sites/odi.org.uk/files/odi-assets/publications-opinion-files/6616.pdf

Peet, Richard, and Elaine Hartwick. *Theories of Development: Contentions, Arguments, Alternatives.* 2nd ed. New York: Guilford Press, 2009.

Pelikan, Jaroslav, and Helmut T. Lehman, eds. "Heidelberg Disputation." In *Luther's Works*, vol. 31, 39–70. Minneapolis: Fortress Press, 2002.

Pieterse, Jan Nederveen. *Development Theory.* 2nd ed. London: SAGE Publications, 2010.

Pfeffer, Jeffrey. "Management as Symbolic Action: The Creation and Maintenance of Organizational Paradigms." In *Research in Organizational Behavior*, vol. 3, edited by L.L. Cummings and B. Staw, 1–52. Greenwich, CT: JAI Press, 1981.

Pope John Paul II. *On Human Work: Encyclical Laborem Exercens.* Washington, D.C.: United States Catholic Conference Publishing, 1981.

Potter, Robert B. "The Nature of Development Studies." In *The Companion to Development Studies*, edited by Vandana Desai and Robert B. Potter, 3rd ed., 16–20. Oxford: Routledge, 2014.

Porth, Eric, Kimberley Neutzling, and Jessica Edwards. "Functionalism." University of Alabama, Department of Anthropology. Accessed March 15, 2016. http://anthropology.ua.edu/cultures/cultures.php?culture=Functionalism

Prati, L. Melita, Amy McMillan-Capehart, and Joy H. Karriker. "Affecting Organizational Identity: A Manager's Influence." *Journal of Leadership and Organizational Studies* 15, no. 4 (2009): 404–415.

Preece, Gordon R. *Changing Work Values: A Christian Response.* Melbourne: Acorn, 1995.

Prisma. *Development Cooperation and Religion: A Prisma Contribution to Reflection and Policy,* December 2014. Accessed August 20, 2016. http://www.prismaweb.org/media/203248/religion%20and%20development%20cooperation%20prisma%20contribution.pdf.

Putnam, Robert D. *Bowling Alone: The Collapse and Revival of American Community.* New York: Simon & Schuster, 2000.

Rahner, Karl. *The Quest for Approaches Leading to an Understanding of the Mystery of the God-Man Jesus.* Translated by David Bourke. New York: Seabury Press, 1975.

Raj, N.T. Sree. "Spirituality in Business and Other Synonyms: A Fresh Look at Different Perspectives for its Application." *Journal from the School of Management Science* 4, no. 2 (2011): 71–85.

Ramalingam, Ben. *Aid on the Edge of Chaos: Rethinking International Cooperation in a Complex World.* Oxford: Oxford University Press, 2013.

Reed, Michael. "Organizational Theorizing: A Historically Contested Terrain." In *The SAGE Handbook of Organization Studies,* edited by Stewart R. Clegg et al, 19–54. London: SAGE Publications, 2006.

Ricoeur, Paul. *Oneself as Another.* Translated by Kathleen Blamey. Chicago: University of Chicago Press, 1994.

Rist, Gilbert. "Development as a buzzword." In *Deconstructing Development Discourse Buzzwords and Fuzzwords,* edited by Andrea Cornwall and Deborah Eade, 19–28. Warwickshire: Practical Action Publishing, 2010.

Robson, Colin. *Real World Research.* 3rd ed. West Sussex: John Wiley & Sons, 2011.

Scheffknecht, Sabine. "Multinational Enterprises – Organizational Culture vs. National Culture." *International Journal of Management Cases* 6 (2011): 73–78.

Schein, Edgar. *Organizational Culture and Leadership.* San Francisco: Jossey-Bass, 2010.

Schneider, Jo Anne. "Comparing Stewardship Across Faith-Based Organizations." *Nonprofit and Voluntary Sector Quarterly* 43, no. 3 (2012): 517–39.

Simmel, Georg. *Essays on Religion.* Translated by H.J. Helle. New Haven, CT: Yale University Press, 1906.

Selznich, Philip. *Leadership in Administration: A Sociological Interpretation.* Berkeley: University of California, 1957.

Sider, Ronald J. *Good News and Good Works.* Grand Rapids, MI: Baker Books, 2004.

——————, and Heidi R. Unruh. "Typology of Religious Characteristics of Social Service and Educational Organizations and Program." *Nonprofit and Voluntary Sector Quarterly* 33, no. 1 (2004): 109–134.

Sparrowe, Raymond. "Authentic Leadership and the Narrative Self." *The Leadership Quarterly* 16, no. 3 (2005): 419–439.

Summer, Andy, and Michael Tribe, *International Development Studies: Theories and Methods in Research and Practice.* Los Angeles: SAGE Publications, 2008.

Scott, W. Richard. *Organizations: Rational, Natural, and Open Systems.* Englewoods Cliff: Prentice-Hall, 1987.

——————. *Institutions and Organizations: Ideas, Interests, and Identities.* Los Angeles: SAGE Publications, 2014.

——————, and Gerald F. Davis. *Organizations and Organizing: Rational, Natural and Open Systems Perspectives.* New York: Routledge, 2016.

Smith, Steven R., and Michael R. Sosin. "The Varieties of Faith Related Agencies." *Public Administration Review* 61, no. 6 (2001): 651–670.

Schulter, Michael, and David Lee. *The R Factor.* London: Hodder & Stoughton, 1993.

------. *The Relational Manager.* Oxford: Lion Hudson, 2009.

Start, Chris and Peirong Lin. "The Search for Spirituality in the Business World." In *Leadership, Innovation and Spirituality*, edited by Patrick Nullens and Jack Barentsen, 31–39. Leuven: Peeters 2014.

Stott, John. *Issues Facing Christians Today.* Grand Rapids: Zondervan, 2006

Stout, Harry S., and D. Scott Cormode. "Institution and the Story of American Religion." In *Sacred Companies Organizational Aspects of Religion and Religious Aspects of Organizations*, edited by N.J. Demerath III, Peter Dobkin Hall, Terry Schmitt and Rhys H. Williams, 62–78. New York: Oxford University Press, 1998.

Summer, Andy, and Michael Tribe. *International Development Studies: Theories and Methods in Research and Practice.* Los Angeles: SAGE Publications, 2008.

Takayama, K.P. "Administrative Structures and Political Processes in Protestant Denominations." *Publius* 4, no. 2 (1974): 5–37.

Taylor, Charles. *Philosophy and the Human Sciences: Philosophical Papers.* Vol. 2. Cambridge: Cambridge University Press, 1985.

------. *The Ethics of Authenticity.* Cambridge, MS: Harvard University Press, 2003.

Taylor, Edward. *Primitive Culture.* London: John Murray, 1903.

Teegarden, Paige H., Denise H. Hinden, and Paul Sturm. *The Nonprofit Organizational Culture Guide: Revealing the Hidden Truths that Impact Performance.* San Francisco: Jossey-Bass, 2011.

The Global Fund. Accessed October 6, 2015. http://www.theglobalfund.org/en/.

Troeltsch, Ernst. *The Social Teaching of the Christian Churches.* Translated by Olive Wyon. Chicago: University of Chicago Press, 1981.

Tsui, Anne S., Sushil S. Nifadkar, and Amy Yi Ou. "Cross-National, Cross-Cultural Organizational Behavior Research: Advances, Gaps, and Recommendations." *Journal of Management* 33, no. 3 (2007): 426–78.

Unruh, Heidi R. "Religious Elements of Church-Based Social Service Programs: Types, Variables and Integrative Strategies." *Review of Religious Research* 45, no. 4 (2004): 317–335.

USAID History. Accessed April 16, 2014. http://www.usaid.gov/who-we-are/usaid-history.

VanDrunen, David. *Divine Covenants and Moral Order: A Biblical Theology of Natural Law*. Grand Rapids, MI: Eerdmans, 2014.

Van den Heuvel, Steven. "The Flourishing of Human Life: Fostering a Dialogue between Theology and the Capabilities Approach Through Dietrich Bonhoeffer." *Theologica Wratislaviensia* 11 (2016): 55–66.

Van Knippenberg, Daan. "Embodying Who We Are: Leader Group Prototypicality and Leadership Effectiveness." *The Leadership Quarterly* 22, no. 6 (2011): 1078–1091.

Van Knippenberg, Tjeu *Towards Religious Identity: An Exercise in Spiritual Guidance*. Assen: Royal van Gorcum, 2002.

Van Velsor, Ellen, Cynthia D. McCauley, and Marian N. Ruderman. "Our View of Leadership Development." In *The Center for Creative Leadership Handbook of Leadership Development*, edited by Ellen Van Velsor, Cynthia D. McCauley, and Marian N. Ruderman, 1–28. San Francicso: Jossey-Bass, 2010.

Verkerk, Maarten. "Spirituality, Organization and Leadership: Towards a Philosophical Foundation of Spirit at Work." In *Leadership, Innovation, and Spirituality*, edited by Jack Barentsen and Patrick Nullens, 57–77. Leuven: Peeters, 2014.

Verstraeten, Johan. "Spirituality as Source If Inspired, Authentic and Innovative Leadership." In *Leadership, Innovation and Spirituality*, edited by Jack Barentsen and Patrick Nullens, 81–98. Leuven: Peeters, 2014.

Volf, Miroslav. *Work in the Spirit: Toward a Theology of Work*. New York: Oxford University Press, 1991.

------. *Flourishing: Why We Need Religion in a Globalized World*. New Haven, CT: Yale University Press, 2015.

Ward, Keith. *Religion and Revelation: A Theology of Revelation in the World's Religions.* Oxford: Clarendon, 1994.

Westerveld, Hendrik S. "Moved by God's Compassion with this World." Master Thesis, University of Tilburg, 2011.

Willets, Peter. "What is a Non-Governmental Organization?" Accessed December 15, 2016. http://www.staff.city.ac.uk/p.willetts/CS-NTWKS/NGO-ART.HTM.

Willis, Katie. *Theories and Practices of Development.* 2nd ed. New York: Routledge, 2011.

Wilson, Suze. "Viewpoint: The Authentic Leader Reconsidered: Integrating the Marvelous, Mundane and Mendacious." In *Authentic Leadership Clashes, Convergences and Coalescences,* edited by Donna Ladkin and Chellie Spiller, 55–64. Cheltenham: Edward Elgar, 2013.

Wink, Walter. *Engaging the Powers: Discernment and Resistance in a World of Domination.* Minneapolis: Fortress Press, 1992.

Winter, G. *The Emergent American Society: Large Scale Organization.* New Haven, CT: Yale University Press, 1967.

Wright, Christopher J.H. *The Mission of God: Unlocking the Bible's Grand Narrative.* Downers Grove, IL: InterVarsity Academic, 2006.

Wright, Nicholas T. *Surprised by Hope Rethinking Heaven, the Resurrection, and the Mission of the Church.* New York: Harper Collins, 2008.

Wolfgang, Fengler, and Homi Kharas. *Delivering Aid Differently: Lessons from the Field.* Washington, DC: Brookings Institution, 2010.

Wolters, Albert M. *Creation Regained: Biblical Basis for a Reformational Worldview.* Grand Rapids, MI: Eerdmans Publishing, 1985.

Wolterstorff, Nicholas. *Justice in Love.* Grand Rapids, MI: W.B. Eerdmans, 2011.

------. *Justice: Rights and Wrongs.* Princeton: Princeton University Press, 2008.

Ybema, Sierk et al. "Articulating Identities." *Human Relations* 62, no. 2 (2009): 299–322.

Yin, Robert K. *Case Study Research: Design and Methods.* 5th ed. Los Angeles: SAGE Publications, 2013.

Young, Ed. "On the Naming of the Rose: Interests and Multiple Meanings as Elements of Organizational Culture." *Organizational Studies* 10, no. 2 (1989): 187–206.

www.ingramcontent.com/pod-product-compliance
Lightning Source LLC
Chambersburg PA
CBHW071224290426
44108CB00013B/1282